WITHDRAWN FROM
TSC LIBRARY
TALLAHASSEE
LIBRARY
COMMUNITY COLLEGE

Sports and Their Fans

Sports and Their Fans

The History, Economics and Culture of the Relationship Between Spectator and Sport

KEVIN G. QUINN

McFarland & Company, Inc., Publishers
Jefferson, North Carolina, and London

LIBRARY OF CONGRESS CATALOGUING-IN-PUBLICATION DATA

Quinn, Kevin G., 1961–
Sports and their fans : the history, economics and culture of the relationship between spectator and sport / Kevin G. Quinn.
p. cm.
Includes bibliographical references and index.

ISBN 978-0-7864-3802-0
softcover : 50# alkaline paper ♾

1. Sports — Social aspects — United States. 2. Sports spectators — United States. 3. Sports — Moral and ethical aspects — United States. 4. Sports — Economic aspects — United States. I. Title. II. Title: History, economics, and cuture of the relationship between spectator and sport.
GV706.5.Q85 2009
306.483 — dc22 2009002426

British Library cataloguing data are available

Manufactured in the United States of America

McFarland & Company, Inc., Publishers
Box 611, Jefferson, North Carolina 28640
www.mcfarlandpub.com

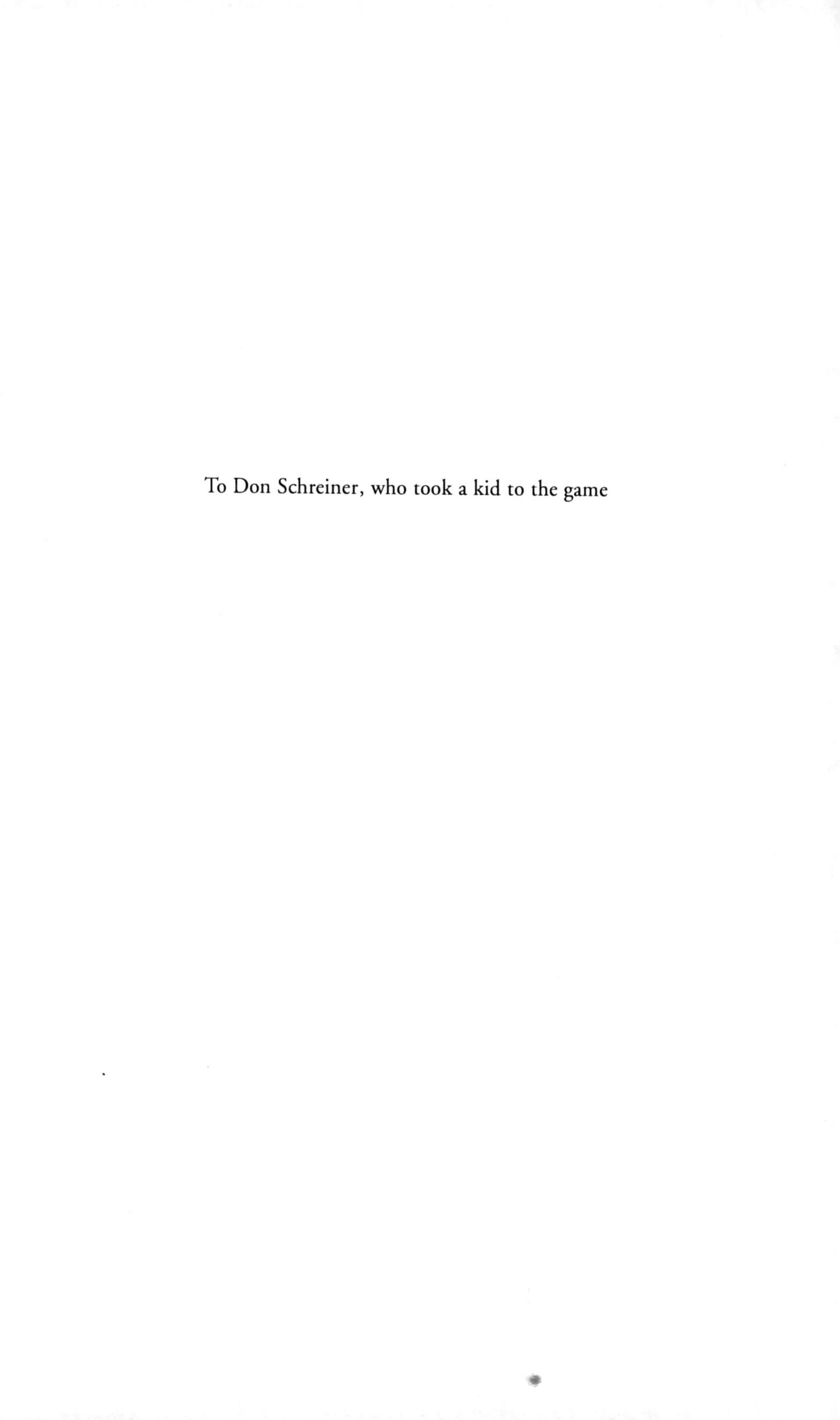

To Don Schreiner, who took a kid to the game

Acknowledgments

A book project requires a lot of help from a lot of good people. I owe many debts of gratitude, beginning with my colleagues at St. Norbert College. Many thanks are due to the SNC library staff, particularly Connie Muelmanns and Kerrie Chang, for their tirelessly cheerful efforts helping me gather research materials. Eliot Elfner, my former associate dean, offered continuing strong support for this project, as has his successor, Jim Benton. My colleagues in the Economics department, Sandy Odorzynski, Marc von der Ruhr and Justin Dubas, have been extremely accommodating during all phases of my research and writing. Wayne Patterson patiently provided the benefit of his experience in writing books, guiding me around a few potential pitfalls in the process. Paul Bursik and I have had countless discussions about all manner of issues in sports — academic and otherwise — which could not help but be reflected in the pages that follow. I have also benefited from many conversations with Chris Borick which, despite his apparently irrational support for Philadelphia teams, have made this a better book.

I am indebted for the financial support that has come from St. Norbert College for the sabbatical during which I began research for this project, as well as for a variety of my other endeavors in the area of sports economics. Thanks to the SNC Office of the Vice President for Academic Affairs and the Office of Faculty Development. Mike Marsden, Darlene Lefevre, Linda Beane Katner, Gayle Lenz, and Cindy Iwen have been helpful in providing and arranging this support beyond any expectation. Invaluable student assistance has come from Lisa Raethz, Melissa Geier, Annie Berkovitz, and Amy Seeger, all of whom were supported by the SNC Office of Admissions. Janice Tesch also provided valuable assistance, and Titletown provided a comfortable place to do my research.

A number of other colleagues also deserve recognition. My understanding of sports has been deepened immensely as a result of my interactions with the sages of the North American Association of Sports Economists and the International Association of Sports Economists. My respect for the members of these two groups is great, but there are far too many to mention here individually. I have been quite fortunate to have gotten to know them, and look forward to their collegiality for years to come. I do owe special recognition to Rodney Fort. Despite being a leading and busy figure in the field, Rod still took some time to mentor me during the very earliest stages of my interest in sports economics. Furthermore, this book, my other work, and my students all have benefited immeasurably from his online sports economics database. The Pro Football Hall of Fame in Canton, Ohio, also kindly provided access to some of their archival material for my background research.

Finally, and by far most importantly, I would like to thank my wife, Terry, for unflagging support and help ever since the idea for this book first took root. She read many, many drafts and provided excellent suggestions that perhaps nobody else could have done. This book reflects much of her input and could not have been completed without her.

Table of Contents

Figures and Tables

Figures

Tables

PREFACE

I taught my first sports economics course at St. Norbert College in the spring of 2000. Unlike today, the field had no textbook specifically tailored to undergraduates. Fortunately, Quirk and Fort's *Pay Dirt* served my students well as a focal point for the main topics covered in the class. Since St. Norbert is a liberal arts institution, it seemed like a good idea to preface the semester by discussing aspects of the historical and social context of sport in modern American life. I set about the assumedly simple task of selecting a book to serve the purpose.

The job turned out to be more difficult than I expected. While there were and are a number of very good sport and society surveys in print, none of them really were what I sought for my students. Some were dry histories, while others were jargon-filled sociological treatises. The majority of available titles seemed to emphasize the important issues of class, race, and gender, but did so to the exclusion of nearly everything else. Many mixed participatory with spectator sports. Perhaps most concerning, I was unable to locate a text that focused on what I thought was most important to my students — the nature of the relationship between spectator sports and their fans.

This book is the product of my decision to try to fill that void. The first task was to decide for whom it should be written. While I certainly hope that this work will be found useful in sports business or other college courses, it is intended for a more general audience. I believe that there are many curious sports fans interested in thinking more intellectually about how they are connected with the games they love. It is for them that this book is offered, and its tone and style reflects this choice.

The material discussed in the chapters that follow is meant to convey the sense of a great deal of academic and popular work that uncountable writers have produced about sports during the last century. However, rather than produce new insights, the book primarily seeks to synthesize the academic and popular writing from a number of disparate fields for the benefit of the nonacademic reader. The success of this project should be judged by the extent to which this synthesis has been accomplished in an academically sound manner without getting too "egg-heady."

It would have been foolhardy to attempt to capture every element of the relationships between sports and fans. Effort instead has been limited to a set of interesting common elements across the different spectator sports and their followers. I find these elements to be intriguing, and suspect that readers will as well.

In the pages that follow, the history of U.S. spectator sports is traced from ancient to contemporary times. The nature of what draws fans to sports over other entertainment forms is developed, followed by the role various media have played in fostering fan interest in sport. The meaning of numbers and statistics in sports is discussed, as are various philosophical notions regarding competitive balance and cheating. Finally, a few thoughts are offered about how a number of social and economic forces may affect big-time spectator sports in the coming decades.

Readers should take note of two items. First, it is impossible to discuss the issues enumerated above without liberal reference to class, race and gender. These matters certainly come up in the book's chapters, but my research has shown them to be extremely well-plowed academic ground. While this book recognizes their importance, it does not pretend to add much that is not already widely known among those likely to read it. Second, since the bulk of American sports fan interest involves the Big Four — the NFL, NBA, NHL, and MLB — so does much of the subsequent chapters. Baseball, in particular, is the oldest organized major American spectator sport — any history of American sport will necessarily overemphasize it, as will any summary of sports research. However, I have taken care to write here about other sports as well, including golf, auto racing, tennis, and college sports. If readers find treatment of these to fall short, they may rest assured that this is simply a reflection of the lack of attention that researchers have paid to those sports.

I hope that what follows makes readers think a bit more deeply about sports and their fans.

1

Fans and Dollars

With apologies to F. Scott Fitzgerald and Ernest Hemingway, why is it that sports are apparently so different from the rest of society and the economy? I have no idea.
—Allen Sanderson[1]

Spectator sports have been with us as long as we have been "us." The ancient Greeks may have had the Olympic Games, but the Egyptians, Minoans, Etruscans, and Romans each had their own athletic spectacles offered for public consumption. We may not know very much about these events, but it is a fair guess that they were a unique part of their lives.

And so it is with Americans, millennia later. The size and scope of our technology and economy may be unprecedented in human history, but our fascination with watching athletes perform in artificial contexts for our entertainment pleasure has not. Spectator sports is big business, of course, but it is more than that. It's our addiction.

What Is a "Sport"?

At first blush, writing a definition of what it means to be "sport" might seem to be an exercise in the academically trivial. After all, even a relatively young child can recognize a hockey game or a tennis match as one, while seeing a play or a ballet as a performance. But how does that child know?

Perhaps the difference hinges on two coincidental criteria: physicality and competition. Clearly, something cannot be considered a sport without some sort of physical exertion. *Jeopardy*, *American Idol*, and games of Old Maid are obviously unscripted competitions, but nobody is about to mistake them for sports. But the exhibition of physicality in the absence of competition is not a sport, either. "Sports" demand that outcomes cannot be known beforehand.

Consider the wondrous physical displays in a Cirque du Soleil show. The incredible skills of the participants are fantastic. But nobody walking out onto Las Vegas Boulevard after seeing *Zumanity* thinks that he or she just witnessed a sporting event. It is not a competition because the precise sequence of movements is known to the participants before the curtain rises. The performers' lives literally depend upon the same outcomes, night after night.

The centrality of spontaneity to a sport is proven when it is taken away. Fixing matches is undoubtedly the greatest sin that can be perpetrated on unsuspecting spectators. To remove the uncertainty of the outcome from a contest is to emasculate it, to kill its essence. "True" wrestling fans follow the Greco-Roman version sponsored by university teams and the Olympics, while sniffing at World Wrestling Entertainment's "matches" as scripted affairs.

There may be a third requirement for consideration of an activity as a "sport." A sports contest needs not only be physical and competitive, but it must also feature an objective measure of the outcome. This point of view relegates anything fundamentally relying upon "judging" to the "not a sport" bin. The distinction is slippery, however, crying out for supremely lawyerly interpretations of what it means to be "fundamentally objective."

Baseball seems to be able to pass the "fundamentally objective" test. Determination of winners and losers according to which team scores more runs seems clear-cut enough, even though balls, strikes, and outs must be judged. Speed skating also passes—finish time is an objective measure—but figure skating and gymnastics do not. Winners must be "chosen" in those sports according to the subjective scores of judges. All-star game home run and three-point shooting contests therefore would make the cut, but dunking contests would not.

A further complication involves the interpretation of "physical." What is the minimum scale of motor activity required?[2] Are darts or bowling sports? How about fishing? Some may feel that "anything that you can do while drinking beer really *isn't* a sport," but those that compete in such activities would strongly disagree. Should the athletic feats observed at a recreational softball league be so blithely condemned? Spotty in quality as they might be, softball seems to be as much a sport as anything else.

What about the degree to which the physical prowess involved in a sport is primarily animal or mechanical instead of human? ESPN's panel of 48 journalists, historians, observers and administrators offered their "Top 100 North American Athletes" of the 20th century as part of the paroxysm of such lists that populated late 1999.[3] A few purists took exception to the inclusion of thoroughbreds Secretariat (#35), Man o' War (#84) and Citation (#100); jockeys Billy Shoemaker (#57) and Eddie Arcaro (#66); and race car drivers A.J. Foyt (#80), Richard Petty (#90) and Mario Andretti (#92). To these critics, the horses and cars do too much of the heavy lifting to count jockeys or drivers as athletes. Devotees of racing, both animal and auto, however, would vehemently object to such narrow-mindedness.

In any case, the lack of a tight definition of sport doubtless has ignited millions of arguments since the Pilgrims first landed at Plymouth Rock. Ranging from gloriously erudite lecture hall discussions to feloniously pugilistic saloon exchanges, it is likely that few of these were settled to the satisfaction of all involved parties. It is wiser to recognize that no sterile definition is to be had. The best course might be to borrow Supreme Court Justice Potter Stewart's wisdom:

> I shall not today attempt further to define the kinds of material I understand to be embraced within that shorthand description; and perhaps I could never succeed in intelligibly doing so. But I know it when I see it.[4]

Stewart may have been writing about pornography rather than sport, but his comments apply here nonetheless. We therefore shall leave the question of definition of sport at that—we fans know 'em when we see 'em.

We Have Met the Fans, and They Are Us

Fifty-seven percent of Americans are not able to name even one current Supreme Court justice, let alone know anything about the late Potter Stewart.[5] How many would fail to recognize a picture of Tiger Woods, Michael Jordan, or Brett Favre? Probably few—sports fandom is hardly a rare thing in this country.

A survey done by the Pew Research Center found that 46 percent of adult Americans followed sports news at least "somewhat closely." A general interest in sports is remarkably consistent across Americans hailing from a variety of other demographic dimensions. Regardless of age, race, educational attainment, household income, or region of the country, just about half of all Americans claim to follow sports.[6] Even so, the interest is not symmetric between the genders—57 percent of men, but only 35 percent of women, claimed to follow sports somewhat closely. Furthermore, more than twice as many males as females follow sports "very closely" (26 percent to 10 percent).[7]

Football, the most uniquely American of all spectator sports, is also most widely appreciated in the U.S. 57 percent of adult Americans claim to be football fans. More than a third (34 percent) said that it was their favorite sport, while 14 percent chose basketball and 13 percent picked baseball. No other sport was chosen by as many as 5 percent, although 12 percent of respondents said they had no favorite. (See Figure 1-1.)[8] All in all, a fair variety of sports can claim fan base of 20 percent or more of the adult American population.[9] (See Figure 1-2.)

Preferences among different sports are connected to racial group membership. For example, 31 percent of African-Americans indicated that basket-

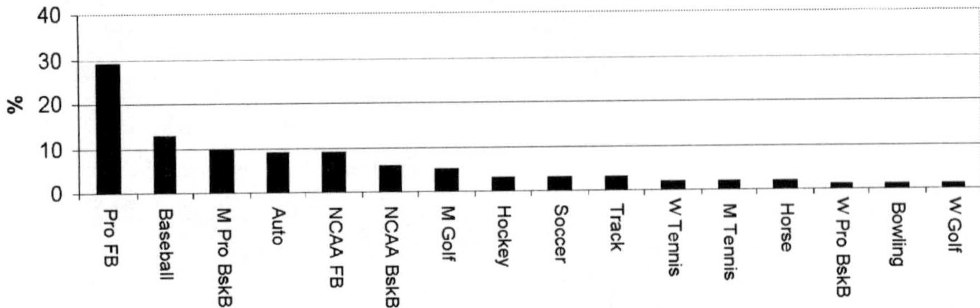

Figure 1-1: Responses to the Question, "What Is Your Favorite Sport?"

Adapted from Polling Report.com. Accessed 10 November 2007 from http://www.pollingreport.com/sports.htm.

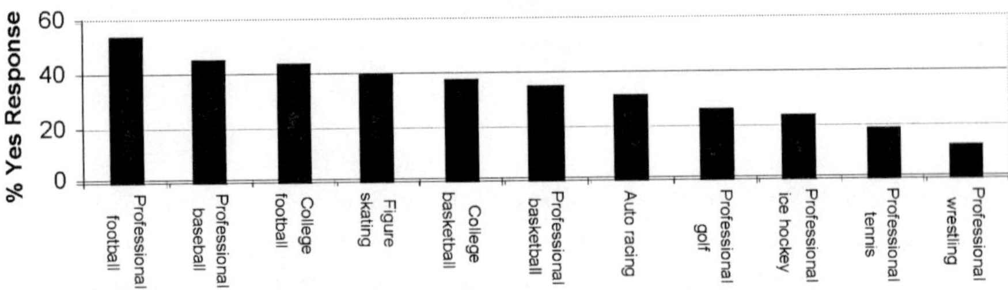

Figure 1-2: Responses to the Question, "For Each of the Following, Please Say Whether You Are a Fan of That Sport or Not"

Adapted from: Polling Report.com. Accessed 10 November 2007 from http://www.pollingreport.com/sports.htm.

ball was their sport of choice, but a mere 4 percent picked baseball. On the other hand, only 9 percent of Hispanics picked basketball, with 24 percent identifying soccer as their favorite sport. Despite these differences, the American myth of the melting pot seems to remain alive and well in sports.[10] "How 'bout those Sox?" is a great conversational ice-breaker, regardless of the color of the collar worn by the participants.

American newspaper coverage of sports reflects these broad fan bases. A 2004 study of sixteen randomly selected newspapers found that 65 percent of sports section front-page stories were about football, basketball, or baseball. NHL hockey was on strike during the survey period, but still accounted for 5 percent, as did golf. Auto racing was featured in 2 percent of stories, while all other sports together accounted for 9 percent. Sports pages are rather a Boys' Town; female teams and players were the main characters in only 5 percent or fewer of stories.[11]

Most of what gets printed today remains old-school sports writing—the job is still to profile players, report scores, and pick out heroes and goats. Only 3 percent of stories were devoted to "sports issues" coverage, such as gender equity or athlete criminal behavior.[12]

Long before the advent of cable news channels or one-sided political blogs, sports editors realized the appeal of targeting the already-faithful. "Homerism"—not the ancient Greek kind—is deeply embedded in the hearts of sports editors. A recent survey found that 39 percent of the editors believed that coverage slanted in favor of the local team was acceptable, and 17 percent of supposedly non–op-ed sports stories included opinion or speculation.[13] While even William Randolph Hearst might have blushed at such bias elsewhere in the paper, partisan fans obviously prefer their sports pages to tell them mostly what they want to hear.

An Economic Bigfoot?

Such loyalty certainly brings them out to the game. A 2002 survey done by the National Endowment for the Arts found that 72 million adults—35 percent of American adult population—attended at least one sporting event that year. Again, sports attendance differs by gender—41.4 percent of males were sports attendees, but only 29.2 percent of females. However, unlike sports interest, sporting event attendance *is* related to other demographic characteristics. Younger adults were most likely to attend a sporting event, although a surprising number of older Americans are spectators—19.7 percent of those aged 65–74 and 11.1 percent of those 75 and older attended at least one sporting event in 2002. Furthermore, perhaps contrary to stereotypes, sporting event attendees are more likely to be better educated and of higher income than the non-attendees, and are more likely to be white than African-American or Hispanic.[14]

The widespread and deep interest in spectator sports has spawned a considerable industry. Just as the machinations of the art auction business has had its effects on painters and patrons alike, so has the spectator sports industry colored the experiences of both athletes and aficionados. Modern spectator sports often seem more like raw commerce than idyllic pastimes. Any weighty discussion about the current state of American sports is sure to include grumbling over how "big money" has affected it.

Such criticism seems fair enough—early 21st century sports pages can read a lot like the business pages with their talk of million-dollar deals, deferred payments, and contractual options. As the grizzled scout types retire from team front offices, they are being replaced by MBAs and JDs with Ivy League pedigrees. Spittoons have made way for computers.

This new breed's understanding of their roles as professional business managers is hardly without warrant. In 2007, over $25 billion was directly spent on U.S. spectator sports, and the industry employs over 100,000 people, less than 10 percent of whom are actually athletes or competitors.[15] And the business is expanding. Between 1998 and 2005, the spectator sport revenues grew at a 5.6 percent annual clip—about twice the rate of inflation.[16]

Still, however large these numbers might be, they are tiny when considered in the context of a $13 trillion economy with 150 million workers. A little perspective: even the American architectural services industry generates slightly more revenue than the spectator sports business, and pays more employees.[17] As culturally interesting as architecture can be—lest we forget, fictional fatherhood icon Mike Brady was an architect—no sane person would suggest that the field even remotely rivals sports in terms of American attention or obsession.

Money Isn't Everything, but the Dollars Tell a Story

So what if spectator sports directly employs only 0.09 percent of American workers and accounts for less than 0.2 percent of American GDP? Clearly there is more to fandom than just a cynical description of consumer behavior in an entertainment market. Nearly every American newspaper has a dedicated sports section, and every local television newscast showcases sports as prominently it does the weather forecast. How can we explain this if sports is no more than a piddling little industry?

Limiting consideration of American spectator sports to its dollar flows is no wiser than talking of Thanksgiving Day solely in terms of money spent on turkeys. Money discussions alone miss all of the important psychological, cultural, political, and spiritual elements of the thing. Even so, dollars can be useful in defining the framework of the American spectator sports economy, and to outline the contours of its reach.

Even the most casual economic analysis of revenues makes clear that the supply side of the U.S. spectator sports industry is dominated by four entities: the National Football League (NFL), Major League Baseball (MLB), the National Basketball Association (NBA), and the National Hockey League. These leagues alone accounted for a total of $16 billion in revenues during 2007, so any treatment of fandom necessarily weighs their activities heavily.[18] Furthermore, these leagues have grown even faster than has the rest of the spectator sports business; between 1999 and 2006, the total annual take by the NFL, MLB, NBA, and NHL rose at a 7.6 percent rate, considerably faster than did U.S. GDP.[19]

The Big Four might be the 800-pound gorilla, but there are a few other animals in the jungle, too. Perhaps most notable among them are the "amateur" athletics programs of Division I of the Collegiate Athletic Association (NCAA). These programs annually generate about $2.4 billion in revenues, the vast majority of which come from football and men's basketball.[20] Some of this money was generated by the NCAA itself, which distributed some of its more than half a billion in revenues to its various member institutions in 2006–7.[21]

Animal and mechanical racing are also billion-dollar businesses. American thoroughbred, harness, and greyhound racetracks earned $7.5 billion in revenues during 2005. NASCAR, the family-run firm that constitutes stock car racing's main organizing body, holds as a closely guarded secret exactly how much it keeps for itself in racetrack, media, licensing, and sponsorship revenues, but rest assured it is a substantial sum.[22] In 2007, the fifteen independent racing teams that compete in NASCAR themselves took in $1.2 billion.[23] Other motor sports, particularly through sponsoring entities such as the Indy Racing League, including the IndyCar Series (formerly CART), and the National Hot Rod Association (NHRA), themselves generate tens of millions each year, but there are no reliable publicly available estimates of exactly how much. Dependable specific estimates also are unavailable for the revenues generated by minor league baseball and hockey leagues, Major League Soccer and Major League Lacrosse, but $3 billion is one educated aggregate estimate of the 2006 revenues of all of the smaller spectator sports together.[24]

These businesses create a lot of their revenues the old-fashioned way—through gate admissions. In 2005, Americans spent about $16 billion to attend sports events in person; by comparison, they spent just under $10 billion going to the movies.[25]

Total attendance for the 2006 or 2006–7 seasons for Big Four league contests alone was 136 million. The average game attendances for their games in those seasons looked like small city populations—67,738 for the NFL, 31,404 for MLB, 17,759 for the NBA, and 16,957 for the NHL.[26] Major League Soccer (MLS) reports that it averaged 15,504 in 2006, totaling just under 3 million fans for the 192 matches.[27] At more than 17,000 per game during the 2008 season, one National Lacrosse League team, the Colorado Mammoth, managed to outdraw the local NBA and NHL franchises that share its venue.[28]

Despite—or perhaps because of—the obvious popularity of doing so, going to major sporting events is not exactly cheap. Team Marketing Report, a publisher of sports marketing and sponsorship information, hit public relations gold with press releases of its "Fan Cost Index" (FCI). The FCI is meant to represent the cost for a family of four to attend a game, and is equal to the cost of two average-priced adult and two average-priced children's game tickets, four small soft drinks, two small beers, four hot dogs, two programs, parking, and two adult-size caps.

NFL games are by far the costliest to attend, with an average 2005 FCI of $329.82, up 5.64 percent from 2004. NBA games were next most expensive at average FCI in 2004–5 of $263.44, up 1.20 percent from 2003–4; and the NHL's FCI in 2006–7 was not far behind at $258.08, up 3.20 percent from the prior season. If MLB is a relative bargain with a 2006 FCI of $171.19, up 4.13 percent from 2005, then minor league baseball is a downright steal. A family of four could catch a typical 2004 minor league contest for a mere $80.61.[29]

Attending a Big Four game represents a major chunk of the typical American household entertainment budget. Their FCI values represent 36 percent of median weekly income for an NFL game, 18 percent for an MLB game, and about 28 percent for an NBA or NHL game.[30] It is no surprise that a look around the crowd during any of these events shows a fairly well-heeled throng. Big-time sporting events simply are not the domain of the skinny-walleted.

In spite of its continuing popularity, direct contest attendance is hardly the dominant form of modern sport spectator consumption. Most fan interactions now take place via various electronic media, which is fine with the teams and leagues. As much as they get from gate receipts, major North American sports also earn substantial revenue from rights fees, particularly from television. In 2006, the major national broadcast television, cable, and satellite rights contract fees—not including local rights fees—totaled nearly $8 billion: for the NFL, the annual media revenues were $4.5 billion; for the NBA, $1.2 billion; MLB, $531 million; the NCAA men's basketball tournament, $545 million; NCAA football, $200 million; PGA Tour, $300 million; and NASCAR, $560 million.[31] These national contracts make up nearly all of the television revenues for the NFL, PGA Tour, and NASCAR, but local contracts represent the vast majority of all media revenues for NHL teams, and about two-thirds for NBA and MLB franchises.[32]

The economic footprint of spectator sports still is not limited to game attendance and media coverage. A number of other industries also rely on sports fan spending. The relatively young video gaming industry, which in part might be considered a derivative form of sports spectatorship, derived a significant chunk of its 2006 $10 billion annual revenue from sports.[33] In 2006, the top-selling video game title was the sports-oriented *Madden 07*, and three of the top ten games in terms of sales that year were sports-related.[34] All told, the revenue that resulted from sports-related publishing, sports agents, sports-related food services, and other peripheral activities in the U.S. in 2007 has been estimated at $173 billion, although this is as much a wild guess as it is science.[35] Suffice it to say that these ancillary revenues dwarf those taken in by the leagues and teams themselves.

The basic advertising-driven model of the entire media industry also depends on sports dollars. First of all, nearly a third of all U.S. advertising—$32 billion of about $110 billion in 2007—is spent on sports advertising.[36] Secondly, numerous radio and television programs specialize in sports fare, and there now are uncountable cable and satellite television networks and television channels dedicated solely to sports. How much of the $7.2 billion that Americans laid out for LCD and plasma televisions in 2005, or of the $330 that the average American spent in 2007 on cable and satellite television, was primarily because of sports?[37] Nobody knows for sure, but it probably isn't an insignificant amount.

This much money changes hands simply because fandom is uniquely intense and pervasive. We spend so much to watch our beloved sports because they mean so much to us.

2

Politics, Robber Barons, and Fans

Widespread in American historical writing is the idea that business leaders in the United States about 1865 to 1900 were, on the whole, a set of avaricious rascals who habitually cheated and robbed investors and consumers, corrupted government, fought ruthlessly among themselves, and in general carried on predatory activities comparable to those of the robber barons of medieval Europe.

—*Hal Bridges*[1]

Politicians and Fans

Where there is money, there will be politicians. The special place sports occupies in so many of our hearts and minds makes it fine political fodder. Politicians who shamelessly drape themselves in Old Glory are only too happy to also capture the reflected glory of successful sports teams. Just as they are willing to stick themselves with the occasional wayward flag pin, our leaders are perfectly willing to risk injury jumping onto the bandwagon should the local boys go on a championship run. The cliché story about a "bet" made between the host city mayors of the two participating teams has become cliché during the two weeks that precede the Super Bowl.

Pols from two-team cities such as New York or Chicago have to tread lightly, of course, although the voters do seem to be tolerant of genuine lifelong allegiances. Mayor Daley is begrudgingly allowed his White Sox preference by Cubs fans already wounded by the Pale Hose 2005 World Series run, while Mets fans responded with little more than perfunctory pique to Mayor Guiliani's Yankee attire during their many post-season appearances.

Politicians can also find that value can be found in being appropriately indignant at slights—real and imagined—of local teams. For example, as chairman of the Senate Judiciary Committee, Utah Senator Orrin Hatch held hearings in October of 2003 regarding the structure of the Bowl Championship Series (BCS). He was particularly interested in why only members of a BCS conference had ever been invited to share in the giant booty that the BCS had created.[2] For the then-upcoming 2004 season, an estimated take of

$80 million was to be divvied up just among the 62 BCS schools of Division I-A (now Division I-FBS). The 55 remaining Division I-A schools were left to split a paltry $6 million.[3]

Hatch made rather direct remarks about remedying this imbalance to the witnesses supporting the BCS system, and offered a not-so-subtle reminder that it was possible that his committee might look into any monopoly behavior in the event that something did not change soon. His threat of congressional intervention into a private and financially successful business was a bit of a departure for Hatch. The conservative Republican had not theretofore been particularly known for his vigorous anti-trust enforcement philosophy. That the three major university athletic programs in Utah hailed from non–BCS conferences perhaps helped shape his perspective on the issue.

Hatch's response was not all that unusual, really. Whenever fans are deprived of their sports, their grumblings are heard by keen ears in Congress and the statehouses. Whether the issue is a league labor disagreement such as the 1994–95 MLB lockout, or an impasse over television carriage such as that which has occurred in the cases of the NFL Network or the Big Ten network, politicians are quick to introduce legislation to "fix" the problem. They risk little downside to such grandstanding.

Political pandering aside, however, the matter of antitrust issues in American sport is hardly new. The very nature of sport means that some level of cooperation among competitors is necessary just to put on a contest. At least, that is the story that leagues want to tell.

Our Favorite Robber Barons

Up to the time they graduate from high school, American schoolchildren are regaled with glorious tales of the post–Civil War industrialists. Among the better-known of these larger-than-life characters are James B. Duke, who dominated the tobacco industry; Andrew Carnegie, who controlled the steel industry; John D. Rockefeller, who cornered the oil business; and J.P. Morgan, who conquered American financial markets. Each got fabulously wealthy through the confluence of a Protestant work ethic, an intelligence to sell something in great demand, and the luck of being in the right place (the U.S.) at the right time (during the American Industrial Revolution's boom). Later in life, these men acquired a sense of noblesse oblige, thinking of themselves as patriarchs and caretakers of the public good via their business dealings. They left fantastic sums to charity. Fans of these men are likely to call them "tycoons."

Others have pointed to their business practices, counting them as immoral, unethical and greedy, and accusing them of stomping all over competitors and consumers without qualms in their quest for greater riches and power. To their critics, they were "robber barons," and their success came only to the detriment of the American way.

They certainly were emblematic of their times. According to one estimate, nearly half of U.S. national wealth in 1900 was held by the richest 1 percent of Americans.[4] The kings of industry ran the American economic show, defining the business environment following the Civil War—just when modern spectator sports leagues had their first stirrings. Like other major American industries, the spectator sports business got its start through the efforts of those trying to corner a market in something: baseball.

Politicians eventually responded to the robber barons' concentration of wealth and power at expense of consumers and other businesses, passing a variety of antitrust legislation beginning with the Interstate Commerce Act in 1887 and the Sherman Act in 1890. Most *verboten* under these laws are attempts to monopolize industries via "unreasonable" restraints of trade, or to fix prices. While these are two of the powers that we generally associate with sports leagues, few seem to complain except for a few noisy lawyers, economists and a labor leader or two.

To be fair, the business of sports is unique among industries—the fiercest and most interesting contest cannot happen without a significant degree of cooperation beforehand between the competitors. GM and Ford might not require the good offices of the Society of Automotive Engineers to coordinate the companies' manufacturing methods and production schedules, but the Yankees and the Red Sox need MLB to set common playing rules, settle on-field disputes, and harmonize game dates. The oil-buying public may not be well-served by an OPEC, but fans are certainly better off when team owners in a sport cede much decision-making to an organizing body or a league.

The importance of a sport's organizing body is made clear by the early days of college football. Game rules differed by location, so each contest was overly unique to where it was played. The home team determined the number of players on a side, the dimensions of the field, the nature of the ball, and what was and was not permitted during play. Not surprisingly, home field advantage was rather robust. As delightful as this might sound for the local faithful, too few game outcomes were in doubt.

It is no stretch to call Yale's Walter Camp the "Father of American Football"—the explosion in the game's popularity was coincident with his standardization of the rules beginning in the 1880s. Similarly, pre–Camp era games were officiated by students or other home squad hangers-on. By 1885, a single formal and impartial referee was a required part of the game, a number that was increased to three in the 1890s. By 1900, as many as 250 colleges were participating in the sport.[5] It is doubtful that this would have occurred without Camp's leadership. It is a short leap, however, between necessary synchronization among competitors and collusively exploiting fans.

The history of the first truly modern sports league, the National League of Professional Ball Clubs (NL), formed in 1876 during the halcyon days of the American Robber Baron, is a case in point. The NL came about directly because its immediate precursor, the National Association of Professional Baseball Players (NAPBP, 1871–1875), fell apart for lack of sufficient cooperation among teams. Teams out of the race often failed to play out contest schedules and game outcomes sometimes turned on questionable rules interpretations. In contrast, the early NL took control of schedule-making and mandated game umpires. Its initial slate of eight teams was intended to cover most of the largest urban centers in the American Northeast, but was closed to cities with less than 75,000. To avoid repeating the NAPBP's failure, the NL concentrated a great deal of decision-making in the person of William Hulbert.[6]

Hulbert was not too shy to use this power. Among his first acts upon becoming president of the league in 1877 was to kick out teams from New York and Philadelphia that had failed to play out their schedules in the league's inaugural season. Hulbert also pushed to clean up the game's "billiard hall" image. He banned for life four players he believed had conspired to throw the 1877 championship.[7] Fans were clear beneficiaries of these efforts.

Hulbert's contributions of cooperation to NL owners' economic success were not limited to playing schedules and rules, however. From the beginning, the league guaranteed team owners exclusive territories, giving them de facto baseball monopoly power over local fans. Imposition of the "reserve clause" and its enforcement was straight from the Robber Baron 101 textbook. Under this system, teams were allowed to "reserve" portions of their roster, protecting them from other teams' attempts to sign their players. The player-poaching ban had the pleasant effect—at least from the owners' point of view—of depressing player salaries. It turned the baseball labor market into one big company mining town.

Fans might not have gotten overly exercised over how players and owners split the pot. On the other hand, they did care about a few of Hulbert's other dictates. His goal of marketing his product as an upscale commodity meant projecting a clean image, so in 1880, the league banned beer sales at games and Sunday baseball. In the era of the six-day work week, fans were not to have Sunday baseball or liquor of any type in Hulbert's gentlemen's league—the working classes be damned.[8]

The NL's blue laws must have looked peculiar to many residents of Victorian-era Cincinnati. Its large German immigrant population did not share Hulbert's view that the Sabbath, baseball, and beer were inconsistent concepts. The Cincinnati ownership believed that it could better serve its fan base—and make more money—by ignoring the league's rules on beer and Sunday ball. Hulbert honored their entrepreneurship by kicking them out of the NL.[9]

The NL league office further discouraged the working classes through its standard game admission price of fifty cents. In 1882, such a price represented the same portion of U.S. per-capita income as did $100 in 2007; by comparison, the average MLB ticket price in 2007 was a bit less than $25.[10] While not in the best interest of fans, surely any Rockefeller or Carnegie would have approved of such blatant price-fixing.

The NL was a deliberate and generally successful effort to create a well-run, money-making spectator sports enterprise. But being "well-run" had resulted in the exit of several teams from large cities; their replacements might have been more malleable to Hulbert's will, but often did not hail from the major population centers. By 1882, seven of the top ten U.S. cities did not have an NL franchise.[11] A lot of potential baseball fans were not being served.

The situation was ripe for a competing league, one that would be more democratic in its attempt reach fans. It arrived in 1882 in the form of the American Association (AA), with the jilted city of Cincinnati among the charter cities. With strong backing from several brewery owners, the AA put teams in several of the largest markets that did not have NL representation, charged half as much as the NL for a ticket, played on Sundays, and served beer at its games. Adding injury to insult, the league did not respect the NL's reserve lists, leading to a bidding war between the two leagues over players.[12]

The AA's strategy was successful—every team in the new league earned a profit in its first year of operation despite ballooning player salaries. Fans might not have cared much about the salary situation, but they were clearly better off now that they had more teams to watch at a cheaper price—plus they could drink beer at the ballpark and take in Sunday games. The AA's success is clear evidence that the NL's robber baronsim had become harmful for fans. The NL lost money in 1882.[13]

Alas, the AA quickly saw value in consorting with the enemy. Following the 1882 season, the two leagues signed an agreement to respect each other's reserve lists. The AA then added four additional teams following the 1883 campaign, foreclosing good opportunities for additional rival leagues, but this did not stop a couple from trying.[14] Both the Union Association (1884) and the Players League (1890) made one-year runs at the NL and AA. They were unsuccessful; however, some of their teams were bought out by the NL and AA, so that by the end of the 1891 season, the AA and NL fielded a combined 17 teams. This spread the spoils too thinly, apparently. The two leagues soon agreed to merge the four strongest AA teams into the NL, buying out the others, thereby making one 12–team league.[15]

As might be expected, most teams in the sleeker NL were profitable for the next decade or so. The mergers had left a lot of cross-ownership among teams, however, and conflicts of interest among erstwhile competitors became problematic from a public relations standpoint. In particular, owners of multiple teams began to treat their smaller-market clubs as step child farm clubs for their big-market teams. The solution was to contract the league further, and the NL became a svelte eight-team operation for the 1900 season.[16] The welfare of fans in the vacated cities was not heavily considered. This was the Gilded Age, and economic Darwinism was all that was needed for anyone looking for philosophical justifications—the Devil take the hindmost.

If the NL thought that their smaller slate would sufficiently satisfy fan demand, they were sadly mistaken. Ban Johnson, president of the Western League, a Great Lakes region minor league, saw an opportunity and recast his organization as the American League (AL). The AL began operation as a rogue major league in 1901, putting three of its teams in cities abandoned by the NL, and a second team in the largest of the other cities. Like the AA had done two decades earlier, the AL made hay by signing away top NL talent in defiance of the reserve clause.[17]

History continued to repeat itself—the clarion call to cartel was powerful, and the two leagues came to a truce over the reserve clause following the 1902 season.[18] After more meetings and a bit more squabbling, the leagues signed a comprehensive peace agreement on September 11, 1903. Under the deal, the leagues were called equals, came to a common set of playing rules, respected each other's reserve lists, and agreed to cooperate on a variety of other matters, including a continuing ban on Sunday baseball.[19] Once again, the interests of fans were subordinated to profits and other owner interests.

Making a Federal Case of It

U.S. population increased by a third during the first decade and a half of the 20th century, from about 76 million in 1900 to slightly more than 100 million in 1915. Furthermore, the percentage of Americans living in cities grew during this time from about 40 percent to about 50 percent, with much of this growth occurring in the cities of the increasingly industrial Northeast.[20] Even so, the AL and NL continued to field the same 16 teams in the same places that they had in 1903, again creating a ripe situation for a rival league to enter.

In 1914, such a contender arrived in the form of the Federal League (FL) and with it, the usual eruption of player bidding wars. This time however, courtesy of the Sherman Act and President Theodore Roosevelt's vigorous attempts at trust-busting, it now looked to be a bit more difficult for the incumbent leagues to maintain their stranglehold on top-tier baseball. Even so, practical application of the Sherman Act had vexed early 20th century federal courts, and initial case law gave little guidance as to how antitrust statutes should be interpreted. Furthermore, Mr. Roosevelt notwithstanding, many of the judges who were to hear Sherman Act cases had been appointed under Republican leadership; they were sometimes unfriendly toward poking the federal proboscis into what they perceived as private business behavior.

There were some early victories for trust-busters, but there were a number of prominent Sherman Act cases that went the other way, too. In 1911, the U.S. Supreme Court ruled that both Duke's American Tobacco and Rockefeller's Standard Oil were to be broken up under the Sherman Act.[21] On the other hand, an antitrust case started that same year by the feds against U.S. Steel—created by J.P. Morgan's merger of other steel firms including Carnegie's company—ended up with a Supreme Court decision that the corporation was not in fact monopoly.[22]

The political landscape had changed dramatically by the time the FL was born, however—there was a new Democratic Congress and a Democratic president, and they were not quite as friendly toward big business as previous regimes. Among the legislation was the Clayton Act, which beefed up antitrust law by specifying particular behaviors that were to be considered illegal. Before the 1915 season, the FL took advantage of the new law, filing an antitrust suit against the NL and AL, citing restraint of trade under both the Sherman and Clayton Acts.[23] The suit found its way to the Chicago courtroom of federal judge Kenesaw Mountain Landis. Meanwhile, the bidding wars continued.

Judge Landis himself had come from a strong Republican family, and two of his brothers served as GOP congressmen. Concerned about the possible ramifications for baseball should he have to decide the case under the new law, he had urged that the parties to settle rather than have the case go to trial. In a hearing held on the case in January of 1915, he asked an attorney representing the FL, "Do you realize that a decision in this case may tear down the very foundations of this game, so loved by thousands, and do you realize that the decision may seriously affect both parties?"[24] His warning found traction. Following the ensuing season, the three leagues came to an agreement to buy out most of the FL owners for a reported total of $400,000 ($20,000 per year for twenty years) in return for the FL's dropping of the antitrust suit.[25]

Not everyone came out a winner, however. The Baltimore and Buffalo FL teams were cut out of the settlement and Baltimore's peeved owners pressed on with the suit, now naming several of their former FL cronies as defendants.[26] In 1919, just as Landis had feared, a jury found organized baseball to be an illegal monopoly, and called for a payment of $240,000 to the Baltimore owners.[27]

NL and AL owners went into a tizzy, claiming this meant the end of baseball as the world then knew it. They brought the case to the appellate court, which set aside the earlier verdict and damage award. The case then went to the U.S. Supreme Court which, in 1922, affirmed the Court of Appeals ruling. In a puzzling opinion, Justice Oliver Wendell Holmes wrote that interstate travel was merely incidental to the game of baseball, which meant that federal antitrust law did not apply.[28]

Not MLB? Then No Soup for You

Major League Baseball took full advantage of their antitrust exemption. It exercised its freedom gleefully, usually at the expense of the players, but fans lost too as MLB chose to keep the same the same teams in the same places. Despite two world wars, the invention of air travel, and dramatic U.S. population growth and shifts, sports pages in 1953 listed the same teams in the standings as they had in 1903.

Other leagues went about their business in the wake of *Federal Baseball* as if they too had antitrust immunity. They certainly seemed justified in doing so. In 1953, a federal appeals court re-affirmed MLB's antitrust exemption in the *Toolson* case, relying on the fact that Congress had not seen fit to take away the exemption in the thirty years that had ensued since *Federal Baseball.*[29] But the rest of the big-time spectator sport industry was not to be so fortunate, even if their fans were.

The carnage began soon after the *Toolson* decision, and the first victim was the boxing business. Prizefighting in the late 1940s and early 1950s had been tightly controlled by a syndicate called the International Boxing Club of New York (IBC). In usual "tycoon" fashion, the IBC had bought out a competing boxing promoter and taken control of the prizefighting business, running all but two of the twenty-one championship bouts held in the U.S. between 1949 and 1954. In addition to the exhibition rights, IBC held all of the television, radio, and movie rights for these fights, attracting government attention under antitrust law.[30] Obviously, this syndicate was able to restrict the number of fights offered to the public as well as to charge higher prices than would have been the case had the business been competitive. This undoubtedly boosted profits, while hurting fans.

In 1955 the Supreme Court found that the protections offered to MLB did not extend to the IBC. While the decision technically turned on the role of television revenues and dissenting opinions were incredulous that the majority had split hairs as it did in its effort to ignore precedent, *International Boxing* was the beginning of a new legal era for American spectator sports.[31]

Courts uneasy with the MLB exemption embraced its limitation to baseball only, and other sports leagues found themselves routed one by one in their own antitrust proceedings. The NBA was denied an MLB–like exemption in a 1956 federal court decision, while the NFL got its own bad news one year later.[32] Over the next couple of decades, a series of other courts failed to extend antitrust protection to professional hockey, golf, tennis, college football, and soccer.[33] By 1960, big-time spectator sports had found itself in a brand new, and uncertain, legal world.

Despite these legal losses, the Big Four leagues still enjoy considerably more political and legal latitude with respect to antitrust than do many other industries. Apparently fans are a bit more tolerant of robber barony in their favorite sports than are as consumers of other products. Owners smart enough to realize this cast themselves as patriarchs who are caretakers of the public amenities that are their teams.

Most of the time, politicians choose to stay out of these relationships, figuring that they are better off cashing campaign contribution checks from owners rather than trying to make cheap electoral hay out of baron-bashing. Two of the ways that politicians permit owners to fatten their profits—at the expense of fans—is by allowing monopoly control of league broadcasting rights, and by letting owners control entry into their little clubs.

Deciding What Fans Watch

Leagues and other sport organizations have had a love-hate relationship with the idea of electronic media coverage of games ever since the invention of broadcast radio. On one hand, such coverage can increase interest and therefore gate attendance. On the other hand, fans may opt for the comfort and economy of their own living room over buying a ticket and going to the game. Economists frame this issue as a question of whether broadcasts and game attendance are complements or substitutes. If radio seemed threatening, then television surely must have really seemed scary. However, early television technology was lacking, and the modern symbiotic relationship between the two was not at all obvious at first.

Television's initial foray into sports came in the form of a University of Pennsylvania football game in 1938. It may be the highest rated program ever—all six television sets in Philadelphia reportedly were tuned in to the contest.[34] The first baseball game telecast took place the following year; presumably a few more viewers got to see the contest between Princeton and

Columbia as NBC provided the coverage.[35] There was only one camera at the game, along the third base line, the image was fuzzy, and the available viewing screens were small—not exactly an attention-riveting combination. Not that it mattered very much, anyway—there were probably less than 1,000 sets in use in the U.S. that year. Even as late as 1949, there were still less than a million U.S. households that had a television. Things changed during the next few years—by 1952, there were more than 15 million American television households.[36]

College athletic programs, many of which had long relied upon fans making hours-long car and train journeys back to the alma mater on football Saturdays, began to worry that television would harm gate receipts and possibly affect competitive balance among teams. In 1952, individual schools ceded control of television broadcasts to the NCAA, directing it to come up with a master plan for TV. Supposedly, the plan was to maximize the number of schools getting exposure on the precious few networks then on the air. By the early 1980s, the NCAA's control of college football broadcasts had become quite strong and its rules quite detailed. The 1982–85 plan included a cap of six broadcasts in which any one school could be included over a given two-year period.[37] Fans of the most popular college programs were not well served by having so few opportunities to see their teams, but ratings was huge when the big guys were on. Of course, that meant that advertisers were willing to pay big bucks for the relatively rare marquee match-ups that were telecast, and the NCAA enjoyed huge rights fees as a result.

These policies had not sat well with some of the most prominent teams or their alums. In 1979, the top programs formed the College Football Association (CFA) and sought to sell TV rights on their own. Shortly thereafter, the University of Oklahoma led a number of schools that sued the NCAA under antitrust law. In 1984, the U.S. Supreme Court found the NCAA's control of college football television broadcasts to be in violation of the Sherman Act.[38] Fans soon benefited as broadcasts of big-program games, as well as games of more regional interest, quickly increased dramatically, while overall revenues declined.[39] In contrast, the NFL and the other members of the Big Four, on the other hand, managed to avoid a similar "catastrophe."

The NFL had taken its 1957 antitrust court loss rather hard, and immediately went on the offensive. An early salvo was a screed in the form of a shrill pamphlet written by then-commissioner Bert Bell (or his lawyers) that predicted a near-term and dire end of professional football unless the NFL got back what it thought it already had had.[40] Bell lobbied Congress hard for an antitrust exemption, but was unsuccessful in getting any legislation passed.

Bell was a veteran of the formative days of the league. As president of the Philadelphia Eagles, the first college draft in 1936 had been his idea, but he did not see how television would catapult the league into what it is today. He had been distinctly distrustful of television coverage's effect on attendance, refusing to allow teams' home games to be broadcast into their local markets. This ban on home game broadcasts continued until 1973, when the league decided to "black out" only those home games that were not sellouts 72 hours before kickoff.

A hint of the league's future came in December of 1958. The Baltimore Colts and Johnny Unitas won a "sudden death" championship game victory over the New York Giants and the Baltimore Colts had riveted viewers across the country. The buzz that the game created put the NFL on the mass culture map in a new way, but Bell was not the man who would capitalize on it.

Bell experienced his own "sudden death" in the form of a fatal heart attack during a 1959 Steelers-Eagles game at Franklin Field in Philadelphia. After seven days of subsequent owner meetings, and twenty-three ballots, a compromise replacement was chosen: Pete Rozelle, the 33-year-old general manager of the Los Angeles Rams. Legend has it that he was in the men's room when he learned of his election.[41]

Despite—or because of—his youth, Rozelle was a visionary. He could see the future, and it had one big eye and lived in people's living rooms. Already familiar with the glaring socialism of the NFL's long-standing strong revenue-sharing rules for the gate, Rozelle proposed that owners consider sharing all their TV money as well. Rather than each team selling its rights individually, he suggested that the league do so as a single entity.

The league's recent setbacks in court and in Congress notwithstanding, Rozelle went ahead and negotiated a deal with CBS for national NFL rights. The deal *might* have passed legal muster—after all, the upstart American Football League (AFL) had already cut a $2 million national deal with ABC to carry its games through 1965—but instead was found by a federal court to violate antitrust law.[42]

The national packaging idea was going to need legislative approval. Given Bell's recent failure on Capitol Hill, Rozelle's initiative was bold indeed, perhaps a bit arrogant, and maybe even crazy. But Rozelle's West Coast media savvy gave him a more modern political touch than Bell had, and he was successful in winning congressional passage of the Sports Broadcasting Act of 1961 (SBA).

Under the SBA, teams in professional football, baseball, basketball and hockey leagues are allowed to collude in their dealings with national broadcasters, without running afoul of the Sherman Act. They are also permitted to share among themselves the revenues generated by those dealings. In order to pass, the law had a number of restrictions added on to it. Legislators worried about the effect on college and high school football inserted a provision prohibiting pro broadcasts on Friday nights or at any time on Saturdays from early September through early December.[43]

The NFL took immediate advantage of the SBA, negotiating a $4.6 million per year contract with CBS. Vince Lombardi's Green Bay Packers dynasty captured the national eye, and ratings increased by 50 percent. Two years later, the NFL cut another two-year deal with CBS for $14 million per season.[44] The league was hot, but fans were not permitted to decide what they could or couldn't watch. That was up to the arcaneries of the national broadcast contracts, and what was best for the networks.

The SBA truly is the "family jewels" for the NFL, and national TV revenues are the mother's milk of the league. Politicians are wise to this fact, and are not above taking advantage of it to get what they want. In December 2007, it only took a threat by Senator Christopher Dodd to revisit the SBA in order to get the 2007 Giants-Patriots game (in which the Pats were going for their last win for a perfect regular season) onto free TV.

Who Gets to Be in the Club?

Rozelle helped New Orleans celebrate All Saints Day 1966 when he blew into town with a surprise announcement: the NFL had granted the city a new expansion franchise. Coincidentally, Senator Hale Boggs of Louisiana, then the House minority whip, had just recently attached a rider to some inflation-fighting legislation that would exempt the just-announced AFL-NFL merger from antitrust law. The bill, which paved the way for the first Super Bowl in January of 1967, was signed into law on October 21, 1966, just days before Rozelle's trip to Louisiana.[45]

Franchise expansion is a fairly rare thing in the Big Four—owners are loathe to share national TV money any more than necessary—and nobody gets a franchise without ponying up hundreds of millions of dollars. The next NFL franchise will likely see an expansion fee of $1 billion or more, but the decision to expand depends on what is best for owners, not for fans.[46] Clearly, more fans would be served if each of the Big Four added a few teams, but fan welfare is not what drives incumbent owners.[47]

The Big Four generally also have been successful in protecting exclusive territories for their teams, even though such arrangements in other industries generally are found to violate antitrust law. For example, in 1953, the courts held that the NFL could create exclusive broadcast territories for teams to protect the gate, even if it meant that fans could be denied watching any but their own home team.[48] While this ruling did not stop the Raiders from moving into the Los Angeles Rams territory in the 1980s following a protracted legal battle, the franchise movement is more an exception than the rule.[49]

Monuments to Fandom

Easter Island has the statues, Egypt has the pyramids, and China has the Great Wall. Chicago has Soldier Field. In fact, there are more than 200 sports stadiums and arenas in the U.S. with a seating capacity of 30,000 or more. (See Table 2-1.) Five thousand years from now, anthropologists will be spinning yarns about our worship of sports, and the monuments that we built to help us practice our cultural religion.

TYPE	Number	Average Capacity	Largest Capacity
Football	144	58,632	107,000
Auto Racing	29	99,138	250,000
Baseball	28	44,893	57,000
Horse Racing	8	70,125	120,000
Basketball	1	32,000	32,000
Soccer	1	56,000	56,000

Table 2-1: List of Stadiums with Capacity of 30,000+ by Type and Capacity

Author's calculations adapted from World Stadiums. Accessed 5 January 2007 from http://www.worldstadiums.com.

Nobody knows for sure how the Easter Island statues were financed. But the pyramids, the Great Wall, and the home of the Bears all were built using plenty of government money. Since 1900, between $30 and $35 billion (in 2007 dollars) was spent to build major league parks and arenas, about $20 billion of which came out of the public coffer, just for teams in the Big Four leagues.[50] Big Four stadiums and arenas may cost obscene sums to build or renovate, but owners remain largely unconcerned as long as the public picks up most of the tab. (See Figure 2-1.)

Much of this public largess has come during the last few decades. As of 1950, only 12 of the 46 facilities in which Big Four teams played were publicly owned, and five of those were in the NBA. No NHL teams and only one MLB team then played in a publicly owned venue.[51] Conversely, about 70 percent of the franchises of the Big Four now play in venues constructed since 1980, and nearly all of these saw a significant public role in their creation. All but three NBA teams played the 2007–8 season in arenas built or significantly renovated since 1987. Opening Day 2008 in Major League Baseball (MLB) featured 20 parks built in 1990 or later. Similarly, 25 National Football League (NFL) teams spent the 2007 season in stadiums that were new or significantly renovated since 1992.[52]

Despite the significant personal wealth of most team owners, the public picked up nearly 65 percent of the roughly $22 billion cost of the 100 or

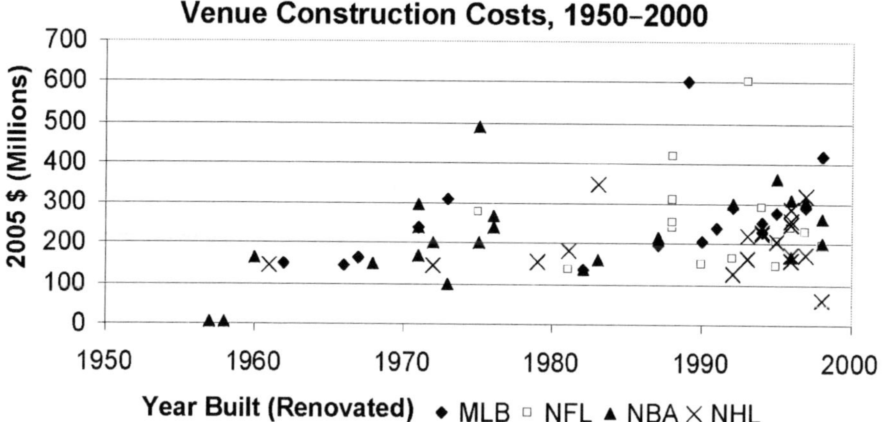

Figure 2-1: Stadium and Arena Construction and Major Renovation Costs for the Big Four Leagues, 1950–2000

Author's calculations adapted from World Stadiums. Accessed 5 January 2007 from http://www.worldstadiums.com.

so major league venues built or renovated since 1990.[53] Add to this subsidy a number of other sweetheart arrangements, such as the team getting to keep venue naming rights (which average more than $2.5 million per year for the 70+ venues that have them), or special low-cost, government-subsidized construction financing.[54] And it all comes out of the pockets of the citizens, fans and non-fans alike.

It is no surprise that owners want new venues. A new stadium is a surefire way to increase game attendance and profits for its first few seasons. Even casual fans feel a need to "check out the new digs," and owners are only too happy to capitalize on that sentiment. A study done on the attendance effects of MLB parks opened between 1950 and 2000 found that the occupied seats count increased by about a third in the parks' debut seasons (taking team winning into account). Ticket prices usually went up, too. This honeymoon effect lingered for two or three seasons for mostly multipurpose parks opened between 1960 and 1974, but for six to ten seasons for the newer facilities.[55]

That "new ballpark smell" is more than just an aphrodisiac for MLB owners—it can put $200 million extra into their wallets, plus extra concessions, naming rights, etc. The only problem is that it costs $250 million to build a new MLB park; fortunately for them, since the public picks up $170 million of it, owners only have to come up with about $80 million in order to get more than a quarter billion.[56]

Owners claim that such public subsidy is a net positive for the public.

They usually offer two arguments to make their point. The first is that their teams have positive economic impacts that more than justify their subsidy. The second is that fans are better off with a winning team, and that the extra revenue that the new facilities generate will improve competitive quality. These claims sound great, but do not really hold water.

During the last twenty years, essentially none of the hundreds of high-quality academic papers investigating economic impacts of major professional and college sports teams have found that they justify multihundred-million-dollar subsidies.[57] Even the biggest teams, such as the Yankees, generate revenues of $300 million per year or less. While this is a lot of money, it is only comparable to a large department store.[58] In a typical big league city, a business like this hardly is a blip in the economy.

Consider the Seattle-Tacoma community, the 15th largest U.S. metropolitan area, which had a $182 billion economy in 2005.[59] The *combined* revenues that year of the Seahawks (who went to the Super Bowl after that season), Mariners, and Sonics (who finished in first place) accounted for $449 million—less than *one-quarter of one percent* of total economic activity in the metro area.[60] Perhaps only the Green Bay Packers, with a home community of less than 250,000 people, is different. Even so, the team's $194 million in revenues represents only 1.5 percent of the surrounding area's $13 billion economy.

Furthermore, the economic "multiplier" effects of big league teams are also fairly insignificant. Once the team's facility is built, most of the jobs that remain are low-paying, and unlike other local businesses, a large chunk of the monies generated leave the local community in the form of player pay.[61] Visitors' spending associated with the team is not all that great because most fans attending games hail from fairly close by.[62] Locals' spending tends to replace other entertainment spending that would have happened anyway—it is not as if the team puts more money into fans' wallets. Of course, such facts do not deter the very high-priced consultants that teams retain for public relations purposes during their stadium drives. The assumptions and methods underlying their reports are considered laughable by most academic economists.

What about the ability of new facilities in helping teams win more games? Unfortunately, owners' claims about this fall flat, too. Only MLB and possibly NHL teams get better in the wake of a new venue, but even there, the effect is small.[63] Rather than re-investing in the team, owners are far more likely to simply pocket the majority of the new-stadium revenue bounty.

Yet despite these inconvenient facts, owners continue to ask for new publicly financed facilities, and generally continue to get them. Their top card to play is the threat of relocating the team if they do not get what they want. And they will get what they want as long as fans continue to love their teams so much, politicians do not want to get blame for losing them, and the federal government allows leagues to keep their clubs closed. We are addicted to our sports, and like most addicts, price is no object in satisfying our carnal sports urges.

3

We Are Sporticus

How did Americans get to be so addicted to sports? Suppressed in Colonial times, spectator sports grew and matured along with the nation. When mass media came about, sports were there, too. A propensity for fandom is hard-wired into our heads, and then our culture installs the software that makes us demand more and more. A sprawling sports media has developed to satisfy that demand. Most Americans' initial exposure to the mathematics of probability came in the form of sports statistics publicized by those media. Now an entire industry—fantasy sports—has been created around those stats. We care very much about competitive balance and fairness, although cheating can provide enormous rewards for those with sufficiently pliant ethics.

Spectator sports fandom is very much a part of who we are.

In the Beginning, There Were Spectator Sports

When most people think of primordial spectator sports, they think of the ancient Olympic Games, which date back to at least 776 B.C.[1] But the Games' origins are shrouded in very old mists and myths. One story is that Zeus himself started the Games to celebrate his victory over Cronos for control of the world. Another tale, attributed to Pindar of the 5th century B.C., is that a Greek hero named Pelops sought the hand of Hippodamia, daughter of King Oenomaus. The king required that Hippodamia's suitors beat him in a chariot race before he would consent to her marriage. He had defeated twelve earlier beaus, and displayed their heads in order to make his point to any others who might be bold enough to pursue his daughter. True love conquers all, however; Hippodamia sabotaged Dad's chariot, whereupon he not only lost, but died in the process. There's nothing new about fixing games or steroids—cheating is even part of one of our earliest sports myths.[2]

Just as small-but-proud American burgs bicker over the genesis of the hamburger—sometimes employing rather creative history—so do patriotic researchers studying their favorite ancient civilizations. Dr. Labib Boutros, former director of athletics at the University of Beirut, suggests that the Olympics have even older roots than the Greek stories would allow. He points to a 15th century B.C. stadium excavation in Amrit, on the coast of northern Phoenicia, facing the island of Arwad. He notes that its topology matches that of the stadium at Olympia, and claims that it was the Phoenicians that brought their religious and cultural traditions, including sports, to the Greeks while exiled in their country.[3] He claims that the Games may have been subsumed by the Greeks into their other ritual tributes to Zeus.

Religion also played a role in the end of the ancient Olympic Games' many-century run when the Roman emperor Theodosius banned the Games as pagan activities in 339 A.D.[4] As if to make a divine point, Olympia was hit by a series of earthquakes beginning in 522 A.D., and resulting river floods buried the place under fifteen to twenty feet of yellow silt.

In any event, a considerable body of archeological work supports the proposition that spectator sports have been part of human culture for a very long time, and that they did not arise out of the ether in ancient Greece. The ruins of the primary civilizations of the world—in Mesopotamia, Egypt, India, and Mesoamerica—all show obvious signs of significant spectator sporting activity. Such evidence dates at least as far back as the Early Dynastic Period of the Sumerian Civilization (3000–1500 B.C.), and perhaps even earlier.[5]

In fact if one rather bold Chinese source is to be believed, stone hunting balls unearthed in Gaoyang County in China's Shanxi Province are over 100,000 years old, and were also supposedly used for shot-put-like competitions.[6] That's a fairly impressive finding, considering that archeologists estimate that the earliest modern humans in Asia arrived or evolved there just around that time.[7] If we allow ourselves to believe this, it is not too much of a stretch to also believe that there surely were other people who watched the throwers ply their skills against each other. No doubt the best of them drew crowds, complete with factions of supporters for each of the participants. Perhaps the most successful of them even enjoyed some degree of local celebrity. Did "chicks dig the long ball" one hundred millennia ago?

Whether such stories are factual or fanciful, archeologists have demonstrated very credibly that the spectator aspect of sporting events probably became fairly sophisticated at a very early date in human existence. Several thousand-year-old drawings on pharaonic monuments indicated that ancient Egypt was rife with spectator sporting competitions that bear remarkable resemblance to our own. Evidence of ball games is found in some of their second millennium B.C. wall-paintings.[8] Like our modern day big leagues, Egyptians gave their sports basic rules, neutral referees, player uniforms, and a means of recognizing winners by awarding them different collars.[9]

It Comes Down to Economics

Ancient Greek and Egyptian civilizations were able to muster and maintain elaborate displays of spectator sports because they had enough resources to do so. Subsistence cultures do not have the luxury of such frivolous use of their time and energy. In any society, economics plays a critical role in the rise of large-scale spectator sports, just as it does for any other form of high culture. A society's economy simply must be capable of generating sufficient food, shelter, clothing, and other basic necessities to free up the plenty that would make spectator sports a viable and worthwhile proposition.

Moreover, it is difficult to imagine an economically thriving society that does not also have a flourishing set of spectator sports to accompany their art, drama, music or other forms of non-participatory entertainment. Digs around the world suggest that sporting spectacles developed in the same ancient civilizations that also created writing, well-developed political and legal structures, and elaborate architecture.[10] Essentially, it is fair to say that spectator sports evolve as part of societies' development of other types of basic social institutions.

A case in point is found in the Minoan period of Crete, in the second century B.C. The Cretans became wealthy and powerful by engaging in sophisticated trade promoted by the strength of their navy, which may have had a greater commercial than military focus. Their trading success spawned an early "leisure society" and there is ample evidence that they were sports crazy. Digs at the ruins of the Palace of Minos at Knossos show that they loved boxing and bull-jumping—and had the means to pay for them.[11]

Thus, we should regard our Thanksgiving Day football, March Madness basketball, and World Cup soccer as modern manifestations of a very old human urge rather than something unique to our own age. The only real difference is the immense wealth that much of our world now enjoys; this affluence, although not universally shared, allows for a grander scale for our spectator sports—and for our other arts—than our ancestors possibly could have imagined.

We Are Sporticus

Life in America now is vastly different than it was three centuries ago. Few think of mainstream 21st century American society as Puritanical; indeed, it is quite the opposite, which is part of the reason why so many religious fundamentalists of all creeds deeply dislike our culture. We have certainly become a much more hedonistic people, and a goodly part of our nearly $10 trillion annual personal consumption is what we spend to entertain ourselves with all kinds of diversions, including spectator sports.

But how did we get here, and why do spectator sports occupy such an apparently outsized corner of the American—indeed, the human—condition? Why do we tie our psyches to the fortunes of our local teams? Why do we find entire sections of general-interest newspapers devoted to sports? And why do we spend princely sums on our beloved teams, not to mention the billions of tax dollars to fund the "American Pyramids" that dot our cities? Couldn't these resources be put to better use solving our society's myriad problems?

They could, but we won't. Rather, watching sports obviously is deeply programmed into our genes; human beings have been doing so as long as they have been sapient creatures. It will always be so, as long as our species wanders the earth. We are *Homo Sporticus.* Not that there is anything wrong with that.

Sports in Colonial and Antebellum America

Not every advanced culture has embraced sports as a positive, or even benign, social force. In fact, America's own family tree includes those with a rather jaundiced view of such frivolities. A telling incident involves William Bradford, the first governor of the Plymouth Colony. Bradford called all the able-bodied Pilgrims in the colony to work on Christmas Day 1621. To the devout Pilgrims, Christmas had become too much of a pagan holiday co-opted by a morally bankrupt and corrupt Roman Catholic Church; it certainly was not something to be celebrated with festivities of any sort. Charles Dickens' thoughts on the subject were more than two centuries in the future. Upon returning to town from his own work for his noon meal, Bradford found some of his constituents "openly at play." He describes them as engaged in such sinful activities as "stool-ball" and "pitching at the bar." A good Puritan, Bradford got his front-buttoned breeches in a bunch over the moral offense of playing these 17th century English folk games on a holy day, and promptly seized their equipment.[12] Later, even the Continental Congress prohibited games, sports, theater, and other amusements they deemed as inappropriate for a nascent country earnestly embarking on its independence.[13] Such heavy discouragement, along with the economic harshness of early colonial existence, caused significant spectator sports to be largely absent in the Colonies, particularly in New England, until the middle part of the 18th century. In the South, however, it was a different story.

A wealthy ruling class began to emerge in the gentrifying and pastoral southern colonies at the beginning of the 18th century. Fed by the institution of slavery, southern society stratified, eroding the appeal of daily, diligent hard work and sober piety. Newly minted gentlemen were drawn to a more leisurely way of life than their northern cousins, one that incorporated such diversions as horse racing, cockfighting, and hunting. Some of these sports, which generally included varying degrees of drinking and gambling, even began to democratize a bit; the genteel sometimes mingled at these proceedings with those much further down the socio-economic ladder.

By the end of the 18th century, the South had developed a thriving thoroughbred breeding and racing industry, and played host to numerous fairs and festivals keyed to the annual rhythms of plantation life. These events frequently included various sporting events as important parts of the festivities, and could feature as many as several thousand spectators.[14]

The northern cities of the early 19th century eventually also found themselves with their own gentry comprised of successful merchants, colonial officials, landowners, and military officers. They too began to develop a more favorable attitude toward leisurely play. While the gentlemen of Philadelphia and New York interested themselves in horse racing and cockfighting, the cities' tavern owners offered tradesmen and laborers more menial games such as darts and bowling. These diversions were not always popular with the whole of the citizenry, however. For example, in 1802 Philadelphia, 1,500 merchants and 1,200 manufacturers signed a petition protesting a local racecourse. The petition was rife with language describing how the track contributed to the "dissipation" of men's characters; the verbiage harkened back to the city's Protestant work ethic roots.[15]

The Genesis of the American Sporting Fraternity

The early 19th century saw an infant United States enter adolescence. Despite the new nation's Puritan legacy, the larger story of pre–Civil War America is one of a country beginning to industrialize. The plow, the land, and the village found themselves supplanted by the machine, the factory, and the marketplace. The movement away from the semi-subsistence rural existence and toward a more urbanized market economy diminished the appeal of the Calvinist celebration of sweat and toil, and created fertile socio economic conditions for the rise of a robust spectator sport culture. The Yankee fruition of the Industrial Revolution led to more than a tripling of the country's population (Figure 3-1) and a near-tripling of economic output per person (Figure 3-2).

American life was profoundly affected by these changes. As the country added miles of railroads—often in spite of very poor returns for investors, incidentally—the three-week stagecoach trek across the West quickly con-

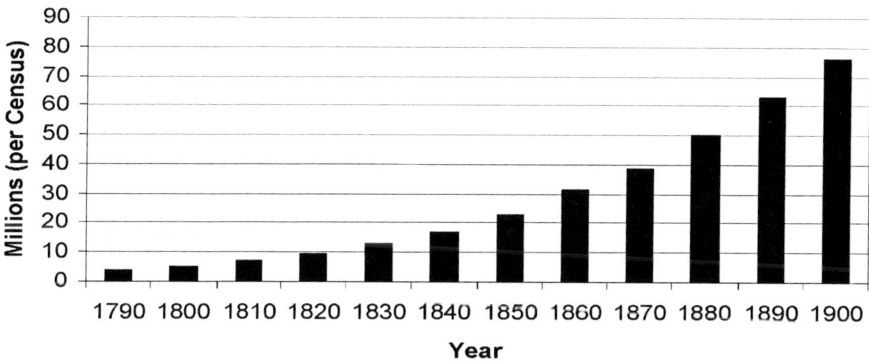

Figure 3-1: U.S. Population, 1790–1900

Sources: U.S. Department of Commerce, Census Bureau. Accessed August 10, 2005, from http://www.census.gov/population/censusdata/table-2.pdf. Values for 2000 and 2005 accessed August 10, 2005, from www.census.gov.

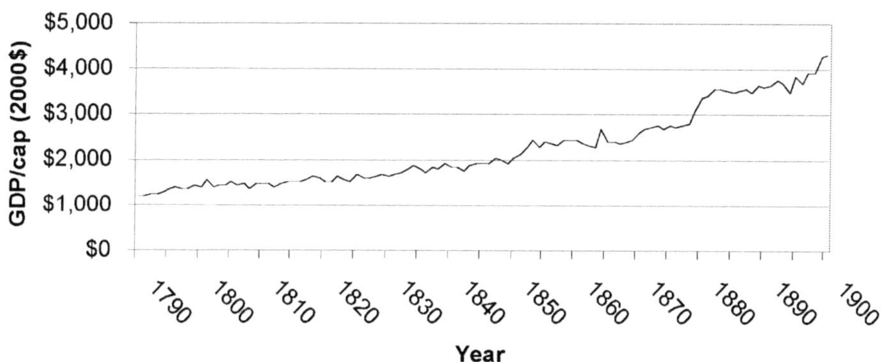

Figure 3-2: U.S. Real GDP per Capita, 1790–1900

Sources: Economic History website, http://www.eh.net, accessed Sept. 26, 2005; U.S. Department of Commerce, Census Bureau, accessed August 10, 2005 from http://www.census.gov/population/censusdata/table-2.pdf.

densed into the three-day train trip. Goods from all over the country and the world became much more easily available. News traveled more easily, too, first by rail, and later by telegraph. The country was becoming a smaller place.

Word of greater economic opportunity encouraged a significant migration to cities, and the great American shift from rural to urban life was on (Figure 3-3). Americans found themselves living in increasingly closer proximity to each other (Figures 3-4 and 3-5). Whereas more than 90 percent of Americans in 1800 lived in rural areas, close to half of the country's population was urban in 1900.[16]

No city exceeded 50,000 residents in 1790, but by 1870, more than fifty cities were even more populous than that.[18] This more concentrated, richer

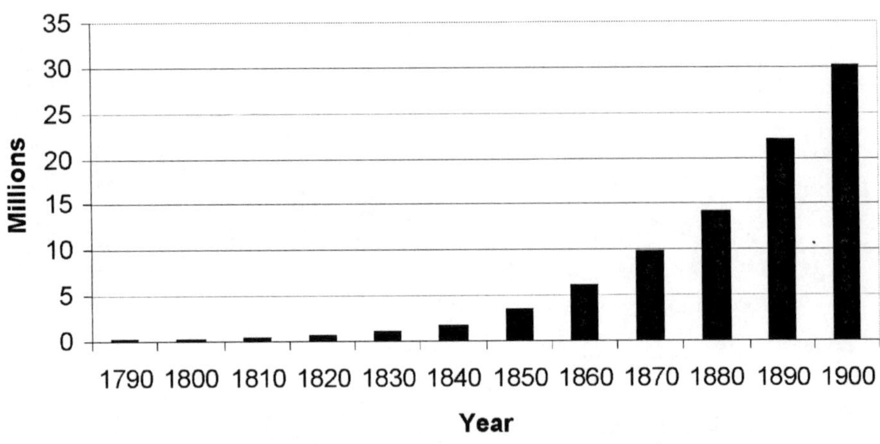

Figure 3-3: Total U.S. Urban Population, 1890–1900

Source: Don Dodd, Historical Statistics of the States of the United States: Two Centuries of the Census, 1790–1990 *(Westport, CT: Greenwood Press, 1993); U.S. Bureau of the Census,* Statistical Abstract of the United States, 1992 *(Washington, DC: GPO, 1992).*

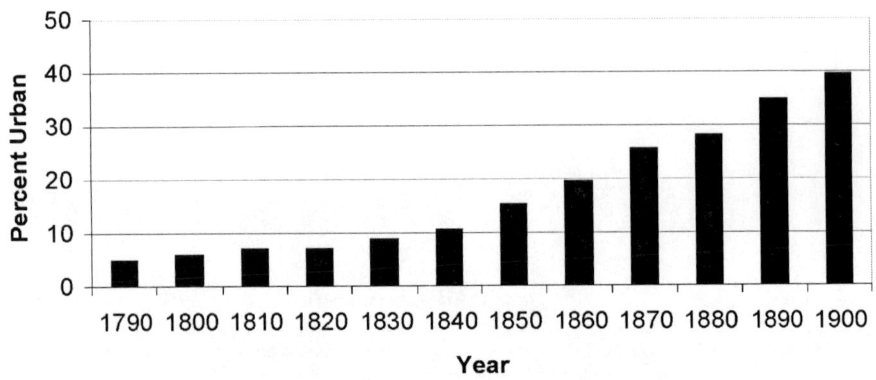

Figure 3-4: Percent of U.S. Population Living in Urban Areas, 1790–1900

Source: Don Dodd, Historical Statistics of the States of the United States: Two Centuries of the Census, 1790–1990 *(Westport, CT: Greenwood Press, 1993).*

population found itself with more leisure time, ever greater means to make more of it than ever before, and ever more and closer neighbors with whom to share it.

Typically, it was the most able of a German or Irish family's males who would make the voyage alone to the New World. They were to send as much money back home as possible, in the hopes that their kinfolk would finally be able to join them in their new life. But many of these new Americans were

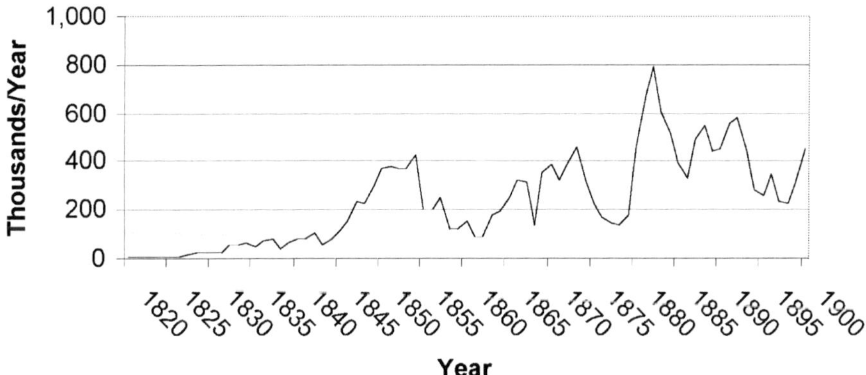

Figure 3-5: Immigration to the U.S., 1820–1900

Source: U.S. Department of Homeland Security, Office of Immigration Statistics, Yearbook of Immigration Statistics: 2005. Accessed at http://www.uscis.gov/graphics/shared/statistics/yearbook/LPR05.htm.

Catholic, not Protestant, and they generally had no truck with Puritan notions about the sinful idleness of spectator or participatory sports.

Not surprisingly, males made up a disproportionate share of the new American urban population. In 1840, for example, there were twice as many men as women between the ages of 20 and 50 living in the important and teeming port city of New Orleans. Twenty years later, the city still had six thousand more males than females. In 1850, almost 40 percent of American men between twenty-five and thirty-five were unmarried. As might be expected, these men—who came from nearby farms as well as from far abroad—sometimes gave way to the temptation of spending some of their beefier income on themselves. The new large, urban, single, often middle-income, male population meant the boom of brothels, gambling halls, and spectator sports.

By the 1840s, it would have been clear to any observer that an urban spectator sporting culture had evolved from almost nothing a half a century earlier. Saloons in New York, homes to city-dwelling workingmen during their off-hours, boasted of hosting illicit prize-fighting contests, and of making available for reading such early sporting sheets as William T. Porter's *Spirit of the Times* and *The Clipper*.

Horse racing, pedestrianism (foot-racing), boxing, rowing, and billiards were the primary professional sports of choice for these early Victorian spectators, and the money involved often was not trivial. In 1849, in a $20,000 bout (nearly half a million in 2006 dollars), Tom Hyer, the "Great American Hope" beat Tom "Yankee" Sullivan, a British boxer who came to the U.S. following England's widespread bans of the sport. It is said that this was the first sports story ever transmitted via telegraph.[18] A billiards championship held in Detroit in 1859 resulted in the winner, one Michael Phelan, reportedly cashing in on the equivalent of about $350,000 in 2006 dollars.[19] The American sporting fraternity was born in the first half of the 19th century.[20]

4

Spectator Sports Become Big Business

It was the American sporting fraternity that fathered the business of spectator sports. The first spawn was baseball, whose own story in many ways is the main thread in all of American sport's history. Early generations of American boys played ball games, just as boys do everywhere. As they grew up, so did the new country's main cities of Philadelphia, New York, and Boston. When these boys became urban men in the late 1820s and 1830s, they had a bit more free time than their rural counterparts, and continued to play and refine their childhood ball games.

In 1831, groups of Philadelphians, seeking to get away from the town's enduring and oppressive Puritanism, crossed the Delaware River to play town-ball in then-bucolic New Jersey. They played pick-up games of "two-old-cat," which before long became well-attended regular Saturday "rounders" and town-ball contests. They combined with another town-ball group from the city in 1831 to form the Olympic Ball Club of Philadelphia.[1]

The men of the Olympic Club apparently liked to have fun and consumed an "adult beverage" or two, which led to varying levels of scolding by the more respectable elements of Philadelphia society. But these hardly were ruffians. Rather, they were young, successful merchants and professionals because those with more meager means would not be able to afford the equipment, the cost of getting across the river or the leisure time to play. In 1837, the club agreed to a formal constitution, the first formal baseball rules document known.[2]

More is known about a similar group, the New York Knickerbocker Club. They regularly gathered in a vacant lot at the corner of Twenty-Seventh Street and Madison Avenue in Manhattan, not far from where Madison Square Garden now stands. After a few years of relatively unstructured play, New York's economic growth pushed them out of this location, forcing them to make other arrangements. Led by Alexander J. Cartwright,

Jr., the group drew up a constitution, codified the game's rules, and secured grounds at Elysian Fields in Hoboken at a cost of $75 per year, including use of the site's dressing rooms. They called themselves the New York Knickerbockers Base Ball Club, and they lasted from 1845 until 1882, well after the formation of the National League.[3] While there were earlier teams in New York and in Philadelphia that played a sport that we now would identify as baseball, the Knickerbockers were given credit as the seminal entity of the game by no less than Henry Chadwick, an English-born cricket reporter for the *New York Times* who became the dean of baseball's earliest writers.[4]

Chadwick, ironically, played a role in the now-discredited myth of Abner Doubleday's invention of the game from scratch, or at least from townball, in 1839. Near the end of his life, in 1905, Chadwick wrote an article about how baseball probably evolved in the U.S. as a descendent of rounders, as claimed by Robin Carver in 1939 in his *Book of Sport*.[5] Such an origin should not strain the imagination; after all, stool ball, the early stick-and-ball game, is mentioned in England writings as early as 1085, during the time of William the Conqueror.[6]

The claim of a British bastard pedigree for the quintessential American game did not sit well with a lot of fin de siecle baseball people. At the urging of sporting goods magnate Albert Spaulding, the Mills Commission, a blue-ribbon panel led by Colonel A.G. Mills of New York, was charged with the determination of baseball's true origins. Mills seemed like a good choice as chair as he had played baseball before the Civil War, and had been the fourth president of the National League (1882–1884). Other august commission members included Morgan G. Bulkeley, the first president of the National League, a former governor, and then–U.S. senator from Connecticut; Arthur P. Gorman, a senator from Maryland; Nicholas E. Young, the fourth president of the National League (1884–1902); Alfred Reach and George Wright, two well-known businessmen and former players; and James E. Sullivan, president of the Amateur Athletic Union.[7]

Three years later, on December 30, 1907, after much investigation, the commission issued its final report. It came down on the side of the Doubleday story, apparently relying largely on the testimony of Abner Graves, a mining engineer from Denver. Graves had attended school with Doubleday in Cooperstown, New York, not coincidentally now home to the Baseball Hall of Fame. Graves claimed to have been in attendance when Doubleday made the decisive changes to the rules of townball, including the creation of the baseball diamond.

Many contemporary scholars, however, suggest that it was Spaulding, who by the early 20th century was making a very good living selling sporting goods to Americans, who pushed hard for the patriotic fairy tale over a less dramatic evolution story. Who better to have invented America's game than Doubleday, the man who allegedly fired the first shot as a captain for the Union at Fort Sumpter?[8]

Whatever the truth about baseball's beginnings, the majority of the early Knickerbockers were primarily white-collar workers, and with a few exceptions, drawn from the city's middle class. Of the forty-four players between 1845 and 1850 whose occupations can be identified, one-third had jobs in commerce and finance. About a quarter were doctors or lawyers, with the rest holding various and sundry other clerical occupations. The Knickerbockers only played each other until 1851, when a rash of other clubs began to come into existence. These clubs also had memberships that of white-collar professionals, small-business proprietors, and skilled craftsmen.[9]

In 1851, one such club, the Washington Club of Brooklyn (later the Gotham Club), challenged the Knickerbockers to a home-and-home series, which quickly became an annual contest. The competition drew some attention, and obviously at least a few spectators. Both the *Spirit* and another newspaper, the *Mercury*, reported on the games as early as 1853. While these reports were usually just three or four lines, they also often were accompanied by a rudimentary box score. The *Spirit* actually helped facilitate the formation of more clubs by publishing the Knickerbockers' rules and a diagram of a playing field in 1855. By the end of that year, there were over 125 teams in the New York metropolitan area, and New York area landowners were known to maintain baseball fields in order to rent them out for profit.[10] It was not long before the first fully enclosed baseball park, the Union Grounds in Brooklyn, was built, in 1862. This style of park soon became popular because it allowed owners to sell food and drink to spectators without competition from street vendors.[11]

The Dawn of a Respectable Professionalism

With its popular success, baseball inevitably began to become less about social intercourse, and more about winning. The increasing fan interest also brought about a significant degree of gambling. The gentleman's amateur game began to feature "revolvers," ringers who would play for different clubs for a few dollars. It was not long before the larger clubs began to pay skilled players under the table, or arrange sham jobs for them in order to represent their squads.

These changes, and the proliferation of baseball teams around New York, led to a call for an overall governing body of the sport as early as 1855. A convention finally gathered in December of 1857, and Dr. Daniel Adams of the Knickerbockers was elected president. With only a few changes, the Knickerbockers' rules were essentially adopted as the official rules of baseball. In 1858, twenty-six of the larger baseball clubs came together to form the National

Association of Amateur Baseball Players. Adopting the rules agreed upon the prior year, the NAABP explicitly forbade professional players, and chose William H. Van Cott as its first president.[12]

The National Pastime

The formation of the NAABP was an important milestone in the history of American spectator sports. While the organization was somewhat weak and ostensibly amateur-only, it was baseball's first example of the type of central body that any spectator sport needs in order to expand. By 1860 there were more than sixty members of the NAABP, and fans were routinely charged admission to their teams' games.[13] The game began to become part of the fabric of American life; a championship game between the Mutual Club of Manhattan and the Atlantic Club of Brooklyn was seen by 20,000 fans.

By the beginning of the Civil War, baseball already was generally accepted as the national pastime. While the war temporarily disrupted the game, it also facilitated its spread across the country. The 1868 NAABP convention had representatives from over 100 clubs from villages and burghs all over the U.S.[14]

Even though the NAABP strictly banned play-for-pay, the practice proliferated; in fact, the basic economic structure of the league almost guaranteed it. By sanctioning admissions fees while outlawing player pay, the NAABP created strong incentives to cheat—just as the NCAA does in its revenue sports today, with many of the same problems.

In 1869 the Wright Brothers of Ohio—Harry and George, not the perhaps better-known Wilbur and Orville—formed the Cincinnati Red Stockings, the first baseball team made up of overt professionals. Paying between $600 and $1,400 per man per season (about $9,000 to $21,000 in 2006 dollars), the Wrights were able to recruit the very best players from all over the baseball nation.[15] They barnstormed across the country, taking on and beating all comers.[16] The team won all 65 of its games during 1869, racking up a grand profit of $1.39 for the season.

On June 14, 1870, following 27 more straight victories, the Red Stockings rolled into New York to play the Brooklyn Atlantics. Fifteen thousand spectators paid fifty cents each to watch the teams play to a five-run tie at the end of nine innings. Henry Chadwick, in attendance of course, was consulted about what to do next. He deemed that the game should be played until there was a winner, a practice that is still held sacred among baseball faithful (as current MLB Commissioner Bud Selig found out following the 2002 All-Star game). The Atlantics finally broke the Red Stockings 92-game winning streak by scoring in the 11th inning.[17]

The loss meant that the magic of the Red Stockings was spent, and interest in the team fell off. The team ultimately folded, and Harry took his three best players east to play in Boston, eventually forming the Boston (then Milwaukee, then Atlanta) Braves.[18]

But the genie was out of the bottle—there was no putting the professional toothpaste back into the amateur tube. The Red Stockings were the first American professional spectator sports team as we now know them, the offspring of the country's burgeoning population and wealth.

In March of 1871, the first truly professional baseball league, the National Association of Professional Baseball Players (NAPBP), was formed at Colliers' Café in New York City. Teams paid a $10 fee to be eligible for the league's championship, and each team was required to play five games against each of the others, although no formal league schedule was created.

Like many pioneers, the league faced its share of serious problems. During its five somewhat rocky years of operation, twenty-five different teams wandered into and out of the league, which had significant competitive balance problems (Table 4-1).

TEAM	1871	1872	1873	1874	1875
Brooklyn Atlantics		0.243	0.315	0.400	0.045
Philadelphia Athletics	0.750	0.682	0.549	0.600	0.726
Boston Red Stockings	0.667	0.830	0.729	0.743	0.899
Baltimore Lord Baltimores		0.648	0.607	0.191	
Chicago White Stockings	0.679				
Cleveland Forest Cities	0.345	0.600			
Brooklyn Eckfords		0.103			
Hartford Dark Blues				0.302	0.659
Fort Wayne Kekiongas	0.368				
Middletown Mansfields		0.208			
Baltimore Marylands			0.000		
New York Mutuals	0.485	0.630	0.547	0.646	0.448
Washington Nationals		.000	0.205		0.179
New Haven Elm Citys					0.149
Washington Olympics	0.500	0.222			
Philadelphia White Stockings			0.679	0.500*	0.544**
Rockford Forest Cities	0.160				
St. Louis Red Stockings					0.211
Troy Haymakers	0.464	0.600			
Keokuk Westerns					0.077

Table 4-1: Winning Percentages of National Association Teams, 1871–1875

Source: Adapted from Rod Fort's "Sports Business Pages," http://rodneyfort.com/SportsData/BizFrame.htm.

* Team was known as the Pearls.

** Team was known as the Phillies.

Teams out of the pennant race often would simply quit traveling and playing; for example, of the thirteen teams that began the league's final season, only seven remained at the end of the year. The reincarnated Red Stockings, now in Boston, were the only team that played out its entire 1875 schedule. Furthermore, gambling and rowdy drunken behavior among fans limited the league's appeal, and roster shenanigans such as revolving eroded the legitimacy of contests. Philadelphia managed to win the league in 1871, but the Boston team took the last four championships easily, posting a ridiculous 71–8 record during the league's final season.[19]

The National Association's fitful start and relatively quick demise is now no more than a sports trivia question for even the most dedicated of baseball fans. But it marks an important milestone in American professional spectator sports history. The association suggested that an American sports league could be a real business.

The National League

By early 1876, it was obvious that the National Association of Professional Baseball Players was a corpse, done in by poor management and fixed games.[20] However, it was equally obvious that good money could be made in this baseball thing, but that firmer oversight of the league was needed. William Hulbert, then owner of the Chicago White Stockings, lured four of Boston's top players to his roster, and then convened the top eight teams, including the cuckolded Red Stockings, from the National Association to create a new league. This league, which exists to this day as MLB's National League, is the first clearly recognizable modern professional spectator sports league in North America. The NL included four western teams (Chicago, Cincinnati, St. Louis, and Louisville) and four eastern teams (Hartford, New York, Boston, and Philadelphia). Some of the more important innovations of Hulbert's new league were a set number of franchises (limited to cities with populations in excess of 75,000), and a balanced 70-game schedule (ten against each of the other teams), which was set in advance.

Hulbert, who essentially controlled the NL until his death in 1882, was not kidding about teams honoring schedules. During the league's inaugural 1876 season, the New York Mutuals (owned by the famed William Marcy "Boss" Tweed) and the Philadelphia Athletics (who were rumored to have been involved with gamblers) failed to play out all of their games.[21] Hulbert kicked them out, and the remaining teams played a 60-game schedule for the 1877 season.

In order to deter the thug element, alcohol was verboten in all NL parks.[22] Gambling also was not tolerated; Hulbert's investigation into the curious manner in which Louisville blew the 1877 pennant resulted in the team's expulsion from the NL. Four Louisville players thought to be involved were banned for life.[23] These events were within living memory when the Black Sox scandal hit in 1919, and had an impact on the later ferocity of MLB's response to that debacle.

The league was not terribly profitable in its earliest years, compelling teams to look for ways to save money.[24] One of the most important of these was allegedly proposed in secret at an owners' meeting in 1879, by Arthur Soden, who was by then the proprietor of the Boston team. Soden suggested that each team be allowed to "reserve" up to five players, who would be off-limits to all other owners. This system quickly proved popular with owners because it depressed player salaries, and by 1890, teams' entire rosters were reserved.[25]

For the next eighty-five years, the reserve clause was the cornerstone on which North American professional spectator sports leagues were built. It stoutly withstood the pressures of Teddy Roosevelt's trust-busting, the labor movement of the 1930s, and the influence of television money well into the late 20th century. The notion that somehow teams are owed the loyalty of their athlete-employees still colors the way that many fans view their favorite players.

The voracity of the Gilded Age's laissez-faire capitalism did not spare professional baseball; rather, it made it among the first national entertainment industries. Between 1890 and 1899, total National League attendance more than tripled, from 777,932 to 2,543,384. But another spectator sport, less pastoral and more in tune with the timed precision of the Industrial Era, began to capture public attention.

5

Entertainment for the New Century

Football: The Sport for an Industrial Nation

About the same time that well-heeled twenty and thirty-somethings were forming amateur baseball clubs, college boys—perhaps as always—were seeking to prove their manhood. During the 1820s, Ivy Leaguers at Princeton and Dartmouth played a rough sport similar to the soccer-like game allegedly invented in 1823 by William Ellis at Rugby College in England. While the game of rugby had codified rules by 1845, it was not until 1871 when the Dartmouth version of the game, "Old Division Football," had its rules written down.[1]

In fact, by the middle of the 1800s, it was common practice for each institution to have its own violent form of a "foot-ball" game, complete with its own unique rules—sometimes unwritten.[2] Schools regularly challenged each other to matches, with home teams commonly providing referees who interpreted the peculiarities of local convention. The first "real" football game is generally acknowledged to have been played in New Brunswick, NJ, in November of 1869 between Rutgers and Princeton.[3] About 100 fans were in attendance.

By 1873, Yale, Princeton, and Columbia had agreed on a set of rules based on the Yale version of the game in which players could not run with the ball; not surprisingly, Harvard stayed out of the alliance. The Crimson Tide favored the "Boston" version of the game in which running was permitted.[4] Eventually, Harvard's rules prevailed, and in the 1880s, Yale's doctor-alum-coach Walter Camp began his relentless lifelong mission to refine and promote the game. Among Camp's many innovations were the ten-yard first down, four downs, eleven-man teams, and the line of scrimmage. Under his direction, the Yale football team won 97 percent of its games between 1883 and 1887.[5]

It wasn't very long before intercollegiate football rivalries began to arise. Yale-Harvard football, for example, seemed as natural as Oxford-Cambridge crew, although with considerably more broken teeth. College faculties took a dim view of the brutal game, and generally banned the sport from campuses. Undeterred, students played off-campus, no doubt drawing local student and townie crowds to their often-bloody spectacles.[6]

While crew, cricket, rifle, lacrosse, bicycling, tennis, polo, cross-country, fencing, basketball, trap shooting, golf, water polo, swimming and gymnastics were also played intercollegiately during the last half of the 19th century, by the 1890s, it was football that sparked the greatest interest among spectators.[7] As early as 1878, the student organizers of a Princeton-Yale game rented a Hoboken field for $300, drawing over 4,000 fans.[8] The annual Thanksgiving Day championship game for the student-run Intercollegiate Football Association, first played in 1876, soon became the premier spectator athletic event in the country. In the 1890s, the game was played at the Polo Grounds in New York City, regularly drawing 40,000 or more spectators.

While the Thanksgiving contenders usually were the august Princeton and Yale, the event was roundly criticized for the violence, drinking, and betting that it begat among spectators. Such tomfoolery did not sit well with frontier religion neo–Puritans. One such group, the Popular Amusements Committee of the 1894 Kansas Methodist Conference, called upon the presidents of their institutions of higher learning to prohibit the game.[9] They were little heeded, particularly on the East Coast, and the game remained popular and vicious. By 1895, perhaps as many as 120,000 college, high school, and club athletes played in 5,000 or more Thanksgiving Day football games.[10]

Harvard and Yale cleared about $50,000 per year each for the 1900 season—over $1 million in 2006 dollars. Ten years later, the two schools were even making about 70 percent more annually from the sport.[11]

Big bucks meant "pay-for-play" cheating and other financial temptations. Amid scandals and a rash of player deaths and serious injuries, President Theodore Roosevelt—a strong proponent of gentlemanly but rigorous amateur sports—called football coaches and athletic representatives from Harvard, Yale, and Princeton to the White House in early 1905. But the ensuing season resulted in the deaths of another 18 players, so Roosevelt convened a second meeting that October at which he leaned on the three schools' representatives to reform the sport. The National Collegiate Athletic Association traces its origins to these 1905 meetings.

Harvard's president, Charles W. Ellis, was particularly proactive in taking Roosevelt's advice, as the school had a new football-only stadium to fill. Costing $310,000 (about $7 million in 2006 dollars), Harvard's stadium was constructed over a four-and-a-half month period using 250,000 cubic feet of concrete. Opened in 1903, it had a capacity of 22,500 fans, which was expanded by 1929 to 57,750.[12] While college faculties might have disdained football—some still do—college presidents don't get to be college presidents by missing significant revenue opportunities.

The other Ivies, naturally, were not terribly far behind in cashing in on the football craze. The 70,869-seat Yale Bowl, replacing the 33,000-seat Yale Field, was opened in 1914 at a cost of $750,000 (about $16 million in 2006). Princeton's now-replaced 45,725-seat Palmer Stadium also opened in 1914, and Brown's 25,597-seat Schoelkopf Field was unveiled the following year. Large venues were built at Dartmouth (20,416) and Penn (52,593) for the 1923 season, and at Brown (20,000) in 1925. Other schools also saw the revenue potential in large college football stadia, particularly in the Midwest and West: University of Wisconsin (1917), University of Washington (1920), Ohio State (1922), Purdue (1924) and Notre Dame (1930). They wouldn't have built 'em if they didn't think they'd come.

The 1920s saw the dawn of a new college football tradition: the bowl game. The first of these had begun in 1902 to help attract more visitors to a struggling Tournament of Roses. The undefeated 1901 University of Michigan team met the Stanford University squad in a match that guaranteed the participating teams a whopping $3,500 (about $85,000 in 2006 dollars). The game was won 49–0 by Michigan, attracting 8,000 spectators.[13] Although the game turned a profit, organizers feared that such a lopsided game would turn off visitors for the next year. They replaced the football game with, of all things, amateur, then professional, chariot racing. Whispers of the races being fixed eventually led back to another featured game in 1916. The event became annual, and was moved to the 57,000-seat Rose Bowl and renamed when the venue was opened in 1923. In 1928, the stadium was expanded to hold 76,000 fans.[14]

With such strong demand for amateur collegiate contests, it was not long before others tried making money at football without the messy burden of college presidents and faculties. In the 1870s and 1880s, young men formed local football clubs across the East and Midwest in much the same way that members of their fathers' generation had done with baseball; however, these were amateur affairs meant primarily as recreational activities. While some of their games surely drew crowds, these events were more like park district softball games than for-profit ventures.

A football game played on November 12, 1882, between the Allegheny Athletic Association and the Pittsburgh Athletic Club changed all this. One of the Allegheny players, one William (Pudge) Heffelfinger, was openly paid $500 for his services. Despite the "huge" payment—equivalent to about $11,000 in 2006 dollars—the Allegheny Athletic Club cleared a profit on the game of $621 (about $14,000 in 2006 dollars).[15] Play it, and they will come—in 1897, the Latrobe Athletic Club became the first football team to play a full season with an all-professional roster.[16]

The Fab Five—The First Rock Stars?

By the end of the 19th century, spectator sports had already spawned a few celebrities—bareknuckle fighter John L. Sullivan and baseballer John Montgomery Ward, for example—but the modern sports-figure-as-rock-star had to wait for the 20th century. The phenomenon of mass media hit its stride during the prosperous 1920s, and Americans truly began living richer and longer. (See Figure 5-1 and Figure 5-2.)

Technological innovation created a middle-class with a little disposable income, leading to the creation of the serious business of leisure. The biggest

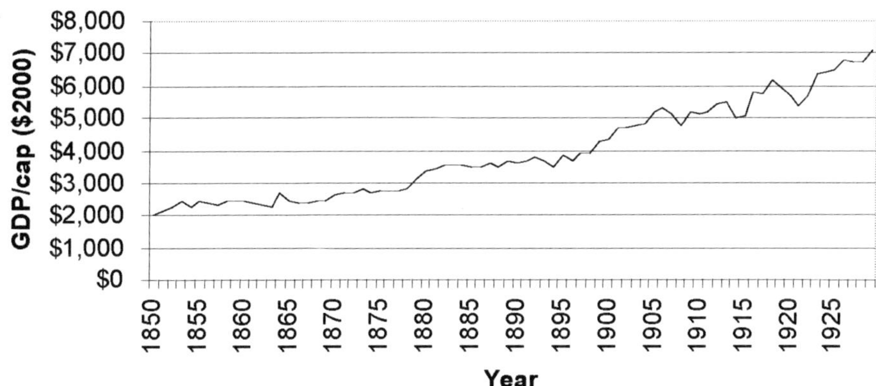

Figure 5-1: U.S. Real GDP per Capita, 1850–1929

Sources: Economic History website, http://www.eh.net, accessed Sept. 26, 2005; U.S. Department of Commerce, Census Bureau, accessed August 10, 2005, from http://www.census.gov/population/censusdata/table-2.pdf.

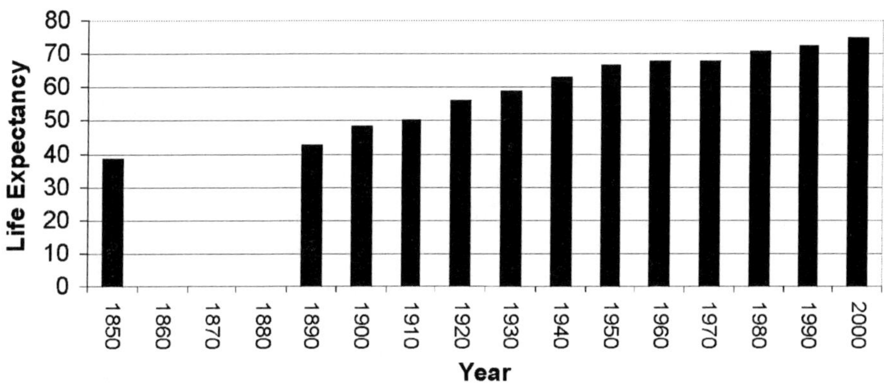

Figure 5-2: U.S. Life Expectancy at Birth, White Males, 1850–2000

Source: Infoplease, "Life Expectancy by Age, 1850–2004." Accessed 4 April 2006 from http://www.infoplease.com/ipa/A0005140.html.

of these, the film industry, was born in 1903 with *The Great Train Robbery*. Another such business, radio, began when the first human voice was electronically transmitted without wires on Christmas Eve 1906. Neither was terribly profitable at the time, but what they started soon became so.

By 1922, the movie industry was boasting average weekly attendance of 40 million—1.56 tickets per household per week.[17] The first commercial broadcasts, benefiting from technological advances resulting from World War I, went live in Detroit and Pittsburgh in 1920. While these broadcasts were initially designed to sell radios, not advertising, the first radio ad is believed to have run in New York City in 1923. The ad-supported business model of broadcasting lives today on the Internet.

The modern recording industry also came of age in the 1920s, doubly encouraged by radio and the spread of the phonograph. The success of the Victor Talking Machine Company's Victrola, first marketed in 1906, led even Thomas Edison, patent-holder for a competing technology, to sell Victrola-compatible disks by 1912.[18] Phonograph production in the U.S. has been estimated at 345,000 in 1909, 514,000 in 1914, and 2.23 million in 1919. In 1910, about 30 million records were sold, but by 1921, it is believed that record sales numbered 140 million for a total of around $106 million in revenues (about $1.2 billion in 2006 dollars).[19]

The social impacts of even the most successful of the wide-distribution magazines of the previous century—*The Saturday Evening Post*, *Collier's*, *Harper's*, and the like—paled compared to the broad, cross-class impacts of radio, records, and the movies. No social phenomenon of this breadth had ever before been seen in the country. Silent-era stars such as Charlie Chaplin, Harry Lloyd, Mary Pickford, and Lillian Gish became household names, as did "Amos and Andy," two fictional African-Americans played on radio by white actors, Freeman Gosden and Charles Correll. The fifteen-minute, five-times weekly serial debuted as "Sam and Henry" in 1926, enjoying great success throughout the Depression and World War II. The program briefly made the jump to television in 1951 with black performers, but the move resulted in social controversy, and soon was off the air.[20] Similarly, the 1920s music business had its stars—Al Jolson, Louis Armstrong, George Gershwin, and many others. But perhaps none of these other mass media stars has had the lasting power of New York Yankees' slugger George Herman "Babe" Ruth.

By 1920, the National League and its once-rival-now-partner, the American League, were also firmly well established as fixtures in America's growing entertainment industry. Until the ridiculous on-field success of the New York Yankees began to take its toll on interest and attendance toward the end of the decade, NL and AL teams averaged a profit of about $1.5 million per year in 2006 dollars (Figure 5-3). Teams in the twenties were drawing an average of well over half a million fans per year (Figure 5-4).

The Yankees were the most successful team of the decade, bringing in an average of more than one million fans each year, and their owners cleared about $4 or $5 million annually (in 2006 dollars). At a time when the average GDP per capita in the U.S. was about $6,500 per year (2006 $), this was real money. And the Babe was the rock star of the team.

Ruth had been purchased by the Yankees from the Red Sox following the 1919 season for the previously unheard-of price of $125,000 (about $1.5

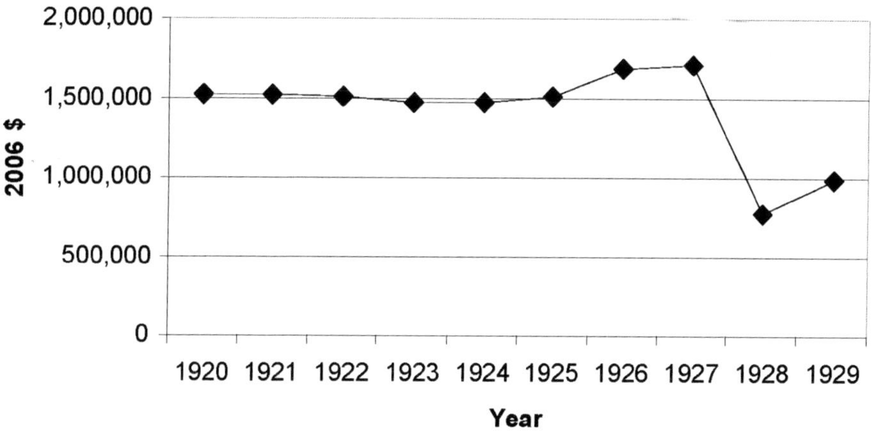

Figure 5-3: Average MLB Team Profit, 1920s (2006 dollars)

Sources: http://roadsidephotos.sabr.org/baseball/data.htm#ofd, and Lawrence H. Officer and Samuel H. Williamson, "Purchasing Power of Money in the United States from 1774 to 2006," MeasuringWorth.Com, 2007.

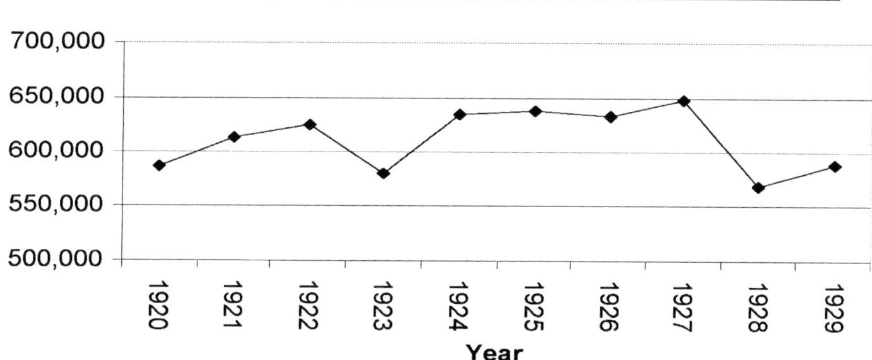

Figure 5-4: Average Home Attendance per Season per Team, MLB, 1920–1929

Source: Rodneyfort.com.

million in 2006 dollars), and in 1920, the team went on to be the first to draw over a million fans. With Ruth's exciting home runs, they won six AL pennants and four World Series in the 1920s. He was the perfect antidote for baseball fans sickened by the sleaze uncovered by the investigations into the 1919 Black Sox scandal.

In 1923, the 53,000-seat Yankee Stadium, dubbed "The House That Ruth Built" opened and the team won its first World Series. Yankee Stadium was huge; the other large parks at the time were far smaller—Boston's Fenway Park then held 35,000, and Chicago's Comiskey Park and Washington's Griffith Stadium each could seat 32,000.

Ruth's salary of $20,000 in 1920 grew to $80,000 by 1930 (about $200,000 and $900,000 in 2006 dollars), far above that earned by any other baseball player at the time.[21] Man o' War, another sports superstar of the era, might have been the only athlete to earn more money in a season than Ruth—but he was a horse, of course. Still, winning 20 of 21 races during a sixteen-month period in 1919 and 1920, and picking up $249,265 in purses (more than $2.5 million in 2006 dollars), was pretty impressive.[22] Ruth was not alone in his celebrity, however. There were four other figures that also captured sports fandom's imagination during this "Golden Era of Sports." They were golf's Bobby Jones, tennis's Bill Tilden, boxing's Jack Dempsey, and football's Red Grange.

Before World War I, golf was considered to be such a trivial sport that it was routinely ignored by newspapers' sports sections.[23] There were only 34 courses in the U.S. as late as 1890, although there were over 100 by 1895. The game at that time was an East Coast hobby; the number of courses grew to nearly 1,000 by 1900 as several Ivies and military academies flirted with it. After the war, however, golf took off, and about 600 new courses were added annually between 1923 and 1929. Many of these were in the North Central portion of the country—by 1931, 41 percent of courses were located there.[24]

Without question, part of golf's 1920s growth in popularity was due to the accomplishments of Robert Tyre "Bobby" Jones, by far the greatest golfer of the time. Although he spent his career as an amateur, he won twenty-three of the fifty-two events he entered, including thirteen of twenty-seven major tournaments between 1923 and 1930. In 1930, he became the only person to win the British Open, the British Amateur, the U.S. Amateur, and the U.S. Open Championship in a single season. His reputation was one of integrity and honesty, traits still associated with even the highest levels of competitive golf.

After retiring from competitive play, Jones wrote numerous books and newspaper columns about the game, and was a co-founder of the Masters Tournament annually held at the course he designed in Augusta, Georgia.

He may have been an amateur, but his golf celebrity translated into money and was a marketing success. His 1931 and 1933 series of instructional films brought in an estimated $250,000 in revenue (about $3.7 million in 2006 dollars).[25]

Bill Tilden was also an amateur during the height of his popularity in the 1920s. Winning Wimbledon in 1920, 1921, and 1930, he was also U.S. singles champion six times and U.S. doubles champion four times during the decade. Known for his powerful serve, Tilden's success changed the public perception of tennis from a milque-toasty, sissy sport into one more in tune with the American middle-class machismo of the early 20th century. Despite his later convictions for solicitation of under-age males, he was a successful editor of *Racquet* magazine, and wrote several books and a novel about tennis.[26]

William Harrison "Jack" Dempsey, another member of the 1920s Fab Five, was the Heavyweight Boxing Champion of the World between 1919 and 1927. Perhaps as many as 500,000 fans saw his five title fights, and millions more listened to them on the radio. An estimated 80,000 attended his 1923 title bout at New York's Polo Grounds with Argentina's Luis Angel Firpo. They didn't get to watch much—Dempsey knocked Firpo out 57 seconds into the second round. After he lost a decision to Jack Tunney in 1926, the following year's rematch drew immense attention. Over one hundred thousand people paid a total of more than $2.6 million (over $30 million in 2006 dollars) to see Tunney again beat Dempsey, albeit not without controversy.[27] After retirement, Dempsey wrote a well-respected book about boxing and spent nearly forty years running a Times Square restaurant in New York City.[28]

The last of the Fab Five, Harold "Red" Grange, helped professional football come out from behind the college shadow. While the college game was already well-organized and well-developed by the end of World War I, the same could not be said of the professional version. Pro teams were ragtag collections of players, rosters were often in chaos, and leagues were not very stable. In August of 1920, several professional teams throughout the Midwest met in an auto showroom in Canton, Ohio, to form the American Professional Football Conference. They were in it to make money—in fact, one of their goals was to stem rising player salaries. Jim Thorpe was chosen as president, and league franchise fees were set at $100 per team (which apparently was never paid by any team).[29]

Only a couple of the new league's teams made any money the first couple of seasons, and there was substantial franchise turnover. George Halas moved his Decatur team to Chicago in 1921 after pocketing $5,000 (about $56,000 in 2006 dollars) from A.E. Staley in exchange for a promise to call the team the Staleys for one more year.[30] The league changed its name to the National Football League in 1923, when it revamped its organization. By

1924, the NFL was much less dysfunctional, and its games were attracting about 5,000 fans per contest. Halas's Chicago Bears were the most successful team in the league, drawing nearly 10,000 per home game.

The following year, the electrifying Red Grange, a gridiron star who had captured the interest of college football fans, completed his eligibility at the University of Illinois. One day later, he signed with the Bears. The team spent the next 11 days playing two league games plus six exhibition games, including a contest with the New York Giants that drew 64,300 fans. All together, Grange and his manager, C.C. "Cash and Carry" Pyle, made about $250,000 in the football business (about $2.9 million in 2006 dollars) during and immediately after the 1925 NFL season. By comparison, player salaries at the time averaged about $100 per game (about $1,100 in 2006 dollars).[31]

Pyle and Grange then asked Halas for a share of the team's gate plus one-third interest in the team. Halas, known to throw around a nickel like he would a manhole cover, and his partner, Dutch Sternaman, balked, and Grange petitioned the NFL for his own expansion franchise in New York. Tim Mara, owner of the New York Giants, vetoed the idea—he did not want to compete locally with the most popular football player in the world. In 1926, Grange started his own league which folded after one season, and Grange went on to star for the Bears between 1929 and 1934.[32]

Drinking and Driving

The end of Prohibition in 1933 was embraced by a large swatch of American society seeking respite from Depression hardship. The social experiment may have been well-intentioned, but it had resulted in a number of rather unpleasant unintended consequences, including making criminals out of the many otherwise law-abiding citizens who chose not be religious observers of the 18th Amendment. It likewise made national cultural icons out rum-running thugs such as Chicago's Al Capone and Detroit's Purple Gang, local idols out of countless, otherwise anonymous, rural bootleggers, and led to the emergence of NASCAR. In the process, Prohibition was responsible for a fundamental change in the nature of auto racing as a spectator sport.

Stock car racing was not the first form of auto racing, which surely has been around as long as there have been autos. However, the sport's early development took the form of an expensive, rich man's, high-tech hobby. Much of the early activity was in Europe, and involved city-to-city rather than track racing. The first American auto race of note was sponsored by the *Chicago Times-Herald* newspaper and was held on Thanksgiving Day 1895. The 54-mile Chicago-Evanston round-trip event was won by Frank Duryea, posting an average speed of 7.5 mph. There was only one other finisher.[33]

But auto technology improved rapidly, and the American car business made significant strides. In 1904, the same year that Ford Motor Company was founded, railroad family scion William K. Vanderbilt established the Vanderbilt Cup in an effort to enhance America's role in international auto racing. The first Vanderbilt Cup race, held that October, drew between 30,000 and 50,000 spectators along its 28.4 mile course in Long Island, New York. The 1906 edition, also in Long Island, drew an estimated 250,000 fans, including one who was killed while straying onto the course.[34] By 1909, the sport, which had branched into a variety of different subtypes, was sufficiently well-developed in the U.S. to support the construction of the Indianapolis Motor Speedway, host of the annual Indy 500 race since 1911.[35] The quest for ever-greater speed became relentless.

The end of the 1920s saw George Cobb, George Eyston, and Malcolm Campbell each employing teams of highly educated internal combustion engineers in efforts to best each other's land speed records.[36] Their proving ground of choice was southwestern Utah's Bonneville Salt Flats. The 200-mph barrier had been broached by one Henry Segrave on March 29, 1927, who shattered by nearly 30 mph the prior record set by Campbell less than two months earlier. By the end of the 1930s, Cobb owned the record of 369.7 mph, which was not officially broken until 1947, again by Cobb.[37]

But thanks to Henry Ford and his mass-produced Model T, automobile ownership, and therefore racing, had by then become a much more democratic affair than it was at the beginning of the century. The availability of relatively affordable cars and Prohibition's stymie of the liquor supply had led to a new group of Americans, who were less educated, more rural, but just as entrepreneurial as the Bonneville drivers.

By 1933, booze-runners in the southeastern U.S. had become quite accomplished at tweaking and tuning their factory-produced cars to outrun the overmatched vehicles driven by government revenue agents. The return of legal booze after tight economic times failed to eliminate the demand for cheap, tax-free backwoods moonshine, or the utility of cars that could speed around curvy dirt roads, even when heavily laden with a couple of dozen cases of moonshine.

Legend has it that one day in the mid–1930s, in the wake of some inevitable disagreement between two bootleggers over whose car was faster, a quarter-mile track was laid in a Stockbridge, Georgia, farmer's cow pasture. Fifty people allegedly showed up to see who would win the argument, and a subsequent race supposedly drew 100 fans. As the number of spectators grew to over a thousand, the farmer—apparently also entrepreneurial—put a fence around his pasture and began charging admission.

Whether this story is true or not, rural stock car racing in the Southeast quickly grew in popularity during Depression, and the best drivers soon could make as much money racing as they could running hooch.[38] In 1948, Bill France, Sr., provided direction and uniform rules to the disorganized sport by forming what eventually became NASCAR, which emphasized the use of everyday cars that could be found on the street.[39]

NASCAR remains among the most democratic of sports—despite a greater reliance on expensive specialized equipment over athletic ability. Its loyal fans remain largely southern, rural, young, and of moderate income, although NASCAR recently has taken great pains in attempting to expand this base.[40] The thirty-six races that comprise the Sprint Cup schedule drew a combined 4.5 million fans in 2006, each paying an average ticket price of about $90. The leading NASCAR teams generated $50 million or more per year in revenue, and were valued at over $100 million each.[41] The top drivers, such as Jeff Gordon, Tony Stewart and Dale Earnheart, Jr., are now rock stars in their own right.

The Movie Business Discovers Sports

Hollywood made its early fortune by identifying and exploiting mass culture, and the studios did not miss the rise of sports as entertainment during the 1920s. They were quick to tap famous athletes for movie roles—boffo big box office did not require acting ability so much as name recognition. With their celebrity already established, the studios did not have to engage their increasingly impressive public relations machinery to manufacture star athletes' notoriety—they already had it.

Babe Ruth was one of Hollywood's early choices, appearing in at least nine films between 1920 and 1942, sometimes even playing himself. Although he was the highest-paid player in all of baseball, Ruth allegedly made more money from his movies than he did playing ball.[42]

Pugilism, even more than baseball, has been part of the motion picture business since there was one. *Boxing* (1892) was one of the first four movies filmed by Thomas Edison using the 35mm format.[43] The sport lends itself perfectly to the stock underdog-makes-good story: Low-born boxer overcomes all manner of adversity to win the championship, the lady, and the hearts of millions.

Not surprisingly, Jack Dempsey, also a member of the Fab Five of 1920s rock-star athletes, was the first boxer to earn a notable Hollywood resume. He appeared in sixteen movies during his life, beginning with the mostly lost fifteen-chapter serial *Daredevil Jack* ("the serial with a thousand punches," 1920) through his role as a reporter in *Damn Citizen* (1958).[44] His long film career and the box office successes of *The Joe Louis Story* (1956), the *Rocky* series (1976–2006), and *Cinderella Man* (2005) are clear evidence that boxing endures as good Hollywood plot fodder.

Perhaps the most successful transition from athlete to movie star was made by swimmer Johnny Weismuller. He had won five gold medals at the 1924 and 1928 Olympics in Paris and Amsterdam, along with 119 other world and national swimming titles. Although he was not a household name like Ruth or Dempsey, he was famous enough to land his first film appearance in *Glorifying the American Girl* (1929). Playing the role of Adonis, he wore a costume that consisted of one strategically located fig leaf.[45]

Weismuller starred in a dozen *Tarzan the Ape Man* films between 1932 and 1948, becoming far better known for his loin cloth and shabby treatment of the English language than he was for his bathing suit and spectacular freestyle crawl.[46] Following his run as Tarzan, he went on make sixteen *Jungle Jim* films, a low-budget series that ran through the mid–1950s. In 1956, *Jungle Jim* was reborn as a 26-episode television series, also starring Weismuller. His last movie, *Won Ton, the Dog Who Saved Hollywood*, was released in 1976.

Much has changed about the American film industry since the 1930s, but the appeal of elite athletes as box office bait remains. Perhaps the best measure of modern mass celebrity is an appearance on television's *Saturday Night Live*. Since its inception in 1975, sports-world hosts have included Fran Tarkenton, O.J. Simpson, Bill Russell, John Madden, Bob Uecker, Alex Karras, Joe Montana, Walter Payton, Carl Weathers, Wayne Gretzkey, Chris Evert, George Steinbrenner, Charles Barkley, Nancy Kerrigan, George Foreman, Deion Sanders, Derek Jeter, Andy Roddick, Tom Brady, and Peyton Manning.[47]

Hooked on Sports

American spectator sports stars have come and gone since this Golden Age. The pain of the Great Depression was eased a little by the Joe DiMaggios, the World War II years by the Sammy Baughs. The 1950s economic boom was made even sweeter by cheering for American Olympians' success against their godless Communist opponents, and the tumultuous 1960s found both energy and respite via the likes of Muhammad Ali and Pete Rose. As the malaise of the 1970s yielded to the 1980s return of "Morning in America," so did the Pittsburgh Steelers dynasty to the San Francisco 49ers.

But it was in the 1920s that we first got hooked on sports in the way that we now know. It's the drug of choice for the millions of Americans that get high or fall low with the fortunes of their favorite teams and athletes.

6

Depression, War, and Diaspora

By the time the stock market crashed in October of 1929, American sports fandom in many ways was similar to the early 21st century version. Elite athletes from baseball, football, boxing, tennis and golf had begun to emerge as mass culture icons alongside top musicians, radio voices, and movie actors. These stars took advantage of their celebrity. Babe Ruth earned an estimated $110,000 in 1930, $40,000 of which was from endorsements.[1] By comparison, in 2006, Tiger Woods took in around $100 million in income, most of which came from personal appearances and endorsements rather than playing golf.[2] The magnitudes may have changed, but the dynamics are largely the same now as they were seventy-five years ago.

Even so, the decades that followed the Roaring Twenties had profound effects on the relationship between spectator sports and their fans. The Great Depression required teams and leagues to invent new ways to generate revenues from fans with little money to spare. World War II brought about the end of the Depression, but presented an entirely new set of challenges to pro sports, including how to produce a saleable product in the face of severe labor supply issues. The beginning of the Cold War in the 1950s turned the Olympic Games and Little League baseball into patriotic duties. Meanwhile, booming consumerism scattered nuclear families across newly formed suburbs, and easier travel and air conditioning led many to leave the cold North and East for the warmth of the Sun Belt.

Sometimes the sports world was a reluctant participant in the face of these forces, while at other times, athletes and executives played leading roles. In the end, society, the sports business, and sports fandom continued their symbiotic evolution in response to the changing social environment.

Chasing Fans in Hard Times

Whatever good feelings that Depression-era sports films and the end of Prohibition may have brought to the country, American life at the time was more than grim for most. By 1935, the Roaring Twenties were long gone, and national income had fallen to less than a third of what it had been in 1927. Unemployment, which had averaged an annual rate of 3.3 percent during 1923–29, shot up to 8.9 percent in 1930, 15.9 percent in 1931, and 23.6 percent in 1932. It remained above 14 percent through 1941.[3] Millions were out of work with no viable options. Food stamps, Medicaid and most of the rest of the social safety net Americans now take for granted were yet a generation away.

Some entertainment industries suffered less than other parts of the economy during the Depression, but business was still bad. Back in giddy 1927, Americans had spent just under $1.4 billion on all forms of recreation, including sporting event attendance. By 1933, such spending had declined by more than 40 percent, to $809 million.[4] However, the portion of national income spent on entertainment actually increased from 6.58 percent to 8.12 percent from 1927 to 1933 as Americans used relatively more of their meager earnings in search of temporary escape from real life.[5]

The movie business, thought to be recession-proof, turned out not to be. Driven by the public's voracious demand for the talkies, the industry had rapidly expanded during the late 1920s. Much of this expansion was financed with enormous debt, which at first seemed to be a good business strategy. In 1930, movie admissions had hit a peak of 80 million patrons per week, or about two tickets sold each week for every three Americans. Two years later, however, weekly attendance had fallen by more than 30 percent to 55 million, and one-fifth of the estimated 20,000 movie theaters operating in 1930 had closed their doors. As the economy continued to implode in 1933, many Hollywood studio giants, including RKO, Paramount and Fox, were forced into bankruptcy court.[6]

The story was much the same in the big-time spectator sports business. Major League Baseball, for which the best data are available, had seen its 1927 attendance crack the five million mark; about 20 percent of the spectators had gone to Yankee stadium that year to watch what many still think is the best MLB team of all time. In 1930, the AL and NL drew a combined 5.4 million. The following year, demand for major league ball succumbed to the faltering economy and fell by a painful 16 percent.

It got worse—much worse. A month into the 1932 season, the economy and the federal government's new 10 percent amusement tax conspired to reduce MLB attendance by 45 percent even from 1931's lousy first month. By the end of the season, total MLB attendance tallied only 3.8 million, and owners had lost a collective $1.2 million. Given that the average MLB franchise sales price between 1925 and 1932 was about half a million dollars, a collective loss of relatively similar magnitude in 2006 would be on the order of $1 billion. Things did not get better in 1933; MLB attendance further declined to under 3.2 million fans, 42 percent below the 1930's high-water mark. The big leagues did not again see five million fans until 1945.[7]

Owners were in a panic, looking for new revenues wherever they might be found. The end of Prohibition provided a little relief, as the 1934 season saw the return of legal beer sales at the ballpark, courtesy of the 21st Amendment's repeal of Prohibition.

The maturation of the radio broadcast business also helped in 1934. World Series national radio rights, which had been given away by the league for free from 1922 (or 1923) through 1933, were sold for the first time to the Ford Motor Company for $100,000 per year for the 1934–1937 seasons.[8] Despite the national rights windfall, some owners worried that free local radio broadcasts were damaging their fragile gate revenues. Earlier that year, both St. Louis teams, the Browns and the Cardinals, had completely eliminated the local radio broadcasts that had been offered since 1923 for just that reason.[9] It may have worked—the Cardinals increased their 1934 attendance by 26 percent, and the Browns by 31 percent, over 1933. However, these increases may have had to do more with better teams; the Cardinals finished in first place in 1934 after finishing in fifth in 1933, while the Browns moved from last to sixth, but won 13 more games.[10]

In any event, MLB and minor league team owners continued to seek other ways to increase Depression-era revenues without increasing ticket prices. The weekend doubleheader, for example, came into existence around this time.[11] Owners also began selling stadium signage more aggressively. It was in 1933 that Wheaties cereal began its long association with sports advertising, when General Mills bought a sign on the left field wall of a minor league park in Minneapolis, and Babe Ruth first appeared in the cereal's print ads that year. The brand's slogan, "Breakfast of Champions," was born shortly thereafter in the wake of a deal to broadcast games of the minor league Minneapolis Millers on radio station WCCO.[12]

Turning on the Lights

The use of technology during the 1930s to generate additional baseball revenue was not limited to radio. The magic of electricity was also tapped in the effort to make the game more accessible to potential paying fans. Night games were thought to be an answer to the problem posed by the gainfully employed fan's inability to attend day games during the week.

Big-league baseball came relatively late to this party, however. The first football game under the lights had been staged long earlier, in 1892, in Mansfield, Pennsylvania, as the highlight of the Great Mansfield Fair that year.

The first contest between Mansfield Seminary and Wyoming Seminary ended in a 0–0 tie, but the event still is annually re-created each September as part of the town's "Fabulous 1890s Weekend."[13]

Even the NFL entered the Electrical Age before MLB. The Providence (RI) Steam Roller lost to the Chicago Cardinals 16–0 under the new lights on the evening of Wednesday November 6, 1929, as one of four games that the Steam Roller played between November 5 and November 10. The two teams had originally been scheduled to play that Sunday, but heavy rains made Providence's home field too soggy to use, so the game was moved to nearby Kinsey Park and its new lights. The football was painted white for better visibility and the game drew a respectable 6,000 fans. At least one player, however, did not share the enthusiasm for night football. According to his 1930 contract, Tony Lattone was paid $125 each for day games, but only $75 for night games, supposedly in order to compensate for the cost of turning on the juice.[14]

While there were amateurs playing night baseball since at least the 1880s, the first "modern" professional baseball game under the lights was played at a minor league park in Des Moines, Iowa, on May 2, 1930. The experiment was a huge success, drawing 12,000 fans to a ballpark that had been averaging about 600 per game. A number of barnstorming teams soon began to use rented lights to draw fans to minor league parks. The Negro League's Kansas City Monarchs also brought portable lighting systems with them on their travels, drawing crowds as large as 30,000 to their games at rival parks.[15]

MLB *paters* continued to believe that night baseball was more of a gimmick than a serious strategy, and kept their game under the sun. But pressure for night ball grew as attendance continued to flag. They gave in to the inevitable when President Roosevelt threw a switch in Washington, D.C., that turned on the lights six hundred miles away in Cincinnati's Crosley Field on May 24, 1935. The Reds defeated the Philadelphia Phillies in a low-scoring affair, 2–1, but the experiment looked like a success. The attendance of 24,422 represented a significantly larger Reds home crowd than that year's average of 5,898.[16]

The last MLB team to succumb to night baseball was the Chicago Cubs, which held out until 1988. Following their purchase of the team, the Tribune Company managed to convince the city of Chicago to give permission for Cub night games—over the strenuous opposition of Citizens United for Baseball in the Sunshine (CUBS), a colorful alliance of Wrigley neighbors and tradition-minded fans. The first game was scheduled against the New York Mets for August 8, 1988. Perhaps Someone Up There is also a traditionalist—the game was rained out. The first Wrigley night game instead was played the following evening, with the Cubs beating the Mets by a score of

6–4. The Cubs went 3–3 in 1988's six Wrigley night games, drawing only a little better than the average home day games that season (30 thousand versus 25 thousand).[17]

All-Star Games

The pursuit of greater fan interest during the Depression also was responsible for the creation of various league All-Star games. MLB's version was the first one played, and was the brainchild of *Chicago Tribune* sports editor Arch Ward. The inaugural game was held at Comiskey Park on July 6, 1933, as part of the Chicago World's Fair. More than 47,000 fans braved a sweltering afternoon to watch the AL beat the NL 4–2. An aging Babe Ruth did not disappoint, hitting the first All-Star Game home run into the right-field stands.[18]

Ward was also the driving force behind football's College All-Star Game. First played in Chicago in 1934, the game pitted the best college players against the best team in professional football. Although the August game soon became the annual one-sided blowout of the prior year's college All-Americans, it served as the ceremonial opening to the professional football season until 1976. During its four-decade run, the event generated a total of nearly $4 million for various Chicago-area charities.[19]

Several college bowl games also trace their origins to local charitable efforts on behalf of the Depression unemployed. The annual Army-Navy football game, played since 1890, had been discontinued due to disagreement following the 1927 season. An appeal to philanthropy was successful where détente between the academies failed, and the game was revived during the 1930 and 1931 seasons as a charity event played in New York's Yankee Stadium. Since 1932, each school annually has made the game its early December regular season finale.[20]

The NFL's Pro Bowl game has its roots in the Depression era as well. In January of 1939 and 1940, the NFL held post-season games in Los Angeles between the newly crowned champions and a group of all-stars from around the league. The 1942 game, held just a month after Pearl Harbor, was moved to New York, after which the event was abandoned altogether. The modern Pro Bowl was instituted beginning with the 1950 season as a post-season game between the stars of the NFL's Eastern and Western Conferences.[21] The NHL named all-star teams beginning at least with the 1930–31 season, although the first official game was not held until 1947.[22] The NBA, which was formed in 1947, played its first All-Star Game in 1951, and a similar event has now become part of nearly every other major and minor North American league sport.

The End of the Depression

The Army-Navy football rivalry has nothing on the one between the New York Yankees and Boson Red Sox. Boston fans in particular are wont to cite the improbable late-inning pennant-winning home runs by Bucky Dent in 1978 and Aaron Boone in 2003 as supporting evidence of their unique level of persecution by the baseball gods. The more honest among them aver that the Sox zero-games-to-three comeback against the Yankees in the 2004 ALCS did much to salve those hurtful memories. Seldom mentioned by even the most victimized Sox fan, however, is a bizarre contest played between the two teams on Sunday September 3, 1939, at Fenway Park.

After losing a wooly 12–11 first game of a double-header, the Yankees scored two runs in the top of the 8th inning of the second game to take a 7–5 lead. The time was precisely 6:21 P.M., a fact made germane by Boston's blue laws, which then imposed a 6:30 P.M. curfew on Sunday baseball. Under the rules, the half-inning needed to end in order for that score to become official, and both teams knew it.

In an attempt to negate the inning and the Yankees' win along with it, the Sox began stalling for time. They first tried to intentionally walk Babe Dahlgren, who refused to acquiesce and swung at the pitches anyway. Meanwhile, two Yankees base runners, Joe Gordon and George Selkirk, got themselves purposely tagged out while casually sauntering toward home. The inning ended, and the game became official.

Savvy but irate Sox fans pelted the field with bottles, Boston manager Joe Cronin protested, the umpires huddled, and the Sox were declared the winners by virtue of a 9–0 Yankee forfeit. American League president Will Harridge later reversed that decision, calling the game a tie, and the Sox couldn't even win for losing.[23]

That same evening, September 3, 1939, President Roosevelt held an eleven-minute radio fireside chat with the nation to explain why Britain and France had declared war on Germany in response to Hitler's invasion of Poland on September 1.[24] Although nobody knew it at the time, the opening of hostilities in Europe meant the closing of the Depression in the U.S.

Between 1929 and the end of 1938, real U.S. GDP per capita had fallen from $7,105 to $6,776 per person (2000 $).[25] Even though the U.S. was officially neutral at first, the beginning of the war brought with it immediate economic expansion. By December 7, 1941, real GDP per capita had grown to $9,908 (2000 $), an increase of more than 46 percent.[26]

Three late-season NFL games were underway when the news broke of the Japanese attack on Pearl Harbor. The public address announcers at New York's Polo Grounds and at Chicago's Comiskey Park each interrupted their commentaries to tell all active servicemen to report to their units. Redskin games at Washington's Griffith Field usually had many high-ranking officers in attendance, and that day's match with the Philadelphia Eagles was no exception. Although several of them were paged during the game, and reporters were told to check with their offices, no specific announcement was made to the crowd about carnage occurring in Hawaii.[27]

All in all, World War II exacted a horrible toll in terms of human life and suffering, but it had a terrific effect on the U.S. economy. Accounting for inflation, U.S. gross national product grew by 71 percent between 1939 and 1945, increasing real per capita disposable income by a welcome 49 percent. Civilian unemployment, which had averaged 18.2 percent during the 1930s, fell to 14.6 percent in 1940, and continued to drop through 1944, when it stood at only 1.2 percent.[28]

Women Go to Work—and Play Ball

Pearl Harbor permanently changed the U.S. in ways analogous to September 11 sixty years later. Families that had survived over a decade of hard economic times soon found themselves facing a different set of challenges, not the least of which were the loss and injury of their loved ones. American casualties during World War II officially numbered more than one million of the sixteen million who served, including 405,000 thousand who were killed.[29] Countless more suffered psychological trauma.

The twelve million servicemen on active duty in mid–1945 represented about one-fifth of the 55 million-person U.S. labor force at the time.[30] With so many male bodies in uniform and unavailable for civilian work, women found themselves trading in their aprons for factory smocks. A total of 2.5 million women entered the work force for the first time, with 1.3 million of them going to war industries.[31] They enabled the out-production of the Axis, and eventual Allied victory in World War II.

The wartime acceptance of the expansion of women's roles into traditionally male jobs included ball-playing. With the financial support of Cubs owner and chewing gum giant Phillip K. Wrigley, the entity that became the All-American Girls Professional Baseball League came into existence as a nonprofit organization in 1943. The game they played was a hybrid version of baseball and the softball that women played recreationally at the time.

Four AAGPL teams (South Bend, Kenosha, Racine, and Rockford) with a combined total of sixty women played a total of 108 games between the end of May and the beginning of September of 1943. The players made between $45 and $85 (or more) per game, the league drew 176,000 fans (1,629 per game on average), and the quality of play was generally considered to be good.

The following year, two new teams (Milwaukee and Minneapolis) were added to the league, which continued to draw well. In 1945, total attendance for the league was 450,000, which continued play after the end of the war. A July 4, 1946, doubleheader drew an estimated 10,000 fans. Attendance peaked in 1948 at 910,000, after which the league began to fade. It ceased its operations in 1954.[32]

Demand Problems Become Supply Problems

Although World War I was well within living memory in 1941, the new war was a different animal. First of all, the sinking of the *Lusitania* in 1915 had nowhere near the immediate psychic impact on the public that Pearl Harbor had. Secondly, the intervening quarter-century had made professional sports a much bigger business than it had been at the beginning of World War I. Sport business leaders were unsure of how to react.

Some spectator sports responded by canceling or greatly curtailing their activities. The Indianapolis 500 was not run during 1942–1945. The USGA cancelled all of its championships and the PGA Tour cut back to only three events in the wake of the federal government's halting of golf equipment manufacturing.[33] Although tournament tennis in England, and with it the annual Wimbledon championship, was cancelled during the war, it continued in the U.S., and Americans dominated international tennis play for several years after the war.[34]

Less than a month after Pearl Harbor, MLB commissioner Kenesaw Mountain Landis wrote to President Franklin Roosevelt, asking for his guidance on whether or not to shut down the sport during the war. Roosevelt quickly responded with his "green light letter" of January 15, 1942, in which he told Landis that baseball could help the country's morale, and to keep on playing:

> I honestly feel that it would be best for the country to keep baseball going. There will be fewer people unemployed and everybody will work longer hours and harder than ever before.
>
> And that means that they ought to have a chance for recreation and for taking their minds off their work even more than before.
>
> Baseball provides a recreation which does not last over two hours or two hours and a half, and which can be got for very little cost. And, incidentally, I hope that night games can be extended because it gives an opportunity to the day shift to see a game occasionally.[35]

Roosevelt was careful to note later in his letter that the war had top priority, and that any players drafted into the military were expected to serve.

The first MLB player drafted following Pearl Harbor was Philadelphia

Phillies pitcher Hugh Mulcahy. More than one hundred other AL and NL players—about a quarter of the players in the big leagues—were drafted during 1942 and 1943. Two of them, Elmer Gedeon and Harry O'Neill, were killed in action, as were more than 40 minor leaguers.[36]

Many players did not wait to heed the siren call of patriotic duty. Perhaps the most notable of these was hitting great Ted Williams. Fresh from the 1941 season and his .406 batting average—the last one posted in MLB—Williams joined the navy in May of 1942, and was called to active service in November. He became an accomplished fighter pilot, although it cost him three of his prime baseball years.[37]

Another volunteer was Hank Greenberg, best known for hitting 58 home runs in 1938 and for leaving the Detroit Tigers during the 1934 pennant race to observe Yom Kippur. Greenberg had been drafted in 1940, and was honorably discharged for being over 28 years old just two days before Pearl Harbor. Nineteen games and two homers into the 1942 season, he voluntarily re-enlisted in the Air Force, serving until 1945. He played in 78 games during the 1945 season as well as in 1946 and 1947, hitting 83 more homers before retiring with a total of 331. Had he played full seasons during 1941–1944, he very well may have hit over 500 career home runs.

The NFL followed MLB's lead in dealing with the issues dealt it by the war. In a March 24, 1942, news release, the league stated that as long as the federal government did not deem otherwise, it would assume that its best contribution to the war would be to continue its operations as normally as possible. Commissioner Elmer Layden was philosophical, taking his cue from the sentiments expressed in Roosevelt's Green Light letter:

> From Aristotle's time on down we have been told, and it has been demonstrated, that sports is necessary for the relaxation of the people in times of stress and worry. The National league [*sic*] will strive to help meet this need with the men the government has not yet called for combat service, either because of dependents, disabilities, or the luck of the draw in the Army draft.[38]

The NFL saw 995 of its personnel serve during World War II.[39] A total of 638 of these were players, including 8 members of the Professional Football Hall of Fame. At least six owners, including George Halas, who had also served during World War I, volunteered before the end of 1942.[40] Nineteen players, an ex-coach, and an executive died in the service of the country.[41]

Appeals to Patriotism

Team owners could plainly see the popularity of the war effort, and thought it good business to make the game synonymous with American patriotism. MLB donated equipment for soldiers' use during down times, held special games to sell war bonds, and raised money for causes such as the Army and Navy Relief Fund.[42] The NFL likewise took an active role in the promotion of War Bonds, accounting for more than $4 million in sales during 1942 alone. The Green Bay Packers' coach Curly Lambeau, quarterback Cecil Isbell, and Don Hutson were credited with selling $2.1 million during a single rally one night in Milwaukee, Wisconsin. The league also donated nearly $700 thousand in revenues from its exhibition schedule to various service charities.[43]

Despite these actions, the manpower shortage caused by the war had significant impacts on the quality of the leagues' offerings to fans.

An Inferior Product

In 1941, the Yankees' Joe Dimaggio had illuminated the sports world with his (still-standing) record 56-game hitting streak. By 1943, the exodus of major league talent to the armed forces had left professional baseball but a weak shadow of what it had been just two seasons earlier. One writer opined that MLB games had become "the fat guys playing the tall guys at the annual company picnic."[44] The labor supply situation indeed must have been desperate—in 1945, the hapless St. Louis Browns even tapped one-armed Pete Gray to play in its outfield.

The perennially terrible Browns were emblematic of what was happening in MLB. Between 1935 and 1939, the team went 266–478 (.278), finishing an average of 47.6 games per year out of first place. Not surprisingly, the team drew quite poorly, averaging only 1,428 spectators per game during the period. An "improved" 1940 edition of the team ended the season "only" 23 games out, the team's highest finish since 1929. This slightly better showing, along with the improving economy, lifted the team's gate to just under 240,000 (3,153 per home date)—still only about a third of the American League average of 680,000 (9,374 per game) for the season. Blaming the two-team St. Louis baseball market, the Browns sought permission to relocate to Los Angeles. Unfortunately for the team, the league meeting to discuss the issue was held on December 8, 1941, and the request was denied.[45]

Just two seasons later, the unthinkable happened: the Browns won the 1944 AL pennant.[46] The following year, in karmic parallel, the Chicago Cubs won the NL. While the Cubs had been a fairly decent team during the late 1930s, they failed to post even one winning season during 1940–44, and their last World Series appearance of the 20th century came as somewhat of a surprise. No doubt these pennants were both due in some part to the effects of the war on MLB talent.

Wartime measures affected the product that was professional baseball in other ways as well. Many of the minor leagues suspended their schedules, and big-league teams reduced travel by training in the North. Late afternoon and night games became more common so that working men and now working women could attend. Even as the game itself resisted racial integration, MLB owners quietly dropped the segregation of their stadiums.[47]

Shortages rendered un–American the use of rubber in the core of baseballs, so MLB searched for a replacement that would ensure that the dead-ball era stayed dead. The first attempt at a substitute resulted in eleven of the first twenty-nine games of the 1943 season ending as shutouts. Within weeks, the Spaulding Company was able to make a workable rubber-free ball, and a more acceptable measure of offense returned to the game.[48]

The lack of manpower had a decided effect on NFL operations, too. The NFL also shortened schedules from 11 to 10 games for the 1943 through 1945 seasons, and began to allow unlimited substitutions and the modern two-platoon game.

When the Brooklyn (football) Dodgers opened their 1943 training camp, only seven of their players from the prior year were available. Chicago Bears running back great Bronko Nagurski came out of a six-year retirement to play for his old team. The Cleveland Rams suspended operations for the whole season, while the Philadelphia Eagles and the Pittsburgh Steelers fielded a combined team, the "Steagles," which went 5–4–1. The Steagles were undone for the 1944 season, when the Steelers merged with the Chicago Cardinals. The awful 0–11 combined team was referred by some pundits as the Car-pets. The Brooklyn team and the Boston Yanks also merged for the 1944 season, playing as the city-less Yanks.[49]

College football also suffered during the war as many schools abandoned their programs. Interestingly, the navy played a significant role in the game as its trainees were encouraged to play at the colleges that they attended; it was not unusual to see players move from team to team as they were transferred from base to base. Navy players helped develop football powerhouse programs at Notre Dame, Purdue, Northwestern, Georgia Tech, and Texas, not to mention the Naval Academy.[50] Later, the wave of returning servicemen attending college made for a golden age of the sport during the late 1940s.

The First Diaspora: The Great Suburbanization

By the time that the atomic bombs dropped on Hiroshima and Nagasaki in 1945, weary Americans were more than ready to return to something that better-resembled normal life. Wartime manufacturing may have pumped up pocketbooks, but rationing had made all kinds of things scarce. Those that had remained back home had little of interest on which to spend their earnings until after the war ended.

With VJ Day came a trickle, and then a torrent, of returning servicemen, eager to reclaim their abandoned jobs from their wives and sisters. The major professional leagues began to look more like their pre-war selves, and the factories that had overwhelmed the Axis powers retooled for a new, consumer-led America. Refrigerators, washing machines, and soap powder replaced warplanes, tanks, and bullets in the GNP accounts. There seemed no end to the pent-up demand resulting from the disbursement of long-deprived consumers' bulging savings accounts.

The automobile finally unshackled the American middle class from the necessity of being close to public transportation, and a great exodus from the big cities began. Families took advantage of cheap land surrounding the nation's metropolises to build homes larger than their grandparents could have imagined living in, and taking advantage of the Eisenhower administration's nod to the German Autobahns. Originally conceived and sold to the public as a national defense project, the Interstate Highway Systems state-of-the-art roads soon became the ribbons by which suburbanites remained tied, ever more tenuously, to their central cities.

The nuclear family became the center of the new American lifestyle. Earlier generations of young parents had lived with their own parents and down the block from uncles, cousins, and other extended family, but the forces of suburbanization were strongly centrifugal. Now they became isolated in sterile Levittown neighborhoods, with other idealist and exuberant families like themselves. Influenced by their own experiences, the Greatest Generation sought to give their Baby Boomer children the idyllic youth they felt had been denied to them.

There was plenty of money with which to do this. The U.S. macroeconomy boomed louder than a thousand atomic bombs, and middle-class wages grew faster than anyone had thought possible even a few years earlier. By the early 1970s, real per capita income in the U.S. was about double what it had been just twenty-five years earlier. (See Figure 6-1.)

As a recovering Europe and Asia rebuilt from the ashes of war, American factories hummed for two and three shifts a day. The good times allowed labor unions to name their wages, and oligopolistic Big Auto, Big Steel, and their ilk were only too happy to oblige. The lack of any competition from abroad allowed the passing on of increasing costs to increasingly affluent consumers. Blue-collar workers with little formal education found themselves able to afford houses with pools, large yards, new cars, and more leisure time than ever in which to enjoy them. The advent of the forty-hour work week

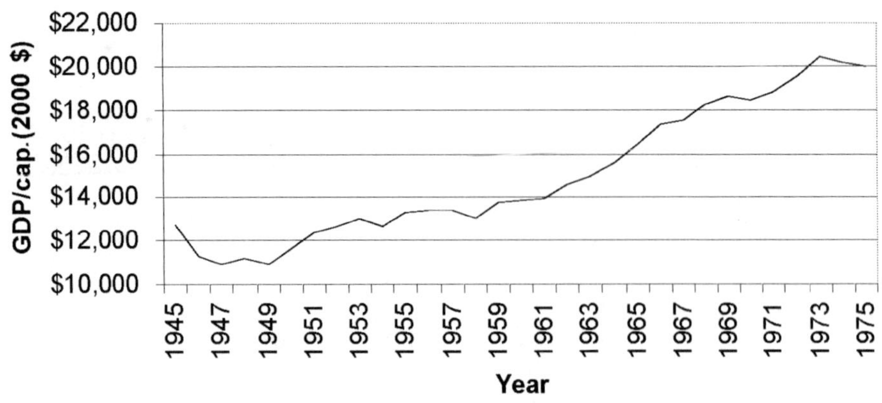

Figure 6-1: U.S. Real GDP per Capita, 1945–1975

Source: Economic History website. Accessed from http://www.eh.net, 26 Sept. 2005.

and generous paid vacations meant that there were plenty of hours for family time.

Not surprisingly, the 1950s also saw the rapid growth of participatory family and youth sports. With the help of the Brunswick Company, dark and seedy bowling "alleys" with foul-mouthed pinboys became brightly lit, family-oriented, automated "lanes"; perfect places for Mom, Dad, and the kids to spend a little quality time during evenings and weekends. Women joined weekday bowling leagues, dropping off their children at the facilities' babysitting services for a little klatching over hardwood.[51] Golf and tennis likewise grew in popularity as expanses of green space were much more affordable in the bucolic suburbs than in the paved-over cities. Little boys joined Little League baseball and Pop Warner football in droves. Their sisters became tumblers and cheerleaders. Dads coached the boys and Moms led the girls, schooling them in the American Way.

By the mid–1950s, such participation had actually become a patriotic duty. The increasing chill of the Cold War between the competing ideologies of the U.S. and the Soviet Union began to touch every part of normal American life. The Olympic Games became much more than just an exhibition of the finest athletes in the world; rather, they were a struggle between the free, God-fearing peoples in the American sphere of influence and the godless Communists and their minions behind the Iron Curtain. It was every parent's duty to raise healthy, well-educated and physically talented children to keep our edge over those evil commies. Two world wars in living memory had done a lot to hone Americans' sense of us-against-them, a sentiment shamelessly exploited by alcohol-sodden demagogue Joseph McCarthy.

The Second Diaspora: Population Migration

Americans weren't just moving to the suburbs. They also were deserting the large urban centers of the Industrial North for the Sunbelt cities of the South and the West. While the country's head count increased during the fifties by over 25 million people, a healthy average annual rate of over 1.7 percent, New York City's population actually shrank at a nearly 2 percent annual rate during the decade. Chicago's population grew at a paltry 1.2 percent. Boston and Pittsburgh fared even worse with about 0.8 percent growth each during the 1950s, but Atlanta, Dallas, Los Angeles, San Francisco, Seattle, and San Diego all grew at annual rates of 4 percent to 6 percent.[52] The increasing prevalence of air conditioning and availability of better intercontinental travel were primary drivers of these changes, but the global experiences of military veterans doubtless made the world seem to be a somewhat smaller place that should be embraced, not shut out.

The major North American sports leagues were very slow to recognize the new reality of the second American diaspora. Of course, hockey remained a Canadian and northern U.S. phenomenon; moreover, there were only six teams, so the NHL perhaps was justified in ignoring the trend, at least at first. Basketball also could be forgiven for not noticing suburbanization. Barely a half-century since its invention, the sport remained a largely eastern urban thing, and the NBA was still in its infancy. But MLB and the NFL should have reacted more quickly than they did. Their sloth resulted in a big-time sports vacuum in fairly large, growing, and prosperous cities. (See Figure 6-2.) These are exactly the conditions that produce rival leagues. And that is what happened.

In mid–1944, the end of the war was coming into view, and the population shifts began to appear likely. Two days before D-Day, a group of millionaires met in St. Louis under the urging of Arch Ward, the entrepreneurial sports editor of the *Chicago Tribune*. Ward saw that end of the war would bring a large increase in both the demand for professional football, as well as in the supply of players. The meeting eventually whelped the All-American Football Conference, which by its first year of operation, in 1946, consisted of the Western Division, with teams in Cleveland, San Francisco, Los Angeles, and Chicago. The Eastern Division was made up of entries fielded by New York City, Buffalo, Brooklyn, and Miami. Given weekly games, it would have been feasible to use trains to get visiting teams to contests, but the league further facilitated their travel by cutting a deal with United Airlines. The eight-team league started playing games in 1946, and often found itself playing in front of good crowds. Over 60,000 watched the Cleveland Browns destroy the Seattle Seahawks on September 6, 1946.[53]

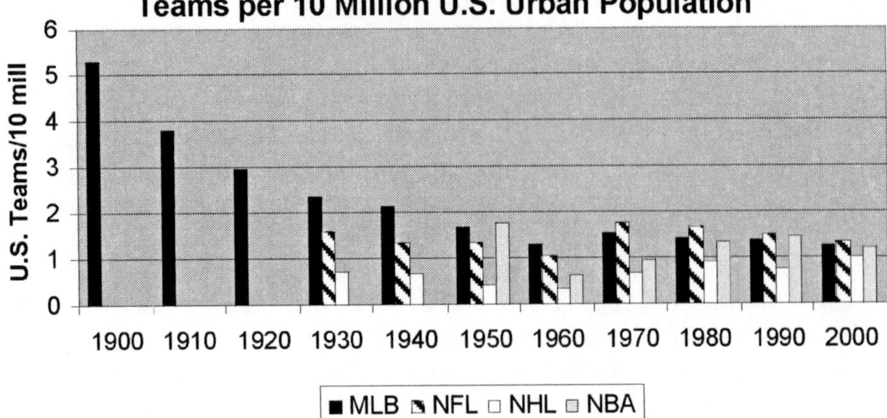

Figure 6-2: American Major Professional Teams per 10 Million of U.S. MSA Population by League, 1900–2000

Source: Don Dodd, Historical Statistics of the States of the United States: Two Centuries of the Census, 1790–1990 *(Westport, CT: Greenwood Press, 1993); U.S. Bureau of the Census,* Statistical Abstract of the United States, 1992 *(Washington, DC: GPO, 1992).*

The Browns were a good team—too good, as it turned out. They went 12–2 in their first year, and won the league championship four straight times. Their dominance of the AAFC quickly led to flagging interest which, along with turbulence in teams' ownerships, led to the AAFC's doom. On December 9, 1949, the NFL assimilated the clubs in Cleveland, Baltimore, and San Francisco. With the inclusion of the 49ers as part of the NFL, Major league sports west of the Mississippi became reality for the first time.

Baseball and Football Finally React

It was not entirely true that there were no high-quality professional spectator sports happening out West before 1950, however. Born shortly after the American League, in 1902, and playing its first season in 1903, the Pacific Coast League initially was made up of baseball teams in six cities: San Francisco, Los Angeles, Sacramento, Portland, Seattle and Oakland.[54] Unlike many other minor leagues bowing to Branch Rickey's "farm system" revolution, in which teams affiliated themselves with major league clubs, the PCL had relatively few such relationships. PCL players became local heroes, more or less independently of the big leagues that were so far away back East.[55] By the 1950, the PCL, boosted by its rapidly growing host cities, was on the verge of becoming a third major league.

Needless to say, this did not go over all that well with the American and

National Leagues. They reacted with a series of what could only be called cartel-like moves, set to crush the possible competition. In 1951, in an effort to push major league ball into the expanding West, Congress held hearings on MLB's use of their antitrust exemption. Not wanting to risk their sacred exemption, and feeling the heat from the PCL, MLB allowed a fair degree of team movement during the 1950s. Among other relocations, the Boston Braves moved to Milwaukee in 1953, the Philadelphia Athletics to Kansas City in 1955, and of course, the Dodgers and Giants moved after the 1957 season from New York to Los Angeles and San Francisco. The latter two moves led to a couple more congressional hearings, but as usual, the inquiries and attendant chest-thumping amounted to very little.

Even all of this change was not enough to slake the mobile population's thirst for big-time sports. The Continental League was proposed in the late 1950s as an eight-team circuit meant to prod MLB into further expansion. Despite the fact that it was a stillborn effort—the league dried up in 1960 without ever playing a game—it did what it set out to do: fulfill baseball's manifest destiny. It was better to get a relocating existing team than an expansion franchise, but the new hometown fans loved their teams. Incumbent owners soon discovered that expansion could be lucrative. (See Table 6-1 and Table 6-2.)

First Year after Move	From	To	3-Yr. Average Win Pct. Before Move	3-Yr. Average Win Pct. After Move	Difference in 3-Year Avg. After Move
1953	Boston (NL)	Milwaukee	0.484	0.576	+0.092
1954	St. Louis (AL)	Baltimore	0.368	0.390	+0.022
1955	Philadelphia (AL)	Kansas City	0.409	0.378	-0.031
1958	New York Giants	San Francisco	0.467	0.524	+0.057
1958	Brooklyn	Los Angeles	0.597	0.519	-0.078
1961	Washington, D.C.	Minneapolis	0.426	0.520	+0.094
1966	Milwaukee	Atlanta	0.530	0.500	-0.030
1968	Kansas City	Oakland	0.404	0.533	+0.129
1970	Seattle	Milwaukee	0.395*	0.416	+0.021
1972	Washington, D.C.	Dallas	0.455	0.408	-0.047
2005	Montreal	Washington, D.C.	0.479	0.500†	+0.021
AVG.			**0.456**	**0.478**	**+0.022**

Table 6-1: Summary of MLB Franchise Relocation, 1953–2005

Source: K.G. Quinn and P.M. Bursik, "Growing and Moving the Game: Effects of MLB Expansion and Team Relocation 1950–2004," Journal of Quantitative Analysis in Sports, v.3, no. 2 (2007): article 4.

*Team only played one year in Seattle before moving to Milwaukee.
†2005 season only.

Year	City	Franchise Fee	Forgone Shared Revenue	Roster Payments to Other Teams	Avg Win Pct of First 3 Years
1961	Washington, D.C.	0	0	2,175,000	0.367
1961	Los Angeles	550,000*	0	2,150,000	.0467
1962	Houston	0	0	1,850,000	0.403
1962	New York	0	0	1,800,000	0.299
1969	Kansas City	100,000	2,062,500 (over 3 years)	5,250,000	0.452
1969	Seattle	100,000	2,062,500 (over 3 years)	5,250,000	0.408‡
1969	San Diego	4,000,000	0	6,000,000	0.384
1969	Montreal	4,000,000	0	6,000,000	0.384
1977	Toronto	1,750,000	0	5,250,000	0.343
1977	Seattle	1,250,000†	0	5,250,000	0.344
1993	Denver	95,000,000	0	0	0.467
1993	Miami	95,000,000	0	0	0.436
1998	Phoenix	130,000,000	39,000,000**	0	0.514
1998	Tampa	130,000,000	39,000,000**	0	0.415
					Avg. = 0.376

Table 6-2: Summary of MLB Expansion, 1961–1998

Source: K.G. Quinn and P.M. Bursik, "Growing and Moving the Game: Effects of MLB Expansion and Team Relocation 1950–2004," Journal of Quantitative Analysis in Sports, v.3, no. 2 (2007): article 4.

Note: Values in nominal dollars.

*Paid to Dodgers for entering their territory.

†Reduced fee included as part of antitrust settlement payment.

‡ Includes one year in Seattle and two years in Milwaukee.

**14 million in forgone 1993 television money, plus 5 million per year for five additional years.

In any event, MLB made up for lost time, putting expansion teams in Los Angeles (Angels, 1961) and in New York (Mets, 1962), turning both cities into two-team markets. The leagues also expanded their geographic reach into Minneapolis in 1961 (from Washington, putting a new Senators expansion team in DC), and into Houston in 1962 with the Colt 45s, who later called themselves the Astros with the opening of their space age indoor stadium. Atlanta got itself a team with the abrupt move of the Braves from Boston in 1966. The Bay area won a second team when Oakland welcomed the Athletics from Kansas City in 1968; the AL continued play in KC that year with the expansion Royals. 1969 saw the birth of baseball in three more new cities as the San Diego Padres, Montreal Expos, and Seattle Pilots all played their inaugural seasons. Seattle's outing was something less than stellar, and the team moved to Milwaukee after one season and became the Brewers. The last move in MLB that would occur for over thirty years happened in 1971 when the perennially dismal Washington Senators relocated to the Dallas market and became the Texas Rangers. MLB attendance skyrocketed as their host cities grew in population. (See Figure 6-3.)

The other major sports did not expand as quickly and consequently were not as successful in fending off rival leagues during the 1960s and 1970s. The American Basketball Association was formed in 1967, lasting until a peace agreement with the NBA in June of 1976 led to the absorption of the ABA's New York Nets, Denver Nuggets, Indiana Pacers, and San Antonio Spurs. A similar history is shared by the now-defunct World Hockey Association. The WHA was formed in 1971, and played from 1972–73 until its more successful teams were subsumed by the NHL following the 1978–79 season. Those teams were the Quebec Nordiques, Edmonton Oilers, Winnipeg Jets, and New England Whalers; all but the Oilers have since relocated to other cities in the U.S.

Generally speaking, these rival leagues rested their fortunes on local economic support. Their franchise owners primarily were counting on gate revenues to pay the bills. The genesis story of the American Football League, the NFL's big rival during the 1960s, was a little different, however.

The NFL, feeling pretty good about its situation, was just as stubborn as the other incumbent leagues during the 1950s. Not only had the league

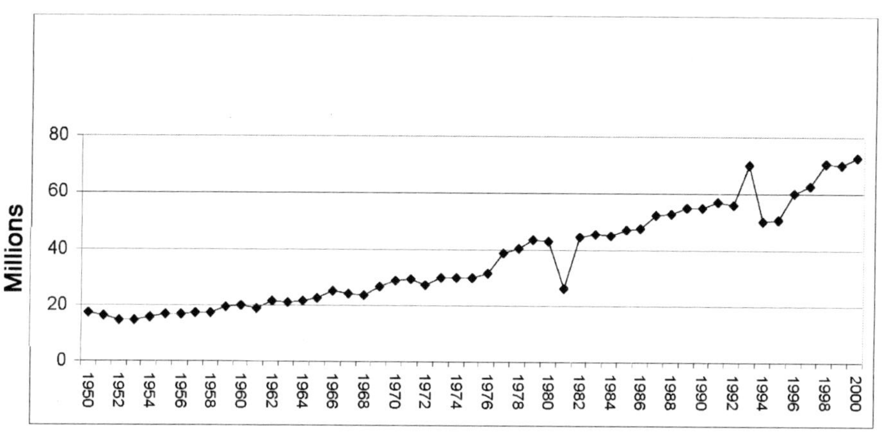

Figure 6-3: MLB Total Attendance, 1950–2004 (millions)

Source: Rodneyfort.com. Note: 1993 was the first year for expansion teams in two large markets (Denver and Miami) that played in large venues. MLB went from 154- to 162-game schedules beginning with the 1961 season. Labor disputes led to cancellation of portions of the 1981, 1994, and 1995 seasons.

beaten back the challenge from the AAFC, with some western representation in St. Louis and San Francisco, but the professional version of the sport was itself poised for a big break into the American consciousness.

Forever living in the shadow of the much more popular college football season, NFL franchises were mostly relatively small, yet moderately successful, family businesses. The league offices were less than modest, with commissioner Bert Bell actually running it out of his kitchen before moving to unpretentious digs in Philadelphia.

Two seemingly random and unlikely events in the late 1950s shook the NFL out of its smugness. The first was the "Greatest Game Ever Played," the 1958 NFL championship game between the Baltimore Colts and the New York Giants. The fourth quarter ended with a tie score of 17–17. In the first-ever "sudden death" overtime period, young Colt quarterback Johnny Unitas calmly led his team on a touchdown drive that electrified the sports fan nation. Pro football was finally on the American fan map on a par with the big boys of MLB and college football.

The second was Bell's unexpected passing from a heart attack in the end zone stands of Philadelphia's Franklin Field with two minutes left in an October 1959 Eagles-Steeler game. His replacement, the compromise candidate finally elected in 1960 by the owners on the twenty-third ballot, was the thirty-three-year-old Los Angeles Rams publicist-cum-general manager named Pete Rozelle.

Rozelle was a man of vision. One of his first acts was to move the league offices to New York City, a symbolic statement that the NFL had arrived. His careful lobbying of Congress for anti-antitrust legislation in the 1960s put the NFL in a position to be a darling of the rapidly growing television broadcast industry. The timing was right—the league had a lot of Catholic roots and ties, and Catholicism was popular in the U.S. John Kennedy had been elected president, the Singing Nun was a big pop sensation, and legendary Green Bay Packers coach Vince Lombardi was the very picture of a midwestern Italian Catholic even though he hailed from the East. But for all of his vision and skill in country-club politics, Roselle was not able to stop the formation of the American Football League.

Lamar Hunt, the son of billionaire oilman H.L. Hunt, had made a pitch for a Dallas NFL expansion franchise in 1959. He was rebuffed, but not deterred, leading him to organize the American Football League. This was actually the fourth "AFL" to take on the NFL (there were three other failed attempts in 1926, 1936–37, and 1940–41), but it was the only one that could be called successful.[56] His Dallas Texans (later the Kansas City Chiefs) were joined in the fall of 1959 by the Houston Oilers, Boston Patriots, New York Titans (later the Jets), Denver Broncos, Los Angeles Chargers, and Buffalo

Bills. There also was a Minneapolis franchise that withdrew before the first year of play, moving to Oakland to become the Raiders.[57]

Predictably, the NFL reacted by granting two expansion franchises in early 1960, one in Minneapolis, which caused the AFL entrant to get cold feet in that market, and another in Dallas, in Hunt's back yard.

The AFL played their first season in 1960, with a few rules that diverged from those of the NFL, meant to increase exciting play. Attendance was sparse, but the league was kept afloat by a five-year television deal with ABC, signed just before the season began.[58] NBC later helped out too, paying over $600,000 to broadcast the league's 1963 championship game, along with a five-year, $36 million deal to broadcast regular season games. The NFL also found the TV trough with a $14 million deal from CBS in 1964 for two years of broadcast rights. The ever-increasing TV dollars fueled a bidding war for players, and the two leagues called a truce in 1966. The deal called for the NFL to absorb the rival league teams as equal partners, paving the way for the league's wide geographic coverage and strong national television presence for the next several decades.[59]

Into the Next Century

By the mid–1960s, all the pieces were in place to drive American spectator sports into the 21st century: affluence, mobility, suburbanization, and continental appeal. And television money.

7

Chadwick to Arledge to Patrick

I always turn to the sports section first. The sports section records people's accomplishments; the front page nothing but man's failures.

—*Earl Warren*[1]

Media Money Madness

It is now difficult to imagine big-time professional spectator sports without its symbiotic relationship with television. Local and national media revenues positively define the current state of the NFL, NBA, NHL, MLB, NCAA, and PGA Tour. While the magnitude of the money might be new, the role that media and journalism play in the nature of spectator sports is as old as the sports themselves.

The NFL is by far the biggest fish in the modern TV pond. Its 1998–2005 contracts with CBS, Fox, and ABC were thought to be incredible at a total of $17 billion, or about $2.1 billion per year, but the ensuing deals are even more astounding. The AFC and NFC Sunday afternoon games during 2006–2011 were sold to CBS and Fox for $3.7 and $4.3 billion respectively—a total of $8 billion, or $1.3 billion per year.[2] Sunday night games are now the property of NBC through 2011 for about $600 million per year. A big part of these deals are a couple of Super Bowls for each of the three networks. With an expected 100 million viewers raptly watching for the next new commercial, these are the most valuable single-event properties in all of media.[3]

Cable and satellite now are a big part of the NFL's television picture, too. ESPN has committed to paying $1.1 *billion* annually for the weekly Monday night games, plus some pre-season contests and access to various NFL assets through 2013. DirecTV is paying $3.5 billion for the out-of-market satellite rights for 2006–10, or $700 million per year. More controversially, a post–Thanksgiving Thursday and Saturday night package is currently running on the fledgling NFL Network, the league's in-house channel.[4] Not counting the Thursday–Sunday package, which likely could be sold for billions, the NFL has contracts on their product for the next six-plus years that total $24 billion dollars.[5] Given the revenue-sharing system among teams and with the players union, any game tickets or t-shirts sold seem to be just money icing on the profit cake.

While MLB's national television bounty cannot match the NFL's, it is not exactly poverty-stricken, either. First of all, 60 percent or more of the league's television money comes from unevenly distributed and relatively lightly shared local arrangements. Second, MLB still sees significant revenues from national contracts.[6] MLB's current deals with Fox, ESPN, and Turner Sports, which run through 2013, are worth a total of $5.5 billion, or about half a billion per year.[7] Like the NFL, MLB also cut a seven-year, $700 million deal through 2013 with DirecTV for an out-of-market package and MLB-only Baseball Channel.[8] When local revenues are included, MLB earns on the order of $1.5 billion per year from television.

The NBA's deal with ABC and AOL/Time-Warner for 2002–3 to 2007–8 paid a total of $4.6 billion, or over $700 million annually, and individual teams in favorable local media markets can earn $70 million or more each year from all forms of broadcast revenues.[9] An eight year, $7.4 billion ($925 million per year) extension with ABC/ESPN and Turner will run through the 2015–16 season, and includes a variety of digital rights.[10] ABC/ESPN also has a deal with the WNBA that runs from 2008–9 through 2015–16, which pays no rights fees, but calls for the network to split TV ad revenues with the league.[11]

Even the lowly NHL was getting about $120 million annually from its American and Canadian contracts before the labor action that cancelled the 2004–2005 season.[12] The league's three-year deal with a rather obscure cable network that began with the 2005–2006 season yielded a much less generous $69 million annually, a sum that risks the NHL's extinction as a major North American league.

The National Collegiate Athletics Association gets its part of the TV pie too, although the "amateur" athletes who serve as the organization's cannon fodder see very little of the massive revenues they generate. While regular season conference and non-conference games are sold by individual schools and conferences, NCAA has sold the rights to 67 of their championships to CBS, and 21 others to ESPN.[13] Notre Dame's own five-year football deal with NBC pays the school $9 million each year.[14]

The granddaddy college property of them all, of course, is the NCAA men's basketball tournament, popularly known—and trademarked—as "March Madness." CBS's eleven-year deal through 2014 for the tournament pays the NCAA a total of $6 billion, or about half a billion each year. After taking whatever NCAA decides to spend on itself, the organization returns these monies to its membership; the largest 300 or so institutions in the club are the primary beneficiaries.

The other huge money-maker in college sports is the Bowl Championship Series. The BCS is an alliance of the six largest conferences (the Big East, the Big Ten, the Atlantic Coast Conference, the Pacific Ten, the Big Twelve, the Southeastern Conference), Notre Dame, and major bowls (the Rose Bowl, the Sugar Bowl, the Orange Bowl and the Fiesta Bowl) formed to stage a national championship game along with some other interesting match-ups after each college football season. The championship game rotates among the four bowls. The current $84 million-per-year deal with Fox for the Orange, Sugar, and Fiesta Bowls runs through the 2010 bowl games, while the Rose Bowl has a separate contract with ABC through 2014 for over $30 million annually.[15]

Other sports also depend on TV dollars to fuel their machines. Thanks in no small part to Tiger Woods, the PGA Tour's TV deals for 2003–2006 with CBS, ABC/ESPN, USA, and the Golf Channel brought in $850 million annually, although there is evidence that these deals may have cannibalized some existing sponsorship money.[16] The PGA Tour did not report the financial terms of the subsequent six-year television deal that began in 2007, although it is widely believed that the new accords pay substantially less. The new deals reconfigure the tournament schedule, cut out the ABC, TNT and USA networks, and include a playoff-ish FedEx Cup at the end of each season. Under the contracts, the number of tournaments annually covered by CBS increases from 16 in 2006 to 19, and by NBC from 5 to 10. In addition, the Golf Channel will cover the early rounds of official PGA events as well as the Champions Tour (for senior golfers) and the Nationwide Tour (for second-tier golfers).[17]

The newest kid on the block is NASCAR, which split its broadcast rights between NBC/TNT and Fox/FX for the six-year contract that concluded with the 2006 season. That deal was worth a total of $2.4 billion, or $400 million annually.[18] The most recent set of contracts with Fox, the Speed Channel, Turner Sports, and ABC/ESPN runs through 2014 for a total of $4.5 billion, or $560 million per year.[19] In addition, Sirius has the satellite radio rights for a five-year period beginning in 2007.[20] (See Figure 7-1, Figure 7-2, and Table 7-1).

Sport/ League	Network	Major Properties Included	Duration of Contract	Contract Value
NFL	CBS	AFC Sunday games and two Super Bowls	2006–2011	$3.7 billion

Sport/ League	Network	Major Properties Included	Duration of Contract	Contract Value
NFL	Fox	NFC Sunday games and two Super Bowls	2006–2011	$4.3 billion
NFL	NBC	Sunday night games	2006–2011	$3.6 billion
NFL	ESPN	Monday night games	2006–2013	$8.8 billion
NFL	DirecTV	NFL Sunday Ticket (out-of-market package)	2006–2010	$3.5 billion
NFL	NFL Network (League-owned)	Thursday and Saturday games after Thanksgiving	N/A	N/A
MLB	Fox and Turner	Weekend afternoon games, playoffs	2007–2013	Approximately $3 billion
MLB	ESPN	Sunday and weekday evening games	2006–2013	$2.4 billion
MLB	DirecTV	MLB Extra Innings (out–of-market package)	2007–2013	$700 million
MLB	Baseball TV (League-Owned)	N/A	N/A	N/A
NBA	ABC/ESPN and Turner	ABC/ESPN: Sunday, Wednesday, and Friday games, playoffs, digital rights. Turner: Thursday night games, playoffs.	2008–9 through 2015–16	$7.4 billion
NBA	NBA TV (League-owned)	Tuesday games	N/A	N/A
NBA	Various carriers	NBA League Pass (out–of-market package)	N/A	N/A
WNBA	ABC/ESPN	Regular season and playoff games	2008–9 through 2015–16	$0, but league and network will share advertising revenues
WNBA	NBA TV (League-Owned)	Regular season games	N/A	N/A
NHL	Versus		2005–6 through 2006–7, plus options through 2010–2011	$207.5 million (including third year option)
NHL	NBC	Stanley Cup games	2005–6 through 2006–7	N/A

Sport/ League	Network	Major Properties Included	Duration of Contract	Contract Value
NHL	Various	NHL Centre Ice (out-of-market package)	N/A	N/A
NASCAR	Fox/Speed, ESPN, Turner	Nextel Cup series, Busch series, Craftsman Truck series	2007–2014	$4.5 billion
NASCAR	DirecTV	Hot Pass (driver vantage point channels during races)	2007–2009	N/A
PGA Tour	CBS	19 events	2007–2012	N/A
PGA Tour	NBC	10 events	2007–2012	N/A
PGA Tour	Golf Channel	Champions League, Nationwide Tour, early rounds of PGA Tour events	2007–2012	N/A
IRL	ABC/ ESPN	Indianapolis 500 and other races	2008–9	N/A
Formula One	Fox/Speed	U.S. Grand Prix, Canadian Grand Prix, and other races	2007–2009	N/A
Arena Football League	ABC/ ESPN	Regular season games and playoffs	2006–	ABC/ESPN purchased minority stake in league that includes broadcast rights
NCAA	CBS	66 Championships, including men's basketball tournament	2004–2014	$6 billion
BCS	Fox	Fiesta, Orange, and Sugar Bowls	2007–2010	$336 million
BCS	ABC/ESPN	Rose Bowl	2006–2014	$300 million
Olympics	NBC	Winter Games and Summer Games	2010 and 2012	$2.201 billion

Table 7-1: Selected Major Television Sports Rights Contracts

Sources: Various assembled by author.[21]

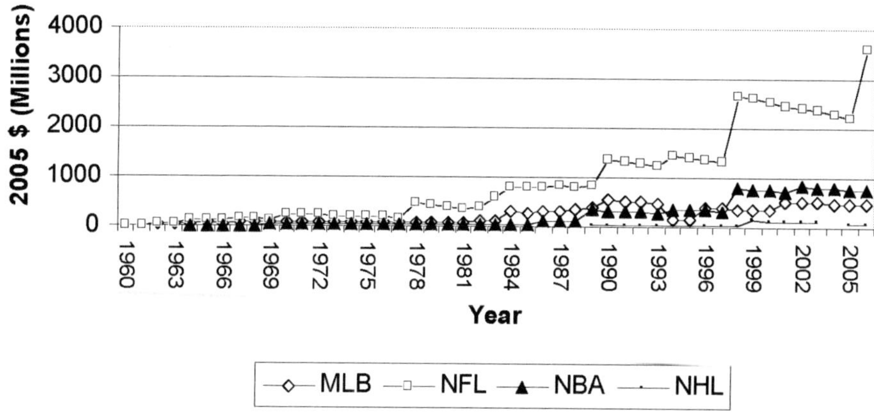

Figure 7-1: Annual League Revenues from National Television Contracts, 1960–2006, in 2005 Dollars

Sources: Rodneyfort.com; G. Foster, S.A. Greyser, and B. Walsh, The Business of Sports: Text and Cases on Strategy and Management *(Mason, OH: Thompson, 2006), and author's calculations. Includes national satellite television revenues.*

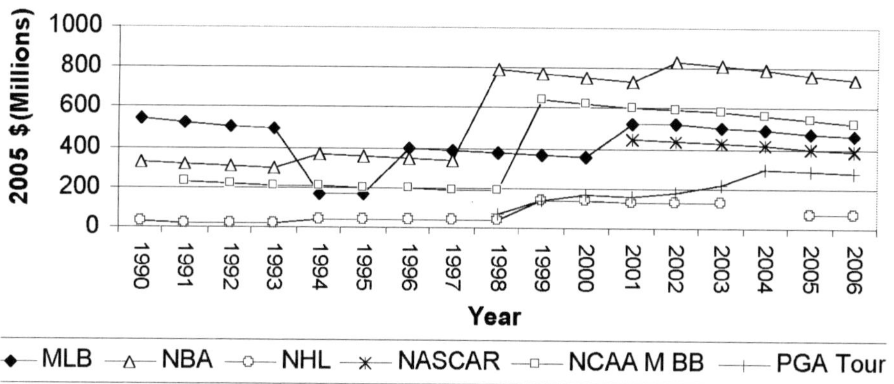

Figure 7-2: Annual National Television Contracts, 1990–2006, in 2005 Dollars

Sources: Rodneyfort.com, G. Foster, S.A. Greyser, and B. Walsh, The Business of Sports: Text and Cases on Strategy and Management *(Mason, OH: Thompson, 2006), various other sources, and author's calculations. Includes national satellite television revenues. (Omits NFL).*

Before Dick Enberg—Sports Reporting in the Ancient World

These stunning figures are not so much a new phenomenon in spectator sports as they are reflections of the technology and the prosperity of our times. As long as sports have been played in front of others, there have been people to bring what happened to those who were not directly in attendance. Sports journalism is as old as the art of telling a story, and so is the celebrity of those who do so.

Also not new are the symbiotic and sometimes overly cozy relationships between the storytellers and the sports that they describe. Those staging the earliest sporting events knew that someone had to get the word out about them. Two thousand years of Egyptian wrestlers' exploits, beginning in the early third millennium B.C., are chronicled as relief sculptures, statuettes, and temple and tomb decorations—mediated spectatorship is as old as spectatorship itself.[22] Internet, television and newspapers are simply today's versions of the ancient monuments, walls, potshards, and a host of other media depicting sports uncovered by archeologists.

The power of the combination of sports and sports media was obvious even to the ancients. Favorable press coverage of leader athletic feats did not originate with North Korea's Kim Jong-Il and his supposed eleven holes-in-one in his first and only round of golf.[23] As early as 2640 B.C., Egyptian pharaohs celebrated their thirtieth anniversaries of their reigns with runs around a ritual track, along with any number of other displays of their omnipotence despite their advancing years. This not-so-subtle reminder to potential usurpers had quite the run: three millennia.[24]

Shulgi, a Sumerian king from the early third millennium—or his advisors—similarly saw political value in legends of superhuman skill. His claim to fame, immortalized in the form of a hymn, was to have done the 200-mile round trip from Nippur to Ur in a total running time of about 30 hours. Since the modern 200-mile running record is slightly under 29 hours, King Shulgi must have had some righteous wheels.[25]

The early Greek Olympics were symbiotic with media in a variety of ways. Many of the games were heralded by a sophisticated public relations apparatus that let people far and wide know when safe passage to the Games was to be had despite the on going Peloponnesian War and other hostilities.[26] Contest rules and results were duly recorded in stone beginning in the sixth century B.C. and continued through the third century A.D. Given stone's limited portability, these inscriptions might have been more monumental than informational, however.[27]

Eventually, stone inscriptions gave way to more convenient forms of tribute. From about 550 to 400 B.C., Greek families would commission poets to create lionizing victory odes (*epinikia*) for their sports hero kin. The lyrical poet Pindar, himself immortalized by his contemporary Plato, is the best known of these hired guns.[28] At least 45 of his odes still exist in full, grouped together into four books based on the four sets of popular games that included the Olympics.[29] Pindar might be considered his era's Red Smith.

Record-keeping is as much part of the long history of sports journalism as is the romantic chronicle of athletic characters. Plutarch, who was born in 46 A.D. and was well known for writing about history's characters, noted that the first comprehensive list of Olympic victors was assembled in about 400 B.C. The list, authored by Hippias of Elis, a sophist made famous in a pair of Platonic dialogues, dated back to 776 B.C., right around the time that scholars place Homer's Iliad and Odyssey epics.[30]

The ancient Etruscans, who ruled Rome before the Romans threw them out in 509 B.C., were big sports fans, too. A tomb painting reports that boxing, foot-racing, discus and javelin throwing, and chariot racing were all present in their society. The early Romans, on the other hand, apparently held a view of spectator sport more in line with John Calvin and Max Weber than with George Will and Bob Costas, seeing it as a distraction from the more pressing business of conquest and commerce. Although chariot races were present at least as early as the fourth century B.C., and gladiatorial contests as early as the third century B.C., Roman spectator sports only took off after their conquest of Greece in 146 B.C.

Even so, sports reporting and romanticizing in ancient Rome fell far short of their Greek antecedents, with only occasional mixed reviews from the literary giants of the day. Cicero and Pliny the Younger noted gladiator bravery only in passing. Ovid and Juvenal were taken in by various sporting spectacles, but Seneca and Martial had a decidedly dim view of such things.[31] Still, the markets for chariot and gladiator tchotchkes around the events suggest that sports were popular with the general public, despite the lukewarm opinions of the literary elite.

After the fall of Rome in 476 A.D., European power and affluence moved eastward to Constantinople. So did the largest sporting spectacles, especially chariot racing. However, spectator sports in Byzantium was more or less the province of the aristocracy, and accounts of the hunt, the joust, and the duel were more about solidification of the social order than updating the faithful.[32]

As feudalism took over Europe, the wealth that the system created was concentrated in the few hands of the landholding elite, as were the major spectator sports of the times. Even so, they were unromantic compared to their Greek forerunners. Hastiludes, which were various forms of martial games such as the melee (free-for-all fighting) and jousting tournaments, became common among the upper crust during the late Middle Ages. Archery contests emerged as soon as that military technology became available. Even so, incessant real warfare limited even the elites' attendance at such events, and sports journalism was not a significant part of their society. The Black Plague of the 14th century, which killed as much as 60 percent of Europe's population, made labor scarce and may have rendered spectator participatory sports overly frivolous.[33,]

Origins of Modern Sports Writing

A century after the retreat of the plague, tennis and a variety of mass ball games, such as the precursors of modern soccer and baseball, began to evolve in England. By 1500, these games were held in low regard by the powers that be. They tended to be accompanied by gambling, brawling, and other behaviors associated with the Great Unwashed. Polite English society was not terribly interested in reading breathless accounts of glorious achievements surrounding these activities.[34] The rise of the English Christian Right—Puritanism—during the 16th and 17th centuries did little to further the cause of sports writing. Puritan influence on English culture nosedived with Oliver Cromwell's death in 1658, and the Restoration that put Charles II back on the throne in 1660.

Charles II was a horseracing buff, and reopened the tracks that had been closed during Cromwell's reign. The sport became popular with the upper classes, and by 1750 the Jockey Club had been established at Newmarket.[35] Around the same time, the game of cricket began to break out of the pastures of rural England, and was soon being played at elite public schools such as Eton and Winchester. As the British Empire grew into the second half of the 19th century, so did English sporting culture.

Fascination with English games and sports created a demand for reading about them, and the sporting publication as a legitimate literary genre emerged by the late 18th century.[36] *The Sporting Magazine* was the first of these, debuting in 1792 as the first English national periodical devoted to coverage of all manner of spectator sports. Other publications devoted to national exposure of British sports soon followed, including *The Racing Calendar, Bell's Weekly Messenger, The Times*, and the *Weekly Dispatch*. There also were a number of regional publications that offered sports coverage, too. Between 1793 and 1815, these periodicals reported on a total of 6,736 organized sporting events throughout the country.[37]

The Sporting Magazine took an eclectic approach to its coverage of material. It covered such topics as agriculture and political opinion, along with dispassionate reports of contest outcomes and juicy gossip concerning the figures of the day. Event calendars and the formal rules of various sports were commonly found in its pages. Anticipating the Web 2.0 revolution, much of the magazine's content was reader-generated, although editors claimed to have been on the watch to ensure accuracy. *The Sporting Magazine* took various moral stands, such as opposition to the war with France in 1795, and was outspoken in its criticism of animal cruelty. By the 1820s, it was the fourth best-selling periodical in London, and sportswriters were emerging as literary celebrities in their own right.[39]

Unlike their more egalitarian British counterparts, early 19th century U.S. newspapers and periodicals were aimed at a relatively snooty audience. An annual newspaper subscription typically cost between eight and ten dollars—a considerable sum for a non-essential—so only the well-off could afford such a luxury. Furthermore, reading was hardly a widespread skill in infant America.[39] Publishing was done more as a labor of love than as a profit-seeking enterprise, even as the country's literacy rate increased.

Of course, there was some sports coverage in early American newspapers. For example, the *Boston Gazette* published a story on a 1773 boxing match. However, such stories were quite unusual.[40] The first American sporting periodicals began to appear in the late 1820s, when, in the U.S. sports were still considered a low-brow activity unfit for the literate. None of the earliest attempts at the genre lasted very long. Slightly more respectable publications such as the *American Farmer* and *The Spirit of the Times* tended to play it safe by covering mostly the "respectable" sports such as horse racing, although there was some treatment of other sports such as boxing. Sports writers were not held in terribly high regard, so journalists often published under pseudonyms so as not to damage their reputations.[41]

As America grew, so did interest in spectator sports. *The Spirit of the Times* quickly became the most successful magazine of its type, and saw its circulation grow to 100,000 by the 1850s. After an apparently unsuccessful effort to hype cricket as the national game in the 1840s, the publication switched its efforts to baseball in the 1850s, about the same time that *New York Mercury* reporter William Cauldwell initiated the first regular baseball coverage, in 1853.[42] That same year, another sports publication, *The Clipper*, was founded, and soon supplanted the *Times* as the country's leading sporting publication. *The Clipper* countered the *Mercury* by employing one Henry Chadwick as the country's first full-blown sportswriter.[43]

Two technological innovations bolstered the growing American newspaper business. In 1844, the telegraph was invented, and one year later, Richard March Hoe invented the rotary press.[44] Not only could information now be transmitted quickly, but newspapers could now be printed cheaply. A "penny press" supplying lower- and middle-class readers with inexpensive newspapers took off. Not unlike today's Internet, the penny press represented quite a threat to the staid "mainstream media" of the day. In 1830, the U.S had only 650 weekly and 65 daily periodicals, with total circulation of the dailies at about 78,000. Ten years later, there were 1,141 and 138 dailies, and the dailies' circulation totaled 300,000.[45]

Sport was a regular staple of penny press pages, mixed in with lurid crime stories, high-society gossip and fashion, and birth announcements. The *New York Herald*, founded in 1835, one of the leaders in penny press sensationalism, occasionally would express regret at the role of sport in society, but covered it anyway. So did the stately *New York Times*, perhaps in response to the popularity of its new competition. By the Civil War, newspaper sports coverage was routine, but remained interspersed throughout the paper.[46]

Just as other American industries became more organized and regular in the latter half of the 19th century, so did sports. Compulsory education was increasing literacy and with it, the sports media market. Sports reporting generally evolved into a respectable profession, with specializations in horse racing, baseball and other sports becoming commonplace. In 1870, the first known American female sports reporter, "Middie" Morgan, began covering races and cattle shows for the *New York Times*.[47]

Throughout the 1870s, papers began to hire sports editors. In 1883, Joseph Pulitzer organized the first sports department and the sports page was born at his *New York World*. Pulitzer recognized a market among the city's tenement-dwelling masses, and encouraged sports as a fitting interest for this market. While horse racing was given the most attention, baseball, boxing, tennis, track, and football were also covered in the *World*.[48]

Soon after Pulitzer cemented the legitimacy of American sports journalism, two new baseball-focused magazines, *Sporting Life* (1883) and *The Sporting News* (1886), were born outside of New York City, cementing the role of sport in American print media.[49] Pulitzer competitor William Randolph Hearst also recognized how sports coverage could attract readers. He even devoted an entire front page to the 1895 Harvard-Princeton football game, complete banner headlines and a huge illustration of the event. The author of the story on the game was Richard Harding Davis who managed to get paid the unheard-of sum of $500 for his efforts, and his name in large type. The edition sold out.[50]

By the turn of the century, the American sportswriter-as-star was a firmly established concept, and bidding wars between competing papers for top talent occasionally broke out. They all owe a debt to the efforts of Henry Chadwick, who amid his other freelancing work had begun to write for the *New York Herald* in 1862.

Henry Chadwick: Journalist and Moralist

Henry Chadwick was born in Exeter in 1824 into a well-known English family.[51] His grandfather, Andrew Chadwick, was a good friend and follower of John Wesley, founder of the Methodist church. Andrew Chadwick took to heart Wesley's messages of strong moral character through education and social justice for the poor. He founded the first four Methodist Sunday schools in Lancashire and was a champion of those most negatively affected by the nascent Industrial Revolution. Andrew's philosophy rubbed off on his son James, Henry's father, who became a crusading English journalist championing the ideals of the American and French Revolutions. Perhaps it was James's penchant for radical politics during George IV's turbulent reign that led to his emigration with his wife and young family to New York City in 1837.[52]

Growing up in Devonshire, far from the political machinations of post–Waterloo London, Henry Chadwick spent his pre-teen years playing ball-and-stick games such as rounders and cricket. He also learned from his father about botany and astronomy, and about the philosophies of John Locke and David Hume. These teachings, both scientific and moral, had profound effects on Henry's world view, his spirit of moral reform, and how he influenced American baseball during his lifetime.[53]

The Chadwicks settled in Brooklyn, which in the late 1830s offered a boy plenty of opportunities for more ball games—including baseball—as well as hiking, hunting, and fishing. Henry would sometimes watch local cricket matches played by fellow English immigrants. He was taken with the scientific grace of the athletes he watched. He turned his father's training in record-keeping and organization into his first real job in 1840 when, despite his tender age, he was hired as an assistant librarian.[54]

Henry apparently inherited his father's attraction for journalism, and got himself hired in 1843 as a writer for the *Long Island Star*. He interspersed sports stories with other pieces criticizing Brooklyn's problems with alcoholism, gambling, and disease, and became an advocate for healthy lifestyles that included participation in athletics and outdoor games. His ideas about exercise and civilized sport coincided with the establishment of gymnasiums by the German-inspired Turner Movement, the YMCA, and Harvard University. By the mid–1850s, he was firmly established as a cricket writer for the *New York Times*. It was in 1856 that Chadwick was struck with the thought of making baseball, which he thought faster-paced and more suited to the American psyche, the U.S. national sport. He was not the first baseball journalist—William Cauldwell of the *New York Sunday Mercury* had been publishing game results as early as 1853—but he was by far the most important.[55]

Chadwick became evangelical about the game. In 1857, he convinced the weekly *New York Clipper* to hire him as a cricket and baseball editor, and to begin publishing regular game summaries. He soon began writing summaries and stories for New York's daily newspapers such as the *Brooklyn Eagle*, where he began to work full-time in 1864.[56] Chadwick also played an instrumental role in standardizing baseball play throughout the New York area. Although the Knickerbockers and Andrew Cartwright had laid out some rules, and several other teams had adopted them, many teams did not. In 1857, a convention was called to address this issue, and Chadwick received an invitation. It was at this convention that 9-inning games and 90-foot base paths became uniform, while later such gatherings set the distance of the pitcher from home plate and established that only balls caught on a fly rather than on a bounce constituted an out. Chadwick participated in these meetings, and used his newspaper bully pulpits to argue his points.[57]

Chadwick continued to promote the game throughout the Civil War, both inside and outside the New York area. In 1860, he published the sport's first guide, *Beadle's Dime Baseball Player*, in which he enumerated the 1857 rules, as well as a listing of twenty-two clubs that had participated in their formation. He also included tips on how to construct a field and play the game. The *Beadle's* guides, which were published annually until 1881, along with their successor, *Spaulding Guides* (1881–1908), were instrumental in popularizing the sport across the U.S.[58]

The game of baseball grew quickly following the Civil War, in no small part due to Chadwick's tireless efforts to objectively chronicle it. Crowds became larger, and the sport became less about health and fitness and more about making money. Professional gamblers saw opportunities to ply their trade, and were frequently believed to arrange the outcome of matches. Chadwick, relying on his father's moral instruction, began to play an increasingly important role as the conscience of the game. He wrote that the factories should support their employees' play of the game for health reasons, that teams strictly adhere to the rules, and that home runs were less elegant than more scientific run-scoring strategies. He condemned the playboy lifestyles adopted by many of the National Association players of the early 1870s.[59]

But it was another journalist, not Chadwick, who was most influential in getting the National League off the ground. By the conclusion of the 1875 season, it was clear that the National Association was suffering from lack of strong leadership. In October of that year, William Hulbert got *Chicago Tribune* sports editor Lewis Meacham to promote the idea of a reformation of the NA through the formation of a closed league with greater control over its players and more forceful rejection of gamblers' influence. Chadwick was held in disdain for what was perceived to be his outsized East Coast influence over the sport. The February 1876 *Tribune* article announcing formation of the National League made a point of referring to Chadwick as an old man who had been a dead weight on the sport. An April article written by Meacham ridiculed Chadwick for naming himself "Father of the Game," which he in fact had not. To his credit, Chadwick soon came to terms with the failure of his beloved National Association, and the necessity for the new structure of the National League.[60]

Chadwick continued publishing various guides and manuals about baseball, football, chess, and other sports and pastimes for the rest of his life. By 1894, the NL recognized his great contributions by naming him a permanent member of the league's Rules Committee, which two years later honored his contributions with a salary of $50 (about $1,200 in 2007 dollars) per month for the rest of his life.[61] Thirty years after his death in 1908, Chadwick was elected to the National Baseball Hall of Fame by the Veteran's Committee.

Sports Print Journalism after 1900

By 1910, nearly every paper in the country was giving regular coverage to major sporting events such as the World Series and Kentucky Derby.[62] By the time American boys went off to Europe to World War I, the sports page had turned sports into something that soldiers from Seattle to Sarasota could have in common. By the end of the war, constant baseball newspaper coverage had embedded it deeply into American culture. In F. Scott Fitzgerald's *Great Gatsby*, when Meyer Wolfson is introduced by Jay Gatsby to Nick Carroway as "the man who fixed the World Series" in 1919, Nick is struck by how "one man could play with the faith of fifty million people—with the single-mindedness of a burglar blowing up a safe."

After World War I, consolidation meant that the number of individual newspapers in the U.S. fell, even as total circulation increased. From town to town, city to city, newspaper formats were becoming much more alike than different. Such homogenization was concomitant with the rise of the wire services, led by the Associated Press.

Growing affluence meant that consumers took on ever-increasing importance in the U.S. economy, and a new business model took over the media industry. Whereas 50 percent of newspaper revenues in 1890 came from advertising, by 1929 this fraction had risen to 75 percent. A new reader-driven focus led to more sports coverage. The average paper in 1890 had devoted only 0.4 percent of editorial content to sport. Ten years later it was 4.0 percent, and by the 1920s sports coverage accounted for between 12 percent and 20 percent of the content of nearly every major American daily. The AP news service by then had its own twelve-person sports department, and the sports page had become a firmly-established American institution.[63]

The complementarity between American media and American sport continued to deepen in the 1920s. Papers continued to find a reliable readership base in sports fans, and this base could be satisfied with material generated at relatively low cost. Spectator sports benefited from much uncontroversial friendly treatment, and steady streams of stories made hometown baseball teams sources of civic pride. The tripling of newspaper college football coverage between 1913 and 1927 evolved the sport's fan base from the elite to the middle class. Teams, of course, were thrilled by the free public relations, and did whatever they could to encourage their local rags to run favorable stories.[64]

The relationship between beat reporters and the sports and athletes that they cover remains quite cozy. Teams often provide free game admission, plush press quarters, the equivalent of media concierges, and free meals to lure reporters to their events. A 1997 survey reported that the typical sports columnist at a major metropolitan newspaper typically was responsible for three or four columns per week, earning more than $90,000 for the effort.[65]

Newspaper stories about professional sports are still more highly read than those about business, entertainment, or even opinion pieces. Fifty percent of male newspaper readers and 31 percent of female readers consider sports coverage important. Younger readers are more likely to have a higher interest in reading about sports in the paper, although a 2003 *Seattle Times* study found that sports story readers were typically male, with an average age of 48.1 and an average income of $72,600. A large majority of readers report that they are satisfied with the quality of sports coverage in their newspapers.[66]

These numbers mean that more than 20 percent of U.S. daily newspaper content is now devoted to sports—more than any other category.[67] Despite the popularity of sports coverage, however, newspaper readership is declining quickly. Total U.S. paid newspaper circulation fell about 7 percent between 2000 and 2007, and the average American spent 12 percent fewer hours per year reading them. Sports magazines have seen declines in their circulation as well, but they remain a solid American institution. In 2006, *Sports Illustrated* enjoyed a paid circulation of 3.2 million, while *ESPN the Magazine* boasted over 2 million. *Golf Digest* and *Golf* each had circulations of about 1.5 million.[68]

Declining readership for periodicals does not mean that Americans are consuming less mediated sports. Rather than doing so via ink-and-paper, they are increasingly turning to electrons and bytes.

Radio and Sports

Sports on the radio dates back to the inventor of the technology, Gugliemo Marconi. In 1898, just one year after patenting his invention in England, Marconi used his device to send news of the Kingstown Regatta to the *Dublin Daily Express*. The *New York Herald* got wind of the report, seeing it as an opportunity to get a leg up on its rivals, and paid Marconi $5,000 to provide wireless Morse code accounts of the America's Cup race from 15 miles off of the Jersey coast. Within a decade, the technology had advanced to being able to carry voice transmissions. Experimental radio stations at universities across the country quickly proliferated. One of these laboratory stations was at the University of Minnesota, which transmitted voice accounts of the school's football games in 1912—the world's first modern sports broadcast.[69] This occasion changed sports media from solely reporting on historical events to contemporaneous accounts of action as it unfolds. Newspaper articles can only summarize what had already happened, but fans taking in a game via electronic media share with in-person fans the sense of uncertainty and drama as it unfolds.

The for-profit possibilities for radio soon became obvious, but World War I saw the U.S. Navy take over the radio business in 1917, and advance the technology further. In 1920, the first commercial radio station, KDKA, was established in Pittsburgh in a Westinghouse employee's garage. The company was only too happy to back the effort, believing that programming was the key to making some real money in selling radios.[70]

Soon after its founding, KDKA turned to sports programming as one of its first staples, and its first such broadcast generally is believed to be the April 1921 broadcast of the Johnny Ray–Johnny Dundee boxing match.[71] The station also provided the first radio broadcast of a Major League Baseball game, between the first-place Pirates and the last-place Phillies, on August 5, 1921.[72] Other stations soon followed suit. The 1921 Yankees-Giants World Series was carried by New York's WJZ, just four days after the station was launched.[73] The following year, the Yankees-Giants series, broadcast by Grantland Rice on WJZ, drew an estimated one million listeners.[74]

The timing could not have been more fortuitous for radio's flirtation with sports. The Roaring Twenties meant that people had money to buy the devices, and both baseball and football were about to explode as mass culture. In 1922, there was only one radio in every 400 American homes; by 1929, one-third of households had radios. The famous Dempsey-Tunney "long count" fight in 1927 alone was estimated to have sold over $90,000 of radios from just one New York department store.[75] Earlier that year, the Stanford-Alabama Rose Bowl had become the first coast-to-coast sports broadcast, courtesy of NBC.

By the early 1930s, NBC and CBS dominated radio broadcasting, and were earning substantial profits from their advertising sales, including sports programming. Baseball was made to order for the new medium. Its pace and the ease with which it could be described made it a natural, and there was money to be made. In 1934, Ford paid $100,000 per year to sponsor the World Series radio coverage for four years. Even so, MLB nearly banned broadcasts of their games, although fear of cannibalizing their gate was not universally held among team owners. During the 1920s, Cubs owner Phil Wrigley put the word out that he would welcome radio coverage of his team as good publicity. Opening Day 1925 saw WGN's first regular season Cubs radio broadcast, and the home team beating the visiting Pittsburgh Pirates, 8–2. Saturday games were also broadcast on WGN the following season, and Chicago baseball radio flourished. At one point during the 1930s, five different stations carried Cubs and Sox games.[76] Other teams, such as the Yankees, were cashing in more directly by selling the broadcasting and advertising rights to their games.[77]

By the end of World War II, over 30 million U.S. households—nearly 80 percent—had radios, and sports on the radio were already a relatively settled part of American life. (See Figure 7-3.) The number of local AM stations doubled between 1945 and 1950, increasing the demand for programming. Mutual Broadcasting's *Game of the Day*, launched after the war, ran until the 1960s.[78]

Local radio baseball announcers became stars in their own right, with fame that sometimes transcended that of the players themselves. Vin Scully, who has broadcast Dodger games since 1950 when they were still in Brooklyn, simply *is* the Dodgers to many fans. Ernie Harwell's 43-year run as the voice of the Detroit Tigers similarly endears him to their fans. Bob Uecker has been the primary radio voice of the Milwaukee Brewers since 1971—the year the team moved from Seattle. In fact, the National Baseball Hall of Fame in Cooperstown, NY, has an award dedicated to broadcasters. The first Ford C. Frick award in 1978 went to Red Barber and Mel Allen, longtime radio

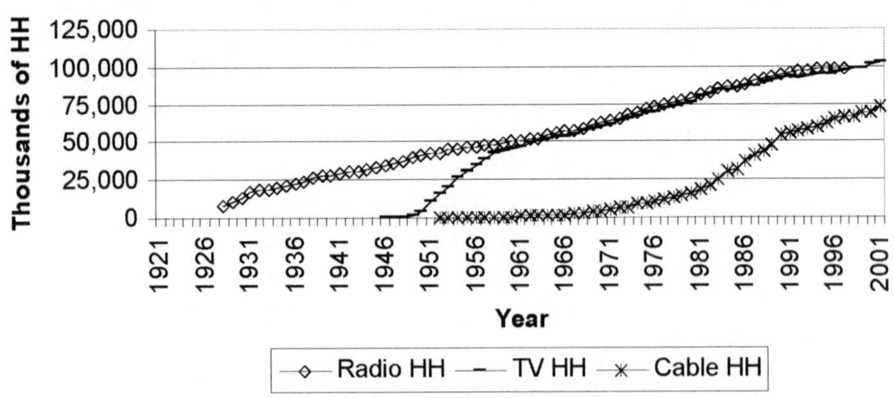

Figure 7-3: U.S. Households with Radios, Television, and Cable Subscriptions, 1921–2001

Source: G.T. Kurian (ed.), Datapedia of the United States: American History in Numbers, *3rd ed. (Lanham, MD: Bernan Press, 2004). Note: Some missing values have been interpolated.*

voices of the New York Yankees.[79] With 150 or more broadcasts annually, fans come to feel as though the baseball announcers are their intimate friends.

By early 1960s, radio's prominent role in American culture was being replaced by television. However, despite the de-emphasis on radio in favor of television, modern annual sports radio rights fees can reach into the millions. While each NFL team retains its own local radio rights, the league's deal with Westwood One radio from 2004 through 2008 paid the league $120 million. The league also gets $220 million for its 2004–2010 deal with satellite radio broadcaster Sirius. ESPN Radio is paying MLB $55 million for 2006–2010 national radio rights, while the league's XM satellite radio rights from 2005 through 2015 will put $650 million in MLB pockets. Even the NHL has lucrative satellite radio rights, with XM paying $100 million for the 2005–6 through 2014–15 seasons.[80]

The cost of radio sports rights is astronomical because of the intensity of fan interest. Broadcasters managed to figure out, however, that they do not need to buy rights in order to have sports talk programming. Call-in sports shows catering to fans grew in popularity during the 1970s and 1980s. In 1987, Emmis Broadcasting bought the only country radio station in New York and changed its call letters to WFAN and its format to 24-hour all-sports programming. Doubts abounded because a variety of other stations in town had well-established evening sports talk shows centered around local teams—how was a station with no sports properties going to attract an audience?[81]

The doubters soon disappeared as the format took off, attracting a relatively affluent male demographic. Within three years, Emmis sold WFAN, tripling its original investment. The format remains quite popular. Of the 10,600 radio stations in the U.S., 553 have sport formats, making it the sixth most common type.[82] ESPN Radio, launched in 1992 as a sports radio network, now provides sports-related programming, including talk, to over 700 U.S. stations, with 215 of them carrying the network 24 hours per day.[83] Its prime competitor is Fox Sports Radio, which is a similar but somewhat smaller operation.

The One-Eyed Monster Takes America

Anyone born before 1965 remembers the rapid penetration of the VCR into homes, and anyone born before 1985 knows how quickly the Internet changed American life. Anyone born before 1940, however, can recount how these phenomena pale in comparison to the velocity with which televisions propelled themselves into living rooms. On the other hand, anybody born in the mid–1950s or later has little or no recollection of radio as the dominant electronic medium.

One of radio's own giants, RCA president David Sarnoff, was a visionary with respect to the technology that would replace radio in the hearts and minds of leisure-seeking Americans. As early as 1939, he had cut a deal with the FCC for NBC to televise some of New York's World's Fair, and was responsible for the first—underwhelming—single-camera baseball telecast between Columbia and Princeton. A later broadcast of a Reds-Dodgers doubleheader added a second camera. The company's chief rival, CBS, did their own early sports telecasts. Their 1939 coverage of the Lou Nova–Max Baer match was the first time that boxing was televised. Television and sports inched hand-in-glove into the New York market until World War II began, and necessary resources were diverted to the war effort.[84]

The post-war return of American prosperity after years of Depression and war deprivation was essential to the new medium's phenomenal growth in the late 1940s and early 1950s. The NBC and DuMont networks established the first regular programming right after the war, and the number of U.S. television broadcast stations exploded from 9 in 1945 to 30 in 1946. Like many new electronic media, the issue of industry standards slowed TVs early growth, but there still was regular network programming over a total of 108 broadcast stations across the East Coast.[85]

The FCC was buried in an avalanche of new station applications, and responded on September 30, 1948, in typical bureaucratic fashion: a temporary ban on new applications. No doubt the move also had something to do with entrenched radio interests seeking to protect their business from the new medium's threat. To be fair, there were a number of technical issues that still needed to be worked out for TV—such as interference between stations, channel allocation, and the ongoing matter of industry standards—and the commission intended to hold hearings about these matters.[86] However, the Korean War extended the application moratorium for four years, and when the freeze was lifted in April of 1952, there were still only 108 stations. However, there was reallocation of the existing licenses so that by 1950, both the Midwest and West Coast were linked to the TV networks. The number of stations nationwide went to 198 in 1953 and 402 in 1954. The American television broadcast industry has grown steadily since then, with about 1,400 stations bringing in total annual revenue of about $36 billion in 2005.[87]

TVs were quite expensive in the late 1940s, so many of the earliest sets sold were bought by neighborhood bars and taverns, which hoped to keep their patrons on their stools a little longer with the novelty of the thing. Even so, unit TV sales were only 14,000 in 1947, and there were only 190,000 of the machines in use in 1948. But as American family incomes grew, and the price of sets came down, more and more of them purchased their first TVs. By 1950, there were nearly four million U.S. homes that owned a television, representing a 9 percent penetration rate. By 1952 almost 35 percent of homes had a TV. By 1958, there were TVs in 83 percent of American homes, about the same percentage as radio.[88]

As had happened in radio, television broadcasting business models evolved rapidly, and there was a lot of experimentation. Early cameras were heavy and difficult to move, and a lot of light was needed. The visual medium required stations to build pricy sets for original programming. Sporting events were attractive because they did not require much set-building, so they appealed to fledgling television broadcasters looking for an inexpensive way to generate interest in the medium.[89]

TV's early technological limitations meant that some sports were more suited to the medium than others. Boxing and wrestling were early TV sport darlings because their action was confined to a relatively small space. Unlike baseball and football, viewers were likely to be able to see those contests better on tiny TV screens than they could in person. Promoters eager for exposure at first did not charge for broadcast rights, but three-minute rounds separated by one-minute breaks were perfectly suited to sell sponsorships and ads. One early sponsor was Gillette, for NBC's *Cavalcade of Sports*. The program featured a heavy dollop of the sweet science, and became a staple of the new medium. The program ran for twenty years. Meanwhile, Gillete saw the market share for its shaving products increase from 16 percent in the 1930s to over 60 percent in the late 1950s.[90] In fact, TV boxing became so popular that it led to a decline in the number of local fight clubs—from 300 in 1952 to only 50 by 1960.[91]

As TV screens got clearer and bigger, other sports began to replace the overexposed boxing and wrestling. Despite having seen radio help rather than hurt gate revenues, team owners were queasy about TV. They feared that suburban fans in comfortable but distant living rooms might skip a drive into the city if able to watch games for free. Eventually, the prospect of profitable television rights deals brought them around. The opportunities were better for the haves than the have-nots, however. The growth of the number of MLB broadcasts is credited with killing attendance for some of the smaller minor leagues in the 1950s.[92]

Roone!

Perhaps no single individual did more to shape modern sports media than Roone Arledge. Born in New York in 1931, after graduating from Columbia University, Arledge worked for NBC for five years before leaving to become VP of Sports for a struggling ABC in 1960. He changed both sports and television during his long career in broadcasting.

In 1959, ABC was the also-ran of the television broadcasting industry. The company was formed when, for antitrust reasons, RCA was forced by the FCC to spin off one of its two NBC radio networks in 1943. It was purchased by Edward J. Noble, who had made his money selling Lifesavers candy, and re-christened as the American Broadcasting Company.[93]

Baseball TV rights in the late 1940s were selling for about $1,000 per game, and college football went for about $3,000 per contest. In 1949, CBS had paid the incredible sum of $100,000 for the rights to the Rose Bowl. Forever lagging its richer competitors, ABC could not compete for these rights, and by necessity developed a culture of programming experimentation. One product of that culture was a televised Roller Derby. Critics hated it, but the "sport" became ABC's most popular programming in 1949, so the network put it on for as much as four prime-time hours per week.[94]

ABC also tried a couple of prime-time football highlight programs in 1950, but with less success. At the time, the NFL was but a minor sport with sparse coverage even from newspapers, while live college game broadcasts apparently were more interesting to viewers than fuzzy highlight packages. Neither of the two shows drew enough viewers to warrant a second season. Meanwhile, viewers tired of the Roller Derby's novelty, and it too was banished from ABC's schedule by 1951.[95] The network continued to similarly lurch its way through the remainder of the decade. In 1953, ABC launched a Saturday MLB game of the week package with Dizzy Dean and Buddy Blattner behind the mic. In spite of—or because of—doing well among non-blacked-out viewers, ABC lost the package to CBS in 1955.

Unhappy with NBC's 1959 decision to cancel *Cavalcade of Sports*, Gillette moved nearly all of its ad account to ABC. At $8 million per year, this sum was more than the combined profits from ABC's television and radio businesses the prior year.[96] Despite a financially unsuccessful attempt to carry the sport during the 1954 seasons, the network used a bit more than $6 million of the money to steal NCAA football rights—by then the most valuable in all of sports—away from NBC during 1960 and 1961. It also spent over $2 million in 1960 for a five-year deal to broadcast the new American Football League.[97] Despite his having nearly zero sports television experience—his main claim to fame was producing the Shari Lewis and Lambchop puppet show—the 29-year-old Arledge was hired away from NBC in 1960 to help produce ABC's new NCAA package.[98]

Arledge proved to be the right genius at the right time. During a 1960 baseball telecast, he had the revelation that while standard telecasts showed only the game on the field, much of the color and experience of the game resided with the crowd. He understood that spectator sports are in fact "reality television," and that the key to success was to "add show business to sports." He managed to convince ABC, NCAA, and Gillette of his vision.[99] The approach, which took full advantage of technological advances in the form of hand-held cameras and strategic microphone placements, was a big ratings hit.

During the ensuing off-season, Arledge pushed the development of functional "slow motion instant replay." He put it to work for ABC's second season of NCAA broadcasts, which continued to grow in popularity—so much so, in fact, that ABC could no longer afford to match CBS's bid for the subsequent rights deal.[100]

Meanwhile, Arledge cut a series of relatively inexpensive TV rights deals with the likes of the Amateur Athletic Union, the Le Mans auto race, and a variety of disparate domestic and international events in soccer, tennis, golf, and other sports obscure to American viewers. ABC cleared out a regular spot on the weekend programming schedule, Arledge hired Jim McKay to host, and *ABC's Wide World of Sports* (*WWS*) was born as summer filler. It debuted on April 29, 1961, and became the longest-running sports program on television before ending in 1997.[101]

WWS was unique. First, it covered theretofore unheard-of sports such lumberjack contests, surfing, cliff-diving, martial arts matches, weight-lifting, skateboarding as well as too many others to list. Second, *WWS* played up soap opera storylines in tightly produced packages meant to tug at heartstrings as well as tickle adrenal glands. In an increasingly homogeneous television sports environment, WWS was a definite exercise in athletic biodiversity.

Arledge also made the bigger-and-more-annoying-than-life Howard Cosell into a big star and household name. Cosell, who had left a successful career as an attorney to become a sportscaster, was equal parts intelligent and abrasive. He made his reputation by asking the tough interview question and by speaking his mind. During a time when sportswriters left the social commentary out of the story, Cosell made hay with his controversial connections between sports and American life.

In 1965, Cosell's style had exiled him to doing pre- and post-game shows for New York Mets local radio and television coverage. The Mets were, um, not good—they set the record for baseball futility, winning only 25 percent of their games in their first season—and Cosell's grating nasal and acerbic tell-it-like-it is commentary only made things worse. It even had gotten him canned from his TV gig after he told viewers that the Mets manager was taking in-game naps.[102]

Cosell's dogged determination and obnoxious style caught Arledge's eye, and the producer made him *WWS*'s boxing expert. Meanwhile, a loud-mouth named Cassius Clay was tearing up the boxing world. Clay's sing-song poetic predictions of pugilistic pummeling harmonized with Cosell's Brooklyn abrasion to make strangely beautiful music in many interviews broadcast on ABC. When Clay converted to Islam, changed his name to Muhammad Ali and refused to submit to the military draft, Cosell was one of the few sportswriters who was in his corner.[103]

While U.S. cities erupted in anti-war and racial protests, Arledge was willing to take a lot of heat for Cosell's commentary, realizing that everyone complaining about him was also watching. During the 1968 Mexico City Olympics coverage, just months after Martin Luther King, Jr.'s assassination, American 200-meter dash medalists Tommie Smith and John Carlos raised their fists in a "Black Power" salute during the playing of "The Star-Spangled Banner." Middle-class white America may have been aghast, but Arledge sent Cosell to talk to Smith, tossing more gasoline on the fire.[104]

By 1969, ABC's NCAA broadcasts were far more interesting and innovative than the CBS and NBC pro football coverage. Arledge had the idea of turning the NFL into prime-time *entertainment* coverage, and managed to sell both ABC brass and Pete Rozelle on the concept. *Monday Night Football* made its debut on September 21, 1970, with veteran announcer Keith Jackson doing the play-by-play, and Howard Cosell and former Dallas Cowboys quarterback Don Meredith providing analysis. Former New York Giant Frank Gifford replaced Jackson on the *MNF* team in its second season. The show was an instant hit, perennially winning its time slot as the uncomfortable chemistry in the broadcast booth was fodder for millions of Tuesday morning conversations.[105]

During his long career, Arledge also produced a total of ten Olympic Games for ABC, each grander than the last. The well-oiled Arlege Olympic machine, including Jim McKay, was put to the test during the 1972 games when terrorists murdered eleven members of the Israeli team. Arledge later became president of ABC News, and then president of the entire network, along the way developing *Nightline, 20/20*, and putting Peter Jennings into the anchor chair for ABC's *World News Tonight.* He died in December of 2002, well-recognized for his impact and achievements.[106]

ESPN: A New Force in Sports

The 1970s saw the number of hours of annual network sports programming grow from 787 to 1,356. By 1984, the number was 1,700 hours, twice what it had been in 1974, and the three networks were selling more than $1 billion in sports advertising annually.[107] Sportscasters enjoyed as much celebrity as the athletes themselves. Network rights fees paid to the NFL, MLB, and NBA were $1.1 billion in 1984, up from about $500 million in

1980. (See Figure 7-1.) Things could hardly have seemed more favorable for the relationship between broadcasters and sports leagues.

But there was an infant underfoot. Early cable television was not initially regarded as a threat by the broadcast behemoths as the startup technology struggled to find its voice in American media. Still, by 1983, cable could be found in twenty-five million American homes, about a third of those with televisions. With zillions of channels, the concept of "narrowcasting" to specialized audiences became the new thing, and a few cable networks such as CNN, MTV, and ESPN hit the jackpot.

ESPN debuted with the first *SportsCenter* on September 7, 1979. There was nothing about the broadcast that suggested what would happen during the next two decades. Only 14 million homes had cable at the time, and only two million of them were able to receive the fledgling channel. It had little in the way of assets, other than a $10 million investment from Getty Oil, which lent the network its early red-and-orange color scheme, and an Anheiser-Busch ad contract. Its home was a nondescript building in Bristol, Connecticut, seemingly far away from the television nerve center of New York, let alone the style of Los Angeles. However, ESPN did have Chester Simmons—for $200,000 annually—who had worked for Arledge on Wide World of Sports before moving to NBC.[108]

The first edition of *SportsCenter* in 1979 was rather inauspiciously followed by a collegiate sports preview, and then by a live slow-pitch softball game. Later that evening, the network carried a live wrestling match, sports highlights, more *SportsCenter*, and a tennis tournament. The next morning's programming featured men running around in short skirts playing field hockey. All in all, ESPN in many ways resembled a cross between a local television in 1948 and an all-day version of the *Wide World of Sports*. While the big networks carried only 18 hours of sports per week, ESPN went 24/7 less than one year after its debut.[109]

ESPN's viewership began to grow during 1980, and Anheiser-Busch re-upped its deal to five years for $25 million. The network continued to lose money, but got noticed, and the NFL agreed to allow the broadcast of its April 1980 player entry draft. Programming continued to include rodeos, Australian Rules football, high school lacrosse, even ping-pong tournaments—anything that could be gotten on the cheap. Of course, hour-long sports news shows were cheapest of all, and continued to be the backbone of the network. Ratings were not a problem because there was no such thing for cable until 1982. Even so, it was becoming obvious that a significant male audience was trading in the three-minute nightly sports cast on the local network affiliate for the more comprehensive *SportsCenter*.[110]

By the end of 1981, 13.6 million homes could get ESPN. With its growing reach, the network was able to land early-round NCAA men's tournament basketball in 1982. On-air talent such as Chris Berman and George Grande honed their ad-libbing skills filling in between too-scarce highlights—the broadcast networks had refused to provide them to ESPN until 1982. But SportsCenter was establishing its own identity, and the network was a hot property. Arledge's ABC bought a 10 percent stake in ESPN in 1982 for $20 million.[111]

ESPN made the decision to turn its *SportsCenter* anchors into stars in their own right. Chris Berman, Dan Patrick, and Keith Olbermann became household names and began to personify sports just as Henry Chadwick, Red Smith, Vin Scully and Howard Cosell had. The program was the emblem of the network's growing clout, allowing it to charge cable carriers per subscriber. Following Getty's takeover by Texaco in 1984, ESPN was sold off in pieces with the biggest one going to ABC. The deal meant that ABC had paid more than $230 million for the programming network. By the end of the 1980s, ESPN was bringing in more than $100 million per year, making it the most valuable property on the cable dial at that time.[112]

During the 1990s and 2000s, ESPN's multiple channels acquired a variety of top-tier sports programming rights. It also fundamentally changed the way in which fans get their sports fixes. But with success came arrogance.

The grace and class of *SportsCenter*'s Patrick and Olbermann days had by the 21st century given way for hype, hyperbole, and celebrity tabloid journalism. As of 2003, ESPN's various networks were broadcasting 23 hours per week of SportsCenter, plus a variety of other sports talk shows.[113] ESPN executives seemed to become more interested in providing entertainment than sports, with scandal and gossip pushing out scores and highlights. ESPN had fallen victim to the 24-hour news cycle and all of its foibles. Thoughtful commentary by well-educated sports journalists has been supplanted by well-tailored talking heads shouting over each other in attempts to be "edgy." Earl Warren would have been saddened.

While ESPN's decision-makers have been marinating in their own egocentric juices, they apparently have failed to sufficiently appreciate the threat posed to them by the regional sports networks (RSNs). ESPN's programming may be glitz-encrusted, with the very latest in Arledge-inspired technological know-how, but to many fans, it feels far removed from where they live. Comcast Sports, Fox Sports Net and a multitude of other independent entities realized the head start that ESPN had in the national cable sports market, and chose to attack it at the edges with locally based programming.

As the first decade of the 21st century comes to an end, RSNs are available on local cable systems as well as the national satellite companies. They own large chunks of local baseball, hockey, and basketball television rights, and offer *SportsCenter*-ish sports news shows that compete with ESPN as well as the local broadcast affiliate. Some of the RSNs are vertically integrated with the teams they carry. Increasingly broadcasting in high definition, they pose significant challenges to ESPN's hegemony in sports programming. In 2003, the RSNs earned over half a billion in advertising revenues.[114] Likewise, the proliferation of channels on cable and satellite is paying the way for more sport-specific channels such as the Golf Channel, the Tennis Channel, TVG (horse racing), and others. Other threats to ESPN's catbird seat come from the Big Four themselves, which are increasingly choosing to own their own television channels.

What's Next?

No longer does the mountain have to come to Mohammed—teams now can come to fans exiled from their home towns. The Internet instantly brings nearly any local American newspaper or sport score to anyone in the world with a computer and a functional modem or broadband link. Daily podcasts generated by wannabe sportsradio talk stars are made available on iTunes for free; "Have watercooler, will travel." Fans can even watch contests in out-of-market locations via the Web and various satellite broadcast packages that are generating new and growing revenues for teams and leagues. And for members of the growing economic elite, fan tourism is a great way to stay connected with a favorite team or sport, and many firms now specialize in weekend trips and bus tours aimed at getting faraway fans their fixes.

Just an Ideal Drug Delivery System?

The last half of the twentieth century saw a fundamental change in which fans get their sports fixes. Newspapers could tell stories, and radio could give play-by-play descriptions, but they could not match the richness of the television sports experience. One thing has not changed, however—and probably never will. Fans use media to stay connected to their favorite sports.

Technological innovations have given fans a whole new way to take their "sports drug." Whatever communication technology the future brings, it will almost certainly be used to bring sports to fans. This just begs the question: What is it about spectator sports that make them such an attractant?

8

FEEDING THE HABIT AND KEEPING THE FAITH

Die Religion ist der Seufzer der bedrängten Kreatur, das Gemüt einer herzlosen Welt, wie sie der Geist geistloser Zustände ist. Sie ist das Opium des Volks. [Religion is the sigh of the oppressed, the soul of a heartless world, as it is the spirit of spiritless circumstances. It is the opium of the people.]

—*Karl Marx,* Critique of Hegel's Philosophy of Right, *1843*

On a structural level of analysis, a vulgar Marxism is sometimes invoked in viewing sports as an opiate and as producing unreality, mystification and false consciousness.

—*Elden E. Snyder and Elmer Spreitzer, 1974*[1]

"FanAddicts"

The "War on Drugs" is a miserable failure, at least insofar as the elimination of American illegal drug use is concerned. A 2006 survey found that 8.3 percent of Americans age 12 or older admitted to having used an illegal drug during the past 30 days. Over half of adult and teenaged Americans drink alcohol, with a quarter of those "binging" at least monthly.[2] This behavior carries with it significant legal risk—over 13 percent of all arrests in the U.S. are for drug abuse violations, while another 10 percent or so are for driving under the influence. An additional 4 percent are for drunkenness.[3]

All told, an estimated half-trillion dollars has been spent on enforcement of U.S. drug laws, and a half-million people are imprisoned for participating in the illegal drug market. Yet the street price of cocaine remains as low as it was in 1993, and it is now more widely used.[4] Prohibition now does not seem to be working any better than it did during the 1920s. If people want booze or drugs, they will figure out how to get them.

If there is a "War on Religion," as some might claim, it too has failed. Since nine out of ten Americans claim to have some religious affiliation, the masses apparently indulge liberally in Marx's opiate.[5] However, of the 40 percent of Americans who tell poll-takers that they have been to church, synagogue or mosque during the last seven days, about half were lying. Actual head counts show that only about a quarter of the U.S. adult population—approximately 55 million people—cares enough about a particular religion to attend services on a weekly basis.[6] But even though both the Fourth and the Ninth Commandments have fallen on hard times, there can be no denying the power and hold of religion on American life.

The unstoppable American yen for alcohol, drugs, and religion might seem far removed from spectator sports, but they are not. The fate of a modern day Puritan revival of the "War on Sports" likely would fail as mightily as it did two centuries ago. Just as the use of mood-altering substances, and religion cut across gender, class, income and geography, so does U.S. interest in sports. Drugs, God, and sports are simply part of American culture.

Filling the Pews

Pastor and pusher alike would love to have the kind of business enjoyed by spectator sports. The Big Four leagues drew just under 140 million in-person spectators during the 2006–7 and 2007 seasons—a number equal to nearly half the U.S population.[7] NCAA men's and women's basketball attendance totaled 41 million during 2005–6, while NCAA football games attracted 48 million spectators in 2006.[8]

And these are only the biggest sports. Baseball and hockey minor leagues together pull in a combined 55 million, while the two arena football leagues sell 3 million tickets per year.[9] Major League Lacrosse, Major League Soccer and the WNBA draw another 2.5 million combined each season.[10] All together, American big-time and near-big-time spectator sports sell about 300 million stadium and arena seats annually—and this number does not count all those who attend auto racing, horse racing, golf, and tennis events.

The ubiquity of sports is even more impressive when the reach of television is included. Americans view a total of about 80 billion hours per year of sports television programming—25 percent of all U.S. TV-watching.[11] In an era of cultural balkanization, enormous swaths of the population still come together at the same times to watch the same games. In 2006, each nationally televised NFL game drew an average of about 16 million Americans viewers. Add to that the CBS and ABC national broadcasts of college football games, which average another four million viewers each—some even attract as many as ten million pairs of eyeballs.[12] All told, national television football telecasts draw on the order of 70 million viewers per week. Football's active congregation rivals any other in its sheer size, and, perhaps, its fervency.[13]

Other televised sports may be smaller denominations, but they have their share of parishioners, too. NASCAR remains a regional sect concentrated in the South, but with an average race drawing about 5 million households throughout the 2007 season, it still fills a lot of living room pews.[14] Network-carried PGA Tour events post ratings consistent with between two and five million viewing households, depending on the tournament.[15] The 2006–7 basketball and hockey seasons saw national NBA broadcasts on ABC draw an average of approximately 1.5 million viewers apiece, while another million watched each national NHL game telecast.[16]

Post-season, the high holy days in each sport, draws more than just the devout—there is an obvious "holly-and-lilly" fan base in each sport. For example, the typical January 2008 NFL playoff game garnered about 20 million viewers; so did the average 2007 World Series game.[17] The 2006 through 2008 Super Bowls each drew in excess of 90 million American households.[18] Aggregate viewership during the 2007–8 college bowl season approached 130 million.[19] An average of 9 million households saw each 2007 NBA Finals contest, while an average of 2 million saw each Stanley Cup Finals game—historically record-low showings, to be sure, but still quite respectable.[20]

Big-time spectator sports enjoy a place in American society that rivals that of religion and recreational drug and alcohol use. Sports fans behave a lot like religious devotees—some of them seem to act more like frenzied drug users than simple consumers. "Vulgar" as it might be to say so, spectator sport has much in common with opiates, and fans are "fan-addicts."

Baptism, or, The Road to Addiction

Ask a fan why he or she supports a particular team, and the result is likely to be a story of a special relative taking a tyke to a first game. Perhaps the answer might even be that the fan can only say that he or she is not sure, but has always been a fan of that team. Just as baby birds glom onto their first impression of a mommy, fans are imprinted early on with barely remembered childhood experiences.

It is not that religion or fan allegiance are inherited, at least not in the genetic sense. But many people are Catholic or Lutheran for largely the same reason they are Dodgers or Brewers fans—their parents inculcated those leanings. These preferences can change later in life, but childhood Ohio State football fans who become Michigan supporters as adults are about as common as American Orthodox Jews who convert to Islam after college. And just as interfaith marriages can work, so can marriages between spouses with rival loyalties, although each has to tread lightly around the other during the holidays.

While mothers often take the primary role in influencing a child's adult religious traditions, fathers have been identified as the most significant individual in a person's journey to fandom. Friends, other peers, schools, and community also contribute to socializing people into values, beliefs, attitudes, and norms of a given fan culture. Interestingly, males tend to find that their parents and friends have the most influence on how they think about sports fandom, while females are more likely cite their schools.[21]

The economics of religious preference formation and practice can shed some light on the phenomenon of sports fan loyalty. Some might take offense with treating the delicate matter of religion with the impersonality of marginal this versus marginal that, but doing so offers a key insight: the more that one has invested in a religion, the more one benefits from further religious practice. Going to church becomes more meaningful as church attendance becomes more frequent.[22] Similarly, the time that a fan spends following the local team today results in greater enjoyment when following the team tomorrow. Interestingly, this theoretical construct traces its genealogy to economic models of drug addiction.

Now, nobody is claiming that religious practice is as destructive as substance abuse. Instead, the resemblance is found in how addicts' drive to pursue their vice depends on their past consumption of that vice. A heroin addict is willing to give up a whole lot more for a fix than someone who never touched the stuff. How much so depends on the addict's history and intensity of past heroin usage as much as it does on his or her own predilection toward getting hooked.[23]

Isn't this precisely what defines a fan? Being one requires a history with a team or a sport; like-minded fans are a fraternity, a congregation, and their thirst to interact with their team is like an addiction. Or a religion.

No Misplaced Loyalties

The nicotine addict is not sated by alcohol, nor does a pious Catholic consider his Sunday Mass obligation satisfied by a Saturday Temple service. Equally implausible is the devotedly addicted New York Jets fan finding fulfillment in a Giants game—unless they lose, of course. Greeks are about as connected to American football as Americans are to European soccer. Consequently, the typical Athenian could not appreciate the 2005 Steelers' unlikely Super Bowl run any more than the average Pittsburgher could revel in Greece's improbable 2004 European Cup win. Drug and sport addictions are specific, they are not interchangeable, nor are other teams substitutes for one's favorite.

A look at New York baseball fans in the late 1950s and early 1960s makes this point beautifully.[24] Back then, the Big Apple was arguably the center of the MLB universe. At least one New York team had won its league's pennant every year from 1950 through 1958, and four more times during the 1960s. The World Series champion hailed from New York eight times during the 1950s, and three more times during the 1960s.

In 1957, the Yankees drew about 1.5 million fans to Ruth's cathedral, the Dodgers about 1 million, and the Giants about 650,000—a total New York MLB attendance of about 3.1 million. The following season saw the New York Giants and Brooklyn Dodgers departed for western climes, leaving the apparently fortunate Yankees with a local MLB monopoly. But the Yankees were not able to cash in on their newfound status. Dodger and Giants fans failed to convert their loyalties. In fact, the Yankees drew 68,000 *fewer* fans in 1958 than they had the prior year—meaning that 1.7 million paying New York baseball fans simply had vanished.

The mysterious fan disappearance cannot be blamed on a bad Yankees team. They had won over 90 games and the AL pennant by at least eight games in both the 1957 and 1958 seasons. The 1958 squad even won the World Series, which was more than the prior year's edition had done. Apparently closing the local mosque and synagogue do not bolster the congregation of the neighborhood Methodist church.

Nor does the opening of a new Unitarian church affect attendance at the synagogue across town. The Yankees' four-year New York baseball monopoly came to an end when the Mets came into existence for the 1962 season. The expansion NL franchise was beyond atrocious, posting a record-low .250 winning percentage in its first season, but still managed to attract nearly 1 million fans. The Yankees' 1962 attendance was down about 250,000 from 1961, but the Mets were probably not responsible for the decline.

In 1961, the Yankees had had a magical year. They won 109 games while featuring the Roger Maris–Mickey Mantle home run derby that saw Maris break Babe Ruth's 60 single-season home run record. A letdown was likely as the 1962 club won 13 fewer games while the two sluggers combined for only 63 homers between them. In fact, the 1962 Yanks won about as many games as the 1958 edition, and drew about as many fans.

All in all, there is no evidence to suggest that the Yankees even tried to act as new monopolists after the exit of the Giants and the Dodgers. They neither decided to lower payrolls nor did they raise ticket prices in 1958. Other teams that gained and lost monopoly status during the 1950s and 1960s had similar experiences, and made similar choices.

Fans' religious allegiance to their teams is apparently less mutable than which brand of beer they drink, which airline they fly, or which car they drive, but maybe not which addictive drug they use. Maybe.

The Pull of the Drug

A weighty academic study found that young people use illegal drugs to change mood, facilitate social interaction, and make other types of social activities easier or more pleasant.[25] A comparable set of motivations could be given for sports fans. Anticipation of a big game elevates the mood and puts a spring in the step, but crashing from a high after a tough loss can make a fan want to swear off the team forever. Likewise, tailgating parties may be more about social interaction than sport, but the imminence of the game affords them a certain urgency and importance. When a favorite team or athlete wins, fans can feel as though a part of the on-field success accrues to them personally. Winning teams find their fans wearing their logos more than losing teams do. Psychologists even have a name for this high—the BIRG effect: "basking in reflected glory."[26]

Personal investment in winning might seem to imply self-loathing in losing. But self-esteem is a tender thing, so extension of team fortunes onto one's own ego is a bit of a one-way street. Losses require shifting responsibility for failure onto scapegoats. Fans who refer to the team as "we" after wins also tend to use "them" after losses. The difficult experiences of Bill Buckner or Mitch Williams following their respective World Series gaffes in 1986 and 1993 are a result of fans trying to distance themselves from particularly painful losses.[27]

Spectators can find both excitement as well as escapism in their favorite sporting events, just as they might from a good scary flick. The artificial stress of a good game can fill a void in an otherwise dull life. The experience can be exhilarating, and fans report feeling "pumped up" after particularly rousing contests.[28] Conversely, the stressed-out can find solace in sports. For three hours or so, viewers set aside their lives to concentrate on what is happening on the field or court. FDR, a brilliant politician, must have known this instinctively when he urged MLB to soldier on during World War II. Sixty years later, baseball's return after the September 11, 2001, terrorist attacks gave Americans a welcome sign of a returning normalcy.[29]

Whether it is in the grace of a double-axel jump or the roughness of a solid check into the boards, there is a unique beauty in the exertions of competing athletes and their attendant rituals and pageantry. Sportswriters can become more Dickens than Hemingway in their attempts to capture the essence of a sporting event. Amid the aesthetic there also dwells the erotic.[30] It is hard to imagine that less-than-wholesome thoughts are entirely absent among audiences taking in Maria Sharapova's backhand or David Beckham's penalty kick. "Women want him, men want to be him" can apply to Derek Jeter or Tom Brady as easily as it does to James Bond.

Putting Fannies in the Seats

The explanation for the failure of American anti-drug policies is economically obvious: it is simply impossible to effectively suppress markets for that which people fervently want to consume. The same is true of sports fandom. True, few would claim that a weekend of watching NCAA tournament basketball to the exclusion of all else puts one in line for 28 in-patient days at Dr. Drew's rehab clinic. Nor do Dodger fans typically stick up gas stations to buy game tickets. On the other hand, dog-fighting and cock-fighting continue to thrive in the shadows despite former Atlanta Falcons quarterback Michael Vick's famous fall from fan grace and substantial legal penalties for staging such contests.

Americans' enduring interest in sports, legitimate and illegal alike, demands satiation. Just like drug dealers, leagues and teams do not really create the underlying need for their products among consumers. They may seek to channel that need, shaping how it is slaked, but the desire to consume springs from something deep within their customers. They are not so much pushers as they are opportunists.

Economists generally are content to accept consumer urges as given, leaving divination of their genesis to their other social science brethren. To their eye, the spectator sport industry is in the business of creating products sufficiently appealing to part fans from their money. The products that teams and leagues offer to their fan-consumers take a variety of forms, but all derive from fan interest. More appealing teams and contests do not only sell more tickets, but more peanuts and popcorn, not to mention parking spaces, t-shirts and giant foam fingers. They also attract more television viewers and better pique the attention of other entities willing to pay to associate themselves with those teams. There is money to be had by offering interesting contests.

A significant amount of research has been conducted to characterize the factors that affect contest ticket demand, which is probably a decent proxy for overall fan interest in those events. One of the more obvious determinants of fan attention is competitive quality. People love a winner, and competitively successful athletes and teams are more popular than losers, all else being equal. Furthermore, winners can live off past glory, at least for one year—most demand studies find that a good season increases ticket sales this year as well as next.[31]

Big stars tend to gravitate to the more populous markets, where owners can cash in on better fan bases. It would seem that local affluence should have a similar effect, as richer locals should be able to spend more on the luxury that is game attendance. However, when other factors are taken into account, attendance studies often fail to find an indication that higher-income communities draw more fans.[32] The reason for these findings remains a mystery to sports economists. Perhaps higher-income people have more and higher-quality entertainment options available, muting the net effect of their spending power on the local team.

Population is not the only determinant of the quality of a local sports market, however. A host community's own peculiar interests are also quite influential in determining local fan interest. For example, colder-weather cities seem to be more hockey-friendly than warmer climes, probably because fans were more likely to have played the sport in their youth. Similarly, NBA basketball seems to sell better in the urban Northeast than it does in the rural Midwest. Other historical accidents are probably responsible for St. Louis and Cincinnati being more baseball than football towns, while Pittsburgh is the opposite.

One sure-fire way to rouse fans is to play contests in a new stadium.[33] Another is to offer various types of promotions such as price discounts, celebrity appearances, giveaways, etc. One study indicated that a typical promotion can raise attendance at an MLB game by an average of 14 percent.[34] Of course, new stadiums and game promotions probably have little immediate effect on those watching on television or listening on the radio, but perhaps can help build an addicted fan base.

Puzzling Pricing

There is precious little in economics as universally endorsed as the negative relationship between price and demand. Barstool references to "Econ 101" frequently invoke it, and students studying principles of microeconomics have impressed upon them the dictum that "the more something costs, the less people are willing to buy it." The law of demand and the cartel nature of leagues result in monopoly power for teams. Owners have significant pricing clout in their local ticket markets.

Drug kingpins have long known about the use of monopoly power in pricing. In the late 17th century, Dutch traders manage to monopolize the opium market in Java, making a fortune in the process.[35] During Prohibition, alcohol sales in some areas were monopolized by criminal enterprises that ruthlessly protected their ill-gotten profit. Many years later, states that had taken full control of the alcohol retail business following repeal were reticent to give up their monopoly windfall to the private sector.[36] In the same vein, a non-trivial contributor to the failure of the War on Drugs may be that enforcement efforts have been focused on the large-scale drug syndicates. Wiping out the big fish might simply make the market more competitive, thereby lowering street prices.

No self-respecting monopolist would seek to maximize consumption by offering a product at the lowest price. Nor would a monopolist set the price so high as to discourage all consumption. Rather, monopoly sellers are guided by "what the market will bear," and choose prices that maximize profit.

And the same should be expected of team owners. Sellouts do not maximize gate revenues if filling every seat requires too low a ticket price. Yet most academic studies of the subject have found that owners tend to underprice their product—there are far more sellouts than can be justified by the profit motive.[37] This might be good news to fans, but it is somewhat disturbing to economists.

A variety of explanations have been offered to preserve both the law of demand and the avaricious honor of team owner-monopolists. First of all, good historical ticket price data is surprisingly difficult to come by, so economists might just have it wrong. Different seating sections have different prices and fill up unevenly; most studies have not taken this into account. Teams with flagging ticket sales offer all manner of promotions and discounts that are not easy to track.[38] Also, owners may not be choosing prices simply to maximize profits from gate receipts; there are concession sales, television, and other revenues that need to be taken into account as well.[39] Furthermore, owners may be willing to forgo some gate profits for public relations purposes. Local politicians and voters may look favorably upon such "philanthropy," and reward owners with special favors such as publicly financed venues. Forgone profits today may be less about being nice than building up local political capital.[40]

Another possible reason for too-low ticket prices draws from sport's addictive nature. Owners may realize that lower prices today can get more people hooked just as schoolyard pushers might give away a first hit. Slightly lower profits today are an investment in larger future fan bases that will generate profits for years to come. In fact, it may even be the case that an owner could choose to "cash out" occasionally, putting a low-payroll loser on the field while taking advantage of the previously amped-up fan base.[41]

A related puzzle is that teams often tend to set identical prices for games with vastly different expected demand. A Tuesday afternoon contest against a league-also-ran certainly can be expected to generate less interest than a weekend event involving a divisional rival. Yet until recently, teams have made very little pricing distinction between such contests, seeming content to create scalper markets for popular contests and playing to small crowds for less attractive events. For many years, teams lobbied state and local governments to prohibit scalping, but those laws were about as successful as other market prohibitions. Furthermore, interstate Internet market entities such as EBay and StubHub have been beyond the reach of local laws.

An explanation for this apparently irrational behavior on the part of owners has to do with risk. Teams put tickets on sale before the start of the season, long in advance of some later-season games. Owners do not know with certainty which games will be most demanded, and may be loathe to set too high a price. In a sense, being conservative on the initial offering price is a form of insurance—selling a ticket at a lower-than-market price guarantees some revenue, albeit at the opportunity cost. This was particularly true before the Computer Age, when printing millions of tickets was an expensive endeavor. Teams were not too keen to do it more than once. Even so, it is difficult to imagine that a Father's Day Dodgers-Giants game will have weak demand. Perhaps this is another example of owners' fear of alienating their fan bases by being seen as "gouging" for better games. More recently, teams have been more willing to risk greedy reputations, and have begun to charge different prices for different games, especially in MLB.

As an alternative to charging different amounts for different games, team owners have offered a variety of seating options at a variety of prices. In fact, when demand was falling during the Great Depression, baseball owners seemed more likely to reclassify seats as less desirable than they were to lower prices.[42] More recently, stadiums and arenas "need" to be replaced as "obsolete" because of their lack of luxury seating—teams apparently are less interested in revamping their pricing models than in building a new factory. It may be that in the years to come, owners will borrow more from the sophisticated approaches of the airline, cruise vacation, and hotel industries for inspiration as to how to maximize their revenues. Given the unique bond between fans and their sports, however, they need to be wary of killing the goose that lays the golden eggs.

Markets for Iconography

Just as the devout keep statues of saints and martyrs, sports fans want to touch artifacts that carry the mojo of their heroes. It is as if having a signed picture of Brett Favre might confer some of his essence on its owner.

Such feelings are quite human, and probably have existed since the days of painted bison hunters on cave walls. Ancient Roman chariot races and gladiator competitions for the masses were accompanied by souvenir markets. Special oil lamps, small statues of the gladiators and charioteers, and other items were offered for sale around the arenas.[43] The gray-market vendor scene surrounding Wrigley Field after a win and the endless line of semis-*cum*-rolling-stores at NASCAR events might be recognizable as such to those Romans fans of yore.

Sports trading cards are one prominent modern example of the primitive need to own a piece of a sports hero. The earliest versions evolved out of the mid– to late–18th century cards that early American tradesmen used to advertise their services. This early form of advertising became quite popular with the invention of relatively inexpensive color lithography during the 19th century, and was adopted by the country's infant consumer products industry. After the Civil War, trade cards became a popular vehicle for national advertising programs for soap, farm products, drugs, tobacco, and other goods. Collecting them became a fashionable Victorian pastime. Harvard Business School's Baker Library has a collection of more than 8,000 of these trade cards that were used from the 1870s through the 1890s, and offers them as windows into the late 19th century American consumer mind.[44]

The popularity of these cards led to yet another connection between sports and drug. Shortly after the Civil War, expensive, hand-rolled, imported cigarettes became associated with an exotic and upscale lifestyle of wealth and leisure. But the line between sophistication and foppishness can be a thin one, and cigarettes were considered by many to be a bit unmanly. The invention of the automatic rolling machine, in 1881, meant that domestic manufacturers could offer their own hand-rolled products at a lower price to the less well-heeled.[45] This new market had demographics that were aspirant to those cultivated by William Hulbert's National League. Even so, hand-rolled cigarettes did not really become entirely acceptable for "regular-guy" consumption until the Spanish-American War.[46]

Part of the Goodwin & Company's effort to position their Old Judge cigarettes as more palatable to an upper-middle class male market included the issue of the first significant set of baseball cards in 1887. The nearly 2,000 different sepia prints, glued onto cardboard backs, depicted various major and minor league star players and other baseball subjects. In 1887 and 1888, the Allen & Ginter Company, another tobacco producer, issued three full-color sets of fifty various sports champions. Other tobacco companies, such as W.S. Kimball, Goodwin & Company, and Buchner Gold Coin Chewing Tobacco, soon followed suit by producing their own sports cards.[47]

When James Duke's American Tobacco Company consolidated the business in 1890—controlling 90 percent of the U.S. cigarette business in the process—it continued the practice of including baseball cards along with its products.[48] By 1898, Duke's company produced the vast majority of the 4 billion cigarettes made in the U.S., a product to which already was attributed "every known disease and crime."[49]

American Tobacco put out the now-famous T206 523-card set of baseball cards between 1909 and 1911. Widely coveted for their high quality, the set includes the celebrated Honus Wagner card, a copy of which sold for $2.8 million in 2007.[50] But like Standard Oil, American Tobacco soon became a trust-busting victim, broken up by the Supreme Court in 1911.[51] Except for a hockey card series in 1924–25, and brief revival by Red Man in the 1950s, the era of tobacco company sports cards largely ended with World War I.[52]

In subsequent years, as baseball became more of a middle class activity, baseball cards found themselves attached to different products, particularly candy and gum. The first gum company to issue baseball cards was John Dockman and Sons, around 1910. The Zeenut Candy Company issued a series of cards that ran between 1911 and 1939, while Cracker Jack had issues in 1914 and 1915. Zeenut's 1916 set included the first card depiction of an African-American player, Jimmy Claxton of the San Francisco Oaks (who passed himself off as a Native American).[53]

By the 1930s, bubble gum was big business, but the Depression made companies fight for consumers' dollars. In 1933, the Goudey Gum Company made their Big League Chewing Gum brand more attractive by putting out a set of 239 cards. National Chicle issued the first football cards, a set of 36 in an art deco style, in 1935. In 1948, Bowman Gum put out their own a set of 108 football cards, as well as a set of 72 basketball cards, the first in that sport.[54]

Of course, one key element of sports memorabilia collecting is the simple nostalgia associated with childhood memories. Sports heroes loom larger than life to youngsters, and the magic associated with owning a piece of it is very strong. By the time Kennedy was inaugurated, collecting sports trading cards had become firmly entrenched part of the typical American boy's existence. As these boys grew up, their desire to collect items associated with sports heroes did not change. They just had more money to spend on it now.

Complete annual card sets from the 1960s now regularly sell for thousands of dollars each.[55] An entire industry of magazines, websites, shows, and auctions has sprung up around the interest in sports memorabilia; one estimate puts it at about $2 billion per year as of 2007.[56] A recent check of EBay showed that there were 643,558 items offered for sale in the "Sports Memorabilia, Cards, and Fan Shop" area. More than half of the items listed, 360,724, involved cards of various kinds, while another 203,448 were for fan apparel and souvenirs. 52,545 others involved autographed materials.[57] Things have come a long way since five-cent packs of unchewable gum.

Win on Sunday, Sell on Monday

Perhaps there is no stronger outward signal of our tribal memberships than what we choose to wear. Gang members rumble over territory, letting all know who is who based on logos and colors. Sporting preferences are displayed in the same manner. While they rarely shoot each other over who rules the streets of Peoria, there still are harsh feelings between blue-wearing Cub fans and red-attired Cardinals faithful.

Marx might have taken as dim a view of speaking via our clothing as he did of religious practice—in *Das Kapital*, he referred to the "murderous, meaningless caprices of fashion"—but fans literally wear their loyalties on our sleeves.[58] Two otherwise-identical garments can fetch wildly different prices if one of them has a small sports logo on it. Corporate America is not unaware of this phenomenon.

NASCAR sponsors are said to have a mantra: "Win on Sunday, sell on Monday." As of 2001, the sport had more than 900 sponsors spending over $400 million per year trying to commingle their corporate identities. NASCAR also had merchandising deals that year with more than 45 companies selling more than $1 billion annually. The Big Four cash in on selling their essence as well. Overall, holders of sports-related properties probably earned $1 billion or more in 2007 from licensing royalties, with MLB accounting for at least $500 million of it.[59]

Individual athletes similarly cash in by lending their names to sell various and sundry wares, and likely have done so as long as there has been advertising. An ESPN producer not too long ago uncovered a list of products that Babe Ruth had hawked. His endorsement revenues were as much as half a million dollars over an eighteen-year period—back when this was real money.[60] His contemporary, Red Grange, is known to have endorsed sweaters, shoes, caps, a Red Grange doll, soft drinks, chocolates, and a host of other stuff.[61]

Marketers are not stupid—they would not pay athletes endorsement fees unless they believed it helped sell their goods. Nike's arrangement with Michael Jordan is a good example. During the 1982-3 season, the company had roughly half of all NBA players under contract. While Moses Malone made $100,000 that season on his deal, most of the others earned between $8,000 and $50,000. Nike decided to change strategy, and focus on only few top, young players for the next season. They opted for Michael Jordan—up until then a loyal Addidas-wearer, incidentally—and planned a shoe and product line around a persona they would build for him. In 1984, Jordan and Nike came to an unprecedented five-year, $2.5 million endorsement agreement for the new line. The deal included royalties on not only all the Nike Jordan products sold, but on all Nike Air shoes above the 400,000 the company had sold the prior year. Jordan even got some Nike Class B stock.[62] By 1996, Jordan's deal with Nike was paying him $20 million per year.[63]

Jordan's endorsement money train made a few stops other than Beaverton, Oregon, along its way. Most notably, he signed a ten-year, $18 million deal in 1991 to endorse Gatorade. He might have played basketball for the Chicago Bulls, but his primary employer was Madison Avenue.

Jordan remained the king of endorsements through the 1990s, but has since passed the torch onto Tiger Woods. In 1996, Woods signed $40 million, five-year endorsement contract with Nike and a $20 million deal with Titleist—not bad for a 21-year old. In 2000, his deal with Nike was renewed for another five years for $85 million, and he got another five-year deal with Buick for $30 million.[64] In 2007, he inked a five-year deal with Gatorade for a reported $100 million.[65]

Tiger's total income in 2007 was estimated to be $100 million, the vast majority of which was from endorsements, making him the fourth highest paid celebrity in the world, behind Oprah Winfrey ($250 million), and producers Jerry Bruckheimer ($120 million) and Steven Spielberg ($110 million). Still, Tiger, Inc., earned more than the Rolling Stones ($88 million) and Elton John ($53 million). Other top athletes on the 2007 money list included boxer Oscar de la Hoya ($43 million), golfer Phil Mickelson ($42 million) and Formula One drive Michael Schumacher ($36 million).[66]

Most of this money comes about because fans are willing to pay more for products that they associate with a favorite athlete. While a consumer has a favorite toothpaste or beer, the fans' "brand loyalty" to their favorite teams and athletes can be a much more intense attraction—more like a religion or an addiction.

9

The Community of the Opium Den

The addiction to sports, therefore, in a particular degree represents the man's arrested development of a moral nature.

—*Thorstein Veblen*[1]

Veblen published his classic *The Theory of the Leisure Class* during an interesting period in U.S. history. As the nation's economy expanded, more and more people found themselves able to think about more than just getting by. He observed that the plethora of affordable consumer goods brought about by the Industrial Revolution began to prey on the human need for status, spawning what he called "conspicuous consumption." To Veblen, sports were a form of such status-driven consumption, and had little innate utility on their own.

His perspective was not without merit. Much of the early interest in American spectator sports indeed was split along class lines—for example, horse racing was for the elite, while fist-fighting belonged to the cruder masses. Classism is not absent from sports even today. Dale Earnhart apparel is simply not done among the country club set, whereas a Tiger Woods–branded set of golf clubs is the cat's meow. A few blocks away in the corner tavern, NASCAR gear is a social elevator, but following anything as effete as tennis risks ridicule.

While we now think of baseball and football as unrelated to social status, this has not always been the case. In their formative years, baseball was the province of upper-middle class urban-dwellers, while college football belonged to Gilded Age scions at Ivy League schools. Obviously, this has changed, in no small part due to the democracy of broadcast television. An important element of the financial success of the Big Four North American leagues is their appeal across class strata. Even so, clear class distinctions in these sports remain—the hoi polloi sit in the "cheap seats" while the upper crust have "luxury" and "club" seating, each with vastly different amenities and price tags.

Some of American sports' "great rivalries" harbor elements of class warfare: Duke versus North Carolina basketball and USC versus UCLA football are not just about geographical proximity, but also pit private schools versus public schools. The Green Bay Packers–Chicago Bears rivalry is not only one of the oldest in the NFL, but features the small town against the big city. Closer to home for many are the thousands of local high school rivalries in which teams from different sides of the tracks go at it each year.

Veblen was not alone among the day's prominent social thinkers in his dismissive opinion of sports. Max Weber, proponent of the theory that capitalistic economic success is the result of rationalism and the Protestant work ethic, similarly had little use for the pure leisure of spectator sport. Such an unnecessary luxury should be shunned by good people unless, of course, a solidly utilitarian purpose can be identified.

There are still some who espouse this point of view. One outplacement consultancy in particular seems to be a bedfellow of Veblen and Weber on the matter of spectator sports. Seeking to grab cheap headlines just before the NFL football season and the NCAA men's basketball, the firm issues breathless press releases about how many billions various office pools and fantasy sports leagues supposedly cost the American economy in lost productivity. Their methodology leaves a great deal to be desired—it simplistically adds up the number of workers who participate in such diversions, multiplies that figure by the amount of time on average that each spends, and multiplies that figure by the average American hourly wage—returning values on the order of a billion dollars or more. Similar thinking would recommend that all toilets be removed from every American workplace.[2]

While it is foolish to assert that spectator sports are an unmitigated positive for society, the good often is overlooked because it is so thickly woven into everyday life. Offices pools and the like *do* generate real value. A shared pleasant history courtesy of a well-managed pool can be a lubricant that alleviates some of the normal interpersonal friction that inevitably accompanies the productive interactions of employees. To treat this issue fairly requires a more nuanced approach. The outplacement firm's methodology is better suited to a high school accounting problem than a nuanced productivity analysis, although it undoubtedly has succeeded in generating publicity.

Properly measured, any costs resulting from time spent on office pools must be balanced against the accumulation of workplace social capital. American firms spend millions—even billions—on all kinds of strategies for team-building and individual motivation, and office pools certainly must be among the least expensive of these.

The contribution of sport to social capital development goes far beyond just the office. Deeply embedded in the fan experience is a sense of tribal belonging. It means something to be a New Orleans Saint fan or a member of Red Sox Nation. Such affiliation can deepen common interests among socioeconomically diverse people which, in turn, might ease the other kinds of social interrelations that a functional civil society needs. How many rich, white, suburban kids grew up worshipping Willie Mays, Michael Jordan or Tiger Woods? In the increasingly diverse world into which these children entered as adults, such childhood experiences certainly must contribute to the social good that is judging others by their merits rather than by racial group membership. Sports can help acculturate children into the American mericratic ideal. Without a Jackie Robinson, would there would be a Barack Obama.

That said, a less-savory part of rooting for your own team is to wish ill on a rival. Knowing that your favorite television program won its time slot is nothing like watching your team beat a despised rival.[3] Ohio State fans are fond of saying that their two favorite teams are the Buckeyes and whoever is playing the University of Michigan Wolverines that weekend. Conversely, the apparent masochism of watching your team get trounced by such a rival is still a form of clannish solidarity. Shared misery is far less sharply felt than solitary misery, but can reinforce tribal bonds.

Sports, Class, Race, and Gender

Perhaps there is no general mythological figure more uniquely American than that of the self-made man. For the majority of the twelve million people who came through Ellis Island between 1892 and 1954, the promise of meritocracy was better than what they perceived Europe's entrenched classism to be. At first blush, U.S. spectator sports of the early 20th century were the embodiment of this American ideal. Nobody cared where you were from, as long as you could play ball or run fast. Unless, of course, you happened to be African-American in the years before Joe Louis, Jesse Owens, Jackie Robinson, and Arthur Ashe pioneered integration of their sports.

This had not always been so. Between the end of the Civil War and the turn of the century, black athletes could be found in major sports more frequently than they could later. For example, thirteen of the fifteen jockeys that rode in the first Kentucky Derby in 1875 were black, as were fifteen of the first twenty-eight Derby winners.[4] The 1899 World Cycling champion was Marshall W. "Major" Taylor, an African-American raised by a well-to-do white family in Indianapolis.[5] In boxing, George "Little Chocolate" Dixon owned the world bantamweight title in 1890 and the world featherweight title 1891–1897 and 1898–1900; in 1908, another African-American, Jack Johnson, won the heavyweight crown.[6]

Between 1884 and 1887, a few African-American players were on team rosters in the various major baseball leagues that existed at the time. The beginning of the end of African-Americans in baseball—followed by other major spectator sports—might be traced to an 1883 incident involving Cap Anson and Moses "Fleetwood" Walker. Anson, who had been born in Iowa when slavery was still legal there, refused to take the field for an exhibition game between his White Stockings and Walker's team, the semi-pro Toledo Mud Hens. When told that Chicago would forfeit its part of the gate unless he played, Anson relented. Walker, the son of a doctor, who himself had attended Oberlin College and University of Michigan law school before becoming a professional ballplayer, went on to become the first black major league player when the Mud Hens joined the American Association, another major league, in 1884. After another, similar incident in 1887 involving Anson's and Walker's teams, owners in the three major leagues (the National League, International League, and American Association) voted not to sign any more black players. By 1897, African-Americans were effectively banned from major league ball.[7]

Professional football had a slightly better, although hardly great, racial track record, at least in the early part of the 20th century. A 1902 photo of the Shelby (Ohio) Athletic Club professional football team includes a black player, Charles Follis. At least five other African-Americans played professional football before the founding of the NFL in 1920.[8] Several other black players were on NFL teams during the 1920s and 1930s, but the league was nearly exclusively white until after World War II.[9] It was legendary coach Paul Brown's willingness to put Hall-of-Famers Marion Motley and Bill Willis on the AAFC's Cleveland Browns 1946 roster that broke the modern pro football color barrier—one year before Jackie Robinson did so in MLB.[10]

Professional basketball, now a model for African-American racial opportunity in sports—79 percent of its players, 40 percent of its coaches, and 34 percent of its front office employees were black in the 2006–7 season—was not always so.[11] It was "whites-only" in the precursor to the NBA, the American Basketball League, which itself was formed in 1924. The ABL had a distinct NFL flavor about it, with George Halas and George Marshall as early team owners, and Joe Carr as the ABL president until 1928 (Carr was also the NFL president from 1921 to 1939).[12]

Two all-black barnstorming teams, the New York Renaissance and the Harlem Globetrotters, were formed in New York and Chicago, respectively, in the 1920s. But blacks were shut out of other major barnstorming teams, such as the Original Celtics, which was formed around 1915 in New York City. These teams did play each other, providing one of the few examples of whites competing directly with blacks in the same game. However, many of these interracial contests were played in front of segregated crowds.[13]

Courtesy of Jackie Robinson, modern racial history of baseball is better known than for other sports. Branch Rickey took quite a risk when he brought Robinson up to Brooklyn and the big leagues for the 1947 MLB season. He bet that Dodgers fans were less turned off by having someone different on the team than they were turned on by having a winning club. He was proven right, and soon other MLB teams began to tap the Negro League for players. Still, teams fretted that "too many" black players would reduce their predominantly white fan base. To the extent that this was a business issue, their concerns were not without merit. There is a body of academic work that suggests that fans preferred to see teams with players of their own race at least until the 1980s. Fortunately, more recent studies generally find that fans have become a lot more colorblind, at least insomuch as rosters are concerned.[14] There remain issues in the coaching and front-office ranks, particularly with respect to big-time (NCAA FBS) college football.[15]

Imperfect as it was and still is, racial progress in spectator sports has led that of most of American society as a whole. By the time that Muhammad Ali's and Howard Cosell's mouths were making each other huge media stars in the turbulent 1960s, Gayle Sayres and Bob Gibson were more quietly dominating their respective sports of football and baseball. Women athletes were not as successful as racial minorities, however. While female Olympic athletes were held up as national heroes—proof that the American Way of Life was superior to that of the Communists—female sports drew relatively sparse crowds and revenues. Women were flexing their social and political muscle in the 1960s, but female spectator sports could hardly even have been considered much of a business.

Some of that changed on September 20, 1973, when Billie Jean King defeated Bobby Riggs in the "Battle of the Sexes." The tennis match drew a crowd of 35,000 paying customers at the Houston Astrodome, while another fifty million Americans watched on television.[16] The fifty-five-year-old Riggs, the self-proclaimed hero of "male chauvinist pigs" throughout the U.S., had challenged King to the match to make his point that women's tennis was inferior to the male version. He had beaten another women's star, Margaret Court, earlier in the year, and believed that knocking off the top female player would complete his point.

In the wake of her win, King led protests against the tennis establishment, shaming them into beefing up anemic purses for women's matches. Her work has been long-suffering—the grandest of all matches, Wimbledon, finally raised the women's purse to equal that of the male tournaments in 2007.[17]

Such equality is possible in tennis because the women's game is at least as popular as men's tennis—perhaps even more so. But for now, lack of fan interest in other women's sports renders equal athlete pay impossible among the major professional ranks. It seems as though it will be a very long time before this changes, and gender equality approaches the progress made along racial lines.

Sports and Violence

Aside from the yawning gulf in fan interest between male and female sports, a fan's own gender plays a role in the ways in which she or he views sport. Women tend to be attracted to those sports with more obvious aesthetic elements, but men seem to appreciate the more violent among them.[18] This difference is echoed in divergent reactions to especially stressful contests. One study of male and female reactions to NCAA men's tournament games found that men most enjoy the most closely contested games, those that were decided by five points or less. Women preferred moderately close games, with final score differentials between six and ten points.[19] There is a reason why weekend television programming pits figure skating against football—they draw different audiences.

Clearly an element of appeal in some sports rests in a measured degree of controlled aggression. Boxing and legitimate wrestling have obvious and prominent violent goals. Football is not far behind, but even the "non-contact" sports of baseball and basketball find violence in some of their most exciting moments—beanballs, collisions, and hard fouls. And hitting someone with a stick is far less discouraged in hockey than it is in figure skating—the person who whacked Nancy Kerrigan's knee got a lot more than a two-minute penalty.

Indeed, the relationship between violence and fan interest in hockey is unique among major spectator sports. While officially outlawed by the rules, NHL game highlights historically have included at least as much fighting as goal-scoring. Conn Smythe, who owned the Toronto Maple Leafs from the 1920s until the 1960s, is claimed to have observed that "we've got to stamp out [fighting], or people are going to keep buying tickets."[20]

Interestingly, there may be some differences between Canadian and American hockey fans in how they view violence in their sport. One study of game attendance during the 1983–84 NHL season suggests that U.S. fans were more likely to attend games that held the prospect of extreme on-ice violence, while Canadian audiences tended to be turned off by it.[21] Another study, of the 1989–90 season, confirmed that fan demand for violence seemed to be more an American than Canadian phenomenon.[22] Fan attitudes may be changing, however. College hockey's popularity is on the upswing, despite taking a dim view of fighting. Even the NHL has worked to reduce the hand-to-hand combat in favor of rules that favor more scoring.

Unfortunately, violence in sport is not limited to contest participants. Perhaps it never has been. As long as spectator sports have been played, there have been incidents—ancient Rome's Coliseum just as surely saw incidents in the stands when the Christians faced the lions just as modern Los Angeles's now does during Raider-Lion games. An account of a 532 B.C. chariot race in Constantinople tells of a riot that had to be put down by Roman soldiers, leaving a reported 30,000 dead.[23] "Don't tase me, bro" apparently doesn't work in Latin, either.

The early days of American baseball, upon which we draw much of our "sports crowd" behavioral norms, certainly had its share of fan violence.[24] Even "Casey at the Bat" refers to the homicidal attitude of the five-thousand-strong crowd toward the umpire following a called Strike One.[25] In more modern times, the worst cases of spectator misconduct seem to come from big-time soccer. Perhaps as many as 10 percent of European soccer matches involve fan violence, which is considerably higher than any parallel estimate for American sports.[26] Consequently, EU police agencies have been forced to deal with these issues far more than their U.S. counterparts. In fact, following a particularly unpleasant incident in Brussels that killed 39 during a 1985 European Cup match between England's Liverpool and Italy's Juventus teams, the British government took stern action. They have found success dealing with soccer hooligans by applying terrorism policy models.[27] In the early days following the September 11, 2001, terrorist attacks, American authorities looked to these approaches for ideas about international traveler identification methods.

A seemingly disproportionate degree of American fan misbehavior is found in college sports, particularly football. One unfortunate example involves various 2002 editions of annual Thanksgiving-time rivalries. A variety of ugly scenes were found in conjunction with games between Michigan and Ohio State game, Stanford and Cal, South Carolina and Clemson, and Washington and Washington State.[28] In college basketball, "rushing the court" following even minor home college basketball victories is now considered to be just part of going to a game by many student fans.

Not that professional sports are immune from fan misbehavior, either. Baseball saw at least 32 in-game deaths during the 20th century in various minor and major league parks; the majority of them were the result of fan misbehavior rather than batted balls.[29] Judge Seamus McCaffery heard cases and assigned fines and jail time *during games* in the bowels of the now-defunct Veterans Stadium in an effort to deal with the legendary misbehavior of miscreant Philadelphia Eagles fans.[30] Sports sociologists point to a variety of environmental factors that fan the flames of fan aggression: noise, crowding, warm temperatures, foul odors, and alcohol and drugs.[31] Apparently stadiums and crack houses have much in common.

Community via Numbers

Much has been written about the behavior of sports fans and about the social implications of the culture of athletes and sport. Entire academic careers have been made on finer points of these subjects. Some, perhaps taking Veblen's cue, have argued vehemently that spectator sports represents all that is bad in American culture, that classism, racism, sexism, substance abuse, and violence in society are reinforced by the sports that fans love. Others point to the good in sports—how they exemplify concepts of community, teamwork, and striving for excellence. Both points of view are valid.

Regardless of whatever debates might be had about the merits of the high cultural profile enjoyed by spectator sports, the fact remains that those that follow any one of them in particular are indeed members of a community. Despite other apparent differences, they each connect with their sport. One of the most important elements of this relationship is through numbers.

10

Lies, Damn Lies, and Fantasy Sports

After all, facts are facts, and although we may quote one to another with a chuckle the words of the Wise Statesman, "Lies—damned lies—and statistics," still there are some easy figures the simplest must understand, and the astutest cannot wriggle out of.
—*Leonard Henry Courtney, 1895*[1]

Stats and Sports

If a "sport" necessarily includes the notion of competition, then it also involves the use of statistics. After all, no game outcome can be described or even conceptualized without some counting of *something*. It might be time, or points, or runs, or wickets, or whatever, but something is measured and recorded—the most basic activity of the discipline of statistics. Similarly, no discussion about the greats in any sporting endeavor is possible without resort to the collection of career data of some sort. Just as mathematics is the language of science, so is statistics for sports.

The necessary coexistence of fandom and statistics goes to the center of what makes sports interesting and distinct from other athletic displays. Sports fans are attracted by the objective and goal-oriented nature of what they watch. While intermission conversations among ballet aficionados may turn to grace, power or invoked emotion, halftime fan talk will invoke the authority of numbers. Feelings are nearly always subordinate to facts in judging the quality of a sports performance. The gap between a .275 and a .300 hitter is monumental, but is the result of only one less hit every two weeks—an invisible difference to the aesthetic eye, but obvious to the statistically sage.[2]

To be a fan is to be in ready mental possession of ten thousand statistics at any given moment. For many, it began in childhood when they memorized the numbers on the backs of baseball, football, basketball, or hockey trading cards. Adult fanhood is displayed and defended by the ability to spout numbers purported to be germane to the sport in question. You lack even a shred of good judgment if you dare contradict the NBA opinions of the guy on the next barstool if he can correctly quote more current field goal percentages than you can. Tennis fans better know the current professional world rankings, or they really aren't fans. NFL devotees are quick to point out injustices in Pro Bowl selections based on differences in player passer ratings—even though a tiny minority of them could even begin to describe how that statistic is calculated. Numbers simply *are* how fans' thoughts are expressed.

There is another reason why stats are so important to fandom—they can provide a sense of the experience of the game to those who were not in attendance, either because of time or distance. To this end, collections of records and stats were collected as far back as Plato's day, long before the invention of the printing press. Early newspaper sports stories seized on the use of statistics fairly early in their reporting of sporting events. Of course, scores were among the first stats published, followed by ad hoc notes regarding individual players' obvious contributions, such as wickets in cricket matches, goals in a soccer contest, or home runs in a baseball game.

The story of statistics in American sport begins with baseball. Since the game descended from English ancestors, it is not surprising that the baseball's numbers tradition is inherited from cricket. The first significant compilation of English cricket statistics is found in the 1864 *Wisden Almanack.* By 1869, the publication was taking advertisements, and it remains to this day the primary statistical reference for cricket.[3] Three years earlier, however, Henry Chadwick's second edition of *Beadle's Dime Base-Ball Player* had introduced a regularized baseball scoring system.[4]

During the last half of the 1800s, baseball statistics proliferated. Even so, top-level English-speaking academic statisticians, probably finding the subject beneath them, generally managed to resist making use of them until the 20th century. In fact, the eggheads did not think much about the issues of probability or statistics in games at all. A rare exception was a 1902 piece published by Sir Francis Galton—a cousin of Charles Darwin—on the optimal way to divide a purse between first and second prizes.[5]

Fifty years later, inspired by a cocktail party question, a real baseball paper finally appeared in a top-level state journal. The paper made use of mathematical machinery that the author, Harvard professor Frederick Mosteller, had developed during World War II as part of his contribution to the war effort. His paper, published in the staid *Journal of the American Statistical Association*, demonstrated that the better team had won the World Series about 80 percent of the time.[6] The article also found that the American League representative had been better than that of the National League about 75 percent of the time.[7] Still, another four decades passed before the American Statistical Association (ASA) bestowed its formal blessing to the study of statistics in sport when it formed a group dedicated to the subject within its organization in 1992. The goal of the ASA's Section on Statistics in Sports is to stimulate academic interest in research into sports statistical theory and methodology.[8] In 2004, the *Journal of Quantitative Analysis in Sports*, began publishing peer-reviewed academic articles exclusively on relationships between stats and sports.[9]

The early 21st century seeker of historical sports statistics is no longer condemned to *Lord of the Rings*–like quests through dusty library shelves to seek out the mysteries held by yellowed printed almanacs. The Information Age has brought nearly every kind of sports-related statistic and analysis thereof just a click away on uncountable websites. Many of these offer their treasure troves free of charge, assembled by leagues and teams to promote their sports, or as labors of love by true fans. In need of a box score from a 1921 baseball game? Check out Sean Lehman's Baseball Archive.[10] How about the number of punts inside the twenty for various NFL teams in 2003? NFL.com keeps track of that for its fans, even including some fancy sorting capability. We live in a golden era for quantitatively inclined fans.

The Statistical Enlightenment

The art of statistics did not come into being to serve sports fans, of course. Rather, the idea of counting things up has its origins in government and politics. It takes an army to conquer a village, and it takes resources to maintain a military. Those resources tend to come from the conquered, but before they can be taxed, their number and wealth must be counted. In fact, the historical relationship between statistics and government is belied by the term itself, which has its origins in the Italian word *stato*, meaning state.[11]

There is evidence that the Egyptians were keeping track of wealth and number of their citizenry as far back as 3000 B.C., while the Chinese were at it by 2300 B.C. A Greek census in 509 B.C. was conducted for taxation purposes. But none of the ancients can match the Romans, who were famous for their complex censuses, surveys, and other record-keeping.[12] They collected and categorized information about their people at least as long ago as 225 B.C. Rome.[13] Of course not all numbers systematically documented in bygone days concerned governmental information—the Babylonians, for example, recorded celestial measurements on clay tablets as early as the third century B.C. The Greeks also carefully recorded heavenly movements around the same time.[14]

After the fall of Rome, however, significant statistical undertakings in Europe became rare, at least as far as historians can tell. There were a few, however. In 762, Charlemagne made an inventory record of his possessions, and William the Conqueror commissioned the still-extant "Domesday Book" in 1085 to count the number and wealth of settlements in his kingdom.[15] In the 13th century, the Italian city-states of Venice and Florence had begun to collect detailed information on their people.[16] In 1530, London began to require parishes to report deaths in "weekly bills of mortality" as a warning system of impending plague outbreaks. Eight years later, the Anglican Church began keeping track of the happier statistics of weddings and christenings.[17]

It is one thing to record statistics; it is a leap ahead to analyze them in scientific fashion. The most elementary form of such analysis is to repeat and combine measurements of the same quantity by taking their average, but there is no historical record of anyone doing so in Europe until Tycho Brahe did so at the end of the 16th century. In his quest to marry the Ptolemaic (geocentric) and Copernican (heliocentric) theories of the universe, Brahe busied himself building large astronomical instruments to gather ever more copious and conscientious measurements of the heavens. He was assisted by one Johann Kepler, who eventually used Brahe's methodologies to formulate his three laws of planetary motion, which later were derived theoretically by Isaac Newton.

The application of statistical tools for social purposes followed a few decades later. The first modern European analysis of collected social data came in 1662 from Captain John Graunt, a successful London haberdasher. By this time, London's *Weekly Bills of Mortality* were available via subscription for those interested in such things. Graunt used these series, begun 130 years earlier, to demonstrate a variety of interesting phenomena such as the excess of male over female births, periods of plague, changes over time in the number of parishes, and categorization of causes of death. His book, *Natural and Political Observations Made upon the Bills of Mortality*, was a commercial hit, and led to Charles II recommending him to be chosen as an original member of the Royal Society.[18] Before long, others refined Graunt's approach to create reliable life-expectancy tables for use by the burgeoning insurance business.[19]

Baseball Creates American Sports Statistics

> In order to obtain an accurate estimate of a player's skill, an analysis, both of his play at the bat and in the field, should be made ... in a uniform manner.
>
> —Henry Chadwick[20]

By the 18th century, the utility of statistical analysis was well-recognized. Governments continued to increase their data collection efforts. Scientists were only too happy to analyze the data collected. Even though the calculations remained laborious, they had been made considerably more tractable by the discovery of logarithms by John Napier in 1614, and the resultant invention of the slide rule a few years later.[21] Theory and practice evolved, and statistical literacy became an essential skill among the government service elite in Europe.

In the 1830s, worker riots in England led to a re-examination of the oppressive Poor Law of 1601, and a 26-member blue-ribbon commission was charged with collection of data related to the country's indigent. The group, led by Oxford professor Nassau Senior, published its detailed findings in a 13-volume set in 1834. Serving as secretary to the group was health advocate and social reformer Edwin Chadwick—Henry Chadwick's older half-brother.[22]

Twenty-four years Henry's senior, Edwin made a name for himself in England beginning with his 1828 article "The Means of Insurance Against Accidents" and its call for sanitary reform. The work made liberal use of statistical data to buttress its points—James Chadwick apparently had imbued both of his famous progeny with a healthy respect for data collection and record-keeping. There is no doubt that Edwin was a significant influence on his brother's life. Although they lived their lives an ocean apart, they regularly corresponded with each other until Edwin's death in 1890.[23]

Henry Chadwick is often credited with invention of the baseball box score. This is not strictly true. The Olympic Club in Philadelphia began keeping rather detailed, box score–like records early on, and local newspapers had been publishing ball game "abstracts" since the 1830s.[24] Elementary box scores had been used in New York for both cricket and baseball since at least since 1845, and possibly even as far back as the 1820s by William Cauldwell.[25] However, these reports were very different from those seen in modern newspapers or on websites such as MLB.com. On the other hand, an Eckford-Atlantic game box score published in the *New York Sunday Mercury* in 1862—probably written by Chadwick—would be unmistakable as such to a 21st century fan's eye.[26]

Henry's affinity for order and record-keeping led to his format for a universal baseball scoring system, derived from cricket scoring, which was first published in his 1861 *Beadle's*. Always a stickler for protocol, he had even insisted that each game have its own official scorer. Chadwick's system was intended to record each player's actions during the game, as well as his individual contributions to the final score. His goal was that anyone picking up the record after the fact would have the ability to recreate the play of the game with scientific objectivity. Never one to forget about dotting i's and crossing t's, he even went so far as to provide a diagram of an example scorebook page in the guide. True to his self-appointed mission as American baseball's foremost evangelist, Chadwick realized that his system was a bit too complex for the average "crank" (the term for a fan of the day). In 1869, he laid out a simplified scoring system meant for game spectators.[27]

Chadwick's scoring philosophy became a springboard for player performance analysis. Henry developed an approach that he called "Analysis of Batting" that divided the number of outs and the number of runs by a player by the number of games he played. One H.A. Dobson of Washington suggested a refinement to Chadwick: divide the number of hits by the number of at-bats. The first modern American sports statistic, batting average, thus was born.[28]

It is difficult to underestimate Chadwick's prescience in his use of statistics to evaluate players. Frederick Taylor, the patron saint of monopoly capitalist management, and his book, *The Principles of Scientific Management* (1911), were still in a far-off future.[29] The "Total Quality Management" revolution led by W.E. Deming in 1960s Japan is merely a modern manifestation of Taylorism. Chadwick and his statistics had anticipated these movements by many decades. By 1887, Chadwick's emphasis on record-keeping became official when baseball writers formed a national association for the purpose of standardizing scoring techniques.[30]

Fans dig the long ball, and always have, of course. Teams and sponsors began to award prizes for the increasingly popular home run hit. Always the purist, Chadwick was having none of it, although he came by this position honestly. His statistical study had found that home run hitters generally had lower batting averages and did not contribute to winning as much as many fans believed.[31] Such enduring interest in ways to scientifically attribute runs to hitters' performances—scooping the Bill James sabermetric revolution by more than a century—led Chadwick to champion the cause of the "runs batted in" statistic. In 1891, the NL's official scorers were ordered to count it as an official box score statistic.[32] It quickly fell into disfavor, however, and was only officially resurrected in 1920 through the sheer force of will another sportswriter, Ernie Lanigan of the *New York Press*.[33]

Sports Stats as a Business

As the American sports industry grew up, so did the numbers that were used to describe its product, and Chadwick's scientific approach found application in other sports. Walter Camp, who played a role in football's evolution akin to Chadwick's in baseball, was the leading proponent of the application to football of the scientific methods then becoming popular in business.[34] His articles in *Harper's Weekly* and other popular magazines emphasized his game's intelligent rather than brutal nature.[35] In 1893, newly-appointed University of Chicago coach Amos Alonzo Stagg published his book about "scientific football," finding a ready academic audience to whom the tome was pitched.[36]

By the time the 20th century began, statistical analysis of all forms of human endeavor was a well-established philosophy. Sports was no different, and the exploding publishing industry gleefully invented uncountable propriety statistics for any form of sport imaginable. Fans turned to their favorite newspapers and magazines for analyses—solid and flaky—of their favorite games and players. Sports columnists, now American institutions unto themselves, could always rely on numbers to break writer's block. There might not be a statistic that measures how many burned-out deadline-beaters have been saved by wringing out 750 words from some random numerical arcanity, but there could be.

As a generation of writers who only knew Henry Chadwick as a historical figure grew up, so did an entire sport statistics reference industry. Of course, the main subject was baseball, which is more intimately connected with numbers than its sporting brethren. *Baseball Magazine* began publishing *Who's Who in Baseball* in 1912, reporting at first only on hitters, and even then only on number of games played, batting average and fielding average. The 1915 edition was expanded to include pitchers' earned run averages, as well as a variety of other hitter stats. The book quickly became a fan favorite, no doubt both starting and deciding tens of thousands of arguments.[37]

Before World War I, baseball record-keeping was in a fairly sorry state. Figures were unreliable, and various sources frequently listed different values for the same player stats. A New York traveling salesman named Al Munro Elias decided to do something about it, and started up a company meant to record and sell high-quality baseball data. Perhaps unbeknown to him, a similar firm had been set up in Chicago by the official AL statistician Irwin Howe in 1911. Long before there were tight rules about intellectual property rights, Howe used the Associated Press feed for his official records, and then repackaged and sold them to various newspapers.[38]

Elias's first target market, newspaper editors, did not pan out at first, but he and his brother Walter did manage to eke out a living by selling shoes as well as fact cards to various local establishments with baseball fan clienteles. By the end of the war, the Elias brothers had found the key to success in the business: providing up-to-date weekly summary data and league-leader lists for inclusion in Sunday newspaper sports sections. NL President John Heydler noticed their work, and hired their firm, now called the Al Munro Elias Baseball Bureau, to be the official keeper of NL stats. The AP soon hired the firm to supply 250 newspapers with their stats. The Elias brothers did as much to popularize and regularize the daily stats page as anyone did, and was able to capitalize on spectator sports as mass culture in the 1920s.[39]

Elias was pretty much the only player in the sports stats business for half a century. As of 2004, the firm was the official league statistician for all of MLB, NFL, NBA, and NHL. Other firms collected data and published yearbooks for sports other than baseball. In addition to its baseball annuals which began in 1876, Spaulding began publishing a yearly college football guide in 1891.[40] The company also published an annual college basketball guide starting with the 1894 season.[41] Street & Smith's put together a college football annual beginning in 1940—some NFL owners used it as their primary scouting preparation for player drafts during the 1940s.[42] The company added an NBA guide beginning with the 1958–59 season.[43] *Nat Fleischer's All-Time Ring Record Book*, which appeared annually from 1942 through 1988, was the authority on boxing records and statistics.[44] The long runs enjoyed by these publications are testimony to their popularity among fans.

By the 1970s, the Elias Sports Bureau was firmly in the hands of Seymour Siwoff, by most accounts a thoroughly unlikable and arrogant businessman.[45] He had bought the then-struggling company in 1952 from the Elias brothers' heirs, and in 1961 managed to sell Pete Rozelle on hiring the firm as the NFL's official statistician. He added the NBA as a client in 1970. True to his accountant roots, his company's statistics were the most accurate available, and giving them away was something simply *not* done by the company.[46]

Nothing about Siwoff would seem to qualify him as a visionary. As self-appointed gatekeeper of access to major sports league stats, he saw absolutely no reason why the great mass of unwashed fans should ever have direct access to his collections—moreover, that data was proprietary and he did not want to risk it becoming publicly available. Furthermore, it was not until 1972, after the AL dumped the Howe News Bureau for the computer-friendly Sports Information Center (SIC), that Siwoff traded in pencils and erasers for bits and bytes. But Elias's 1975 mammoth computer baseball analysis was only marketed to teams, not fans.[47]

As computer technology continued to improve, Siwoff missed on another opportunity to jump from accumulated statistics into play-by-play data. He airily dismissed an unsolicited 1980 proposal from a baseball fan named Steve Mann, who had managed to land a one-year stats gig with the Houston Astros. To be fair, SIC passed on it too, but they were nicer about it. SIC's Pete Palmer, the company's computer guru, put Mann in touch with an MIT Ph.D. programmer Dick Cramer. The two brought in sports marketer Matt Levine to help launch the company, but not before Cramer and Levine threw Mann under the bus. In 1981, Mann's original idea became STATS, Inc., but he only got $8,000 out of it. By 1984, the company was collecting detailed stats on every MLB game, and five years later was selling various products to

ESPN, which was enjoying its own meteoric rise. In 2000, STATS, Inc., was sold to the News Corporation for a lot more than eight grand.[48]

Now, in the Internet Age, numbers have gotten ridiculously easier to calculate and disseminate, changing the very nature of what it means to be a fan. Not near a television? Click onto NFL.com, CBSsportsline, ESPN.com, MLB.com, NBA.com, etc., and watch your favorite contest unfold through the magic of real-time live statistics. It may lack the sights and smells of the stadium, but you are in much the same situation that Dutch Reagan was when broadcasting Cubs away games on the radio during the 1930s.

Tens of millions of modern-day Chadwick wannabes now put together online shrines to their favorite sports and athletes, many from the womb that is their parents' basements. Some of their efforts are awful but some, such as FootballOutsiders.com are incredibly insightful and have the respect of the academic community. And just as Chadwick did, some of them are even changing their beloved sports.

Wiki-Stats

A committed customer base is the key to success in any business. Oprah Winfrey is a very, very rich woman because she has managed her following's loyalty so brilliantly as to border on the cultish. For two decades, Starbucks was alone in its ability to sell coffee for $4 a pop because its drinkers perceived a measurably diminished quality of life on those days when they miss their fix. NASCAR's insistence on its standardized "Car of Tomorrow" monkeys with the family jewels insomuch as it risks diminishing the role of auto brand loyalty in its sport.[49]

There is a downside to cultivating such devotion, however. Fans of successful television programs can feel as if they personally know their actors, rendering their private lives nearly impossible. Popular singers have to hire burly thugs to keep away the paparazzi and the adoring fans who pay for their pictures. For sports teams and athletes, fans who "know" how to run things better are the bane of existence.

It is quite the love-hate relationship between management and fans. Without an addicted fan base, game tickets are not sold, television and radio ratings are non-existent, logo apparel does not sell, and revenues are meager. Just as every man is sure that he knows how to make love better than Valentino, and can comment on economic policy more authoritatively than Volker, so does every fan think he or she can run their favorite team better than its current management. Sports talk radio would be absolutely lost without the cadre of phone calls critical of local team management to fill the minutes separating beer and erectile dysfunction commercials.

Isaiah Thomas's skippering of the New York Knicks notwithstanding, fandom's arrogation of such expertise unto itself is in nearly every case unjustified. Or at least, this is what economic rationalism would predict. Who has more at stake in a team's success than its coaches and front office? Who has better specific information about the game, the opposing team, and the team's own players? Who knows more about how the game should be played and how to win in general? Certainly not some average fan—any coaching or front office professional no better than the average fan certainly would be devoured by the other professionals in the business, and soon be out of work.

But not every fan is average. Fan bases in American sport number in the tens or hundreds of millions. It would be unreasonable to believe that there is no Newtonian or Shakespearian genius among them. The monumental issue, of course, is to distinguish an Isaac or William from the sea of Ikes and Bills. Teams understandably don't even bother. They draw their management from those who "paid their dues" by "coming up through the ranks." There are few Cinderella stories among major American sports management—just about every significant decision-maker in the industry has the requisite pedigree. But there is one such inspiration.

The Boston Red Sox started off the AL-NL era in rather promising fashion, winning five of the first fifteen World Series played. Unfortunately, the rest of the 20th century did not go so well, and the team failed to win the series even once after 1918. Following the 2002 season—*another* second-place finish behind the detested Yankees—the Sox hired Bill James as a special consultant.[50] Apparently James was the antidote for the curse of the Bambino—the team won the 2004 and 2007 series. In 2006, *Time* called baseball writer and historian James one of the 100 Greatest Thinkers in the World, listing him among the sixteen scientists and other brains on their list.[51]

James's baseball industry career trajectory was not exactly textbook, nor could he have possibly imagined his eventual success when he first began his work. After stints in the U.S. Army and a little graduate school, James found himself in the mid–1970s as the night watchman at a Stokely Van Camp pork and beans factory. He must have been good at his job—there is no record of any terrorist assaults under his watch.[52]

Trained at the University of Kansas in economics and literature, James turned the boring hours at the factory into productive ones about his first love, baseball. He turned his work into a self-published pamphlet titled, *1977 Baseball Abstract: Featuring 18 Categories of Statistical Information That You Just Can't Find Anywhere Else.* The 1977 *Abstract* sold seventy copies at $3.50 a piece, which he took as a sign to do a 1978 version, which sold 300 copies. He continued to publish the *Abstract* annually through 1988, each successive version doing better than the last. His work was introduced to millions when *Sports Illustrated* writer Dan Okrent—an *Abstract* reader since the beginning and later, the first public editor of *The New York Times*—got a story on James published in the magazine in 1981.[53] Ballantine Books took a chance on the publication, then selling 2,600 mimeographed copies annually, and began publishing the *Abstract.* Sales took off to as many as 150,000, putting the nightwatchman-fan's work on the *New York Times* bestseller list.[54] He has sporadically published enormously successful works since.

James's contribution was not so much to question the usefulness of the main baseball stats that had been reported in newspapers and fan guides for two generations—although he did that, and probably better than most. Just as Chadwick had done a century earlier, James had the audacity to rethink from scratch which measures actually *said* something about which players and strategies actually helped win games. He used his economics background to mathematically model run generation as a production process. His insights and impact on the way fans look at their favorite game make one of the giants of baseball's rich history.

But it is only fair to recognize that James is as much the face of a fan movement as he is a pioneer in his own right. Surely there have been fans who have messed around with numbers as long as baseball box scores have been reported in the newspapers. Some of them had to have come up with better ways to measure player productivity, but obviously were dismissed as crackpots by several generations of baseball insiders sure that they knew better.

In 1971, a group of hard-core baseball fans, meeting in Cooperstown, NY, and led by Bob Davids, founded the Society for American Baseball Research (SABR). The organization is decidedly wiki-like in its investigations of baseball history and statistics. Some of its member-fans are extremely accomplished statisticians who are more than qualified and willing to provide better tools. Despite the high quality of much of their quantitative work, they too were ignored by the baseball cognoscenti. Like James, their advice was nearly universally ignored outside of their own circles for quarter century. More than just ignored, these "sabermetricians" were rejected by MLB's establishment like a mismatched kidney.

Rather, James deserves every word of his favorable press mostly because of his tireless determination to get the word out to other fans. He doggedly tried to get Siwoff's Elias Sports Bureau to provide him with collated data so that he did not have to assemble it by hand from newspaper box scores. He was haughtily dismissed, resulting in a long-running feud. James reacted by calling upon the collective goodness of scorecard-collecting fans everywhere, asking them to send in what they had to build a historical game database. He called the effort Project Scoresheet.[55]

During the 1980s, a few teams, most notably the Oakland A's, began to consider and use new stats that came from STATS, Inc., which was able to get itself considered part of baseball's establishment. But between its high annual cost ($100,000) and weak statistical reports where it counted (for example, the firm botched Rickey Henderson's stolen base analysis before his arbitration hearing), the firm was dropped by the impoverished A's following the 1983 season. The firm managed to survive, in no small part by acquiring Project Scoresheet's data set. The company was struggling, however—in 1986, its revenues from its two major clients, the Yankees and the White Sox, amounted to only about $50,000.[56]

Timing is everything in life. In 1987, while STATS was imploding due to internal rancor and a lack of big-money clients, NBC hired the company to give its World Series viewers Arledge-like statistical tidbits that had never before been seen. 1990 was a watershed year for the company—publishing upstart *USA Today* replaced its AP baseball service with STATS, and the meteoric ESPN chose the company as its data provider for its newly acquired MLB coverage. By 1992, STATS was bringing in $2 million in revenue. The firm invested $1 million in technology in 1994 to provide real-time stats. Few knew it at the time, but the Internet was about to take off, and with it, fans' expectations for ever more detailed real-time numbers.

It seems as though MLB, and even a few other sports, are finally seeing the light, although it certainly has taken them long enough. Even then, teams' usage of fan-derived expertise has more the look and feel of Bill Veeck–like promotion than serious effort to be better at their business. The St. Louis Cardinals created a "One for the Birds" contest in which fans were invited to be "cyberscouts" and submit their own reports on promising "under the radar" college prospects in advance of the June, 2008 player entry draft. Under the radar players are defined as NCAA Division II, Division III, NAIA or Junior College players. The team will attribute one player that it took or "nearly took" to on-line reports submitted by a fan. The contest description encourages fans to "Please identify a player's tools and his actual performance. If his performance to date is not reflective of his tools, explain why." The winning fan will win a trip to a pair of Cardinals games.[57] Perhaps our British cousins are a bit ahead of the curve on this—in November 2007, a well-known English Premier League fantasy sports site bought a lower-division team, and will run the team by allowing its 20,000 paid subscribers to vote on trades, player selection and other decisions.[58]

The wiki-fan movement seems to be catching on beyond baseball. All major North American sports now have fan-driven SABR-like groups. Fans with even a modicum of computer savvy can download and analyze to their hearts content vast databases about their favorite sports from sites like databasesports.com. Bill Jameses in other sports are beginning to emerge, mostly from among academic economists—basketball has Dave Berri, football has Aaron Schatz, hockey has Neil Longley and Marc Lavoie, and golf has Stephen Schmanske. They might be professors, but they are also fans, and their work will drive new insights for the sports that they love.

Of course, some of those who care most about statistics are doing so less out of passion for the game than raw financial interest. Contest scores, the most elemental of all statistics, are to gambling what water is to an ocean.

Take a Chance on Me

> The theory yields much, but it hardly brings us closer to the Old One's secrets. I, in any case, am convinced that He does not play dice.
>
> —Albert Einstein (1926)[59]

Einstein was speaking of quantum mechanics, not sports, but the relationship between numbers and sports traces its origins to the earliest games of chance, long before relativity theory hit the human scene. "Random" number generators for dice-like games date back to at least the third millennium B.C. and perhaps even to the very dawn of *homo sapiens* four hundred centuries ago.[60]

The ancient Greeks, who may not have enjoyed leisure more than prior peoples even if they were more assiduous about recording it, used four-sided animal knucklebones as dice at least as far back as 900 B.C., and maybe even earlier. By the first century A.D., fairly sophisticated Yahtzee-like dice games had spread, courtesy of the Romans, from Greece into Egypt, Rome, and even to Britain. Apparently the dice generally were sufficiently fair so as not to have players notice differences in the likelihood of different outcomes, and scant evidence exists of any ancient attempts to calculate probabilities mathematically. Even if someone had wanted to think about probabilities, they would have been stymied by the clumsy number systems of the day. Furthermore, the natural philosophers then in vogue were more interested in determinism and repetition than in learning about variant outcomes.[61]

The Christian Church of the Dark Ages took a dim view of dice games, and did what it could to discourage them. While it clearly was unsuccessful in this quest, there is no evidence of any scientific attempts to calculate probabilities, probably in no small part due to an attitude that divination of random events was more the domain of pagans than of good Christians.[62] Albert Einstein's perspective has a venerable Western intellectual history.

Mathematics might have been moribund in the Roman Catholic world of the Dark Ages, but the same was not true in the East, where scholarship heretically remained beyond the Church's hierarchical reach. Arab thinkers took the best from what Hindu and Babylonian mathematicians had to offer, and their work spread mathematics across the Mediterranean. European mathematics finally began to show signs of revival in the 12th century as the Crusades put Catholic elites in contact with Eastern scholarship, leading to the concept of the European university. Constantinople's sacking in the early 13th century unleashed a flood of manuscripts of all kinds into the West, paving the way for an intellectual renaissance that included early investigation into probability and statistics.[63] Even as it was getting rolling, the progress of European intellectualism remained slow while the Black Death and Hundred Years' War occupied much of England and France during the 14th and 15th centuries. The invention of the printing press in the mid–15th century changed everything, and sparked a wave of inquiry across Europe that had not been seen in a millenium.[64]

Cheap printing led to an increase in the popularity of card games and with them, increasing interest in probabilities. Within fifty years of the invention of movable type, pragmatic Italian thinkers began to wrestle with the matter of how to equitably divide the stakes in a prematurely stopped game. Even the great Galileo took a break around 1620 from his telescope and the Tower of Pisa to consider the problem. The solution vexed scholars for another half century, but was finally solved in 1654 by the great mathematicians Pascal and Fermat. This discovery is generally marked as the founding of modern probability theory.[65]

During the next couple of centuries, scientists and mathematicians unlocked more secrets of the natural world than had been done in all prior human history. Like Pascal and Fermat, some of the greatest of these men turned at least some of their attention to analyzing games of chance, including Leibniz, James and Nicholas Bernoulli, Huygens, de Moivre, and Gauss.[66]

When James Bernoulli died in 1705, he left behind his unpublished work on "the art of conjecturing." Posthumously published in 1713, the work included as an appendix a thirty-five-page letter to a friend about probabilities in lawn tennis. In it, he distinguishes between games of pure chance and those involving athletic skill—an observation that he apparently made as early as 1685, thirty years after a public court had been constructed in his hometown of Basel. The letter includes treatment of a variety of different problems relating to the game, which was well-known at the time.[67]

No doubt Bernoulli's interest in the sport of tennis had been piqued by some form of gambling on the outcomes of games. In this way, at least, a lot of Americans have much in common with elites of the French Enlightenment.

The Sports Gambling Industry

Gambling on sporting events, of course, predates 17th century France. The ancient Mesopotamians engaged in a form of sports wagering as far back as 1600 B.C.[68] Ancient Rome's Circus Maximus was used as a racetrack, where crowds as large as a quarter million would sometimes place bets on race outcomes. Across the Atlantic, Native American populations were known to bet on footraces and ball games.[69]

Horse racing has the longest pedigree in American sports wagering. Despite Puritan preferences to the contrary, the first track that featured regularly scheduled meets was built in Long Island in 1665. Pari-mutuel betting—wherein odds are determined systematically by bettors' choices rather than arbitrarily by bookies—became common after the Civil War.[70]

Early baseball and gambling had gone together cheek-by-jowl in the early years of Reconstruction, much to the consternation of the likes of patricians Henry Chadwick and William Hulbert. It is overwhelmingly likely that betting on college football began as soon as the sport started drawing crowds; the same goes for basketball and hockey. Gambling, sports and otherwise, was quite popular until the 1890s, when it was directly prohibited by law across the country, although church bingo and horse races were legalized in the 1920s. Nevada legalized all gambling in 1931 in order to combat a dying economy.[71] The state is still the only place in the country where sports wagering is legal, although during 1989 through 2007 Oregon ran a lottery in which players attempted to beat the point spreads in NFL games. The state also ran a parallel NBA lottery during 1989–90.

There is a reason why most major newspapers and sports statistical websites offer game odds, point spreads, and injury reports—a lot of their readers find them relevant and useful. Sports gambling is now a very big business in the U.S., although nobody really knows exactly how big. According to the American Gaming Association, in 2006 the 187 legal sports books in Nevada took in $2.43 billion in sports bets. However, they also estimate that this figure represents less than 1 percent of all U.S. sports betting—illegal wagers accounted for another $380 billion that year.[72]

NFL football is by far the most popular sport on which Americans bet, accounting for 40 percent of legal wagers. $8 billion or more was bet in the U.S. on the 2007 Super Bowl alone, with perhaps half of all Americans having some sort of wager on the game. Another $2.5 billion rode on outcomes during the 2007 NCAA men's basketball tournament. Add to these figures about another $15–20 billion bet each year on horse racing, and the scale of the industry becomes apparent.[73]

There is a lot of money in sports gambling simply because there are tens of millions of Americans who choose to play. An academic study published in 2002 indicated that 20 percent of American adults engage in sports betting each year, doing so 15 times per year on average. One out of every five of sports gamblers made bets once a week or more. An additional 7 percent made bets at horse or dog racing tracks, doing so 15 times per year on average. 2 percent engage in off-track race betting an average of 36 times per year.[74] Nobody really knows how many participate in office football or NCAA basketball tournament pools—it is probably the case that a sizable minority, if not a majority, of participants might even fail to think of the activity as "gambling."

The study also found males were more likely than females to engage in sports betting (46 percent versus 22 percent), while whites (35 percent) and Hispanics (34 percent) were more likely to gamble on sports than blacks (18 percent) or Native Americans (18 percent). Younger people are more likely to make sports wagers than older people—44 percent of those between 18 and 30 did so at least once per year, while only 18 percent of those age 61 or more did.[75]

Many of these bets are made directly between private parties rather than involving a bookmaker. A survey of California gamblers published in 2006 found that 18 percent of private wagering involved sports (as opposed to card-playing, dice, etc). Private bettors were twice as likely to be male than female, and were more likely than the general California population to have gone to college, and to have annual incomes above $75,000.[76]

There can be no doubt that sports gambling adds something to watching a game. But there also is no denying that some minority of participants meet the definition of "problem gambler" or "gambling addict." Gamblers Anonymous offers a list of twenty questions that suspected problem gamblers should ask of themselves—answering yes to more than seven is indicative of a problem.[77] The American Psychiatric Association's *Diagnostic and Statistical Manual of Mental Disorders*—the organization's field guide to nuttiness—provides a list of ten criteria; if a patient hits five of them, he or she qualifies as a pathological gambler.[78]

The federal government's latest effort to protect betting fans from themselves has targeted off-shore on-line wagering sites. The Clinton and George W. Bush Justice Departments were staunch opponents of these businesses, claiming that they violate the 1961 Federal Wire Act.[79] Legal scholarly opinion on the topic is mixed, although a Federal Appeals Court strangely found that the Wire Act applies to sports gambling, but not other forms of wagering.[80] In 2006, Bush signed the Unlawful Internet Gambling Enforcement Act into law (as part of the Safe Ports Act), which prohibited U.S. financial companies from processing Internet gambling transactions.[81]

Trying to stamp out sports wagering has been about as successful as the War on Drugs. As long as fans remain so interested in betting, *someone* will be willing to take their money. But one of the most pervasive forms of sports gambling—is it sports gambling?—is simply exploding in popularity: fantasy sports.

"Fan" Stands for Fantasy Sports

As a child, noted San Francisco Giants and ESPN baseball announcer Jon Miller fell in love with Strat-O-matic, a baseball simulation dice game. Alone in his bedroom one summer, he replayed the entire 1966 NL season, doing play-by-play and adding sound effects for hundreds of imaginary contests—and no doubt causing his parents a bit of concern about his future, although they did feed his addiction by allowing him to buy a tape recorder.[82]

If Strat-O-Matic is craps based on real players, then its predecessor, All-Star Baseball, is roulette. The game was developed in 1941 by former MLB player Ethan Allen (who later became George H.W. Bush's coach at Yale) and was based on a simple, but brilliant, premise. The probabilities of particular batting outcomes for any given hitter were represented by wedges of varying size on a paper disk. If a player's stats indicated that on average he hit a home run once in every 72 plate appearances, the size of the HR wedge on his paper disk was set to be $5° = 360°/72$. As long as the spinner apparatus that held each disk was fair, outcomes would reflect the actual probabilities of the ballplayers they represented.[83]

The game took off quickly with kids. Players could simulate choosing a roster via whatever means they deemed interesting and workable, and teams would be pitted against each other in realistic games. Except for their hitting, pitcher statistics were ignored, as were fielding stats. While this was not a problem for the vast majority of those playing the game, one eleven-year old named Hal Richman was affronted by the realism shortfall.

In 1948, Richman was a fifth-grader with a natural understanding of probabilities. He was able to use multiple dice to more realistically simulate baseball games based on the player stats he found in annual *Sporting News* guides. By 1954, at the ripe old age of 17, he had sufficiently refined his game to be awarded a U.S. patent. He put his game aside for a while, and got his accounting degree from Bucknell, finally launching the Strat-O-Matic company in 1961. He was able to sell only 350 of the 1,000 games he made during his first year, but the game caught on fairly quickly, thereafter at first among boys. He has since sold more than one million of the games, and its adult adherents read like a sports *Who's Who*.[84] A number of other similar baseball, football, and hockey board-and-dice simulation games, such as those marketed by APBA, are now available. While they have migrated over to the computer, they are less about dazzling Madden-ish graphics than they are about game strategy.

In 1960, in a modest apartment in Cambridge, Massachusetts, William Gamson, a lecturer in the social science unit of the Harvard School of Public Health, along with two his Antioch College alum roommates, invented the forerunner of what has become fantasy baseball. His "National Baseball Seminar"—so titled to evade bookie-averse postal inspectors—had colleagues choosing rosters and then earning points based on their players' batting averages, RBIs, wins, and ERAs. He took it on the road when he taught at the University of Michigan, where it was picked up by Bob Sklar—later Daniel Okrent's freshman advisor.[85]

Gamson's league has endured for nearly half a century. As of the 2006 season, the Baseball Seminar commissioner was Harvey Schubothe, an Oregon Department of Corrections budget analyst. The now-retired Gamson went on to a highly distinguished academic career at Boston College, and his curriculum vitae is the envy of any academic sociologist. His accomplishments include one of the highest honors in his profession, election as president of the prestigious American Sociological Association (1993–94). He even co-wrote an academic paper on the sociology of scapegoating. Gamson has applied the idea of simulation games to a variety of other social issues and phenomena, although it is difficult to imagine their participants are more dedicated than are fantasy sports owners.[86]

Despite Gamson's contributions, Okrent is often credited with inventing fantasy baseball, although he gives Gamson the credit for doing so. In 1979, on a plane between Austin, Texas, and New York, he redefined Gamson's game, and introduced it to a group of his Philadelphia Phillies friends. The first player draft among them was held in April of 1980, and the group met weekly for lunch at an East 52nd Street in Manhattan restaurant, the Rotisserie Française restaurant on East 52nd Street. Word of the group quickly spread, and to this day, fantasy baseball is often known as Rotisserie baseball.[87] Various entities, such as RotoAuthority.com and the *RotoTimes*, are named in honor of Okrent's contribution to the game.

The critical difference between the Gamson-Okrent simulation and Strat-O-matic and its ilk—even modern video simulation sports games—is that player stats are "live," i.e., based on the ongoing season, rather than on past performance. This makes player selection a more strategically realistic affair—as soon as the 1979 season ended, Strat-O-Matic owners *knew* how Jim Rice had performed that season, but not how he would do in 1980. Unlike Strat-O-Matic players, Rotisserie owners could suffer the same frustration as real team owners when injuries or slumps occurred, and the same elation when finding a sleeper star.

Rotisserie baseball took off as STATS, Inc.'s *USA Today* statistics page provided easy fodder for new leagues. Before the Internet, fantasy league commissioners had to calculate weekly statistical performances by hand, a labor of love if there ever were one. In the late 1990s, a variety of online services began to do all the heavy lifting, further fueling the fantasy sports boom.

According to one story, fantasy football also got its start in the early 1960s. Oakland businessman Wilfred Winkenbach, also a limited partner in the then-new AFL Raiders franchise, developed a gambling game based on football performance. Winkenbach put together the game's rules in a New York hotel during a team road game weekend with Raiders Public Relations manager Bill Tunnel and reporter Scotty Starling. The resultant league, called the Greater Oakland Professional Pigskin Procrastinators League, was open only to football "insiders" such as team administrative staff, journalists—or purchasers of at least ten Raiders season tickets (they would do anything to sell AFL tickets in the league's early days). Team "owners" drafted players, and then got weekly payouts based on their teams' statistical performances. In 1969, an Oakland restaurant owner offered a points-based version of the game to his patrons.[88]

Fantasy sports are now a big business, complete with its own industry association, the Fantasy Sports Trade Association, and even its own writer's guild, the Fantasy Sports Writers Association. 6.5 percent of adult Americans, an estimated 20 million people, played fantasy sports in 2007, creating a market on the order of $1.5 billion annually.[89]

The NFL has eclipsed MLB as the favorite sport fantasized about—an estimated 93 percent of fantasy players do so for football, even though many players run teams in multiple sports. Aside from baseball and football, there are now leagues for hockey, auto racing, basketball, soccer, cricket, and golf.[90] The phenomenon has crossed the ocean with two major English Premier League fantasy leagues, Premiereleague.com and Fantasyleague.com, which attracted more than two million unique visitors in August of 2007.[91]

Websites offer free or low-cost fantasy league management to drive traffic and boost their ad revenues. It works—in September of 2007, just as the NFL season was getting underway, Yahoo, CBSsportsline, and ESPN, the largest fantasy league providers, saw their page views increase to 15 million unique visitors per day to their sites—double July 2007's traffic.[92] Furthermore, these visitors spend a lot of time on their favorite fantasy sites—CBSsportsline estimates that each of their fantasy football players spent an average of 96 minutes per visit just before the 2007 NFL season opened.[93]

The typical player earns an annual W-2 income between $60,000 and 100,000 from his or her "real job," making him or her an attractive consumer demographic.[94] In 2007, an estimated $727 million was spent for sports website advertising. $150 million of this sum went into fantasy sites in order to reach primarily male, primarily upper-middle-class players.[95] There are lots of magazines, companion websites, even television programs now devoted to the fantasy player. The average football fantasy-er watches two to three more hours of NFL television game coverage per week than non-players. Not surprisingly, this affects how the games are covered, with individual player statistics becoming a more important part of the broadcasts.[96]

The popularity of fantasy sports has spread to the real players themselves. While nobody is yet worried about a player throwing a real game to win his fantasy league, anything that smacks of gambling makes the real league commissioners nervous.[97] The commissioners have been more concerned, however, about the fact that their leagues get a relatively small chunk of the action.

In the 1980s, STATS, Inc., began to challenge Seymour Siwoff's stodgier Elias Sports Bureau by producing real-time sports statistics. Rather than trying to outdo STATS by putting out a better product, he responded by trying to clobber STATS, Inc., legally. He certainly had a point—a 1918 case resulted in the prohibition of news services from simply repeating the news put out by the Associated Press.[98] Since then, courts had generally been willing to grant property rights associated with the facts generated during sports broadcasts. However, while the 1976 Copyright Act protected the broadcasts themselves, it liberated facts for release into the public domain.[99]

Motorola began offering STATS's real-time data via its pagers, and the NBA, prodded by Siwoff, filed suit in March of 1996 to protect what it believed was its copyrighted data. Already, the value of such data to Internet ventures was becoming clear, and the NBA had no interest in not cashing in on it. After some initial setbacks, Motorola and STATS won the case in early 1997.[100] The numbers were free.

Or were they? In 2006, MLB decided to up the license fee to use their names and stats online from $25,000 to $2 million per year, prompting a lawsuit from CBC Distribution and Marketing, one of the many relatively small "mom-and-pop" fantasy sites. The specific legal question referred to the right of a player to his own publicity.[101] MLB's legal strategy was based on a 1953 case finding that Topp's Chewing Gum could not print cards with players' likenesses without their permission.[102] Fortunately for fantasy sites and players, a St. Louis court ruled in 2006 against the MLB, i.e., affirming that the stats are historical facts that belong to anyone and everyone.[103] Had the outcome favored MLB, fans could have expected sharp increases in the price of one of their favorite hobbies. Fantasy is safe, at least for now.

11

Balance, Schmalance

Celebrity Culture

> But I, wretched young man that I was—even more wretched at the beginning of my youth—had begged You for chastity and had said, "Make me chaste and continent, but not yet."
>
> —St. Augustine[1]

Chastity is not winning the American pop culture wars in the early 21st century, at least not to the extent that it has diminished public interest of the likes of Britney Spears, Lindsay Lohan, and Paris Hilton. Every day, radio, television, blogs, and books buzz with the latest tell-all account about what new debaucheries these young ladies have plumbed. Moral leaders express outrage at such depravity, some pointing out that it is only possible because of huge sums of ill-gotten money the perpetrators have earned in the entertainment industry or, worse yet, inherited. Paparazzi make small fortunes catching images and videos of said debauchery by selling their pixels to media making large fortunes feeding the delighted clucking public. Americans simply love their dominating celebrities. They also love to see them rise, and better yet, fall—and even better still, rise again. Such is the human condition—why fight it?

Spectator sport has its celebrities, too—the teams and athletes that dominate their sports. Fans love to see a new competitor rise from relative obscurity, reign for a while, and then get knocked off by the new kid in town. Such is the human condition—why fight it?

Yet fight it leagues do, and even the fans that love their sports Goliaths pay lip service to the fight. Spectator sports organizing bodies, fans, and commentators seem endlessly engaged in laments about lack of "competitive balance." Why do we turn on our heroes this way?

Dynastic Dominance and Sports' Golden Ages

> Until this century, dynastic families have provided most of the rulers over the human race.
>
> —John King Fairbank[2]

China is not only the earth's most populous nation, but it is also one of the oldest continuous countries on the world map. Its long political history can be viewed in terms of dynastic periods, some of which went on for centuries, including the Shangs, who ruled northern and central China from about 1766 to 1027 B.C., the Zhous (1122 to 256 B.C.), and the Qings (1644–1912). Most took power by force, and were knocked off in the same way by the next dynasty.[3] But dynasties were not unique to China, nor was China the first country to have them. The ancient Egyptians, Greeks and Romans all were ruled by family dynasties at one point or another. So were many Arabs and Europeans, some until World War I blew up their dynasties or rendered their monarchs mere figureheads.

Still, just as the world has had its Tudors, Habsburgs and Romanovs, North American spectator sport has had its Yankees, Canadiens and Celtics. Political dynasties might chafe their subjects, but fans do not seem to mind competitively dominant teams nearly as much. In fact, the halcyon days of various sports seem to coincide fairly neatly with their respective dynastic eras.

Consider MLB's "Golden Age"—from the time of Babe Ruth through Ted Williams through Mickey Mantle. Between 1921 and 1964, the New York Yankees captured more than two out of every three American League pennants, winning twenty of forty-four World Series played during that span. Meanwhile, AL attendance grew by 150 percent while U.S. population increased by 68 percent—with much of that population increase occurring in the South and West, where MLB had no representation.[4]

The NCAA Division I men's basketball tournament is one of the premier annual events in American spectator sport. Yet as recently as the 1960s, the NCAA tourney was considered second fiddle to the National Invitational Tournament (NIT) in New York. Many factors contributed to the NCAA's rise, but among them must be counted the part played by the UCLA Bruins, who won ten out of twelve NCAA Division I men's basketball tournaments held between 1964 and 1975. Far from damaging the tournament, history suggests that the Bruins' run probably helped—total NCAA Division I men's basketball tournament attendance increased by 30 percent during the UCLA years.[5] Furthermore, television coverage of the tournament was fairly inconsequential until 1969, when a large audience tuned in to see if UCLA would take an unprecedented third straight title. They did.[6]

The NBA experienced a similar dynasty-attendance growth phenomenon, when the Boston Celtics made it to eleven of thirteen NBA Finals played between 1957 and 1969. They won ten of them, including eight in a row (1959–1966). Again, there is little to suggest that their run hurt the league—NBA total attendance grew by more than 350 percent.[7] A few years later, between 1980 and 1991, the Los Angeles Lakers were in nine of twelve finals played—and total league attendance jumped by more than 80 percent.[8] During the Chicago Bulls' 1991–1998 run of six of eight NBA titles, attendance grew by an additional 11 percent.[9] These *uber*-teams certainly did not kill fan interest in the league.

To hear hockey hard cases talk, the greatest days of the NHL preceded helmets, face masks and big player contracts. During the leagues first six decades, the Montreal Canadiens played in more than *half* of Stanley Cup Finals, winning them three times as often as they were runners-up. In fact, the story of the league through the 1980s seems to be one of utter domination. Montreal claimed five straight cups in 1956–1960, and four straight in 1976–1979. The New York Islanders then helped themselves to four in a row (1980–1983), after which the Edmonton Oilers won five of the next seven (1984–1990).[10] Again, there seems to be scant evidence that fan interest in the league waned during these dynastic runs. Total league attendance may have fallen during the Canadiens' late 1970s run—perhaps due to competition from the WHA, which was averaging about 8,000 fans per game in NHL markets—but increased by 64 percent between 1978–79 and 1989–90.[11] By contrast, the dynasty-less early 21st century saw total league attendance grow by only 2.5 percent while six different teams won the six Stanley Cups (2001–2007).[12]

Similarly, the early decades of college football—when the sport experienced its meteoric rise in popularity—was ruled by just three programs. Yale, Harvard, and Princeton accounted for all but five of thirty-one national champions between 1883 and 1913.[13] NFL championships, on the other hand, historically have been spread around more evenly. Even so, the league's 1960s growth spurt was defined by Vince Lombardi's Green Bay Packers, who won five of seven league titles between 1961 and 1967. Meanwhile, the sport became a television darling and total NFL attendance increased by 50 percent—despite the challenge by the upstart AFL.[14]

Too Much of a Good Thing?

It is possible to be *too* successful, however, at least in a relative sense. Competitive outcomes must have a degree of uncertainty to be interesting. Fans may love—or love to hate—a dynasty, but there are limits. Overly successful teams have been blamed for the extinction of more than one American sports league. The National Association collapse following the 1875 season is popularly attributed in part due to the Boston Red Stockings' .776 average season winning percentage during the NA's five-year run.

The demise of the All-American Football Conference (AAFC) is similarly blamed on the outsized success of the Cleveland Browns. Founded in 1944 by *Chicago Tribune* sportswriter Arch Ward (of all-star game fame) as World War II was winding down, the eight-team league played from 1946 through 1949. The Browns won all four championships, along the way posting a 54–4–3 record that included a two-year, 29-game winning streak.[15] Yet another example of a dominating team harming attendance is found in the 1950s New York Yankees. While the Yankees ruled the AL, the NL was significantly more competitive. AL attendance stagnated during the decade, while NL attendance saw healthy increases.[16]

Superstars

Sports fans tire of dynasties just as moviegoers reject series that go on too long—*Terminator XII: The California Scrapheap Years* wouldn't sell many tickets. But film producers are well aware of the box office effects of a big-name star. Why did Johnny Depp earn an estimated $78 million of the roughly $423 million total domestic take for *Pirates of the Caribbean: Dead Man's Chest*?[17] The answer is straightforward—imagine how much less the movie would have made without him. Similarly, fans seem to like to watch superstars.

Sports often can mark their heydays by periods of domination, with golf offering perhaps the most striking example. Bobby Jones literally put golf on the spectator sports map during the 1920s by winning six U.S. Amateurs, four U.S. Opens, three British Opens, and one British Amateur between 1923 and 1930. In fact, Jones finished first or second in 90 percent (18 of 20) of his entries in those tournaments during the period, even winning all four of them in 1930.[18] Another golf Golden Age came during the 1950s and 1960s when Ben Hogan won 32 percent (9 of 28) of the four annual majors held between 1946 and 1953, Arnold Palmer captured 42 percent (5 of 12) of 12 majors he entered during 1960–1962, and Jack Nicklaus won one-third (7 of 21) of majors between the 1962 and 1967 U.S. Opens. Fan interest grew considerably, and so did the prize money available.

More recently, Tiger Woods has defined the notion of supremacy in a sport, winning nearly one-third (13 of 44) of all the major golf championships he entered between 1997 and 2007. His presence is so overwhelming that there is evidence that it actually diminishes other golfers' effort levels when they face him in PGA Tour tournaments.[19] While less effort would seem to reduce fan interest, such is not the case with Tiger. Neilson ratings for tournaments televised by CBS and NBC in 2007 were 111 percent higher when Tiger won or finished in the top five compared to when he was not playing or not in contention.[20] Those one or two million extra viewers make a big difference in how much advertisers are will to pay for spots—Tiger on the leaderboard equals money for the network.

Tiger's success has paid him well. He earned a total of $76 million in career prize money through the 2007 season—an amount greater than the GDP of the small island nation of Kiribati ($73 million in 2007).[21] But Tiger has done as much for the sport as it has done for him. He may have topped the 2007 world money list with over $11 million in winnings, but there was plenty of loot left over for others. Runner-up Phil Mickelson earned $7.3 million. Tiger's positive impact on golf economics is made even more obvious when noting that during 1996, his first year as a pro, the world money list leader (Masashi "Jumbo" Ozaki) earned just $1.9 million in prizes.[22]

Tennis, too, can thank its dominating stars for winning American fans' hearts. The first seven U.S. Opens, beginning in 1881, were won by Richard Sears, but the sport hardly died as a consequence of his success.[23] A couple of decades later, Bill Tilden was the show. He won an amazing 94 percent of the 969 matches he played between 1912 and 1930. Between 1918 and 1930, he scored a total of 21 major championships in singles, doubles, and mixed doubles tennis—including six straight U.S. Open singles championships between 1920 and 1925, and a seventh in 1929.[24] Like his contemporary Bobby Jones, Tilden's success did far more to promote than to damage interest in his sport. His American female counterpart was Helen Willis Moody, who won 52 of the 92 tournaments she entered between 1919 and 1938. She posted a 0.919 match record along the way, even winning 158 matches in a row during 1933.[25] The popularity of tennis in the U.S. enjoyed another boom during the 1970s and 1980s—when the likes of Bjorn Borg, John McEnroe, and Jimmy Connors hoisted an outsized share of Grand Slam trophies.

Fans of the sweet science recall the glory days when the undisputed champion was Jack Dempsey or Rocky Marciano or Joe Louis or Muhammad Ali or even Mike Tyson. But as such figures have left the stage, so has most of the mainstream American interest in boxing. In the early 21st century, the lack of real stars has allowed other sports, such as "ultimate fighting," to push boxing out of the limelight.

There are similar superstar effects in team sports, although they have a somewhat more complicated character. A few studies have suggested that big-time MLB free agents may get paid more than they are worth in terms of winning games, perhaps because name recognition means fannies in seats.[26]

Individual owners may not be able to fully cash in on their own stars, however. In the case of NBA basketball, home fans seem more impressed by winning than brand names on home rosters, while visiting teams' stars do pump up the home gate.[27] NBA games that involve a superstar also generate more television interest than those that do not. One estimate calculates Michael Jordan's superstar value during the 1991–92 season at $53 million dollars *above* what the Bulls generated from him.[28]

The five-year Major League Soccer contract signed by David Beckham for an alleged $250 million in 2007 indicates that at least MLS is well aware of such spillover star effects.[29] The contract was only possible because of MLS's "single-entity" ownership structure. Teams are all owned by the league as a whole, while individual franchise operators are partners in the league. Consequently, all of them can cash in on one team's big star.[30] In the NFL, it is the significant television and gate revenue-sharing schemes that allow teams to each earn a piece of other teams' marquee draws.

Distribution of Sports Championships Since 1970

1970 is a convenient place to mark the "modern age" of American spectator sport. In addition to preceding the dawn of big-money free agency and periods of sports league expansions, the year also saw the debut of *Monday Night Football*, the culmination of Roone Arledge's "sports as entertainment" movement. Even the most casual non-fan observer would note the post–1970 era as one of a significant rise in the cultural profile of the big-time sports. Just as with the Golden Ages of the various specific sports, a systematic analysis shows that championship success has smiled on only a relative handful of teams and players since 1970. (See Tables 11-1 through 11-12.)

Team	Championships	Runner-Up	Champion or Runner-Up
New York Yankees	6	4	10
Oakland A's	4	2	6
Atlanta Braves	1	4	5
Cincinnati Reds	3	2	5
Los Angeles Dodgers	2	3	5
St Louis Cardinals	2	3	5
Baltimore Orioles	2	2	4
Boston Red Sox	2	2	4
New York Mets	1	2	3
Philadelphia Phillies	1	2	3
Cleveland Indians	0	2	2
Detroit Tigers	1	1	2
Florida Marlins	2	0	2

Team	Championships	Runner-Up	Champion or Runner-Up
Kansas City Royals	1	1	2
Minnesota Twins	2	0	2
Pittsburgh Pirates	2	0	2
San Diego Padres	0	2	2
San Francisco Giants	0	2	2
Toronto Blue Jays	2	0	2
Anaheim Angels	1	0	1
Arizona Diamondbacks	1	0	1
Chicago White Sox	1	0	1
Colorado Rockies	0	1	1
Houston Astros	0	1	1
Milwaukee Brewers	0	1	1

Table 11-1: Distribution of World Series Championships and Runners-Up in MLB, 1970–2007

Team	Championships	Runner-Up	Champion or Runner-Up
Dallas Cowboys	5	3	8
Denver Broncos	2	4	6
New England Patriots	3	3	6
Pittsburgh Steelers	5	1	6
Miami Dolphins	2	3	5
San Francisco 49ers	5	0	5
Washington Redskins	3	2	5
Buffalo Bills	0	4	4
New York Giants	3	1	4
Minnesota Vikings	0	3	3
Oakland Raiders	2	1	3
Chicago Bears	1	1	2
Cincinnati Bengals	0	2	2
Green Bay Packers	1	1	2
Los Angeles Raiders	1	1	2
Philadelphia Eagles	0	2	2
St Louis Rams	1	1	2
Atlanta Falcons	0	1	1
Baltimore Colts	1	0	1
Baltimore Ravens	1	0	1
Carolina Panthers	0	1	1
Indianapolis Colts	1	0	1
San Diego Chargers	0	1	1

Team	Championships	Runner-Up	Champion or Runner-Up
Seattle Seahawks	0	1	1
Tennessee Titans	0	1	1
Tampa Bay Buccaneers	1	0	1

Table 11-2: Distribution of Super Bowl Championships and Runners-Up in the NFL, 1970–2007

Team	Championships	Runner-Up	Champion or Runner-Up
Los Angeles Lakers	9	7	16
Boston Celtics	5	2	7
Chicago Bulls	6	0	6
Detroit Pistons	3	2	5
New York Knicks	2	3	5
Philadelphia 76ers	1	4	5
Balt/Wash Bullets	1	3	4
Houston Rockets	2	2	4
San Antonio Spurs	4	0	4
Portland Trail Blazers	1	2	3
Seattle SuperSonics	1	2	3
Milwaukee Bucks	1	1	2
New Jersey Nets	0	2	2
Phoenix Suns	0	2	2
Utah Jazz	0	2	2
Cleveland Cavaliers	0	1	1
Dallas Mavericks	0	1	1
Golden State Warriors	1	0	1
Indiana Pacers	0	1	1
Miami Heat	1	0	1
Orlando Magic	0	1	1

Table 11-3: Distribution of NBA Finals Championships and Runners-Up in the NBA, 1970–2007

Team	Championships	Runner-Up	Champion or Runner-Up
Montreal Canadiens	8	1	9
Boston Bruins	2	5	7
Edmonton Oilers	5	2	7
Philadelphia Flyers	2	5	7

Team	Championships	Runner-Up	Champion or Runner-Up
New York Islanders	4	1	5
Detroit Red Wings	3	1	4
New Jersey Devils	3	1	4
Calgary Flames	1	2	3
Chicago Black Hawks	0	3	3
New York Rangers	1	2	3
Anaheim Ducks	1	1	2
Buffalo Sabres	0	2	2
Carolina Hurricanes	1	1	2
Colorado Avalanche	2	0	2
Dallas Stars	1	1	2
Minnesota North Stars	0	2	2
Pittsburgh Penguins	2	0	2
Vancouver Canucks	0	2	2
Florida Panthers	0	1	1
Los Angeles Kings	0	1	1
Ottawa Senators	0	1	1
St Louis Blues	0	1	1
Tampa Bay Lightning	1	0	1
Washington Capitals	0	1	1

Table 11-4: Distribution of Stanley Cup Championships and Runners-Up in the NHL, 1970–2007

Team	Championships	Runner-Up	Champion or Runner-Up
Miami-FL	5	4	9
USC	3	5	8
Nebraska	4	2	6
Notre Dame	3	3	6
Oklahoma	4	2	6
Ohio St.	1	4	5
Alabama	3	1	4
Florida St.	2	2	4
Florida	2	1	3
Penn St.	2	1	3
Georgia	1	1	2
LSU	1	1	2
Michigan	1	1	2
Pittsburgh	1	1	2
Texas	1	1	2
Washington	0	2	2

Team	Championships	Runner-Up	Champion or Runner-Up
Arizona St.	0	1	1
Auburn	0	1	1
BYU	1	0	1
Clemson	1	0	1
Colorado	1	0	1
Georgia Tech	0	1	1
Oregon	0	1	1
SMU	0	1	1
Tennessee	1	0	1
Virginia Tech	0	1	1

Table 11-5: Distribution of Football Championships and Runners-Up in NCAA Division I-A (or FBS), 1970–2007

Team	Championships	Runner-Up	Champion or Runner-Up
UCLA	6	2	8
Duke	3	5	8
Kentucky	3	2	5
Indiana	3	1	4
Michigan	1	3	4
Florida	2	1	3
Georgetown	1	2	3
Kansas	1	2	3
North Carolina	3	0	3
Syracuse	1	2	3
Arizona	1	1	2
Arkansas	1	1	2
Connecticut	2	0	2
Houston	0	2	2
Louisville	2	0	2
Marquette	1	1	2
Michigan St.	2	0	2
North Carolina St.	2	0	2
Villanova	1	1	2
Florida St.	0	1	1
Georgia Tech	0	1	1
Illinois	0	1	1
Indiana St.	0	1	1
Jacksonville	0	1	1
Maryland	1	0	1
Memphis St.	0	1	1

Team	Championships	Runner-Up	Champion or Runner-Up
Ohio St.	0	1	1
Oklahoma	0	1	1
Seton Hall	0	1	1
UNLV	1	0	1
Utah	0	1	1

Table 11-6: Distribution of Men's Basketball Championships and Runners-Up in NCAA Division I, 1970–2007

Golfer	Majors Won	Golfer	Majors Won
Tiger Woods	13	Ben Crenshaw	2
Jack Nicklaus	11	Bernhard Langer	2
Tom Watson	8	Curtis Strange	2
Nick Faldo	6	Dave Stockton	2
Lee Trevino	5	David Graham	2
Seve Ballesteros	5	Fuzzy Zoeller	2
Gary Player	4	Greg Norman	2
Ernie Els	3	Hubert Green	2
Hale Irwin	3	John Daly	2
Larry Nelson	3	Johnny Miller	2
Nick Price	3	Jose-Maria Olazabal	2
Payne Stewart	3	Lee Janzen	2
Phil Mickelson	3	Mark O'Meara	2
Ray Floyd	3	Retief Goosen	2
Vijay Singh	3	Sandy Lyle	2
Andy North	2		

Table 11-7: Distribution of Major Men's Golf Championships Won, 1970–2007

Note: Includes only multiple winners of one or more of the following: British Open, Masters, PGA Championship and U.S. Open.

Player	Grand Slam Events Won	Player	Grand Slam Events Won
Pete Sampras	14	Gustavo Kuerten	3
Roger Federer	12	Jan Kodes	3
Bjorn Borg	11	Ken Rosewall	3
Andre Agassi	8	Rafael Nadal	3
Ivan Lendl	8	Arthur Ashe	2
Jimmy Connors	8	Ilie Nastase	2
John McEnroe	7	Johan Kriek	2

Player	Grand Slam Events Won	Player	Grand Slam Events Won
Mats Wilander	7	Lleyton Hewitt	2
Boris Becker	6	Marat Safin	2
Stefan Edberg	6	Patrick Rafter	2
John Newcombe	5	Sergi Bruguera	2
Guillermo Vilas	4	Stan Smith	2
Jim Courier	4	Yevgeny Kafelnikov	2

Table 11-8: Distribution of Men's Grand Slam Tennis Championships Won, 1970–2007

Note: Includes only multiple winners of one or more of the following: Australian Open, French Open, U.S. Open, and Wimbledon.

Player	Grand Slam Events Won	Player	Grand Slam Events Won
Steffi Graf	22	Hana Mandlikova	4
Martina Navratilova	18	Evonne Goolagong	3
Chris Evert	18	Jennifer Capriati	3
Margaret Smith-Court	9	Lindsay Davenport	3
Monica Seles	9	Evonne Goolagong-Cawley	2
Serena Williams	8	Justine Henin	2
Billie Jean King	7	Maria Sharapova	2
Venus Williams	6	Mary Pierce	2
Justine Henin-Hardenne	5	Tracy Austin	2
Martina Hingis	5	Virginia Wade	2
Aranxta Sanchez-Vicario	4		

Table 11-9: Distribution of Women's Grand Slam Tennis Championships Won, 1970–2007

Note: Includes only multiple winners of one or more of the following: Australian Open, French Open, U.S. Open, and Wimbledon.

Boxer	*Ring Magazine* Fighter of the Year Awards	Boxer	*Ring Magazine* Fighter of the Year Awards
Muhammad Ali	4	Marvin Hagler	2
Evander Holyfield	3	Mike Tyson	2
George Foreman	2	Sugar Ray Leonard	2
James Toney	2	Thomas Hearns	2
Joe Frazier	2		

Table 11-10: Distribution of Fighter of the Year Awards Won, 1970–2007

Note: Includes only multiple winners of Ring Magazine's Fighter of the Year—some years featured two winners.

Driver	Number Times NASCAR Points Champion
Dale Earnhardt	7
Richard Petty	5
Jeff Gordon	4
Cale Yarborough	3
Darrell Waltrip	3
Jimmie Johnson	2
Terry Labonte	2
Tony Stewart	2

Table 11-11: Distribution of NASCAR Points Championships Won, 1970–2007

League	Total Number of Teams in 2007	Number without Championship Appearance 1970–2007	Percent of 2007 Teams w/o Appearance
MLB	30	4	13.3%
NFL	32	5	15.6%
NHL	30	5	16.7%
NBA	30	8	26.7%
College Football (D-IA/FBS)	120	93	77.5%
Original BCS Teams Only	*67*	*41*	*61.2%*
Men's College Basketball (D-I)	336	303	90.2%
Top 12 Conferences by RPI in 2007 Only	*136*	*103*	*70.7%*

Table 11-12: Percentage of 2007 Teams Failing to Appear in at Least One Championship Game/Series, by League, 1970–2007

Sources: Sources for data included in Tables 11-1 through 11-12: Shrpsports, accessed 23 March 2008 from shrpsorts.com; Ring Magazine; NASCAR.com.

The top fifth of each of the Big Four represent about half of all of the championship series or game appearances in their respective leagues between the 1970 and 2007 seasons. The top six MLB clubs accounted for 42 percent of World Series berths, while the top six NFL teams took 48 percent of Super Bowl slots. The top six NHL teams and NBA teams each accounted for a bit more than half of those leagues' final series appearances. Comparable dynastic domination has occurred in the two biggest college "amateur" sports. The top six programs in NCAA Division I-A (FBS) football account for 52 percent of National Champions or runners-up, while the top six Division I men's basketball programs were NCAA Tournament champs or runners-up 51 percent of the time.

The Big Four leagues each saw a clearly dominant team during the 1970–2007 period. The Yankees appeared in 27 percent of World Series, while the Dallas Cowboys were in 21 percent of the Super Bowls held between 1970 and 2007. The Lakers appeared in 43 percent and the Canadiens in 24 percent of the final series during those years.

Systematic imbalances also have typified the major individual sports since the time *Monday Night Football* first entered American living rooms. Tennis saw its top six male tennis players taking 40.1 percent of Grand Slam titles, and top six women players taking exactly 50 percent between 1970 and 2007. The top six NASCAR drivers accounted for 58 percent of the annual points champions, while the top six boxers took 40 percent of the "Fighter of the Year" nods between 1970 and 2007. Interestingly, the top six male golfers account for only 25 percent of the majors won during that time, despite the efforts of Jack Nicklaus and Tiger Woods.

It indeed would seem hard to make a case for dynasties harming big-time spectator sports. Yet, the families Adams, Kennedy, Bush and Clinton aside, American moral political sensibility tends to bristle at the notion of dynastic rule. Every U.S. grade school history curriculum paints a rather unflattering portrait of King George III, inculcating every child with "all men are created equal"—a line generally credited to the slave-owning Thomas Jefferson. Perhaps nowhere in American culture is meritocracy held in higher regard than in sport. Fans love a winner, at least for a while. Sometimes, it is a long while.

Level Playing Fields

> Justice [fairness] originates among approximately equal powers.
>
> —Friedrich Nietzsche[31]

The notion of fairness plays a fundamental and critical role in human thinking, and not just in sports. However, it is not at all a simple concept. Mainstream economic theory, which can get mathematically inconvenient when equity issues are introduced, has not until recently treated fairness issues with respect.[32] On the other hand, psychologists, sociologists, team owners, and every member of your grandmother's quilting circle already know that people care about fairness. Furthermore, there is evidence that our brains have evolved to value fairness, as various primates, and perhaps even other species, respond negatively to obvious inequities.[33]

Predilection toward level playing fields has obvious implications for spectator sports' organizing bodies. But to what degree? Do people want to see Tiger Woods forced to play with inferior clubs, à la Vonnegut's Harrison Bergeron, just to give the rest of the field a chance? Should leagues act as handicappers general? Not really.

The child's game Rock-Paper-Scissors is commonly used to create random outcomes, for example, in deciding who picks first in a pickup softball game. It is handy when a coin flip is impractical, as there is no strategy that would provide one player with an advantage over another. In that sense, Rock-Paper-Scissors is perfectly balanced from a competitive point of view.

For adult recreational players of the game—and there are some, apparently—there is the USARPS League, a Rock-Paper-Scissors sanctioning body. The USARPS League holds an annual Rock-Paper-Scissors tournament in Las Vegas—the 2007 edition was sponsored by Bud Light, with the winner paid $50,000. ESPN even televised the event.[34]

Despite its "perfectly" competitively balanced outcomes—in that every participant has an equal chance of winning—nobody is looking at Rock-Paper-Scissors as the ideal spectator sport. There is much more to the optimal design of competitive conditions than simply making sure that events mimic coin flips.[35] Rather, the primary purpose of the rules of a sport is to limit competitive efforts so as to "level the playing field" in some areas in order to celebrate interesting inequalities in others.

In the 1956 paper considered to be the founding of the field of sports economics, Simon Rottenberg noted that a league needs competitors of "equal 'size'" in order to be financially successful.[36] The second major paper in sports economics, by Walter Neale in 1964, echoed this sentiment, noting that in the absence of legitimate strong contenders, Joe Louis would have nobody to box, and therefore no income. Neale suggested, with no apology to St. Augustine, that the team prayer of the then-dominant Yankees ought to have been, "Lord, make us good, but not that good."[37] A similar theme is sounded in the third major paper in the field, by El-Houdiri and Quirk in 1971.[38]

There has been considerable recent investigation into what competitive balance does and should mean. A thoughtful essay published in 2002 by University of Chicago economist Allen Sanderson lays out the ying and the yang facing any sports organizing body: it must decide upon what dimensions participants should and should not compete. In effect, such bodies must determine what competition is "fair" and what is "unfair." Some of these distinctions might be made on the basis of participant safety (e.g., requiring helmets), or to increase owner profits (e.g., by setting salary caps), or to emphasize athleticism over technology (e.g., by banning certain kinds of golf clubs).[39]

Other perspectives on the correct approach to the notion of competitive balance range from the moralistic to the pragmatic. Andrew Zimbalist, a well-known sports economist, has claimed that "economic theory tells us that the optimal level of balance in a sports league is a function of the distribution of fan preferences, fan population base, and fan income across host cities."[40] He argues that fans care about fairness. Consequently, the most important role for a league in this regard is to ensure that contest outcomes are in considerable doubt before they begin.[41]

Some of Zimbalist's peers disagree with this point of view, claiming that his perspective is overly moralistic and narrow. They claim that different competitive balance concepts should guide leagues when considering different questions.[42] For example, a focus only on contest outcome uncertainty would cause a league to insufficiently address how playoffs work and the degree to which winning teams can dominate leagues over the course of many seasons.

Uncertainty Is Good

> Competitive balance is like wealth. Everyone agrees it is a good thing to have, but no one knows how much one needs.
>
> —Andrew Zimbalist[50]

There is yet as no definitive theory as to how to set up a sporting league from a competitive balance point of view, although the notion of "every team has a chance" does seem to have a legitimate claim as an overarching principle. However, there are at least three different dimensions across which such a principle might be applied. The first of these concerns individual game outcomes (game uncertainty), the second refers to the distribution of competitive success across teams in a given season (within-season uncertainty), and the third considers the degree to which individual teams' relative success or failure in one season predicts the following season's success or failure (between-season uncertainty). The unifying principle among these concepts is that outcomes—be they from games, standings or championships—must be uncertain to be interesting.

Game uncertainty is perhaps the most intuitive of the three. Of course, the absolute quality of a contest's participants matters—a Division III women's basketball game is more intriguing than watching a group of fat fifty-year old men play Saturday morning pickup ball. But even though the Green Bay Packers are among the best in the world at what they do, fans are not likely to be interested in watching them play the Ashwaubenon High School varsity, unless they happen to be local orthopedists trying to pay off med school loans. This is the reason why sports have leagues of varying levels (e.g., the NL vs. AA leagues), boxers and wrestlers are separated into weight groupings, high school basketball teams are placed into classes based on school size, thoroughbred horses are divided into groups, and tennis tournaments have seedings so as to generate the most competitive matches in the final rounds.[44]

Zimbalist's philosophy would focus attention on the degree to which fans care about differing degrees of game uncertainty. Quite a bit of analysis of this topic has been undertaken by sports economists, including some of the earliest work in the field. The general sense is that it matters, although the evidence is not as clear as might be expected.[45] Even in the same sports, some researchers have found that attendance increases with more game uncertainty while others find the opposite result.[46]

Perhaps these results have been colored by homerism. To the faithful, the most appealing contest is not just a coin flip, but one in which the home team enjoys a strong, but not complete, edge. In fact, several studies of MLB games have shown that, all else being equal, home attendance peaks when the probability of the home team winning is about 66 percent or so—meaning that the home squad should have about twice the chance of winning as the visitors.[47] Fans want to see their teams win, but they want to have a little excitement along the way, at least in baseball. Furthermore, league attempts to improve game uncertainty, and therefore attendance, may backfire if done at the expense of absolute competitive quality.[48]

Leagues seem aware that a 2–1 home team win probability can goose up attendance. Most sports leagues—particularly those that rely on the home gate for the bulk of team revenues—allow or create a degree of home field advantage. One review found that home teams win about 53 percent of baseball and football contests, and over 65 percent of hockey and basketball games.[49] Similar advantages have been found in professional soccer, with the greatest home edge found in collegiate and high school sports.[50] While some of this may come from the psychological effects of crowds cheering on home team players, leagues do not completely discourage it in other ways. In fact, some home advantages, e.g., differing field dimensions and taunting scoreboard animations, are allowed to continue.

Maximizing demand thus might be different in the case of "neutral site" contests, or for broadcasts to national audiences in which more interest might be generated via a more even balance between competitors. Given the increase in "fan tourism" wherein attendees are increasingly likely to hail from outside the host city, it may behoove leagues to reduce home advantages. In fact, there may be some evidence that this has been happening in recent years among the Big Four leagues, which seem to be experiencing declining home-winning percentages.[51]

College football conferences also seem to be sensitive to making sure that they stage games between teams that generally are of similar competitive quality. Fans of big-time college football do seem to be more interested in competitive games that matter, but apparently react negatively to teams that "run up the score."[52] Over time, conferences tend to realign or shuffle their membership in response to too many seasons with insufficiently equal teams.[53]

Within-Season Balance

The second dimension of competitive balance, within-season balance, has obvious connections to game uncertainty. This concept considers the distribution of success among teams in the league as a whole, which of course depends on the degree to which individual contests are up for grabs. There are a variety of ways that sports economists have suggested to get at this idea. For example, they measure how tight various pennant or playoff races were during the season, or how deep into the season a majority of teams remained in playoff contention. Not surprisingly, there is evidence that closer playoff races generate measurably more interest, which of course translates into more revenues for teams and leagues.[54]

More commonly studied measures of within-season balance consider the spread of winning percentages among teams at season's end. One method is to compare the winning percentages of the best and worst teams to gauge the spread between them.[55] Another approach also is rooted in the notion of coin flips. The method compares the actual dispersion of wins across teams in a league during a season to an "ideal" dispersion. The "ideal" dispersion is considered to be what would result if each contest during the season were an exact 50–50 shot. The standard deviation is most commonly used to gauge these dispersions, so the measure of interest is the ratio of the actual standard deviation to the "ideal" standard deviation. If this ratio were to be equal to one, then the league standings would represent the distribution of winning percentages expected if each game outcome during the season were a true coin flip.[56] By this measure, the NBA has long exhibited the least within-season balance, while the NFL has the highest degree of such parity. (See Figure 11-1.)

There are other ways to get at the concept of within-season balance, some of them borrowing from economists' approaches to income or wealth distribution. However, all of these techniques tend to provide the same general insights, so arguments about which technique is superior best remains in the domain of the academically pedantic. The primary interest here is similar to Zimbalist's; i.e., how do fans react to changes in within-season competitive balance?

Evidence of a relationship between balance and fan interest is a bit clearer in the case of within-season uncertainty than for game uncertainty—fans show a distinct preference for more balanced leagues, although that may not

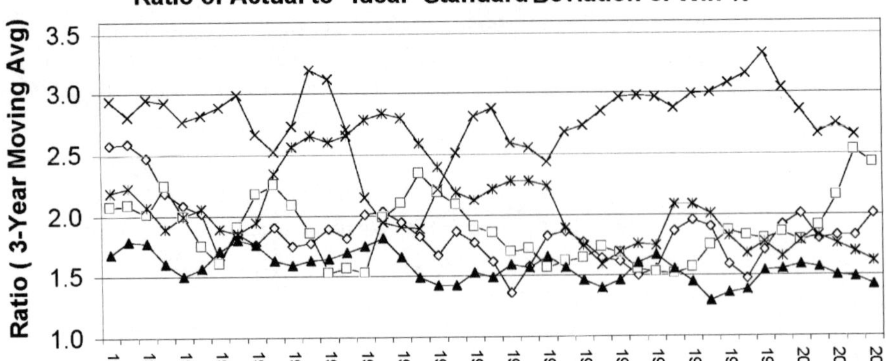

Figure 11-1: Comparison of Within-Season Competitive Balance Across Major North American Sports Leagues, 1926–2004

Source: R.D. Fort, 2006, Sports Business Pages, accessed various dates from http://rodneyfort.com/SportsData/Biz Frame.htm.

always be the way to generate the most revenue in a league.[57] Studies generally indicate that league attendance increases in those years with less dispersion among teams' winning percents.

"Playoffs? Don't Talk About—Playoffs?"

> Proper competitive balance will not exist until every well-run club has a regularly recurring reasonable hope of reaching postseason play.
>
> —Report of the Independent Members of the Commissioner's Blue Ribbon Panel on Baseball Economics[58]

At first blush, the association between within-season balance and higher attendance may seem surprising. It apparently would contradict the anecdotal evidence regarding dynasties and league golden ages. However, it is important to note that there is a bit of a difference between distribution of championships or playoff appearances from year to year, and the distribution of wins in any given season. Interest may be responding to dynasties in that they represent the very highest quality of play—something fans clearly appreciate. High-quality play may be able to trump any negative effects due to unbalanced contests—especially when the home teams in large markets are the dynasties—or due to unbalanced standings at the end of a season.[59] A case in point is the considerable attendance effect of visiting superstars in the NBA.[60] Even so, there are limits—too much domination can harm a league.[61] The challenge facing leagues is to balance these countervailing effects so as to maximize demand. How does a league create the Yankees of the 1940s and 1950s without also creating the St. Louis Browns of the same era? Or the 2007 New England Patriots without the 2008 Detroit Lions?

This matter of between-season competitive balance was the primary concern voiced in 2000 by the august panel members of MLB's "Blue Ribbon" panel. Appointed by commissioner Bud Selig, Richard Levin (president of Yale University), George Mitchell (former U.S. Senate majority leader), Paul Volcker (former Federal Reserve chairman), and George Will (noted political columnist and baseball fan) wrote that revenue disparities were leading to competitive disparities in MLB. They fretted that payroll arms races between teams were leading to escalating ticket prices, and even shutting out smaller market clubs' hopes of playing for something in October. The Chicago Cubs and sold-out Wrigley Field notwithstanding, the commission called attention to the damage that would be done to the league if most teams began April knowing that they would not play games in October that matter. They called for a philosophy that would demand economic reforms generally meant to share revenues more evenly among MLB teams than was the status quo.

Most MLB owners, especially those in smaller markets, were only too happy to agree with the report's recommendations. Such reforms would tend to produce downward pressure on star player salaries, something rarely regarded by the barons of the sport as a bad thing. But the vast majority of fans, baseball and otherwise, of course, do not really care one way or the other about whether it is the owners or the players that get to gobble the bulk of the spoils created by their rabidity. But they do care whether or not their team gets a shot at the hated dynasty. They want at least a fighting chance to knock the king down.

Who Doesn't Love an Underdog?

> I returned, and saw under the sun, that the race is not to the swift, nor the battle to the strong, neither yet bread to the wise, nor yet riches to men of understanding, nor yet favor to men of skill; but time and chance happens to them all.
>
> —Ecclesiastes 9:11

> The race is not always to the swift, nor the battle to the strong, but that's the way to bet.
>
> —Commonly attributed to Damon Runyan

Perhaps the greatest value of a dynasty to a sport comes from furnishing someone to root against. As long as our species has been telling stories, it has had its underdog tales. The majority of recorded human history is spanned by the first telling of David's slingshot prowess and the DVD release of *Hoosiers*. There might be nothing so delicious as the underdog knocking off the giant, but there is no David without Goliath.[62] Public opinion researchers have long known about how people identify with underdogs, and politicians frequently harness the idea as a primary campaign theme.[63] Underdogs and upsets certainly have played important roles in generating fan interest in the two biggest annual events in American spectator sports.

The June 8, 1966, merger agreement between the NFL and upstart AFL is responsible for the most important annual contest in American sports spectator sports: the Super Bowl. The deal called for the AFL champ to play against the NFL champ in a new post-season game, until the leagues could be more closely integrated with the expiration of the AFL's lucrative television contract with NBC. NFL commissioner Pete Rozelle wanted to hype the new event as "The Big One" but AFL pooh-bah Lamar Hunt thought that "Super Bowl" fit better with the theme of big post-season college football games.[64] Moreover, the name was close to the space-age "superball" toy by Wham-O.

The first two "big ones" did exactly nothing to dispel the widely held belief that the AFL had an exceedingly inferior product. The mighty Green Bay Packers had blown out the Kansas City Chiefs 35–10 in Super Bowl I following the 1966 season, and then victimized the Oakland Raiders 33–14 in Super Bowl II.

Super Bowl III, set between the NFL's 13–1 Baltimore Colts against the AFL's 11–3 New York Jets at Miami's Orange Bowl had all the makings of another wincing embarrassment for the AFL. The Colts had crushed the Cleveland Browns in the NFL Championship Game by a score of 34–0, and were 17-point Super Bowl favorites. Interest in the January 1969 game was a nothing like what it would soon become—tickets cost a measly $12 each, and a commercial spot sold for only $54,000.[65]

The Colts lost the game and, unlike the Jets' Joe Namath, did not look pretty doing it. The monumental upset provided magic that helped propel the Super Bowl into the biggest annual sporting event in the country, and perhaps the world. Four decades later, the New England Patriots, seeking to be the first team in NFL history to post a 19–0 season, lost to the New York Giants, an 11.5 point underdog. The contest was the most-watched sporting event in history.[66]

Upsets are part and parcel of what makes the NCAA Division I men's basketball tournament so popular—enough so for CBS to pay billions for the right to televise it. A #2 beating a #15 in the first round is a ho-hum, but it is "man bites dog" when a #15 Hampton shocks a #2 Iowa State, as happened in 2001. Likewise, the compelling narrative of the 2006 tournament was not that Florida won, but that #11 seed George Mason made it to the Final Four. Each year, the network hopes not so much for all of the #1 seeds to make the Final Four as for that occasional supposed also-ran to make the Sweet Sixteen—as #14 seeds Cleveland State did in 1986 and Tennessee-Chattanooga did in 1997. Ratings gold occurs only once in a blue moon, when a Villanova (#8 seed in 1985) or a North Carolina State (#6 seed in 1983) wins it all.

Sports underdogs can even cross over to become part of broader popular culture. By playing upon Seabiscuit's underdogism rather than his success (33 wins in 89 starts), the 2003 movie about the thoroughbred did over $120 million at box office.[67] There has been no such major motion picture glorification of other champion horses, not even Man-o-War (20 wins in 21 starts) or Secretariat (16 wins in 21 starts).[68]

Sports mega-events, with audiences that include many who would not call themselves sports fans, also can offer plenty of similar fairytale fodder. A lot more people around the world can provide details about the 1980 "Miracle on Ice" U.S. men's gold medal hockey team than could name the winning team in any subsequent winter Olympics. Women's soccer might be a horrendous sports business concept, but Brandy Chastain's sports bra following the Team U.S.A. win in the 1999 World Cup is an enduring image. Even less-successful underdogs are recalled fondly—Eddie the Eagle and the Jamaican bobsled team captured millions of Olympic hearts but no Olympic medals.

Parity Efforts

North American sports leagues differ from European soccer leagues in many ways, but one of the more significant has to do with which teams are even in the league. The Big Four have a relatively fixed slate of member "franchises," with relocation or league expansion a relatively rare thing. Not so for our friends across the Atlantic—their leagues are based on a system of "promotion and relegation." For example, the English Premier League (EPL) is comprised of 20 clubs, with each team playing all the others twice (home-and-home) for a 38 week schedule. At the end of the season, which begins in August and ends in May, the bottom three teams get relegated to the second-best league, now called the Football League Championship (formerly the Football League First Division). The three relegated teams' spots in the EPL are then taken by the best teams in the Football League Championship: the top two get promoted automatically and there is a playoff between the third through sixth teams for the remaining EPL slot.[69]

If MLB had a promotion and relegation system in place for the 2007 season, the 2008 Tampa Bay Rays and Pittsburgh Pirates might be playing in the International or Pacific Coast Leagues, while the Scranton/Wilkes-Barre Yankees and Nashville Sounds would be in the AL or NL. On the other hand, both the Rays and Pirates would have had something significant to play for at the end of 2007. Furthermore, the threat of relegation would have beefed up the teams' lousy 2007 attendance—which at 1.6 million and 1.4 million were 28th and 29th, respectively, of the 30 MLB teams. Only the Florida Marlins, at 71–91 another lousy team in 2007, put fewer fans in the stands.[70]

Even though fan interest is stimulated by promotion and relegation, the effect on competitive balance is something less clear. Teams that get promoted to the higher league often have very little chance of doing sufficiently well to avoid relegation in the following year. A team with no hope of sticking around has no incentive to spend money on good players, so they are content to serve as doormats for a year, packing their fans into their stadium to see the big-time visiting teams and their stars.[71] In the EPL, five teams account for all twenty-five first-place finishes from 1983 through 2007, and only nine teams have avoided relegation more than five times during that span. Only three teams during that quarter-century were able to win more games than they lost or tied.[72]

North American leagues engage a wide variety of rules purported to improve the various measures of competitive balance in their leagues. Many of these have little measurable impact on balance, but do deliver the delightful consequence (from the owners' perspective) of depressing player salaries. In general, anything that reduces the competitive impact of better players, or makes it more expensive to win more games, is going to make signing top talent less attractive. Owners are not stupid—it is difficult to amass and maintain the personal fortune required to own a team if one is in the habit of overpaying the hired help—and are only willing to pay players what they are worth in terms of their ability to help the team win is worth.

The oldest scheme sold to promote competitive balance is the reserve clause, with roots in the NL's earliest years. If players are free agents, so the story goes, then all the top talent will migrate to the biggest-market teams. If talent is too heavily concentrated in those markets, then fans around the rest of the league will lose interest—which will damage the league as a whole. It is a great tale, but with very little support from either history or economic theory.

During MLB's reserve clause period, which ran from the 1903 AL-NL peace agreement until the birth of free agency in 1975, New York was unquestionably the most attractive baseball market in the country. Its population was extremely large and extremely affluent compared to others across the country, and splitting it among three teams did not change its appeal to a team owner. During 1903–1975, 201 team-seasons, the New York Yankees, Brooklyn Dodgers, and New York Giants posted a combined 16,898 wins and 13,929 losses, which works out to an average season record of about 84–69—a 0.548 winning percentage. The three teams went 0.500 or better 71.1 percent of the time, and took first place in 27 percent of their seasons in New York. Such concentration of talent and success is not exactly consistent with the "reserve clause promotes improved balance" argument. Furthermore, the post–free agency eras in each of the Big Four generally—but not universally—have been associated with increases in within-season competitive balance measures.[73]

Simon Rottenberg's 1956 landmark paper provided a simple and elegant theoretical explanation for the failure of the reserve system to ensure competitive balance. If players can be bought and sold by teams, then there are strong economic incentives for the most talented to migrate away from smaller to larger, more lucrative, markets.[74] This is because a great player is worth more to a big market club than a small market club—Wayne Gretzkey simply can generate more ticket and TV revenue in Los Angeles than he can in Edmonton. Consequently, the big market team can make a cash offer to a small market team for an amount that is less than what the player is worth in the large market, but more than he is worth in the small market. As long as player talent markets work efficiently, good players will flow from weak to strong markets—although league commissioners can and have tossed sand in the gears of player exchange markets on occasions when transfers were considered *too* grossly consistent with Rottenberg's theory.[75]

There is little evidence to support the assertion that free agency has had clear effects on a league's competitive balance—it does not change the fact that players move, but allows the player instead of the small market owner to cash in on the value of his talent.[76] However, free agency may lead to more roster turnover, which has been found to harm hometown fan interest in a team, at least in MLB.[77]

Another scheme sold to enhance competitive balance is a reverse-order-of-finish draft system, the likes of which began in the NFL before the 1936 season. Again, both history and theory suggest that the draft does more to lower player salaries than it does to promote competitive balance.[78] The NL's competitive balance did not change in the wake of MLB's institution of an entering player draft in 1965, and while competitive balance in the AL improved, this probably had more to do with poor management by the Yankees' then-owners—the team's 1965–75 World Series drought seemed to coincide with CBS ownership of the team.[79]

Entering player drafts are iffy affairs—it is not at all clear that the best players are those taken earliest, despite millions of dollars of expenditures by teams seeking to draft more efficiently. For example, only about two-thirds of MLB first-round picks ever even play in a big-league game, while the average quarterback in the 1999–2006 Super Bowls was picked at the end of the third (of seven) round—and three of those appearances were by undrafted QBs.[80]

In any event, players are very often not drafted in accordance with reverse-order-of-finish. The NBA and NHL have lottery systems to reduce the incentive to tank games at the end of a season in order to improve draft position. NFL drafts include "compensatory picks" at the end of Rounds 3 through 7 that are awarded to teams based on losses of veteran players with limited free agency. Furthermore, there is a lot of horse-trading of draft picks among NFL teams. All told, more than 40 percent of the draft picks made by NFL teams in 2007 were *not* in reverse-order-of-finish.[81]

The root of any enduring competitive imbalance problem is an enduring problem of roster quality imbalance. Teams in North American leagues compete for players in a common labor market, but sell much of their product—game tickets, local broadcast, etc.—in different markets. In general, any league-wide scheme that makes talent cost more for bigger-market teams (e.g., "luxury taxes" that make the cost of signing a player more than his salary) or reduces the benefits to winning more for big-market than small-market teams (e.g., revenue sharing) will improve balance—bigger teams have less incentive to have dominating rosters. However, these plans can get quite complex, and some work better than others at improving balance—in fact, MLB even once managed to come up with a plan that incentivized bad teams to lose more.[82]

Finally, leagues can impose payroll or salary caps in their efforts to reduce the competitive disparities between the haves and the have-nots. The theory behind caps is that they can prohibit a well-financed team from spending its way into a championship. This sounds like an obvious way to go, but the devil is in the details—several devils, actually. First, collective bargaining over caps tends to produce *very* complicated systems loaded with loopholes. Agents of top players conspire with cash-flush owners, and quickly figure out how to get around the cap system. Teams hire "capologists," whose main responsibility is to invent, exploit, and manage the arcaneries of the league's system—which in itself becomes an area of competition among teams. Those loopholes generally can only be addressed during the next union contract battle, and the supposed fixes can open up other go-arounds. The "Larry Bird" exemption in the NBA and amortizing signing bonuses over long-term contracts in the NFL are two clear examples of such loopholes.[83]

Second, modern sports history is rife with examples of big-salary signees that went bust. While nobody seriously argues that on average, higher salaries can attract better athletes, the state of the art of teams' player evaluation is sufficiently bad so that it remains a very inefficient process. Furthermore, players are not free agents until several years in their careers—Michael Lewis's 2003 *Moneyball* suggests that front offices have yet to figure out how to optimally spend their salary dollars.

The bottom line is that the teams with the highest payrolls do *not* always win, although teams that spend far too little do not win, either. In fact, systematic studies of the relationships between payroll spending and team winning, particularly in baseball, yield inconclusive results.[84]

So what is the bottom line on fans' desire for competitive balance? Like chastity, we really do not want too much of it, nor do we really want it too soon. Fans are quite content to watch dynasties appear, dominate, and fade in the face of the new dynasty.

"The King is dead. Long live the King!"

12

FANS "KANT" PUT UP WITH CHEATING

For when the One Great Scorer comes to mark against your name, He writes—not that you won or lost—but how you played the Game.

—*Grantland Rice*[1]

Sports' Categorical Imperative

It is impossible to separate the rich philosophy that underpins the notion of spectator sports from fan interest in them. Any discussion about the "right" amount of competitive balance from the fan perspective necessarily invokes concepts of a Rawlsian justice—that decisions about what is competitively fair or unfair need to be made *before* the schedules are set and the games played. Indeed, fans might even consider competitive justice to be the first virtue of any organizing body in a sport.[2]

Competitive balance is not the only desirable moral quality that fans consider, however. There is an entire set of critical core values that make sports different from other forms of entertainment, both for participants and spectators alike. These values fall into two camps: sportsmanship, the internal set of virtues that govern personal behavior, and contest legitimacy, the competitive authenticity of a contest or league.[3] Violation of either is a transgression of sports' Kantian categorical imperative. True fans can see no end that can justify a means compromising these sacred principles. The sensationality of scandals that breach the imperatives prove the depth at which they are held. (See Table 12-1.)

Scandal	**Sport/League**	**Type**
Black Sox World Series	MLB	Game-fixing
Ty Cobb and Tris Speaker Game-Rigging	MLB	Game-fixing
Jim Thorpe Loses His Gold Medals	Olympics	Violation of Amateurism
1940s-50s Basketball Point-Shaving	NCAA	Game-fixing

Scandal	Sport/League	Type
Suspension of Alex Karras and Paul Hornung	NFL	Gambling
West Point Football Cheating Scandal	NCAA	Personal Behavior
SMU Football "Death Penalty"	NCAA	Violation of Amateurism
Pete Rose Gambling Scandal	MLB	Gambling
Tonya Harding and Nancy Kerrigan Incident	Olympics	Personal Behavior, Contest-fixing
University of Michigan Basketball Payments	NCAA	Violation of Amateurism
Marge Schott's Various Racist and Insensitive Remarks	MLB	Personal Behavior
Jim Harrick University of Georgia Basketball Exam Scandal	NCAA	Personal Behavior
Danny Almonte Little League Age Falsification	Little League Baseball	Ineligible Players
George O'Leary Resume Fabrication	NCAA	Bribery
2002 Winter Olympic Bid-Rigging	Olympics	Personal Behavior
NBA Las Vegas All-Star Game Weekend	NBA	Personal Behavior
2005 Minnesota Vikings "Love Boat"	NFL	Personal Behavior
Operation Slapshot Investigation into Rick Tocchet Gambling Ring	NHL	Gambling
Floyd Landis Tour de France Scandal	Bicycling	Doping
Series of Separate Incidents Involving Michael Vick, Pacman Jones, Tank Johnson, and Chris Henry	NFL	Personal Behavior
NBA Referee Tim Donaghy Gambling Scandal	NBA	Game-fixing
Steroids in Baseball	MLB	Doping
New England Patriots "Spygate"	NFL	League Rules Violations

Table 12-1: Selected North American Spectator Sport Scandals

Assembled by the author from various sources.[4]

So Why Cheat?

Winning isn't everything. It's the only thing.

—Vince Lombardi[5]

Where psychologists and sociologists have built complicated theories about why people cheat in sport, economists have opted for the parsimony of rationality: decisions get made by comparing benefits to costs. Since great monetary and psychic rewards come with winning, they can provide strong incentive, particularly to those sufficiently talented and motivated to become elite-level athletes in the first place. Fans see also-rans as very poor substitutes for winners—even if the also-ran is better than all but three or four other competitors on earth.[6] Winning Olympic gold brings great fame and fortune; a fourth-place finish barely earns a home-town parade. Sportsmanship ideals might seem far less important if abandoning them could provide a winning edge. Only pathologically partisan fans are likely to overlook such a compromise.

Similarly, the temptation to participate in a contest-fixing might overpower an athlete's sense of right and wrong. Matches will be thrown when gamblers can offer enough athletes far more money to throw a game than they could ever earn legitimately. While the penalties for being caught generally are quite severe, the likelihood of being caught can be very small. If discovery is deemed sufficiently unlikely and the ill-gotten gains big enough, then the coldly rational will succumb to the money and compromise the contest.

Of course, such decision calculus is hardly unique to athletes. Occasions of temptation have faced people since the dawn of human sapience. Every day, people have to decide whether or not to cheat on their taxes or spouses, whether to give their best or slack off at their jobs, and whether or not to treat their fellow man well or poorly. Athletes, coaches, referees, and owners might make their choices more publicly than the rest of us, but not any differently.

A culture or society in which all decisions were made according to a stark naked rationality would not be a particularly satisfying one, at least if the speculations of post-apocalyptic literature have any predictive ability. Fortunately, this usually is not the case as human groups tend to evolve ethical systems for themselves. Ethics provide a bulwark against raw self-interest by internalizing some of the external costs of selfish decisions. Violation of one's own ethical code, whether observed by others or not, brings with it its own disutility. Ethics still may fail to prevent cheating when the rewards to doing so are great enough, but they do raise the bar.

The world in 2000 was a far wealthier place than it was in 1900. The 21st century is likely to see several billion more people rise out of the desperation of impoverished subsistence. As they do, as their basic needs for food, clothing, and shelter are met, they will begin to spend more money on cultural pursuits, including spectator sports. As huge as the money is now for those at the top of their games, it will pale compared to what it will soon become. Some superstar somewhere in the world before long will sign the first $1 billion contract. Meanwhile, second-tier stars will earn far less, although a $50 million contract is nothing to sneeze at. The ethos of sport may prove to be fans' only enduring hope against mounting temptations facing sports participants.

The list of what a person would *not* do in order to get $1 billion versus the $50 million contracts that second-tier stars will sign is brief indeed. "Compromising my integrity" perhaps is the only item likely to be common across different athletes' lists. In order to make it on those lists, however, athletes must place an extraordinarily high value on their integrity. This value must derive from a broader sporting ethos, one that has to be rooted in fans and in greater society. It is incumbent upon all that care about spectator sports to send a clear message that honor and integrity have a greater value than any monetary reward imaginable. The integrity of spectator sports cannot otherwise withstand the already enormous and growing economic forces that define them.

The Big Four leagues' self-serving arguments in favor of the reserve system offer only a weak defense of it. The system does not prohibit migration of good players to good markets. As long as leagues operate as cartels, and teams are not free to move from weaker markets to stronger ones, inherent disparities in revenue opportunities will endure. However, the leagues may have missed perhaps the only potentially legitimate argument in favor of reserve clauses: blunting the tournament incentives for free agent athletes.

Tournament organizers in general are in the business of creating events that generate the most interest among spectators. This goal is accomplished by attracting the most talented participants and then motivating them to put forth their best efforts. However, if the returns to efforts are "too high," negative unintended consequences can result.[7] Such may be the case with the current reserve-free agent systems in the Big Four. Each player has a number of years of indentured servitude at a salary typically lower than his economic value to his team. When the player becomes a free agent, he can auction his services to the highest bidder—the top players hit the jackpot, often signed by auction-fevered owners that victimize themselves with the winner's curse.[8]

During each league's free agent season, the top player at each position hits the jackpot for far more money than the second-, third-, and fourth-best—even if he is only marginally better than his cohort. Similarly, the athletes picked earliest in player entry drafts tend to make gobs more money than those chosen later—despite being an unknown quantity. Changing these reward systems to become flatter will surely reduce incentives to compromise integrity to move up the food chain.

However, any artificial depressing of market-derived salaries conflicts with another sports ethos: meritocracy. The situation is trickier in individual sports, particularly those represented in the Olympic games. The rewards to winning come from outside the sports themselves. Nationalistic pride elevates athletes to patriots, so corporations pay kings' ransoms to buy athletes' reflected glory for their products. Again, only if the sporting public changes its winner-take-all ethos will athletes' over-incentivization be quelled—not a very likely scenario.

Instead of strengthening, it may be that the culture of sporting ethos may in fact be deteriorating, at least in the U.S.[9] Victorian sensibilities of fair play seem to be bested now by a new Darwinism. While financial scandals are as old as finance, it would be difficult to refute a proposition that the scale and scope have ballooned during the last couple of decades. Furthermore, this phenomenon may be broader than just in sport, and the trend may be more prevalent among the young—college cheating is on the rise as students fall to the easy lure of academic dishonesty offered by the Internet.[10]

Enforcement of the integrity via police methods certainly has to be part of any solution to curb cheating, in sports and elsewhere. It is highly unlikely to be enough, however. Plagiarism cannot be curbed solely by turning professors into prosecutors, nor can greedy corporate CEOs be stopped solely by constant board monitoring. They must be accompanied by an internal sense of honor heavily reinforced both by one's peers as well as by society at large. Self-regulation may seem like a joke, but it may offer the only hope against rising rewards to breaking the rules, in sports and otherwise.

There Are Rules, and Then There Are Rules

Nice guys finish last.

—Commonly attributed to Leo Durocher[11]

All sports have rules. Some rules exist to enhance the appeal of watching the sport, while others are there to protect the safety of the participants.[12] But perhaps the most interesting are rules meant to preserve the balance between competitors that is believed to constitute the essence of the sport in question. They determine exactly how participants compete in that sport.

To a great degree, a sport's form rulebook represents the current state of balance in a constant cat-and-mouse game among its contestants. Because those that make their living in professional spectator sport tend to be quite competitive, they are in the business of finding ways "within the rules" to get an advantage on their opponents. Successful strategies will be copy-catted by others, so ignoring such new strategic behaviors is not an option for a sport's rule-making body. It must explicitly forbid them or approve them, as choosing not to act would constitute condoning the strategy.

Sometimes innovations are accepted by spectators and participants alike as smart coaching. For example, the set of strategic philosophies that evolved into Bill Walsh's "West Coast offense" led the San Francisco 49ers to dominate the NFL between 1981 and 1988. The team went 120–35–1 (.704) during these eight seasons, winning 6 divisional championships and three Super

Bowls.[13] Nobody ever suggested that Walsh showed poor sportsmanship simply because he found a new way to play offense in the NFL, even if this new way confused and bedeviled opponents. Soon his coaching protégés colonized sidelines across the NFL, as his system became adopted by a significant number of team offenses.

On the other hand, a new strategy can instead be rejected by a sport's culture like a mismatched kidney transplant. One example is the "attack offense." Deployed by Walsh disciple Sam Wyche in the late 1980s when he was coach of the Cincinnati Bengals, the gimmick involved the way in which the Bengals would conduct their pre-play offensive huddle. By including thirteen or fourteen players instead of the usual eleven, opposing defenses would not be able to determine which specific Bengal personnel package would be on the field, and therefore be unable to counter appropriately with their own personnel packages. It worked well for the Bengals during the 1988 NFL season—the team posted a 12–4 record, and earned the right to represent the AFC in that year's Super Bowl. They lost 20–16 to Walsh's 49ers. [14]

Like Walsh's West Coast innovations, Wyche's attack offense was held by all parties to be legal under prevailing NFL rules. However, unlike Walsh, Wyche was found by opposing coaches, and eventually the NFL, to have violated good sportsmanship, and the attack offense was banned after the 1988 season.[15] The NFL's post-season deliberations that led to the ban determined that Wyche had committed the sin of inconsistency within "the spirit of the game." Such deliberations form the "case law" associated with any given sport, and evolve so as to be reflective of its core values.

Whereas respect for the game and its rules is a highly prized virtue in sports, so is being clever in finding new ways that are both "around them" and "within them."[16] The consequence of the tension between this competitive innovation and competitive restriction is that sports rulebooks become very thick and legalistic.

No matter how comprehensive a rulebook becomes, it can never encompass the entirety of the ethos governing its sport. In addition to its fully specified codes, every sport also has a set of "unwritten rules," perhaps more properly understood as the etiquette or a culture that is unique to that sport. Penalties for violations of unwritten rules are just as real as for written rules, although perhaps more subjective.

Fans and participants alike may regard the unwritten rules to be more morally considerable than the written ones. For example, some strategic violations of the written rules, such as by fouling late in a basketball game, are treated favorably by fans as marks of smart play, not failures of sportsmanship. Conversely, "legal" breaches of etiquette, such as stealing a catcher's signals to the pitcher or making noise during an opponent's putt, are held in very low esteem. Many a NASCAR driver has been put into a wall in retribution for sins of etiquette.

Unwritten rules need some sort of self-enforcement, or they will fade away. Baseball perhaps provides the most obvious examples of how this works. Stealing signs? The next pitch is coming at the batter's head. Throwing at our batter's head? Your batter will have to hit the dirt in the next inning. Sliding into second base spikes-high, beyond what is considered "good play"? More high and inside pitches.

But the greatest self-enforcement impetus comes simply from the cultural forces that socially punish unwritten rules violators. Economists use the term "sabotage" to represent negative activities beyond what is considered to be legitimate defensive play. Such dirty play may be within or outside of the written rules, but the specific status is not terribly germane to defining the line between good strategy and sabotage. In fact, some of the most interesting moral controversies in sports involve debates on just these issues. Frequently it is not the rule-making bodies that make the call about whether a given strategy constitutes sabotage or not; it is the manner in which fellow competitors react.

Athletes whose strategic choices tip the scales toward hypercompetitiveness or sabotage are shunned by their peers and by history. For example, Ty Cobb is—rightfully—remembered for being a "violent psychopath" as much as he is for being one of the most productive hitters in MLB history. His contemporaries likely regarded his sharp spikes with greater deference than his sharp batting eye.

Player violence can be a complex issue. Some sports, such as football and boxing, include strong physical aggression as an integral part of their play. However, a boxer is not wronged if his opponent scores a knockout punch, but a basketball player is.[17] "Cheap shots" are intentional actions meant to injure opponents outside the rules. Aside from Cobb, players known for illegitimate use of violence to gain competitive advantages include Karl Malone (NBA), Bill Lambier (NBA), Ulf Samuelsson (NHL), Conrad Dobler (NFL), and Bill Romanowski (NFL).[18] Each will be forever best known as a rogue—outside of their teams' home towns, that is. In the same way, Christopher Columbus, a villain in Native American circles, is still a hero to the Italian-American community.

Sportsmanship

There perhaps is no more honored figure in college football than John Heisman. Heisman went to Brown University for two years before transferring to the University of Pennsylvania in 1889, where he played varsity football for three seasons. During his career, Penn played against Walter Camp's Yale University, losing all three times—by a combined score of 128–10. Heisman's fame, however, came after his playing days were over. Ivy League law degree in hand, he went on to a distinguished three-decade coaching career at Oberlin College, Auburn University, Penn, Georgia Tech, Washington and Jefferson College, and Rice University. In his retirement, he became the first athletic director of New York's Downtown Athletic Club, where he set up a voting system meant to identify the best college player in the country each year.[19]

Heisman's most-enduring achievement came as a result of his successful badgering of rules-committee patriarch Camp for the legalization of the forward pass, which finally occurred in 1906. However, Heisman's name is also associated with the most lop-sided score in college football history. On October 7, 1916, Heisman's Georgia Tech football team avenged an earlier 22–0 baseball loss to Cumberland College wherein Cumberland had been suspected of using ringers. Even though Cumberland had actually disbanded its football team prior to the 1916 season, Heisman insisted that they honor their contract, which included a $3,000 payment to Tech in the event of forfeit. Cumberland assembled a ragtag team that Tech eviscerated 222–0 in the biggest blowout in college football history.[20]

It is difficult to imagine that the 870 individuals now entrusted with annual Heisman trophy ballots would not take into account the sportsmanlike character in making their choices—O.J. Simpson notwithstanding. Georgia Tech's 1916 whomping Cumberland would cause a firestorm among college football fans were it to happen today, particularly under the circumstances. It would be considered poor sportsmanship in the extreme as it overemphasizes the ideal of maximum effort at the expense of the ideal of respect for opponents.[21]

Spectators tend to react with more disgust than admiration to college football coaches who choose to embarrass weaker opponents after a contest is clearly won.[22] In 2002, leaders of the Bowl Championship Series reacted in pragmatic fashion to fans' distaste for shameless blowouts by eliminating "margin of victory" as an element considered by BCS computer ranking models.[23]

Participants in a sporting contest are expected by fans to hew to an internal compass of treasured virtues captured by the sweeping notion of "sportsmanship." A precise definition, however, remains elusive, although some have tried to nail it down.[24] One of the difficulties in doing so is that part of what is considered sportsmanship is not unique to sports, but instead reflects a broader set of cultural values that can evolve with society. Part of being a good sportsman or sportswoman is simply being a good man or woman, whatever that means at the relevant time and place. Fans hold their heroes in high regard as human beings, seemingly expecting them to never fail to meet minimum standards of personal behavior, both on and off the competitive battlefield. Perhaps this perspective springs from how fans want to worship their sports heroes, and a refusal to admit that athletic prowess can be driven from moral character.

However, there clearly is something a bit more enduring to the concept of sportsmanship than general societal expectations of behavior. Certainly a good sportsman must reflect these, but he or she must also balance values of doing one's personal competitive best against notions of fairness, trustworthiness, and generosity.[25] While the integrity of competition must be honored by offering maximum competitive effort, a line is drawn short of violating either written or unwritten rules of play. Sportsmanship is honored insofar as a strangely balanced version of the Golden Rule applies: I will try my best to beat you fairly, and expect the same of you. However, the realization of this philosophy can be sticky.

Sportsmanship is an internal concept, so intention matters. A distracted driver who mistakenly runs a red light, killing an innocent bicyclist, is morally guilty of something different than someone intentionally trying to run down an ex-spouse. Negligence is not the same as murder, nor is a murder of passion the same as premeditated homicide.

When Sammy Sosa was found to be using a corked bat in a 2003 game against the Tampa Bay Devil Rays, there was no doubt that doing so violated the rules. A corked bat is considered to create an advantage over an opponent that is clearly against MLB Rule 6.06(d).[26]

But was Sosa guilty of bad sportsmanship? The answer depends on intent. Sosa claimed that he picked up a corked batting practice bat by mistake, not by intention. MLB apparently did not buy Sosa's protests that he was more dumb than crooked—he was suspended for eight games.[27]

Sometimes good intentions can even trump written rules. In a 1983 game between the Kansas City Royals and the New York Yankees, George Brett hit a two-run homer with two outs in the top of the ninth inning to give his Royals a 5–4 lead. With a little help from Yankees manager Billy Martin, who charged out of the dugout in protest, umpires immediately found that Brett's bat had violated MLB Rule 1.10(b)—pine tar too far up the bat handle. The home run was disallowed on the spot, and he was ruled out, ending the game with a 4–3 Yankee win. (Brett's rather animated reaction to the decision is considered one of the more amusing videotaped moments in MLB history.) Four days later, AL president Lee McPhail overturned the umpires' decision on the basis that Brett's bat did not "violate the spirit of the rules." The home run was re-allowed, and the final four outs of the game were replayed three weeks, four days, four hours, and fourteen minutes later. After 12 more minutes, the Yankees had lost, 5–4.[28]

Scandalous!

> It is not easy as it might initially be thought to define cheating in sport, and just as difficult to specify precisely what is wrong morally with such behavior, and why fair play should be prized.
>
> —Oliver Leaman[29]

Poor sportsmanship and sabotage take from fans something they clearly treasure about a sport: its sense of moral virtue. But if sabotage is thievery, then match-fixing is murder, and doping is treason.[30] Conspiracies to predetermine contest outcomes kill that which distinguishes sport from other entertainment. Doping betrays the human dimension that distinguishes athleticism from engineering. These two violations of competitive legitimacy are far worse transgressions against fans' moral sensibilities than poor sportsmanship or even sabotage.

Immanuel Kant argues that a person should not be treated solely as means to an end. Nor should the legitimacy of a contest ever be compromised for utilitarian goals. To predetermine the course and outcome of a wrestling match cannot be justified, no matter how much it would please unsuspecting fans. Such a match is not sport but show business, and an affront to the moral sensibilities of the spectator. It is no accident that match-fixing incidents, generally the result of gambling, headline the hall of shame of modern sport scandals.

Gambling has a history as long as that of spectator sport; so no doubt match-fixing via bribes or threats to athletes or referees do as well. The ancient Olympic games apparently had a bit of a problem with this, with powerful military and governmental officials finding oddly favorable outcomes in chariot races.[31] In fact, the judges of Olympic equestrian events themselves were allowed to enter horses until the practice was banned in 372 B.C. following a little too much competitive success.[32] Everyone's favorite Roman emperor, Nero, apparently bought a race victory in 67 A.D.—despite falling out of the chariot in the process.[33] Corruption plainly has been part of the Olympic games since their inception, despite the lofty ideals generally associated with them.

In this context, there was nothing particularly innovative about the Olympic figure skating controversies of 1994 and 2002. In 1994, associates of skater Tonya Harding attempted to get competing skater Nancy Kerrigan out of the U.S. Figure Skating Championships, and off the U.S. Olympic team, by whacking her across the knee with a bat. Kerrigan did have to drop out of the U.S. competition, but she still was able to participate in the Lillehammer Olympics games several weeks later. The incident became a media circus, with tickets to the final program going for an unheard-of $1,000 a piece. The event generated the highest television ratings ever for an Olympic broadcast, and the fourth-largest audience in the history of television. Kerrigan became a star, even hosting NBC's *Saturday Night Live* three weeks later. The program garnered *SNL* higher ratings than it had gotten in the prior six years.[34] The Kerrigan hit was a popular hit, too.

Two winter Olympiads later, figure skating saw yet another scandal, this time an apparent vote-trading scheme among judges. To the extent that it appeared to be an institutional rather than a personal violation of competitive integrity, the second affair was much more serious. Under the alleged plan, a French judge was to help ensure that a Russian pair would win one competition in exchange for a French team winning one a few days later. But the judge's uniquely low marks for a Canadian pair's performance in the first competition aroused suspicion, and the scheme was outed. The International Olympic Committee banned both the judge and the head of the French skating organization, also believed to be a co-conspirator, for three years—a seemingly light sentence given the gravity of the alleged offense.[35] Perhaps the punishment reflected a lurid development in the case—the connection of a Russian organized crime figure, widely thought to have had ties to Russian arms trading and art smuggling. During the hearings, the Russian was indicated as a driving force in helping convince the two French skating officials to participate in the trade. Supposedly involved with the incident as part of a convoluted effort to facilitate the renewal of his French visa, the crime figure had also been implicated in a plot to extort $10 million from the Russian ice skating federation chief.[36] Outside of elite skating circles, surprisingly little has been made of the incident since it happened, although the IOC has publicly taken a very dim view of the sequence of events.

Neither one of the recent skating scandals was ever shown to have involved gambling. However, the complicated relationship that modern sports has with gambling is testimony to the centrality of the legitimacy of matches. On one hand, a little action on the side has an obvious positive impact on a fan's interest in a sporting event—which is always welcomed by profit-seeking organizing bodies. On the other hand, robust gambling markets create moral hazard for contest participants—the opportunities to succumb to temptation and profit from fixed matches is simply too great to tolerate. As a result, betting on one's own game is strictly *verboten* by any responsible league or organizing body. Nearly without exception, discovered violations of gambling bans have swift and strong consequences for the participants, and figure prominently in any collection of sports scandals.

Early American sports had its share of competitive legitimacy issues, gambling and otherwise. For example, many supposedly gentlemanly amateur baseball players were only too happy to share in the gate receipts in return for their talents long before the National Association of Professional Baseball Players (NAABP) formerly recognized pay-for-play. 19th century college football was rife with amateurism and other roster irregularities during its quick rise in stature. But the early association of baseball and gamblers was a real source of concern to Henry Chadwick, and later, to William Hulbert.

The granddaddy of all North American gambling-related match-fixing tales, the Black Sox scandal, came long after the amateurism question seemed to have been settled, at least in baseball. Gamblers seeking to fix the 1919 World Series attempted to bribe a number of White Sox players to throw games. In the wake of the incident, eight players were banned from baseball for life, and the position of baseball commissioner was established. The first occupant of that office was owner-friendly Judge Kenesaw Mountain Landis.

As North American sports grew in popularity, so did the money, and along with it, the booty associated with fixing games. Despite baseball's vigorous response to the Black Sox incident, MLB still saw later gambling-related scandals in 1943, when Landis ordered Philadelphia Phillies owner William Cox to sell his team in the wake of several admitted small wagers earlier in the season. Commissioner Happy Chandler banned Brooklyn Dodgers manager Leo Durocher for the entire 1947 season for consorting with gamblers. In 1970, Detroit Tigers pitcher Denny McClain was suspended for three months by commissioner Bowie Kuhn for a 1967 incident involving bookmaking. Of course, the owner of MLB's all-time hits record, Pete Rose, was banned from baseball by Commissioner Fay Vincent in 1989 for not only betting on MLB games, but on the Cincinnati Reds, then managed by Rose. Two years later, Vincent put the Phillies' Lenny Dykstra on a one year probation for admitting to having lost between fifty and one hundred thousand dollars in illegal poker games in Mississippi following the 1989 season.[37]

The invention of point-spread gambling in Chicago by Connecticut math teacher-turned-bookie in the 1940s revolutionized sports gambling.[38] Easy to understand and administer, the method made games between competitively unbalanced teams eminently more interesting to bettors. Spread betting also eased the cost of match-fixing to athletes on heavily favored teams. No longer would a suspicious loss be required to make a fix profitable—all that was needed would be to win by less than the point spread. Before the days of free agency, the relatively low pay for athletes, while still above the average American salary, created a hospitable environment for point-shaving. Ethically flexible players could be more easily convinced to buy in—

point-shaving would not really hurt their teams as they would win anyway, just by fewer points than expected.

The 1946 NFL Championship game pitted the New York Giants against the ten-point favorite Chicago Bears. Just the prior Sunday, the Bears had been only slight favorites, but a mass of money had come in on them during the week. The spread jumped, and with it a few law enforcement eyebrows. Government wiretaps put to work on the matter confirmed that the fix might be in, and that a couple of New York players might be in on it.

A meeting was hastily arranged at Gracie Mansion between prosecutors, NFL Commissioner Bert Bell, and the New York mayor the night before the game. Two Giant players, fullback Merle Hapes and quarterback Frank Filchock, were called in and confronted with what had been learned. Hapes admitted that he indeed had been offered a $2,500 bribe by gambler Alvin Paris to lose the game by more than the spread. The deal would also include the proceeds from a $1,000 bet on the Bears. Filchock denied having been offered the deal. Bell rewarded Hapes's admission by suspending him indefinitely for failing to report the bribe attempt sooner, but let Filchock play. Filchock threw six interceptions, and the Giants lost the game in a wagering "push," 24–14. He later admitted to the offer, and was also suspended by Bell.[39]

The legal case against the NFL fixers dragged into 1947. It got a great deal of press attention in New York amid growing public awareness of the infiltration of sport by gamblers. Shortly before, the headiness of impending military victories in Europe and Japan had been bruised by a similar point-shaving scandal in college basketball.

Unlike modern-day, highly-paid sports superstars with multi-million-dollar salaries at stake, "amateur" athletes then and now are particularly vulnerable to gamblers' offers. The athletes have relatively little of their own money at stake, even if caught. Furthermore, a missed shot or careless turnover in basketball is difficult to attribute to ill intentions, but can change a game's outcome. In January 1945, two Brooklyn gamblers were taken into custody for paying five Brooklyn College players $1,000 to throw the following day's game against the University of Akron. The deal included a promise to pay the players an additional $2,000 following the game.[40] As the scandal unfolded, it became obvious that not only was college basketball riddled with big-time gambling connections, but that many officials had been warned of that fact and had chosen to do nothing.

Political opportunists took advantage of the Brooklyn College affair to demagogue, holding hearing after hearing on the matter. Estimates surfaced of $10 million a day in wagers on East Coast basketball games and $20 million on two Notre Dame–Army football games alone.[41] Ned Irish, chief of

New York's Madison Square Garden, was called on the carpet to explain the threat posed by his big-time college basketball for-profit tournament extravaganzas.[42] Despite all the public attention, big-money tournaments continued to be played, and gamblers' presence in college basketball continued to increase.

In early 1951, *New York Journal American* sports editor Max Kase grew suspicious of the low victory margins by two local powerhouse basketball teams, Long Island University (LIU) and defending national champion City College of New York (CCNY). After burning a little shoe leather chasing sources in seedy bars and bookie joints, he became convinced that there were players being paid to shave points. He took his evidence to district attorney Frank Hogan, who apparently found Kase's evidence credible. Hogan arrested three members of the CCNY squad along with a gambler, and then arrested three LIU players three weeks later. The breadth of the scandal spread like contagion, eventually involving thirty-two players from seven different schools, including Manhattan College, Bradley University, the University of Toledo, and the University of Kentucky.[43]

Point-shaving scandals did not disappear from college basketball or football even in the wake of the CCNY scandal. About every decade or so since, another one pops up. In 2006, an academic paper published in the most prestigious academic journal in economics claimed that there is good statistical evidence to suggest that point-shaving may remain quite widespread in NCAA college basketball.[44] The findings are consistent with a recent NCAA survey in which 1.5 percent of players knew of a teammate that had taken money for playing poorly.[45]

As long as college players remain unpaid, or lightly paid, for their contributions, they will face continued temptation to shave points or throw games that have high public interest. Minor professional leagues do not enjoy such attention. Big, strange wagers on Major League Lacrosse or Slamball are going to raise alarms, so there is insufficient opportunity for gamblers to make money there. Big-time pro sports do get enough attention for robust gambling markets, but their highly paid players are far harder to entice with money. Starting pitchers and quarterbacks might be able to tank games with enough reliability to attract game-fixers, but they make far too much to be bribed.

Multi-million-dollar players are tough to buy, but they can be extorted. Threats of exposure of personal misbehavior, such as marital infidelity or drug use, can dry up the endorsement gravy train and stop the fat paychecks. The real concern associated with the 1999–2001 Atlanta Gold Club scandal was that athletes might have been blackmailed by shady associates of the club's owners over sexual relations with dancers. Interestingly, the media infatuation with the sordid celebrity gossip details of the story generally failed to consider this possibility. Instead, it tended to focus on how the players had let fans down via their carnality.[46]

Unlike top athletes, referees, umpires, and coaches tend to make relatively modest pay, even in the biggest of spectator sports. The 2007 NBA scandal involving referee Tim Donaghy was the result of his gambling problem, but the fact that NBA referees earn between $85,000 and $300,000 per year also played a role. MLB umpires and NHL referees earn somewhat similar salaries, while NFL referees (a part-time position) earn about half of that.[47] This is far more than most Americans, but not enough to resist multi-million-dollar windfalls or threats of public humiliation or physical violence.[48]

Head coaches in the Big Four often sign multi-million-dollar salaries, but their assistant coaches typically do not. While they are not generally in a position to fix games, subordinate coaches and trainers do have inside information regarding issues such as player injuries that can be useful to gamblers. In 2006, Phoenix Coyotes assistant coach Rick Tocchet was implicated in a gambling ring thought to be facilitating bets among other coaches and players. While Tocchet was not accused of wagering on NHL contests, the league was quite concerned about his involvement. Tocchet was reinstated as a coach in 2008, however.[49]

The Big Four leagues' recent queasiness with their players' participation in fantasy sports has hinged on the question of whether or not it constitutes gambling. A recent lawsuit raised just this question, but a New Jersey court found that fantasy is not gambling.[50] For now, leagues have decided not to address the matter—and each of the Big Four's official websites offers its own fantasy sports games. While fantasy sports are off the hook, match-fixing will be with us as long as there is money to be made by doing so.[51]

Oh, the Humanity!

Science!

—Magnus Pyke[52]

Viagra is a godsend for the older man unready to throw off the shackles and hassles of sexual desire when nature presents him with the opportunity to do so. Other than long-suffering wives preferring to be left alone, few complain about Viagra on the grounds that it is a performance-enhancing substance. Elder sex is not generally viewed as a competitive spectator sport, no matter how dull life in the nursing home may get.

Like ardent lovers, athletes also seek to display the highest level of skills that can be mustered. But spectators take more into account than simply the best performances—the causes of a great display matter as much as the display itself. Fans paradoxically want that which constitutes "the best" to be limited by an inherent humanity. Even though video games are inching ever closer to perfection in their simulations, the entities generated remain reflective of actual people's skills and blemishes.

As the novelty of computers beating humans in chess subsides, it seems doubtful that attendance at computer tournaments will supplant interest in human contests. The RoboCup German Open, a tournament in which over 80 teams of researchers in 2008 fielded teams of robot soccer players, will not soon replace FIFA's World Cup.[53] The United States Golf Association (USGA) used to test balls and clubs using a golf driving machine called the Iron Byron (after Byron Nelson) that could drive a ball 350 yards dead straight ten thousand times in a row—something that even Tiger Woods cannot do.[54] It remains unlikely, however, that the U.S. Open will lose audiences to a tournament dominated by a fleet of tweaked-in Robo3000 golfbots. "The thrill of victory and the agony of defeat," *Wide World of Sports's* greatest contribution to the American vernacular, is about human emotions, not great engineering triumphs and failures.

However, this is not to say that medical and technological advances are not welcomed in sports. Sports spectators are willing to pay the most to see athletes display the highest level of skills humanly possible, and technology is part of the equation. It is difficult to imagine that track-and-field fans would prefer a return to a day before good diets, precise training, and high-tech coaching—today's product is a lot better. Billy Kilmer and his beer belly wouldn't survive very long in today's NFL, whose players are bigger, faster, stronger, and hit a lot harder than they did a generation ago.

Top-level athletes suffering serious injury now have access to nearly magical surgical procedures and rehabilitation programs. These generally do not raise hackles, although not every restorative technology is considered acceptable. The limited use of steroids by athletes to aid healing injuries is OK, but using them to ward off the natural ravages of age is not. Injury recovery is human, but so is aging.

Of course, the use of substances and technology to improve performance is not limited to love or athletics. Adam and Eve ate the forbidden fruit to gain godlike wisdom. Warriors preparing for battle long have made use of substances, from ancient cannibals seeking to subsume their rivals' strength to the legendary Norse berserkers of the 11th century, who may have taken some form of hallucinogen, to modern fighter pilots keeping awake with coffee and caffeine pills. Ancient Greek Olympians also ingested various mushrooms thought to enhance performance, while Roman gladiators mixed stimulants with alcohol in efforts to improve their endurance.[55] Modern athletes drink Gatorade and take all manner of legitimate—if sometimes goofy—dietary supplements they hope will give them an edge.

Separating Training from Doping

What constitutes the difference between good training and illicit use of performance-enhancing technology? Three criteria are useful in answering this question. First, would an athlete ingest a substance or make use of a technology in the absence of any perceived competitive benefit? Second, does use of the substance or technology come with a significant risk to the health of its user? Third, is use of the substance or technology not part of a medical response to an illness or injury?[56] If the answer to each of these is "yes," then use of the substance or technology would seem to cross a line.

A sport's organizing body would not necessarily have to be paternalistic toward athletes in order to prohibit such a technology. If its use sufficiently dehumanizes the sport in the eyes of enough fans, then there are perfectly utilitarian reasons for the body to issue a ban. However, the use of risky technologies also can bring with it undesirable externalities, providing further reasons for organizing bodies and even governments to get involved.

Consider the case of anabolic steroids. In 1899, Charles Edward Brown-Sequard, a prominent physiologist, gave a paper to the Society of Biology in Paris extolling the fountain-of-youth effects of injections of extracts from dogs or guinea pigs. Shortly thereafter, in 1896, an article published about such extracts concluded with a call for more research into their effects on athlete training. More study ensued.

Modern Olympic athletes had begun to experiment with a variety of substances as early as the turn of the century. Most of these, such as strychnine, were eventually found to be impotent or even harmful, but male hormones showed some promise. Some German athletes were rumored to have taken testosterone in preparation for the 1936 Berlin games, although this claim has not been fully verified. In 1941, the first verified report of testosterone doping was confirmed when a 19-year-old racehorse implanted with the stuff returned to the form of his youth.[57]

World War II brought a culture of respect for the notion of "better living through chemistry" in many phases of American life. Sports was no exception. Testosterone began to catch on with some West Coast bodybuilders during the 1950s, and the Russian weightlifting team allegedly was using it by 1954. Their competitive success led in 1954 to the production of Dianabol by Ciba Pharmaceutical Company. By the 1960s, word of the success of artificial testosterone had spread widely, and so had its use among athletes.[58]

There is no doubt that anabolic steroids can increase the effectiveness of an athletic training program. The problem is that they are not kind to athletes' health. Short- and long-term use comes with many negative side effects, including liver and heart damage, various cancers, as well as increases in male sex drive, acne, body hair, and aggressiveness.[59] Steroids are not the only substances that improve athletic performance at the expense of the health of the user. Stimulants, for example, can provide a competitive edge, but have been shown to have negative psychological and physiological side effects.

In addition to concern over the dehumanization of their sports via performance-enhancing technologies, organizing bodies must also attend to the "arms race" issue that they create. If a technology provides a sufficient edge, then every athlete must take advantage of it in order to compete. To the extent that these technologies are safe training methods deemed consistent with the spirit of a sport, then there is no problem. On the other hand, if athletes must engage in personally injurious activities just to remain competitive, the organizing body will see a need to act.[60]

The incentive to engage in a dangerous performance-enhancing activity in order to compete has ramifications that can be far broader than just across an organizing body's jurisdiction. Those wishing to become athletes of sufficiently high caliber so as to come under the body's purview are similarly coerced into the practice. College football players seeking an NFL job must play like NFL athletes, even if it means taking human growth hormone and steroids. High schoolers vying for college football scholarships will soon have to do the same, and so it goes on down. In these cases, it can be incumbent upon government to interfere in athletes' liberty to engage in a practice, despite their fully informed consent.[61]

As technology marches forward, athletes will drive demand for ever-more-difficult-to-detect doping regimens, while governments and organizing bodies will respond reactively. It is likely that the athletes will always remain one jump ahead of the medical testers, although statistical methods may begin to prove effective at the detection of cheating.[62] The challenges now facing testers involve human growth hormone, genetic manipulation, and blood doping, all undetectable at the present time.[63] Furthermore, it is not at all clear in what ways—if any—genetic modification or blood doping would be health-damaging, and therefore worthy of bans. Nor is it clear to what extent such practices would dehumanize the sports in which they might be used.

As with any form of cheating, policing will not be enough. A sport's own ethos must instill in its athletes a personal sense of honor. Furthermore, it must do it so widely as to make doping a deviant behavior that will be self-enforced into a small existence.[64] The sporting public must also play a role. Fan demand for ever-greater achievements must be moderated. The sad truth is that we are all complicit. We still cheered on the 1998 home run record derby between Mark McGwire and Sammy Sosa despite half-believing they were 'roided-up.

Big Brother Is Watching

Leagues pay similarly close attention to the personal and private behavior of their employees. They engage a well-oiled apparatus in response to an offensive statement or legal skirmish involving one of their players, coaches, or owners. The concept of the institutional moral police is not exactly new, however—nor are its reasons.

Henry Ford's assembly line Model T was an incredible consumer marketing success. As demand for his product increased, so did his company's need for workers. His timing was fortuitous—the second decade of the 20th century saw millions of southern and European immigrants come to the U.S. Many of them found their way to Detroit, lured by the promise of jobs at factories in the booming auto business.[65]

In 1912, Ford produced 94,662 Model T's. In 1913, production was 224,783 units, and it took a labor force of 13,600 to make them. The company had significant human resources issues, however. Absenteeism was on the order of 10 percent per day, and turnover was appalling. The firm had to make more than 52,000 hires in 1913. Ford's business model was threatened. It critically relied upon a disciplined production workforce able to repeat reliably the same activity hundreds of times daily, but its employees were not up to the task. In 1914, Ford tried a radical approach: the Five Dollar Day.[66]

Since the typical Ford production worker in 1913 was paid $2.34 per day, the Five Dollar Day more than doubled worker pay as it also called for three eight-hour shifts rather than two shifts of nine hours. However, the fine print was that it was in reality a very liberal—$10,000,000—profit-sharing plan. More than 12,000 employees would be added to the payroll, but none would be fired except for "proved unfaithfulness or irremediable inefficiency."[67]

Ford's program came with some significant strings attached, many of which were held by the newly formed Ford Sociological Department. The department claimed broad rights to interfere in all manners of a Ford employee's home life, enforcing all manner of middle-class American values upon its immigrant employees. They were lectured about cleanliness, sobriety, chastity, and industry. Workers failing to meet the department standards for domestic life and workplace productivity were denied half their pay.[68]

Corporate statements accompanying the announcement of the program were calculated to play to the Progressive movement. The company sought to cast itself as a practitioner of paternalistic capitalist welfare seeking social justice, which it claimed "begins at home." They mentioned their discomfort with "a division of our earnings between labor and capital [that] is unequal."[69] A casual observer might have believed that humanitarianism rather than self-interest was primarily responsible for the Five Dollar Day.

The Big Four leagues' behavioral policies have a similarly pragmatic goal, but they couch it in terms of social concern, not unlike the way Ford did nearly a century ago. The leagues' know that much of what they sell is about public relations. Bad athletes mean bad feelings among fans, which risks lower revenues. The leagues' efforts are more capitalism than social engineering. The driving force behind the NBA's 1997 $50,000 fine for Dennis Rodman's offensive remarks about Mormons was at least as much about placating Utah Jazz fans as it was about any moral outrage on the commissioner's part.[70]

Sport as a Forum for Moral Discussion

> The battle of Waterloo was won on the playing fields of Eton.
>
> —Commonly attributed, incorrectly, to the First Duke of Wellington[71]

Only a lout, a fool or a fierce partisan would unleash a strong opinion on presidential politics to an unsuspecting stranger during the last week of a leap-year October. In fact, discussion of any number of topics—money, sex, religion, or politics—among any but the most intimate of friends is considered an expression of at least mildly bad manners. Conversations about those third-rail subjects invariably reveal one's uniquely personal ethical system, risking offending other participants in the discussion. Consequently, these issues are typically given their own special and safe forums, most notably universities and churches. There is, however, still one socially acceptable avenue by which comparison of ethical points of view among close friends, casual acquaintances, and perfect strangers alike is still acceptable: sports.

Sports metaphors provide a convenient and non threatening shorthand to trade moral concepts in all walks of life. Overly harsh political attacks are "blows below the belt." An overanxious colleague in a sales presentation might "jump the gun." An unsuccessful suitor made "an incomplete pass," so he may have "decided to punt" on his target. Like sports, American life is a complex balance of cooperation and competition. The agonies of sports are a microcosm of the agonies of competitive life.[72]

With interests that can cut across class, race, income and even gender, spectator sports provide daily material for easy conversation, even about otherwise difficult topics. Few would be offended by the occupant of the neighboring barstool venturing an opinion on a player's personal habits. Some of the most controversial ethical questions are considered polite game in the context of sports, even when the same discussion would be taboo if about a politician.

The personal behavior of athletes has become a focal point for discussions surrounding that which we expect in general out of ourselves and others. A 24/7 media environment means that any figure even mildly in the public eye can expect what they do privately to become public. Prominent athletes are no exception—like politicians, they are not given the same pass as they were a generation ago. Mickey Mantle's personal choices were kept as quiet as John F. Kennedy's, even as they succeeded in their public lives. However, both Wade Boggs and Bill Clinton erred in believing that their marital infidelities would be kept mum. The sports journalism code of silence on private lives began to unravel with Howard Cosell, with ESPN completing the job in the 1980s. While it is clear that more than a few of the legends had skeletons in their closets, the public perception of modern athletes is that many carry significant blemishes.

However, a legitimate question to ask is the extent to which big-time spectator sports shape mass morality versus simply reflecting it.[73] The cultural struggle between communitarianism and individualism has been part of the American scene at least since de Tocqueville. The tension between those ideals remains reflected in American team sports. On the other hand, the sports business was ahead of the social curve in the struggle for racial equality, but much less so in gender issues.

The 1960s and 1970s challenged American public trust institutions of all kinds. The favorable attitude toward government and the military that resulted from World War II was shattered by Vietnam and Watergate. Corporatism, once the goal of American salaryman life, became a dirty word with news of ITT's alleged role in a plot to assassinate Argentine President Salvador Allende in 1974—during an era of windfall corporate oil profits. Even marriage and family took a hit with exploding divorce rates. As was the case with respect to race and gender, changing societal norms in these elements of daily life had effects on spectator sports. Even today, mores regarding excess alcohol use, profanity and other lifestyle issues are sparking discussions about how fans behave at the ballpark. Not least controversial is the degree to which children going to the game should have to put up with less-than-stellar adult displays. Perhaps booing may one day be banned for fear of harm to developing self-esteems.[74]

13

THE END OF THE DINOSAURS?

The future ain't what it used to be.
—Commonly attributed to Yogi Berra

By the end of the 1960s, broad social forces, such as the women's and civil rights movements, had become reflected in American pastimes. Muhammad Ali transcended sports, and with the ample assistance of Howard Cosell, became as much a political figure as an athlete. The raised fists of Tommie Smith and John Carlos on the podium of the 1968 summer Olympics in Mexico City told the whole world that all was not right in American culture. The Billie Jean King versus Bobby Riggs "Battle of the Sexes" found suburban husbands surprised by their wives' support of the "wrong" contestant. No longer could fans consider sports to be a refuge from the ills of society; they were smack-dab in the middle of it.

By the late 1970s, the American economic giddiness of the 1950s and 1960s had been replaced by brooding malaise. Inflation, unemployment, and energy shortages projected a glum forecast of future prosperity for American families. At the same time, exploited indentured-servant athletes began to break the chains of league reserve systems, providing unheard of paydays for players. Players' unions flexed their muscles and an economic gulf began to widen between athletes and fans, threatening the bond between them. That bond did not break, but it certainly changed. Fans now identify with sports stars in much the same way they do with other celebrities. Sports media in many ways now resemble entertainment media more than they do "hard" news outlets.

Early 21st century fans largely are at peace with the vast sums that big-time athletes earn, and thoroughly understand that social issues affect sports just as they do other aspects of American life. The sports page might read like a business section or local police blotter, but fandom now incorporates knowledge of salary caps, revenue sharing, and participant misconduct as much as it does on-base percentage, third-down conversion rates and field goal average. They are just different tiles in the mosaic that is American spectator sports.

If there is one thing that can be counted upon in the relationship between spectator sports and their fans, it is that it will continue to evolve. An inquiry into the pressures that will shape this evolution can provide insight into how that relationship might change in the coming decades. Perhaps the three most significant influences in this regard will be cultural change, globalization, and technology.

The Revenge of Gen Y

Modern American spectator sports were the product of the World War II generation and their Baby Boomer children. But just as suburbanization profoundly changed American life, so will helicopter parents and their offsprings' strong sense of individualism. Who knows what *their* kids will be like?

A new generation of fans weaned on Myspace and text messaging is likely going to demand a personalized connection with their sports. The revenue stream possibilities for team owners and athletes seem limitless, but they have to be ready to embrace them. But will a societal movement away from "loyal corporatism" be reflected in the decline of team sports at the expense of individual sports, particularly extreme sports?

So far, so good for the Big Four, however, as the first decade of the 21st century has brought them financial success. The NFL has big, fat television contracts that will take it well past 2010. MLB, an economic basket case in the early 1990s, appears to have weathered its competitive balance and doping issues. The NBA, while longing for the days of Magic, Bird and Jordan, has found a gold mine in Europe and Asia. Even the NHL, despite a relatively pauperish network television existence and bruising labor strife, is filling its arenas. Still, there may well be trouble ahead.

The cost of major league sports continues to price average families out of their Taj Mahal stadiums. Furthermore, many are beginning to feel that the stands at major sporting events are dens of increasingly uncivil behavior. It is getting easier for parents to opt not to buy a $75 ticket just so their 10-year old can spend three hours listening to alcohol-sodden 30-somethings drop F-bombs. These families are turning more and more to minor leagues, which are only too happy to provide family-friendly environments where the game often is only part of the entertainment package.

MLS soccer, for example, seems to be building a solid brand. It continues to add teams and build new soccer-only stadiums. Minor league baseball, hockey and baseball are as economically healthy as they were before television—maybe ever. They provide affordable alternatives to the big leagues in small, medium, and large cities across the country. As the Big Four relentlessly seek and mine ever richer revenue veins, they risk turning off a generation of fans. It may be that the community theater of the minor leagues could eclipse the Hollywood of the Big Four.

The increasing biodiversity of the American spectator sport landscape is not limited to just the major sports. The suburbs' first crop of parents and children grew up playing sandlot baseball, pick-up football, YMCA hoops, and backyard ice rink hockey. The sporting world Boomers have made for their children looks very different from their own upbringing, however.

Boomers' kids grew up scheduled to the point of exhaustion, with all of their team sports highly regimented and organized by adults. Ownership of their little league soccer and baseball must have seemed to most of these kids to be held more about their parents than themselves. Youth sports have become increasingly professionalized and eliticized. Training and practice have become year-round, and the opportunity to be a true multi-sport athlete is largely gone by the time a kid is 15 or 16 years old.

Is it any surprise, then, that so many kids hitting college are turning toward supposed minor sports such as lacrosse, rugby, and even Frisbee golf? Then there are all the "extreme," "action," and "adventure" sports, such as skateboarding, snowboarding, BMX, and Moto. Not surprisingly, new generations far removed from the social institutionalism predominant in the middle of the 20th century are increasingly opting for individual sports.

As participation grows in these off-brand sports, spectator interest will not be far behind. ESPN has been hard at work for more than a decade fostering its "X Games." At least for the moment at least, the X Games are far cheaper to put on its television, radio, Internet, and mobile channels than the older mainstream sports. However, as their popularity grows, so will the tournament prizes and media rights fees. This trend bodes well for American media as well as for fans with increasingly varied tastes. However, it will come at the expense of commonality and community, core social values enhanced by the Big Four as they currently stand. As American sports balkanize, the easy social lubrication sports now offer will diminish.

The World Is Getting Smaller

During the height of the Cold War, spectator sports were considered emblematic of American culture—the inability to identify the reigning World Series champion was considered an effective profiling technique to catch spies.

Nationalism, a big part of interest in the Olympic Games, played a much larger role when the outcome of the Cold War's ideological struggle was in doubt.

Only NHL hockey offered any kind of a "foreign" element. While suburbanization blossomed and bloomed, very few NHL players were American, and a third of its six teams called Canada home. Some were not even English-speakers. As late as 1967, only 2 percent of NHL players were Americans.[1] Even so, only 6.25 percent of NHL players between 1943 and 1967 were French-Canadian.[2]

But the NHL was no more than a regional sport in the U.S., with interest confined to a few large cities of the industrial North. The other major sports might have been integrating black players during the 1950s and 1960s, but they were almost exclusively U.S.-born. It is fair to say that American sports back then were, well, very American.

Things have changed during the last half-century. As has been the case in other phases of American life, the increasingly visible hand of globalization has not left our beloved sports unmolested. As of the end of the 1990s, American-born players constituted 14.2 percent of NHL players, but non–North American players represented 23.9 percent of NHL rosters.[3] While American football has yet to gain a foothold abroad, the same is certainly not true of baseball and basketball. During the 1950s, only 3.8 percent of MLB All-Stars were foreign-born during the 1950s, but more than 12 percent were during the 1990s.[4] By 2007, 31 percent of MLB players and 19 percent of NBA players were internationals.[5] Interestingly, in MLS soccer, a sport considered by many Americans to be inherently foreign, only 21 percent of players during the 2006 season were internationals.[6]

These supply-side changes are the result of intensifying global searches for talent.[7] No longer is the Chicago kid who grew up playing baseball or the Philly teen shooting hoops competing only with other hopeful Americans. Their skills are being compared against those of kids around the world by increasingly sophisticated international scouting systems. These systems are getting better at identifying and developing the truly best talents, regardless of country or continent of origin. The superstar effect means that second-tier players will continue to be poor substitutes for the best of the best, blurring the lines between American and other leagues in the same sport.

The leagues are well aware of this blurring. For some years, they have worked to colonize other nations' sporting cultures. Their imperialism has met with varying degrees of success. The NBA has had connections with European basketball for a long time, while MLB has pushed a World Cup–like baseball tournament and even played regular season games abroad. The NFL tried to sell an American football league in Europe, but it flopped. The league has since refocused its international efforts on playing games in other countries, with a bit more success. Apparently Europeans can tell the difference between the real thing and its poor cousin.

North American leagues that ignore the rest of the world put themselves in peril. For example, the NHL's 2004–5 labor strife apparently had enduring positive effects on the European leagues. In fact, Russian energy tycoon Alexander Medvedev and Russian Hockey Federation president Vladislav Tretiak signed a deal in Moscow in early 2008 to create a 20-club Russian league meant to rival the NHL in quality.[8] To show that they meant business, they hired former NHL players' union head Bob Goodenow to help with the start-up.[9] Let the player poaching begin.

Globalization has had demand effects as well. Soccer was once thought by most Americans to be an odd sport with a fan base nearly entirely confined to recent arrivals. Immigrants to the U.S. certainly do retain their interest in the "beautiful game," however, two generations of American kids have now grown up playing soccer as a first participatory sport. They have become aware of, and follow, the English Premier League, the Champions League, and the World Cup. There might be more Kobe Bryant than Ronaldinho jerseys to be seen in American shopping malls, but the disparity is diminishing. Boxing, too, has been re-energized by immigrants, particular those from Latin American countries.

Continuing globalization will change the economics of spectator sports. The seven major emerging economies of the world could very well grow at twice the rate of that of the seven largest economies between 2005 and 2050.[10] China, and India alone accounted for about 40 percent of the world population in 2007, but their per capita incomes were only 11.5 percent and 5.9 percent, respectively, of that in the U.S. However, their economies were growing at about 11 percent and 7 percent, respectively.[11] This means that by 2050, a huge number of the nearly 300 million Chinese and Indian people now living in abject poverty will join the global middle class. They will repeat the American experience, at least in one regard. Emergent American middle-class wealth in the 20th century produced new entertainment and sports industries, forever changing spectator sports. So it will happen again, this time an order of magnitude bigger, as hundreds of millions of Chinese and Indians clamor for their own sports during the coming century.

Both the influx of immigrants to the U.S. and the emergence of a middle class in developing countries will provide opportunities for those sports and leagues clever enough to take advantage them. An interesting question will be how the various international leagues in the same sport decide to compete or cooperate with each other. Will the NBA subsume the various European basketball leagues, turning them into farm systems à la MLB? Or will the NBA's hegemony over the top echelon of the sport fade in favor of a FIFA model, as is the case in world soccer?

In either scenario, huge sums of money will flow into top-tier sports, perhaps so much as to turn the tens of billions in current Big Four revenues into hundreds of billions for some sort of Big Eight or Big Nine. Borders may melt away across leagues that no longer think of Eastern versus Western conference distinctions but in terms of Asian versus European conferences. Elite player pay will be astronomical, or will have to be held down artificially by some sort of global reserve system. If the latter comes true, expect perpetual attempts to beat the system, with corruption serving as the defining element of world sport.

One thing is certain: just as other American industries have faced the Darwinist choice of either becoming competitive on a world scale or disappearing, so will the spectator sports business.

A Bit about Bytes

International media, particularly the Internet, are the reason that globalization likely will force the creation of super leagues. The entrenched powers-that-be, particularly in broadcast media, will deploy every weapon at their disposal—technological, economic, and political—to maintain their stranglehold on spectators. They are losing the war, however. In the absence of broad agreement among the governmental powers of the world that the World Wide Web is a threat and should be curtailed, the net will continue its inexorable march to democratize information.

The Web means that fans in any location whatsoever can keep close tabs on their teams, regardless of where in the world they play. No longer will traditional media companies control what viewers can watch—the Web provides the ultimate "watch-on-demand" opportunity. In a sense, the Internet represents the existence of an infinite number of channels. Those that own channels will be losers, but those that provide content will be winners.

Sports leagues know this. Despite their heavy reliance upon the flow of money from national television media, they have begun to define sophisticated Internet strategies. After a relatively slow start, league websites have come a very long way since the mid–1990s. They now offer their products online, cutting out the network middlemen. They continue working to figure out more ways to tap new technological innovations. Today, mobile phones are the new frontier—who knows what it might be in a couple of decades?

Ready access to their sports via technology could well erode some of the divide between teams and athletes, and their fans. As long as the spectator sport industry remains primarily a public relations business—as it always has been—something will fill the role of the long-suffering homer beat reporter. Blogs, podcasts, and other fan feedback mechanisms are going to put team managers ever closer to the raw emotions of their fan bases. New generations of fans, jaundiced and immune to the Boomers' traditional PR baloney, will have to be reached in new ways through these media. It is likely that they will have to feel far more consulted in league and team decision-making if they are to be expected to open their hearts and wallets.

The End of the Dinosaurs?

Nothing is forever. In 1950, it would have been difficult to imagine that by 2010, the Union Pacific Railroad would have nothing to say about American passenger travel. Or that Ford and GM would become also-rans in the American auto manufacturing business. Or that AT&T would struggle in the phone business. Yet, here we are.

It would seem foolish to think that Americans, or any other people with a few bucks to spend, will ever not see spectator sports as part of their lives. History offers a clear lesson on this point: spectator sports are as human as art, drama, music, or any other indicator of civilized culture. From the Egyptians to the Greeks to the Romans, from Tudor England to 18th century farmers of the American South to Brett Favre: fandom is a permanent facet of the creatures that we are.

However, this is not to say that the sports that we follow, or how we follow them, themselves are immutable. No longer are foot races or chariot races or gladiatorism major elements of the modern spectator sporting scene. Jousts and melees might still take place, but the crowds are small, and the interest in them is just part of a yearning for anachronism. Two centuries ago, the sports of the Big Four—baseball, football, hockey, and football—did not recognizably exist in their current forms. Two centuries hence, they may well no longer exist, either.

But there will be fans. And they will be passionate about their sports, whatever they may be.

CHAPTER NOTES

Chapter 1

1. A. R. Sanderson, 2004, "The Puzzling Economics of Sports," accessed 3 May 2004, at *http://www.econlib.org/library/Columns/y2004/Sandersonsports.html.*

2. University of Michigan sports economist Rodney Fort claims that the physical skill exhibited must feature "large scale motor function" in order to be considered a sport. R.D. Fort, July 2003, personal communication with the author at the Western Economic International meeting, Denver, Colorado.

3. ESPN, "Top N. American Athletes of the Century," accessed 3 November 2007 from *http://espn.go.com/sportscentury/athletes.html.*

4. *Jacobellis v. Ohio*, 378 US 184 (1964).

5. Findlaw, 2005, "Findlaw's Supreme Court Awareness Survey," accessed 10 November 2005 from *http://public.findlaw.com/ussc/122005survey.html.*

6. Pew Research Center, 14 June 2006, "Americans to the Rest of the World: Soccer Not Really Our Thing.

7. Ibid.

8. Polling Report.com, responses to the question, "What is your favorite sport?" Accessed 10 November 2007 from *http://www.pollingreport.com/sports.htm.*

9. Polling Report.com, responses to the item, "For each of the following, please say whether you are a fan of that sport or not." Accessed 10 November 2007 from *http://www.pollingreport.com/sports.htm.*

10. Pew Research Center, "Americans to the Rest of the World."

11. Pew Research Center, "Box Scores and Bylines: A Snapshot of the Newspaper Sports Page," 22 August 2005.

12. Ibid.

13. M. Hardin, 2005, "Survey Finds Boosterism, Freebies Remain Problem for Newspaper Sports Departments," *Newspaper Research Journal*, v. 26, no. 1 (Winter); as reported in Pew Research Center, "Box Scores and Bylines."

14. National Endowment for the Arts, 2004, "2002 Survey of Public Participation in the Arts," Research Division Report #45, Table 28.

15. J.W. Plunkett, 2007, *Plunkett's Sports Industry Almanac 2008* (Houston: Plunkett Research).

16. Author's calculation based on CPI and GDP data as reported by the U.S. Department of Labor, Bureau of Labor Statistics; U.S. Department of Commerce, Bureau of Economic Analysis; and on Plunkett, *Plunkett's Sports Industry Almanac 2008.*

17. In 2002, the architectural services industry had revenues of $25.3 billion, and employed 186,293 people. U.S. Census Bureau, 2004, *Architectural, Engineering, and Related Services: 2002,* Report EC02–541–03 (October).

18. Includes some Canadian revenues generated by MLB, NBA and NHL. Plunkett, *Plunkett's Sports Industry Almanac 2008.*

19. Author's calculations based on *Forbes* magazine data as reported on the Sports Business Data area webpage maintained by University of Michigan sports economics professor Rodney Fort (rodneyfort.com); and on Plunkett, *Plunkett's Sports Industry Almanac 2008.*

20. Author's calculation based on data from U.S. Department of Education, Office of Post-Secondary Education, Equity In Athletics Data Analysis Cutting Tool website, accessed most recent years; available on 3 November 2007 from *http://ope.ed.gov/athletics/.*

21. NCAA, 2007, National Collegiate Athletic Association Revised Budget for Fiscal Year ended August 31, 2007, accessed 3 November 2007 from *http://www1.ncaa.org/finance/2006–07_budget.pdf.*

22. B. O'Keefe, 2005, "America's fastest growing sport," *Fortune,* 5 September.

23. J. Gage, 2007, "The Most Valuable NASCAR Teams," *Forbes,* 15 June.

24. Estimates according to Plunkett, *Plunkett's Sports Industry Almanac 2008*.

25. Includes professional and amateur sporting events, as well as horse, dog, and auto racetrack admissions. U.S. Census Bureau, 2007, *The 2007 Statistical Abstract,* Table 1217, accessed 3 November 2007 from *http://www.census.gov/compendia/statab/arts_entertainment_recreation/consumer_expenditures/*.

26. Regular season totals according to ESPN.com were: MLB, 76.0 million; NBA, 21.8 million; NHL, 20.9 million; and NFL, 17.6 million. Plunkett, *Plunkett's Sports Industry Almanac 2008*.

27. Adapted from information on MLSnet.com.

28. J. Paton, 2008, "Mammoth sales," *Rocky Mountain News* (21 March), accessed 23 April 2008 from *http://www.rockymountainnews.com/news/2008/mar/21/mammoth-sales/*.

29. NHL dollar values converted to U.S. dollar equivalents. Team marketing report, accessed 3 November 2007 from *www.teammarketing.com*.

30. Author's calculations based on 2006 median annual family income of $48,201 (before taxes). Income data from C. DaNavis-Walt, B.D. Proctor, and J. Smith, 2007, "Income, Poverty, and Health Insurance Coverage in the United States 2006," (U.S. Census Bureau, August), accessed 3 November 2007 from *http://www.census.gov/prod/2007pubs/p60–233.pdf*.

31. MLB and NBA figures do not include local broadcast and cable fees. NCAA basketball figure includes only the tournament, but not the regular season. NCAA football figure includes the regular season and four BCS games. PGA figure includes regular season and four PGA majors. NASCAR figure includes Nextel Cup and Busch Series. Plunkett, *Plunkett's Sports Industry Almanac 2008*.

32. MLB value represents 2001 and NBA value represents 1996, based on author's calculations and R.D. Fort, 2007, *Sports Economics* (Upper Saddle River, NJ: Prentice-Hall).

33. Estimated by PriceWaterhouseCoopers as reported by J. Cheng, 2007, "Report: Video Game Spending To Surpass Music Spending This Year," *Arstechnica,* 23 June, accessed 3 November 2007 from *http://arstechnica.com/news.ars/post/20070623-report-video-game-spending-to-surpass-music-spending-this-year.html*.

34. NPD Group, 2007, "2006 U.S. Video Game And Pc Game Retail Sales Reach $13.5 Billion Exceeding Previous Record Set In 2002 By Over $1.7 Billion," press release, 19 January, accessed 3 November 2007 from http://www.npd.com/press/releases/press_070119.html.

35. Plunkett, *Plunkett's Sports Industry Almanac 2008*. Figure based on Plunkett's estimate of 42.2% of all sports revenue.

36. Estimate of annual company advertising for sports in 2007 from ibid. Estimate of total U.S. ad spending in 2007 from Advertising Age, 2007, *Advertising Age Datacenter: 2007 Marketer Profiles Yearbook,* accessed 3 November 2007 from *http://adage.com/images/random/lna2007.pdf*.

37. U.S. Census Bureau, 2007, *The 2007 Statistical Abstract,* Tables 1004 and 1110, accessed 3 November 2007 from *http://www.census.gov/compendia/statab/arts_entertainment_recreation/consumer_expenditures/*.

Chapter 2

1. H. Bridges, 1958, "The Robber Baron Concept In American History," *The Business History Review*, v. 32, no. 1: 1–13.

2. The BCS conferences are as follows: Atlantic Coast Conference, Big 12 Conference, Big East Conference, Big 10 Conference, Pacific Ten Conference, and Southeastern Conference. Notre Dame has no conference affiliation, but is also a member of the BCS.

3. Figures taken from notice of hearing before the House Judiciary hearings that were held on 4 September 2003, just before the Senate hearings. The complete statement can be found at *http://judiciary.house.gov/Legacy/news090303.htm*.

4. B. DeLong, 1998, *Robber Barons* (Berkeley: University of California at Berkeley), accessed 4 January 2008 from *http://econ161.berkeley.edu/Econ_Articles/carnegie/DeLong_Moscow_paper2.html*. By comparison, the share was 33.4% in 2004, up from the American historical low of about 18% in the late 1970s. A.B. Kennickell, 2006, *Currents And Undercurrents: Changes In The Distribution Of Wealth, 1989–2004* (Washington, DC: Federal Reserve Board), accessed 4 January 2004 from *http://www.federalreserve.gov/pubs/oss/oss2/papers/concentration.2004.5.pdf*.

5. R.M. Ours, "Introduction: A Brief History Of College Football," in *College Football Encyclopedia,* accessed 28 December 2007 from *http://www.footballencyclopedia.com/cfeintro.htm*. Chapter 2 includes more discussion about the history of college football in the U.S.

6. Hickok Sports. "Baseball History — The First Major League (1876–1889," accessed 4 January 2008 from *http://www.hickoksports.com/history/baseba04.shtml*.

7. Ibid.

8. Ibid.

9. Ibid.

10. S.H. Williamson, 2007, "Six Ways to Compute the Relative Value of a U.S. Dollar Amount, 1790— 2006," MeasuringWorth.Com,

accessed 4 January 2008 from *http://www.measuringworth.com/uscompare/.*

11. J. Quirk and R.D. Fort, 1997, *Pay Dirt: The Business of Professional Team Sports* (Princeton, NJ: Princeton University Press).

12. Ibid.

13. Ibid.

14. "The Base-ball Field," 1883, *New York Times,* 14 October, p. 7. It may have been that the AA's action was in response to the potential threat posed by the Union Association's plans.

15. Quirk and Fort, *Pay Dirt.*

16. Ibid.

17. Ibid.

18. "Pulliam Is President," 1902, *New York Times,* 13 December, p. 11; "Baseball Season Near," 1903, *New York Times,* 1 March, p. 16.

19. "Sunday Baseball Barred," *New York Times,* 3 March, p. 7.

20. U.S. Census Bureau, Selected Historical Decennial Census Population and Housing Counts, Urban and Rural Populations, Population 1790 to 1990, http://www.census.gov/population/www/censusdata/files/table-4.pdf.

21. United States v. American Tobacco Co., 221 U.S. 106 (1911); Standard Oil Co. of N.J. v. United Sates, 221 U.S. 1 (1911).

22. *United States v. United States Steel Co.,* 221 U.S. 106 (1911).

23. "Federal League Charges a Trust," 1915, *New York Times,* 6 January, p. 14.

24. "Judge Landis May End Baseball War," 1915, *New York Times,* 27 April, p. 10.

25. "Long Baseball War Is Settled," 1915, *New York Times,* 23 December, p. 10.

26. "Claims Baltimore Club Was Ignored," 1917, *New York Times,* 12 June, sports section, p. 10; "Ask Huge Damages of Ball Magnates," 1916, *New York Times,* 30 March, p. 10.

27. "Baseball Moguls See Dire Changes," 1919, *New York Times,* 14 April, p. 10

28. Federal Club v. National League, 259 U.S. 200 (1922).

29. *Toolson v. New York Yankees,* 346 U.S. 356 (1953).

30. L.A. Huston, 1955, "Theatre and Boxing Ruled Subject to Antitrust Laws," *New York Times,* 1 February, p. 1. Another source indicates that IBC controlled 47 of 51 bouts. Business Reference, "Company Histories: Wirtz Corporation," accessed 27 December 2007 from *http://www.referenceforbusiness.com/history/Vi-Z/Wirtz-Corporation.html.*

31 *United States v. International Boxing Club,* 348 U.S. 236 (1955).

32. *Washington Professional Basketball Corp. v. National Basketball Assn.,* 147 F. Supp. 154 (S.D.N.Y. 1956); *Radovich v. National Football League,* 352 U.S. 445 (1957).

33. *Deesen v. Profl. Golfers' Assn.,* 358 F.2d 165 (9th Cir. 1966). *Natl. Collegiate Athletic Assn v. Bd. of Regents of the Univ. of Okla.,* 468 U.S. 85 (1984). *Volvo N. Am. Corp. v. Men's Intl. Profl.* Tennis Council, 857 F.2d 55 (2d Cir. 1988). *Fraser v. Major League Soccer,* 97 F. Supp. 2d 130 (D.Mass. 2000).

34. According to the NCAA football television committee's 1981 briefing book, as reported in Footnote 3 of *NCAA v. Board of Regents,* 468 U.S. 85 (1984).

35. Broadcast History Timeline, "A Timeline of TV History, 1900–1992," accessed 25 March 2005 from *http://www.tvhandbook.com/History/History_timeline.htm.*

36. G.T. Kurian, ed., 2004, *Datapedia of the United States: American History in Numbers,* 3rd Edition (Lanham, MD: Bernan Press).

37. P.L. Pacey, 1985, "The Courts And College Football: New Playing Rules Off The Field?" *American Journal of Economics and Sociology,* v. 44, no. 2, pp. 145–154.

38. NCAA v. Board of Regents, 468 U.S. 85 (1984).39. Pacey, "The Courts and College Football.

40. The failure of this approach is attested by the fact that one of the few remaining copies of this pamphlet is available on microfiche in the archives of the Pro Football Hall of Fame in Canton, OH.

41. M. Brewster, 2004, "The NFL's MVP: Pete Rozell," *Business Week,* 24 November, accessed 4 January 2008 from *http://www.businessweek.com/bwdaily/dnflash/nov2004/nf20041124_5773_db078.htm.*

42. M. Cave and R.W. Crandall, 2001, "Sports Rights and the Broadcast Industry," *The Economic Journal,* v. 111, no. 469: F4-F26.

43. 15 USC 1291.

44. L. Soonhwan and H. Chun, 2002, "Economic Values of Professional Sports Franchises in the United States," *The Sport Journal,* v. 5, no. 3, accessed 28 December 2007 from *http://www.thesportjournal.org/2002Journal/Vol5-No3/economic-values.asp.*

45. J. Duncan, 2006, "Political Ploy Gave Birth to Saints 40 Years Ago," *New Orleans Times-Picayune,* 30 October, accessed 18 December 2007 from *http://www.nola.com/newslogs/tpupdates/index.ssf?/mtlogs/nola_tpupdates/archives/2006_10_30.html.*

46. J. Vrooman, 1997, "Franchise Free Agency in Professional Sports Leagues," *Southern Economic Journal,* v. 64, no. 1: 191–219.

47. L. Kahn, 2007, "Sports League Expansion And Consumer Welfare," *Journal of Sports Economics,* v. 8, no. 2: 115–138; R.G. Noll, 2003, "The Economics Of Baseball Contraction." *Journal of Sports Economics,* v. 4, no. 4: 367–388.

48. *United States v. National Football League,* 116 F. Supp. 319, 323–26 (E.D. Pa. 1953).

49. For more discussion of exclusive territories in sports, see Vrooman, "Franchise Free Agency."

50. Author's calculation based on a variety of sources, including R.J. Keating, 1999, "Sports Pork: The Costly Relationship between Major League Sports and Government," in The Cato Institute, *Policy Analysis* No. 339, April 5, accessed 5 January 2008 from *http://www.cato.org/pubs/pas/pa339.pdf*.

51. Quirk, J. and R.D. Fort. 1997. *Pay Dirt: The Business of Professional Team Sports*. (Princeton, NJ: Princeton University Press).

52. Author's calculations based on a number of sources, including S.Fastis, 2004, "Salaries, Promos and Flying Solo," *Wall Street Journal*, 9 February, p. R4.

53. Not including major college sports venues. Author's calculations based on a number of sources, including J. Seigfried and A. Zimbalist, 2000, "The Economics Of Sports Facilities and Their Communities," *Journal of Economic Perspectives*, v. 14, no. 3: 95–114.

54. Author calculations based on ESPN, "2007 Stadium Naming Rights," accessed 5 Jan. 2008 from *ttp://espn.go.com/sportsbusiness/s/stadiumnames.html*.

55. C.M. Clapp and J.K. Hakes, 2005. How Long a Honeymoon? The Effect of New Stadiums on Attendance in Major League Baseball," *Journal of Sports Economics*, v. 6, no. 3: 237–263.

56. Z.X. Zygmont and J.C. Leadley, 2005, "When Is the Honeymoon Over? Major League Baseball Attendance 1970–2000," *Journal of Sport Management*, v. 19, no. 3: 278–299; L.H. Hadley, 2004, "Review: Zygmont and Leady, 'When is the honeymoon over?'" working paper, Western Oregon University, accessed 6 January 2008 from *http://www.roadsidephotos.com/baseball/hadley04.htm*; D. Coates and B.R. Humphreys, 2005, "Novelty Effects of New Facilities on Attendance at Professional Sporting Events," *Contemporary Economic Policy*, v. 23, no. 3: 436–455.

57. The list of such papers is far too long to include here. For a good summary of them, see R.D. Fort, 2006, *The Economics of Sports*, 2nd Edition (Upper Saddle River, NJ: Prentice-Hall), or M.A. Leeds and P. von Allmen, 2007, *The Economics of Sports*, 3rd Edition (Boston: Addison-Wesley).

58. R. Noll, 1982, "Major League Sports," in *The Structure of American Industry*, ed. W. Adams (New York: Macmillan).

59. As measured by Gross Metropolitan Product, the local equivalent of Gross Domestic Product for countries. Bureau of Economic Analysis, U.S. Department of Commerce, "Regional Economic Accounts, Gross Domestic Product by Metropolitan Area," accessed 6 January 2008 from *http://www.bea.gov/regional/gdpmetro/*.

60. *Forbes* magazine reported that 2005 revenues were $189 million for the Seahawks, $179 million for the Mariners, and $81 million for the Sonics. Accessed 6 January 2008 from *http://rodneyfort.com/SportsData/BizFrame.htm*.

61. Players often live in other cities during the off-season; moreover, they tend to save a much higher portion of their money than do lesser-paid employees.

62. Again, the Packers might be different because such a large portion of game day fans come from outside the area.

63. K.G. Quinn, P.B. Bursik, C.P. Borick, and L.M. Raethz, 2003, "Do New Digs Mean More Wins? The Relationship between a New Venue and a Professional Sports Team's Competitive Success," *Journal of Sports Economics*, v. 4, no. 3: 167–182.

Chapter 3

1. The Olympic Games were one of four sets of contests; the other three were the Isthamian Games, the Nemean Games and the Pythian Games. They were integral parts of important religious festivals. See Leeds and von Allmen, *The Economics of Sports*.

2. Onereed.com, 2002, "Ancient Calendars and the Race against Time," accessed 23 July 2005 from *http://www.onereed.com/articles/vvf/olympics.html*.

3. L. Bourtros, "Phoenician Sports Founded Olympic and the Stadium," accessed 23 July 2005 from *http://phoenicia.org/phoenicianolympics.htm#Stadium*.

4. Leeds and von Allmen, *The Economics of Sports*.

5. K. Blanchard, 1985, *The Anthropology of Sport* (South Hadley, MA: Bergin & Garvey).

6. "China through a Lens, Sports in Ancient China and Greece," Accessed 23 July 2005 from *http://www.china.org.cn/english/features/olympics/100651.htm*.

7. Smithsonian Institution, Human Ancestors Hall—*Homo Sapiens*, accessed 1 April 2007 from *http://www.mnh.si.edu/anthro/humanorigins/ha/sap.htm*.

8. Blanchard, *The Anthropology of Sport*.

9. Touregypt.net, "Egypt: Ancient Sports," accessed 23 July 2005 from *http://www.touregypt.net/historicalessays/ancsportsindex.htm*.

10. Blanchard, *The Anthropology of Sport*.

11. Ibid.; also see R. Hooker, "History of the Minoans," accessed 23 July 2005 from *http://www.wsu.edu:8080/~dee/minoa/history.htm*.

12. B. Rader, 1983, American Sports: From

the Age of Folk Games to the Age of Spectators. (Englewood Cliffs, NJ: Prentice-Hall).

13. E. Gorn, 1997, "Sports through the Nineteenth Ccentury," in *The New American Sports History: Recent Approaches and Perspectives*, ed. S.W. Pope (Urbana: University of Illinois Press).

14. Ibid.

15. Ibid.

16. Go.HR.com, accessed 10 August 2005 from *http://go.hrw.com/ndNSAPI.nd/gohrw_rls1/pKeywordResults?ST9%20Cities%201900.*

17. B. Rader, 1983, *American Sports: From the Age of Folk Games to the Age of Spectators* (Englewood Cliffs, NJ: Prentice-Hall).

18. Hickock Sports, "History — Bareknuckle Boxing in America," accessed 4 April 2007 from *http://www.hickoksports.*com/history/boxing02.shtml.

19. Rader, *American Sports.*

20. Ibid.

Chapter 4

1. G.B. Kirsch, 2003, *Baseball in Blue and Gray: The National Pastime during the Civil War* (Princeton, NJ: Princeton University Press).

2. Ibid.

3. M.L. Adelman, 1997, "The Early Years of Baseball, 1845–60," in *The New American Sports History: Recent Approaches and Perspectives*, ed. S.W. Pope (Urbana: University of Illinois Press).

4. Baseball historians have noted that baseball-like games were played as early as 1823 in New York, and 1791 in Pittsfield, Massachusetts. J. Freyer, M. Rucker, and J. Thorn, 2005, *Peverelly's National Game.* (Mount Pleasant, SC: Arcadia).

5. Adelman, "The Early Years of Baseball.

6. Thebaseballpage.com, "Tracing the Origins of Baseball," accessed 15 August 2005 from *http://www.thebaseballpage.com/features/2001/origins/origins.htm.*

7. Baseball Hall of Fame, "Origins of the Baseball Hall of Fame and Museum," accessed 15 August 2005 from *http://www.baseballhalloffame.org/about/history.htm.*

8. Ibid.

9. Adelman, "The Early Years of Baseball, 1845–60."

10. Ibid; West Michigan Whitecaps, "History," accessed 31 October 2005 from *http://www.whitecaps-baseball.com/KIDS/CLASS/history.html.*

11. West Michigan Whitecaps, "History."

12. Adelman, "The Early Years of Baseball, 1845–60."

13. Thebaseballpage.com, "Tracing the Origins of Baseball."

14. Ibid.

15. Library of Congress, "American Treasures of the Library of Congress," accessed 15 August 2005 from *http://www.loc.gov/exhibits/treasures/tri077.html.*

16. Ibid.

17. K.D. Cornette, "The Story of the 1870 Red Stockings, or Why the Red Sox Lost the 1986 World Series," accessed 15 August 2005 from *http://www.rEds.oxdiehard.com/story/stockings.html.* See also Lawrence H. Officer and Samuel H. Williamson, 2007, "Purchasing Power of Money in the United States from 1774 to 2006," MeasuringWorth.Com.

18. Ibid.

19. Hickocksports.com, "Baseball History — The Professionals Take Over," accessed 15 August 2005 from *http://www.hickoksports.com/history/baseba03.shtml.*

20. A. Feldman, "Baseball's Transition to Professionalism," accessed 31 October 2005 from *http://www.sabr.org/cmsFiles/Files/feldman%20JKA%202002.pdf.*

21. Ibid.

22. The American Association, a rival major league that played 1882–1891, *did* allow alcohol at its games, and was dubbed the "beer and whiskey league" by derisive National League wags.

23. Baseball Library, "National League," accessed 31 October 2005 from *http://www.baseballlibrary.com/baseballlibrary/ballplayers/N/National_League.stm.*

24. Ibid.

25. "The Collective Bargaining Agreement for Fans, the 1800s," accessed 31 October 2005 from *http://www.cbaforfans.com/1800s.html.* According to another source, teams' entire rosters were reserved by 1883. Feldman, "Baseball's Transition to Professionalism."

Chapter 5

1. S. Meacham, 2006, "Old Division Football, the Indigenous Mob Soccer of Dartmouth College," Dartmo.com, accessed 1 April 2006 from *http://www.dartmo.com/football/Football_Meacham.pdf.*

2. There is evidence that such a game was being played at Yale as early as the 1790s. See ibid.

3. I. Waddington and M. Roderick, 1996, "American Exceptionalism: Soccer and American Football," The *Sports Historian* (University of Leicester Center for Research into Sport and Society), no. 16, accessed 1 April 2006 from *http://www.aafla.org/SportsLibrary/SportsHistorian/1996/sh16f.pdf.*

4. J. Nauright, 1996, "Writing and Reading

American Football: Culture, Identities, and Sports Studies," accessed 1 April 2007 from *http://www.aafla.org/SportsLibrary/SportingTraditions/1996/st1301/st1301k.pdf.*

5. R.A. Smith, 1988, "A Failure of Elitism: The Harvard-Yale Dual League Plan of the 1890s," *The New England Quarterly*, v. 61, no. 2.

6. Meacham, "Old Division Football."

7. R.A. Smith, 2001, *Sports and Freedom: The Rise of Big Time College Athletics* (Oxford: Oxford University Press).

8. "Introduction," *College Football Encyclopedia,* accessed 1 April 2007 from *http://www.footballencyclopedia.com/cfeintro.htm.*

9. H.D. Sears, 1992, "The Moral Threat of Intercollegiate Sports," *Journal of Sport History*, v. 19, no. 3 (Winter).

10. R. Crepeau, 2006, "Stuff Another Football in the Turkey, 11 November, accessed 1 April 2007 from *http://www.poppolitics.com/archives/2006/11/stuff_another_football_in_the.*

11. D.L. Westby and A. Sack, 1976, "The Commercialization and Functional Rationalization of College Football: Its Origins," *The Journal of Higher Education*, v. 47, no. 6.

12. A. Brooks, 2003, "Harvard Stadium, 1903–2003," *Harvard University Gazette,* accessed 1 April 2007 from *http://www.hno.harvard.edu/gazette/2003/10.23/00-stadium.html.*

13. Hickok Sports, "History — College Bowl Games," accessed 4 April 2007 from *http://www.hickoksports.com/history/collbowl.shtml.*

14. "Rose Bowl Stadium," accessed 4 April 2007 from http://www.rosebowlstadium.com/RoseBowl_history_154_facts.htm.

15. Pro Football Hall of Fame, "Nov. 12 — Birth of Pro Football," accessed 1 April 2007 from *http://www.profootballhof.com/history/general/birth.jsp*. A facsimile of the record of Heffelfinger's payment can be accessed at *http://www.profootballhof.com/history/general/birth_certificate.jsp.*

16. National Football League, "NFL History," accessed 5 April 2007 from http://www.nfl.com/history/chronology/1869–1910.

17. "Media Timeline — 1921–1925," accessed 4 April 2007 from *http://www.ketupa.net/timeline3.htm.*

18. "Recording History — The History of Recording Technology," accessed 4 April 2007 from *http://www.recording-history.org/HTML/phono_technology1.php.*

19. P. Gronow, 1983, "The Record Industry: Growth of a Mass Medium," *Popular Music*, v. 3: 53–75.

20. M. Watkins, 1991, "What Was It about Amos and Andy?" *New York Times*, 7 July, accessed 4 April 2007 from *http://query.nytimes.com/gst/fullpage.html?res=9D0CEFD9143EF934A35754C0A967958260.*

21. Baseball Almanac, "Babe Ruth Baseball Stats," accessed 4 April at *http://www.baseball-almanac.com/players/player.php?p=ruthba01.*

22. L. Schwartz, "Man o' War Came Close to Perfection," ESPN.com, accessed 4 April 2007 from *http://espn.go.com/sportscentury/features/00016132.html.*

23. J. Nauright, "The Emergence of Golf as a Sporting Spectacle 1904–1935," accessed 5 April 2006 from *http://www.aafla.org/SportsLibrary/NASSH_Proceedings/NP2002/NP2002s.pdf.*

24. R.L.A. Adams and J.F. Rooney, 1985, "Evolution of American Golf Facilities," *Geographical Review*, v. 75, no. 4: 419–438.

25. Golf Links to the Past, "Biography — Bobby Jones," accessed 5 April 2007 from *http://www.golfspast.com/page/E/CTGY/HBJB.*

26. F. Deford, 1976, *Big Bill Tilden: The Triumphs and the Tragedy* (New York: Simon and Schuster).

27. This was the famous "long count" fight in which Dempsey failed to take a neutral corner after knocking down Tunney. It is estimated that Tunney took 14 seconds to get back up. International Boxing Hall of Fame, "Enshrinees — Jack Dempsey," accessed 4 April 2007 from *http://www.ibhof.com/dempsey.htm.*

28. R. Roberts, 2003, *Jack Dempsey, the Manassa Mauler* (Urbana: University of Illinois Press).

29. National Football League, "NFL History," accessed 5 April 2007 from *http://www.nfl.com/history/chronology/1911–1920.*

30. Roberts, *Jack Dempsey.*

31. J. Quirk, J. and R.D. Fort. 1997. Pay Dirt: The Business of Professional Team Sports. (Princeton, NJ: Princeton University Press).

32. J. Quirk and R.D. Fort, 1997, *Pay Dirt: The Business of Professional Team Sports* (Princeton, NJ: Princeton University Press).

33. HickokSports.com, "History — Auto Racing — Early History," accessed 20 June 2007 from *http://www.hickoksports.com/history/autorace01.shtml.*

34. Ibid.

35. Indianapolis Motor Speedway, "History of the Indianapolis Motor Speedway," accessed 20 June 2007 from *http://www.indianapolismotorspeedway.com/history/.*

36. M. Allison, 2007, "A Need for Speed," *The Telegraph,* February 3 and March 2, accessed 19 June 2007 from *http://www.telegraph.co.uk/motoring/main.jhtml?view=DETAILS&grid=A1YourView&xml=/motoring/2007/02/03/nosplit/mfspeed03.xml.*

37. CNN, 1997, "List of World Land Speed Record Holders," October 15, accessed 19 June 2007 from *http://www.cnn.com/TECH/9710/15/brits.land.speed/list.reut.html.*

38. R.G. Hagstrom, 2001, *The NASCAR*

Way: The Business That Drives the Sport (Somerset, NJ: John Wiley & Sons), pp 22–23.

39. NASCAR, "Evolution of the Stock Car: Part I," accessed 19 June 2007 from *http://www.nascar.com/2002/kyn/history/evolution/02/06/stockcar/index.html.*

40. Irwindale Speedway, "NASCAR Brand Review," accessed 20 June 2007 from *http://www.irwindalespeedway.com/ISdemo05.pdf.*

41. J. Gage, 2006, "Racing for Success," *Forbes,* 5 June, accessed 20 June 2007 from *http://members.forbes.com/forbes/2006/0605/126.html.*

42. IMDB, "Biography for Babe Ruth," accessed 20 June 2007 from *http://www.IMDB.com/name/nm0751899/bio.*

43. IMDB, "Trivia for: Boxing (1892)," Accessed 22 June 2007 from *http://www.IMDB.com/title/tt0241266/trivia.*

44. IMDB, "Jack Dempsey (I)," accessed 20 June 2007 from *http://IMDB.com/name/nm0218727/.*

45. IMDB, "Biography for Johnny Weissmuller," accessed 20 June 2007 from *http://www.IMDB.com/name/nm0919321/bio.*

46. The Tarzan Movie Guide (1995 and 2001), "The Weismuller Films (1932–1948)," accessed 20 June 2007 from *http://www.tarzanmovieguide.com/index.htm.*

47. SNL Archives, accessed 21 June 2007 from *http://snl.jt.org/.*

Chapter 6

1. CMG Worldwide, 1998, "50 Years after His Death, the Legend of the Bambino Lives On," accessed 22 June 2007 from *http://www.baberuth.com/flash/about/viewheadline.php?id=946.*

2. "#2 Tiger Woods," 2007, *Forbes,* accessed 22 June 2207 from *http://www.forbes.com/lists/2007/53/07celebrities_Tiger-Woods_WR6D.html.*

3. R. VanGierzen and A.E. Schrenk, 2001, "Compensation from before World War I through the Great Depression," *Compensation and Working Conditions,* Fall, accessed 18 June 2007 from *http://www.bls.gov/opub/cwc/cm20030124ar03p1.htm.*

4. J. Inberger, 1948, "The Money Spent for Play: An Index of Opinion," *The Public Opinion Quarterly,* v. 2, no. 2: 249.

5. Ibid.

6. T. Balio, 1996, "Surviving the Great Depression," in *Grand Design: Hollywood as a Modern Business Enterprise 1930–39.* (Berkeley: University of California Press), pp. 13–15.

7. CC. Alexander, 2002, *Breaking the Slump: Baseball in the Depression Era.* (New York: Columbia University Press), p. 52; Rodney Fort, "Sports Business Pages," accessed 15 June 2007 from rodneyfort.com.

8. D. Pappas, 1997, "1997: 75 Years of National Baseball Broadcasts," *Outside the Lines* (national SABR Business of Baseball Community Newsletter), accessed 20 June 2007 from *http://roadsidephotos.sabr.org/baseball/nationalbroadcast.htm.*

9. "Year in Review: 1934 National League," *Baseball Almanac,* accessed 20 June 2007 from *http://www.baseball-almanac.com/yearly/yr1934n.shtml.*

10. Fort, "Sports Business Pages."

11. J.L. Vaughn, 2002, "Baseball's Importance during the Great Depression." Master's thesis, Central Connecticut State University, accessed 18 June 2007 from *http://fred.ccsu.edu:8000/archive/00000016/01/etd-2002–16.pdf.*

12. "1930s: Sports and Games," 2002, in *Bowling, Beatniks, and Bell-Bottoms: Pop Culture of 20th Century America,* ed. S. Pendergast and T. Pendergast (Farmington Hills, MI: UXL); General Mills, "Wheaties History," accessed 16 June 2007 from *http://www.wheaties.com/history/index.aspx.*

13. Greater Mansfield Chamber of Commerce, Inc., "History of Mansfield," accessed 21 June from *http://www.mansfield.org/history.htm.*

14. V. Spadafora, 2006, "Football under the Lights," *The World Almanac 2007,* accessed 21 June from *http://www.worldalmanac.com/blog/2006/11/football_under_the_lights.html*; Professional Football Hall of Fame, "History — Providence Steam Roller," accessed 22 June 2007 from *http://www.profootballhof.com/history/decades/1920s/providence.jsp*; Fort, "Sports Business Pages."

15. D. Pietruza, 1997, *Lights On! The Wild Century-Long Saga of Night Baseball* (Lanham, MD: Scarecrow Press); Minor League Baseball, "History: Timeline," accessed 15 June 2007 from *http://web.minorleaguebaseball.com/milb/history/timeline.jsp.*

16. "Famous Night Games," *Baseball Almanac,* accessed 15 June 2007 from *http://www.baseball-almanac.com/firsts/first10.shtml*; Fort, "Sports Business Pages."

17. B. Clarke, 2006, "Cubs Night Games at Wrigley Field," on Cubdom, accessed 21 June 2007 from *http://www.thecubdom.com/features/wrigleyfieldnightgames.html.*

18. "History of the MLB All-Star Game — 1933," *The Sporting News,* accessed 15 June 2007 from *http://archive.sportingnews.com/features/allstar/1933.html.*

19. "College All-Star Football Game." Encyclopedia of Chicago. Accessed 15 June 2007 from *http://www.encyclopedia.chicagohistory.org/pages/3215.html.*

20. Hickok Sports, "College Bowl Games,"

accessed 15 June 2007 from *http://www.hickok sports.com/history/collbowl.shtml.*

21. In 1940 and 1942, there was a second all-star game played, one in December pitting the all-stars against the prior year's champions, and another in January against the newly crowned champions. Hickok Sports, "The Pro Bowl," accessed 15 June 2007 from *http://www.hickok sports.com/history/probowl.shtml.*

22. Hickok Sports, "NHL All-Star Teams," accessed 15 June 2007 from *http://www.hickok sports.com/history/nhlallstarteams.shtml.*

23. A. St. John, 1999, "Home Away from Home: A Yankee Fan's Guide to Fenway Park," *The Village Voice,* accessed 15 June 2007 from *http://www.villagevoice.com/news/9927,stjohn,68 88,3.html.*

24. Franklin D. Roosevelt Presidential Library and Museum, accessed 15 June 2007 from *http://www.fdrlibrary.marist.edu/39.html.*

25. L.D. Johnston and S.H. Williamson, 2005, "The Annual Real and Nominal GDP for the United States, 1790—Present," Economic History Services, accessed 21 June 2007 *http:// www.eh.net/hmit/gdp/.*

26. Ibid.

27. Professional Football Hall of Fame, "Football and America: World War II," accessed 15 June 2007 from *http://www.profootballhof. com/history/general/war/worldwar2/page1.jsp.*

28. "Economic Report of the President," 1947, Appendix B, Table I and Table V, accessed 19 June 2007 from *http://fraser.stlouisfed.org/pub lications/ERP/issue/1630/download/7538/ERP_19 47_January.pdf*; R. Higgs, 1990, "Wartime Prosperity during World War II?" presented at Economics in Times of Crisis (Cliometric sessions at the 1990 Allied Social Science Associations meetings, Washington, D.C.), accessed 19 June 2007 from *http://eh.net/Clio/Conferences/ASSA/ Dec_90/Higgs%20Abstract.*

29. Ibid.

30. Ibid.

31. J.P. Jacobsen, 2007, The Economics of Gender, 3rd Edition (Malden, MA: Blackwell), p. 407.

32. J. Lesko, 2005, "League History," for AAGPBL Players Association, Inc., accessed 22 June 2007 from *http://www.aagpbl.org/league/ history.cfm.*

33. United States Golf Association, "USGA history 1931–1950," accessed 20 June 2007 from *http://www.usga.org/aboutus/usga_history/1931_ 1950.html.*

34. "The Tennis Grand Slam," accessed 22 June 2007 from *http://www.all-about-tennis.com/ tennisgrandslam.html.*

35. "President Franklin Roosevelt Green Light Letter—Baseball Can Be Played during the War," *Baseball* Almanac, accessed 22 March 2005 from *http://www.baseball-almanac.com/prz _lfr.shtml.*

36. "Year in Review: 1941: American League," *Baseball Almanac,* accessed 22 March 2005 from *http://www.baseball-almanac.com/yearly/yr1941a. shtml.* Gene Stack of the Chicago White Sox actually was the first drafted player to die on active duty, but he did so of a heart attack following an army baseball game. "Year in Review: 1942: American League," *Baseball Almanac,* accessed 22 March 2005 from *http://www.baseba ll-almanac.com/yearly/yr1942a.shtml.* National Baseball Hall of Fame and Museum, "The Uncertainty of Peace," accessed 15 June 2007 from *http://www.baseballhalloffame.org/exhibits/onli ne_exhibits/baseball_enlists/peace.htm.*

37. Williams also left MLB to serve during the Korean War.

38. Professional Football Hall of Fame, "Football and America: World War II," accessed 15 June 2007 from *http://www.profootballhof. com/history/general/war/worldwar2/.*

39. Professional Football Hall of Fame, "Football and America: World War II Honor Roll," accessed 15 June 2007 from *http://profoot ballhof.com/history/general/war/worldwar2/honor _roll.jsp.*

40. Ibid.

41. C. Ellenport, 2001, "From the Football Field to the Battlefield," on NFL.com, accessed 15 June 2007 from *http://www.nfl.com/features/ 2001/military.html.*

42. National Baseball Hall of Fame and Museum, "War Dominates Baseball," accessed 15 June 2007 from *http://www.baseballhalloffame. org/exhibits/online_exhibits/baseball_enlists/dom inates.htm.*

43. Professional Football Hall of Fame, "Football and America: World War II," accessed 15 June 2007 from *http://www.profootballhof. com/history/general/war/worldwar2/page1.jsp.*

44. National Baseball Hall of Fame and Museum, "A New Ball Game," accessed 15 June 2007 from *http://www.baseballhalloffame.org/ex hibits/online_exhibits/baseball_enlists/new.htm.*

45. BaseballLibrary.com, "St. Louis Browns," accessed 15 June 2007 from *http://www.baseball library.com/baseballlibrary/ballplayers/S/St_Louis _Browns.stm.*

46. Ibid.

47. National Baseball Hall of Fame and Museum, "A New Ball Game."

48. National Baseball Hall of Fame and Museum, "Baseballs Like Concrete," accessed 15 June 2007 from *http://www.baseballhalloffame. org/exhibits/online_exhibits/baseball_enlists/con crete.htm.*

49. Professional Football Hall of Fame, "Football and America: World War II."

50. B. McCarty, "Football's Greatest

Decade," *College Football Historical Society Journal*, v. 1, no. 1: 2–6. Accessed 15 June 2007 from *http://www.aafla.org/SportsLibrary/CFHSN/CFHSNv01/CFHSNv01n1b.pdf.*

51. K. Jay, 2006, *More Than Just a Game* (New York: Columbia University Press).

52. U.S. Census Bureau, various years, *Statistical Abstract of the United States.*

53. Professional Football Researchers Association, "All American Football Conference," accessed 24 March 2005 from *http://www.footballresearch.com/articles/frpage.cfm?topic=aafc.*

54. PCL 100, "Centennial News, the Formation of the Pacific Coast League," accessed 25 March 2005 from *http://www1.infinitydesign.net/virtual/pclbaseball.com/www/pcl100/news/?id=2277.*

55. Homerunweb, "Excerpts from *The Book of Baseball Literacy,*" *The Book of Baseball Literacy*, 2nd Edition, accessed 25 March 2005 from *http://www.homerunweb.com/ch3text.html.*

56. J. Quirk and R.D. Fort, 1997, *Pay Dirt: The Business of Professional Team Sports* (Princeton, NJ: Princeton University Press).

57. Answers.com, "American Football League," accessed 25 March 2005 from *http://www.answers.com/main/ntquery;jsessionid=13872xegu7jv8?method=4&dsid=2222&dekey=American+Football+League&gwp=8&curtab=2222_1&sbid=lc04b.*

58. CNNSI.com, 2001, "The AFL: A Football Legacy," *http://sportsillustrated.cnn.com/football/news/2001/01/22/afl_history_1/.*

59. CNNSI.com, 2001, "The AFL: A Football Legacy," *http://sportsillustrated.cnn.com/football/news/2001/01/22/afl_history_1/.*

Chapter 7

1. *Sports Illustrated*, 1968, 22 July.

2. ESPN, 2004, "Late Season Games Can Be Moved to Monday Nights," 9 November, accessed 9 February 2008 from *http://sports.espn.go.com/nfl/news/story?id=1918761.*

3. Brandweek.com, "NBC, ESPN Snap up NFL Packages," accessed 17 May 2005 from *http://www.brandweek.com/brandweek/search/article_display.jsp?schema=&vnu_content_id=1000885303.*

4. ESPN.com, 2004, "Late Season Games Can Be Moved to Monday Nights," 9 November, accessed 25 March 2005 from *http://sports.espn.go.com/nfl/news/story?id=1918761.*

5. P.J. Gough, 2004, "NFL Inks $11.5 Billion in Pacts with CBS, Fox, DirecTV," *Hollywood Reporter,* 9 November, accessed 9 February 2008 from *http://www.hollywoodreporter.com/hr/search/article_display.jsp?vnu_content_id=1000708995.*

6. MLB teams in 2004 got anywhere between under $600,000 (Expos) to $180 million (Yankees) in local media rights. See M.A. Leeds and P. von Allmen, 2007, *Sports Economics,* 2nd Edition (Boston: Addison-Wesley).

7. B.M. Bloom, 2006, "TV Deals OK'd in Quiet Meetings," MLB.com, 16 November, accessed 9 February 2008 from *http://mlb.mlb.com/news/article.jsp?ymd=20061116&content_id=1741845&vkey=news_mlb&fext=.jsp&c_id=mlb.*

8. J. Donavan, 2007, "MLB, DirecTV Strike Deal," *Sports Illustrated,* 8 March, accessed 9 February 2008 from *http://sportsillustrated.cnn.com/2007/writers/john_donovan/03/08/directtv/.*

9. R.D. Fort, "Sports Business Pages," accessed 25 March 2005 from *http://users.pullman.com/rodfort/SportsBusiness/BizFrame.htm.*

10. R. Sandomir, 2007, "N.B.A. Renews Pacts, Adding Links to Digital Use," *New York Times,* 28 June, accessed 10 January 2008 from *http://www.nytimes.com/2007/06/28/sports/basketball/28sandomir.html?fta=y.*

11. J. Consoli, 2007, "WNBA Expands TV Rights Deal with ABC/ESPN," Mediaweek.com, 16 July, accessed 10 January 2008 from *http://www.wnba.com/media/fever/070716_MediaWeek_wnba.pdf.*

12. J. Zuglad, 2004, "Business of the NHL — league's TV Deal May Suffer," *Minneapolis Star-Tribune,* 21 January, accessed 25 March 2005 from *http://www.startribune.com/stories/1330/4330146.html.*

13. NCAA, "NCAA Broadcast Information," NCAA.com, accessed 25 March 2005 from *http://www.ncaasports.com/broadcast/mlacrosse.*

14. D. Kiley, 2007, "NBC: Blindsided by Notre Dame," *Business Week,* 20 December, accessed 9 February 2008 from *http://www.businessweek.com/magazine/content/07_53/b4065037218411.htm.*

15. L. Robbins, 2007, "A Football Final Four," *New York Post,* 17 July, accessed 9 February from *http://www.nypost.com/seven/07172007/sports/a_football_final_four_sports_lenn_robbins.htm.*

16. "The PGA Tour: Where's the Green?" 2002, *Business Week*, 20 May, accessed 9 February 2008 *http://www.businessweek.com/magazine/content/02_20/b3783108.htm.*

17. B. Kelley, "About Golf," accessed 16 August 2006 from *http://golf.about.com/b/a/234789.htm.*

18. P. Penelope, 2003, "NASCAR Pulls into Prime Time," *Forbes*, 7 October, accessed 9 February 2008 from *http://www.forbes.com/2003/10/07/cx_pp_1007nascar.html.*

19. Edmunds.com, 2005, "NASCAR Announces New Lucrative Television Contracts,

but without NBC," *Edmund's Inside Line*, 8 December, accessed 9 February 2008 from *http://www.edmunds.com/insideline/do/News/articleId=108437*.

20. "Sirius Satellite Will Broadcast NASCAR," 2005, *USA Today*, 22 February, accessed 9 February 2008 from *http://www.usatoday.com/sports/motor/nascar/2005-02-22-sirius-nascar_x.htm*.

21. Autoracingsport.com, 2006, "Fox Sports and Speed TV to broadcast F1 races in U.S. through 2009," 28 November, accessed 9 November 2008 from http://autoracingsport.com/uncategorized/fox-sports-and-speed-tv-to-broadcast-f1-races-in-us-through-2009/; R. Cohen, 2007, "NBA extends TV deals with ESPN/ABC, TNT, ESPN," 27 June, accessed 9 November 2008 from http://www.usatoday.com/sports/basketball/2007-06-27-3096131424_x.htm; *Deseret News*, 2007, "WNBA unveils new television contract," accessed 9 November 2008 from http://findarticles.com/p/articles/mi_qn4188/is_/ai_n19370272; ESPN, 2004, "Late season games can be moved to Monday nights," 9 November, accessed 9 November 2008 from http://sports.espn.go.com/nfl/news/story?id=1918761; ESPN, 2005, "NASCAR agrees to 8-year deal with ESPN, ABC," 8 December, accessed 9 November 2008 from http://sports.espn.go.com/rpm/news/story?series=wc&id=2251049; J. Garcia, 2008, "What to Watch: Obama Need Second Term to Fix BCS," accessed 9 November 2008 from http://www.mysanantonio.com/sports/What_to_Watch_Obama_Need_Second_Term_to_Fix_BCS.html; M. Harris, 2004, "Source: ABC, ESPN to extend TV contract with IRL," *USA Today*, 26 May, accessed 9 November 2008 from http://www.usatoday.com/sports/motor/irl/indy500/2004-05-26-notebook_x.htm; MLB, 2007, "MLB, DIRECTV expand multi-year agreement," 8 March, accessed 9 November 2008 from http://mlb.mlb.com/news/press_releases/press_release.jsp?ymd=20070308&content_id=1833910&vkey=pr_mlb&fext=.jsp&c_id=mlb; PRnewswire.com, 1999, "CBS Sports and National Collegiate Athletic Association Reach Long-Term Agreement for NCAA Division I Men's Basketball Championship," 18 November, accessed 9 November 2008 from http://www.prnewswire.com/cgi-bin/stories.pl?ACCT=104&STORY=/www/story/11-18-1999/0001079506&EDATE=; D. Sessa, 2006, "Baseball expands TV coverage with Fox, Turner deals," Bloomberg News, 11 July, accessed 9 November 2008 from http://www.bloomberg.com/apps/news?pid=20601089&sid=a4weBYzzyNtc&refer=home; R. Sandomir, 2003, "OLYMPICS; NBC's Olympic Run Is Extended to 2012 With $2 Billion Bid," *New York Times*, 7 June, accessed 9 November 2008 from http://query.nytimes.com/gst/fullpage.html?res=9E00E6D91739F934A35755C0A9659C8B63&sec=&spon=&&scp=3&sq=olympics%20tv%20rights%20deal&st=cse; R. Sandomir, 2008, "Versus extends contract with N.H.L." *New York Times*, 23 January, accessed 9 November 2008 from http://www.nytimes.com/2008/01/23/sports/hockey/23versus.html?ref=sports; UPI, 2008, "NBC Sports extends NHL TV contract," accessed 9 November 2008 from http://www.upi.com/Sports_News/2008/04/24/NBC_Sports_extends_NHL_TV_contract/UPI-13211209063880/.

22. T.F. Scanlon, 2006, "Sports and Media in the Ancient Mediterranean," in *Handbook of Sports and Media*, ed. A.A. Raney and J. Bryant (New York: Erlbaum).

23. CNN, 2004, "Birthday Praise for N. Korea's Kim," 16 February, accessed 2 February 2008 from *http://edition.cnn.com/2004/WORLD/asiapcf/02/16/kim.birthday.reut/*.

24. Scanlon, "Sports and Media in the Ancient Mediterranean."

25. E.S. Sears, 2001, *Running through the Ages* (Jefferson, NC: McFarland).

26. Scanlon, "Sports and Media in the Ancient Mediterranean."

27. Ibid.

28. Ibid.

29. B. Suzanne, 1998, "Characters of Plato's Time and Dialogues: Pindar," accessed 2 February from *http://plato-dialogues.org/tools/char/pindar.htm*.

30. P. Christesen, 2007, *Olympic Victor Lists and Ancient Greek History* (Cambridge: Cambridge University Press); Scanlon, "Sports and Media in the Ancient Mediterranean."

31. Scanlon, "Sports and Media in the Ancient Mediterranean."

32. R.D. Mandell, 2003, "Europe, 500–1750," in *Sport*, ed. E. Dunning and D. Malcolm (London and New York: Routledge).

33. T. Hendricks, 2003, "Sport in the Later Middle Ages," in *Sport*, ed. Dunning and Malcolm. The relative scarcity of capital (land) and labor changed dramatically as a result of the plague, which had the effect of increasing wages. This may have encouraged rather than discouraged more spectator sports, although this is not known with certainty.

34. Ibid.

35. J.I. Day, 1950, "Horseracing and the Parimutual," *Annals of the American Academy of Political and Social Science*, v. 269 (May): 55–61.

36. R.W. McChesney, 1989, "Media Made Sport: A History of Sports Coverage in the United States," in *Media, Sports and Society*, ed. L.A. Wenner (Newbury Park, CA: Sage).

37. A. Harvey, 2004, *The Beginnings of a Sporting Culture in Britain, 1793–1850* (London: Ashgate).

38. Ibid.

39. M. Schudson, 1978, *Discovering the News: A Social History of American Newspapers* (New York: Basic).

40. W. Wanta, 2006, "The Coverage of Sports in Print Media," in *Handbook of Sports and Media*, ed. A.A. Raney and J. Bryant (New York: Erlbaum).

41. McChesney, "Media Made Sport."

42. D. Block, 2006, *Baseball before We Knew It: A Search for Roots of the Game* (Lincoln: University of Nebraska Press).

43. McChesney, "Media Made Sport."

44. A.J. Schiff, 2008, *"The Father of Baseball": A Biography of Henry Chadwick* (Jefferson, NC: McFarland).

45. Schudson, *Discovering the News.*

46. McChesney, "Media Made Sport."

47. J. Bryant and A.M. Holt, 2006, "A Historical Overview of Sports and Media in the United States," in *Handbook of Sports and Media*, ed. Raney and Bryant.

48. J. Holtzman, 2005, Jerome Holtzman on Baseball: A History of Baseball Scribes (Champagne, IL: Sports Publishing, LLC).

49. Bryant and Holt, "A Historical Overview oOf Sports."

50. Holtzman indicates that the game was between Harvard and Yale, and took place in 1885 (Holtzman, *Jerome Holtzman on Baseball*); M. Oriard, 1993, *Reading Football: How the Popular Press Created an American Spectacle* (Chapel Hill: University of North Carolina Press).

51. There is at this time only one full book-length biography of Henry Chadwick. The material in this section draws heavily from that work: Schiff, *"The Father of Baseball."*

52. Ibid.

53. Ibid.

54. Ibid.

55. Ibid.

56. Holtzman, *Jerome Holtzman on Baseball.*

57. Schiff, *"The Father of Baseball."*

58. Ibid.

59. Ibid.

60. Ibid.

61. S.H. Williamson, 2007, "Six Ways to Compute the Relative Value of a U.S. Dollar Amount, 1790—2007," on MeasuringWorth. Com, accessed 16 February 2008 from *http://www.measuringworth.com/uscompare/*; Schiff, "The Father of Baseball."

62. McChesney, "Media Made Sport."

63. Ibid.

64. McChesney, "Media Made Sport"; Bryant and Holt, "A Historical Overview of Sports and Media in the United States."

65. Wanta, "The Coverage of Sports in Print Media."

66. Ibid.

67. Northwestern University Readership Institute, 2001, "Newspaper Industry Content Analysis Report: Data Tables and Definitions," accessed 7 January 2008 from *http://www.readership.org/content/content_analysis/data/industry_content_report.pdf.*

68. Magazine Publishers of America, "2006 Average Total Paid and Verified Circulation for Top 100 ABC Magazines," accessed 10 February 2008 from *http://www.magazine.org/circulation/circulation_trends_and_magazine_handbook/22175.cfm.*

69. J.W. Owens, 2006, The Coverage of Sports on Radio," in *Handbook of Sports and Media*, ed. Raney and Bryant.

70. Owens, "The Coverage of Sports on Radio."

71. Ibid.

72. *Baseball Almanac,* "Famous firsts in the lively ball era," accessed 10 February 2008 from *http://www.baseball-almanac.com/firsts/first3.shtml.*

73. New York Radio History, accessed 9 June 2006 from *http://www.tangentsunset.com/newyorkradiohistory.htm.*

74. Owens, "The Coverage of Sports on Radio."

75. McChesney, "Media Made Sport."

76. S. Shea, 2007, "Cubs Broadcast History," Society for American Baseball Research, Business of Baseball Committee, 26 July, accessed 10 February 2008 from *http://bob.sabrwebs.com/index2.php?option=com_content&do_pdf=1&id=119.*

77. McChesney, "Media Made Sport."

78. Owens, "The Coverage of Sports on Radio."

79. Ibid.

80. Sports Business Journal, 2006, *2006 Sports Business Resource Guide and Fact Book* (Charlotte, NC: Street & Smith's).

81. J. Mills, 1987, "Radio's All-sports Gamble," *The New York Times,* 4 August, accessed 10 February from *http://query.nytimes.com/gst/fullpage.html?res=9B0DEFD91639F937A3575BC0A961948260.*

82. Owens, "The Coverage of Sports on Radio"; Radio Advertising Bureau, 2007, *Radio Marketing and Fact Book 2007–2008,* 11 October, accessed 10 February 2008 from *http://www.rab.com/public/MediaFacts/2007RMGFB-150-10-11.pdf.*

83. ESPN, 2008, "Frequently Asked Questions — ESPN Radio," 7 February, accessed 10 February 2008 from *http://espnradio.espn.go.com/espnradio/story?storyId=1457975.*

84. J. Neal-Lunsford, 1992, "Sport in the Land of Television: The Use of Sport in Network Prime-time Schedules, 1946–1950," *Journal of Sport History*, v. 19, no. 1: 56–76.

85. Neal-Lunsford, "Sport in the Land of Television"; G.T. Kurian, ed., 2004, *Datapedia of the United States: American History in Numbers,* 3rd Edition (Lanham, MD: Bernan Press).

86. K. Massey, "Museum of Broadcast Communications. Freeze of 1948," accessed 17 February 2008 from *http://www.museum.tv/archives/etv/F/htmlF/freezeofl/freezeofl.htm.*

87. Kurian, *Datapedia of the United States*; Neal-Lunsford, "Sport in the Land of Television"; U.S. Census Bureau, 2008, *2008 Statistical Abstract,* Table 1113, accessed 17 February 2008 from *http://www.census.gov/compendia/statab/tables/08s1113.pdf.*

88. B.J. Baran, "Sports and Television," Museum of Broadcast Communications, accessed 17 February 2008 from *http://www.museum.tv/archives/etv/S/htmlS/sportsandte/sportsandte.htm*; Neal-Lunsford, "Sport in the Land of Television"; Kurian, *Datapedia of the United States*; Annual TV Households, "Number of TV Households in America," accessed 25 March 2005 from *http://www.tvhistory.tv/Annual_TV_Households_50–78.JPG.*

89. Baran, "Sports and Television."

90. Neal-Lunsford, "Sport in the Land of Television."

91. Baran, "Sports and Television"; McChesney, "Media Made Sport."

92. V. Adams, 1954, "News of TV and Radio," *New York Times,* 30 January, p. X15.

93. G. Noyes, "American Broadcasting Company," Museum of Broadcast Communications, accessed 17 February 2008 from *http://www.museum.tv/archives/etv/A/htmlA/americanbroa/americanbroa.htm.*

94. Neal-Lunsford, "Sport in the Land of Television."

95. Ibid.

96. Ibid.

97. V. Adams, 1960, "A.B.C. Signs Pact for Pro Football," *New York Times,* June 10, p. 63; R.A. Smith, 2001, *Play-by-Play: Radio, Television, and Big-Time College Sport* (Baltimore: Johns Hopkins University Press).

98. R. Arledge, 2002, *Roone* (New York: HarperCollins).

99. Ibid.

100. Ibid.

101. Ibid.

102. Ibid.

103. R.O. Davies, 1994, *America's Obsession: Sports and Society since 1945* (Fort Worth, TX: Harcourt Brace).

104. Arledge, *Roone.*

105. Ibid.

106. Ibid.

107. Lawrence A. Wenner, 1989, *Media, Sports and Society* (Newbury Park, CA: Sage Publications).

108. M. Freeman, 2001, *ESPN: The Uncensored History* (Lanham, MD: Taylor Trade).

109. Ibid.

110. Ibid.

111. Ibid.

112. Ibid.

113. D. Brown and J. Bryant, 2003, "Sports Content on U.S. Television," in *Handbook of Sports and Media,* ed. Raney and Bryant.

114. A. Romano, 2004, "Regional Appeal," *Broadcasting and Cable,* 15 March, accessed 17 February 2008 from *http://www.broadcastingcable.com/article/CA403509.html.*

Chapter 8

1. E.D. Snyder and E. Spreitzer, 1974, "Sociology of Sport: An Overview," *The Sociological Quarterly,* v. 15, no. 4: 467–487.

2. Substance Abuse and Mental Health Administration, 2007, "Results from the 2006 National Survey on Drug Use and Health: National Findings," Office of Applied Studies, NSDUH H-32, DHHS Publication No. SMA 07–4293.

3. U.S. Census Bureau, 2008, *Statistical Abstract of the U.S.,* Table 318, accessed 27 January 2008 from *http://www.census.gov/compendia/statab/tables/08s0318.pdf.*

4. "Powdered Wigs," 2007, *Economist,* 13 December; B. Wallace-Wells, 2007, "How America Lost the War on Drugs," *Rolling Stone,* 27 November, accessed 24 January 2008 from *http://www.rollingstone.com/news/story/17438347/how_america_lost_the_war_on_drugs.*

5. C. Bader, K. Dougherty, P. Froese, B. Johnson, F.C. Mencken, J.Z. Park, and R. Starr, 2006, "American Piety in the 21st Century: New Insights to the Depth and Complexity of Religion in the US," Baylor University, Institute for the Studies of Religion, accessed 15 January 2008 from *http://www.baylor.edu/content/services/document.php/33304.pdf.*

6. Gallup Polls, "Religion," accessed 7 January 2008 from *http://www.gallup.com/poll/1690/Religion.aspx*; T.W. Smith, 1998, "A Review of Church Attendance Measures," *American Sociological Review,* v. 63, no. 1: 131–136.

7. Data collected from various official league websites.

8. U.S. Census Bureau, 2008, *The 2008 Statistical Abstract,* Tables 1217 and 1218.

9. Author calculation based on various sources.

10. Author calculation based on various sources.

11. S. Szymanski, 2003, "The Economic Design of Sporting Contests," *Journal of Economic Literature,* v. 41, no. 4: 1137–1187.

12. NCAAfootball.com, 2008, "TV Ratings and Bowl Games Highlight America's Passion for College Football in 2007," accessed 26 January 2008 from *http://www.ncaafootball.com/index.php?s=&url_channel_id=34&url_article_id=11994&change_well_id=2.*

13. Author calculations based in part on M. Hiestand, 2007, "NASCAR Ratings Drop Again; Remain Strongest in the South," *USA Today*, November 13, accessed 27 January 2008 from *http://www.usatoday.com/sports/columnist/hiestand-tv/2007-11-13-nascar-ratings_N.htm.*

14. Ibid.

15. Author calculations based on T. Bonk, 2008, "Tiger Tale: To Have or Have-not," *Los Angeles Times,* 23 January, accessed 26 January 2008 from *http://www.latimes.com/sports/la-sp-tigertv23jan23,1,2991626.story?coll=la-headlines-sports&ctrack=1&cset=true.*

16. That's Racin,' 2008, "Media Center: NASCAR on 2008 Fox Schedule," 25 January, accessed 27 January 2008 from *http://www.thatsracin.com/119/story/10203.html*; Neilson ratings as reported by J. Seidman, 2007, "Sports Ratings: Challenged at the National Level," 5 September, accessed 15 January 2008 from *http://tvbythenumbers.com/2007/09/05/ted-asks-why/502.* Other calculations based on various sources.

17. B. Gorman, 2007, "Does NFL Sunday Night Scheduling Help Ratings?" accessed 15 January 2008 from http://tvbythenumbers.com/2007/11/11/does-nfl-sunday-night-scheduling-help-ratings/1723; B. Gorman, 2007, "Neilson Top 20 Sports TV Ratings — Week of September 10–16," accessed 15 January 2008 from http://tvbythenumbers.com/2007/09/22/top-20-sports-shows-week-of-sept-10-16/812; B. Gorman, 2007, "Neilson Top 20 Sports TV Ratings — Week of October 22–28," accessed 15 January 2008 from http://tvbythenumbers.com/2007/11/02/top-sports-shows-oct-22-28/1596.

18. P.R. LaMonica, 2007, "CBS Scores with Super Bowl Ratings," CNNMoney.com, 5 February, accessed 15 January 2008 from *http://money.cnn.com/2007/02/05/news/companies/superbowl_ratings/index.htm*; Neilson Media Research, 2008, "Neilson's Recap of 2008 Super Bowl Advertising," 7 February," accessed 27 February 2008 from *http://www.nielsenmedia.com/nc/portal/site/Public/menuitem.55dc65b4a7d5adff3f65936147a062a0/?vgnextoid=697760772bfe7110VgnVCM100000ac0a260aRCRD.*

19. NCAAfootball.com, 2008, "TV Ratings and Bowl Games Highlight America's Passion for College Football in 2007," accessed 26 January 2008 from *http://www.ncaafootball.com/index.php?s=&url_channel_id=34&url_article_id=11994&change_well_id=2.*

20. MSNBC, 2007, "NBA Finals TV Ratings Were Record Low," accessed 26 January 2008 from *http://www.msnbc.msn.com/id/19253444/.*

21. D.L. Wann, M.J. Melnick, G.W. Russell, and D.G. Pease, 2001, *Sports Fans: The Psychology and Social Impact of Spectators* (New York: Routledge).

22. L. Innaccone, 1998, "Introduction to the Economics of Religion," Journal of Economic Literature, v. 36, no. 3: 1465–1496.

23. G. Becker and K. Murphy, 1988, "A Theory of Rational Addiction," Journal of Political Economy, v. 96, no. 4: 675–700. It should be noted that a similar approach to modeling consumer brand loyalty was undertaken in Houthakker and Taylor's 1966 monograph and its 1970 second edition: H.S. Houthakker and L.D. Taylor, 1966 and 1970, *Consumer Demand in the United States, 1929–1970* (Cambridge, MA: Harvard University Press).

24. Material for this section is drawn from K.G. Quinn and D. Surdam, 2007, "The Case of the Missing Fans," St. Norbert College and University of Northern Iowa, mimeograph.

25. Other reasons included in the study were physical effects, and to manage the effects of other substances.

26. R.B. Cialdini, R.J. Borden, A. Throne, M.R. Walker, S. Freeman, and S.R. Sloane, 1976, "Basking in Reflected Glory: Three (Football) Field Studies," Wann, Melnick, Russell, and Pease, *Sports Fans.*

27. Cialdini, Borden, Throne, Walker, Freeman, and Sloane, "Basking in Reflected Glory"; Wann, Melnick, Russell, and Pease, Sports Fans.

28. A.A. Raney, 2006, "Why We Watch and Enjoy Mediated Sports," in *Handbook of Sports and Media*, ed. A.A. Raney and J. Bryant (Hillsdale, NJ: Erlbaum); D.L. Wann, 1995, "Preliminary Validation of the Sports Fan Motivational Scale," *Journal of Sport and Social Issues,* v. 19, no. 4: 377–396.

29. Wann, Melnick, Russell, and Pease, *Sports Fans.*

30. Wann, Melnick, Russell, and Pease, *Sports Fans*; A. Guttman, 1996, *The Erotic in Sports* (New York: Columbia University Press).

31. Nearly every sport demand study has found this result. For a comprehensive compendium of significant attendance demand studies see A. Zimbalist, ed., 2001, *The Economics of Sport* (Northampton, MA: Elgar).

32. For example, see D.J. Berri, M.B. Schmidt, and S.L. Brook, 2004, "Stars at the Gate: The Impact of Star Power on NBA Gate Revenues," *Journal of Sports Economics,* v. 5, no. 1: 33–50. For another example, see A. Krautmann and L. Hadley, 2006, "Demand Issues: The Product Market for Professional Sports," in *Handbook of Sports Economics,* ed. J. Fizel (Armonk, NY: M.E. Sharpe).

33 How Long a Honeymoon? The Effect of New Stadiums on Attendance in Major League Baseball," *Journal of Sports Economics*, v. 6, no. 3: 237–263.

34. M.A. McDonald and D. Rascher, 2000, "Does Bat Day Make Cents? The Effect of Promotions on Demand for Major League Baseball," *Journal of Sport Management*, v. 14, no. 1: 8–27.

35. J.C. van Ours, 1995, "The Price Elasticity of Hard Drugs: The Case of Opium in the Dutch East Indies, 1923–1938," *The Journal of Political Economy*, v. 103, no. 2: 261–279.

36. R. Room, 1987, "Alcohol Monopolies in the U.S.: Challenges and Opportunities," *Journal of Public Health Policy*, v. 8, no. 4: 509–530.

37. A. Krautmann and L. Hadley, 2006, "Demand Issues: The Product Market for Professional Sports, in Handbook of Sports Economics, ed. Fizel.

38. Krautmann and Hadley, "Demand Issues."

39. R.D. Fort, 2004, "Inelastic Sports Pricing," *Managerial and Decision Economics*, v. 25, no. 2: 87–94.

40. R.D. Fort, 2004, "Subsidies as Incentive Mechanisms in Sports," *Managerial and Decision Economics*, v. 25, no. 2: 95–102.

41. Quinn and Surdam, "The Case of the Missing Fans"; S.C. Ahn and Y.H. Lee, 2003, "The Attendance Demand of Major League Baseball," Paper presented at the 2003 Western Economic Association International meeting, Denver, CO, July.

42. D. Surdam, 2007, "Mr. Keynes, Meet Mr. Ruppert: The New York Yankees during the Great Depression," Paper presented at the annual meeting of the Social Science History Association, Chicago, IL, November.

43. T.F. Scanlon, 2006, "Sports and Media in the Ancient Mediterranean," in *Handbook of Sports and Media*, ed. A.A. Raney and J. Bryant (Hillsdale, NJ: Erlbaum).

44. Harvard Business School, Exhibits — 19th Century Trade Cards — Historical Collections — Baker Library, accessed 14 January 2008 from *http://www.library.hbs.edu/hc/19th_century_tcard/*.

45. P.G. Porter, 1969, "Origins of the American Tobacco Company," *The Business History Review*, v. 43, no. 1: 59–76.

46. J. Adler, 2005, "Coffin Nails — The Tobacco Controversy in the 19th Century," *HarpWeek*, accessed 14 January 2008 from *http://tobacco.harpweek.com/hubpages/CommentaryPage.asp?Commentary=Introduction*.

47. S. Wong, 2005, *Smithsonian Baseball: Inside the World's Finest Collections* (New York: Harper Collins).

48. Porter, "Origins of the American Tobacco Company."

49. E.S. Martin, 1899, "This Busy World," *Harper's Weekly*, 19 August, p. 809.

50. L. Hemphill, 2008, "No Card This Month," on Thestate.com, 12 January, accessed 15 January 2007 from *http://www.thestate.com/sports/story/282573.html*.

51. *American Tobacco Co.*, 221 U. S. 106 (1911).

52. J. Zoss and J. Bowman, 2004, *Diamonds in the Rough: The Untold Story of Baseball* (Lincoln University of Nebraska University Press).

53. Ibid.

54. *Tuff Stuff*, 2007, December (collectibles guide magazine).

55. Ibid.

56. J. Yastine, 2007, "Superbowl-sized Sports Memorabilia Sales," *Nightly Business Report*, 2 February, accessed 7 January 2008 from *http://www.pbs.org/nbr/site/onair/transcripts/070202c/*.

57. Count done at 2:05 p.m. CST on 7 January 2008 by the author.

58. Quoted in D.W. Robinson, 1961, "The Economics of Fashion Demand," *The Quarterly Journal of Economics*, v. 75, no. 3: 376–398.

59. B.J. Mullin, S. Hardy, and W.A. Sutton, 2007, *Sports Marketing* (Champaign, IL: Human Kinetics); D. Rovell, 2003, "Seven Licensees Will Pay the Bulk of the Fees," on ESPN.com, 4 August, updated 6 August, accessed 26 April 2008 from *http://espn.go.com/sportsbusiness/news/2003/0804/1590167.html*; author's estimate based on 2000 sports licensing revenues of $721 million as reported by tcdtrade.com, 2001, "Licensing Industry Prospers, but Sports, Entertainment Categories Soften," accessed 7 January 2008 from *http://www.tdctrade.com/imn/01062802/trade01.htm*.

60. R. Sandomir, 1998, "TV Sports; It's a Summer Doubleheader for Babe Ruth Fans," *New York Times*, 14 July.

61. Benjamin G. Rader, 1983, *American Sports: From the Age of Folk Games to the Age of Spectators* (Englewood Cliffs, NJ: Prentice-Hall).

62. J.B. Strasser, 1993, *Swoosh! The Unauthorized Story of Nike and the Men Who Played There* (New York: HarperCollins).

63. B. Herbert, 1996, "In America; Nike's Pyramid Scheme," *New York Times* (10 June).

64. C. Brown, 2000, "Golf; Nike Deal for Woods Said to Be the Richest," *New York Times*, 15 September.

65. J. Gorant, 2007," "New Flavors," on Golf.com, 7 September, accessed 8 January 2008 from *http://www.golf.com/golf/tours_news/article/0,28136,1660194,00.html*.

66. "The Celebrity 100," 2007, *Forbes*, 14 June, accessed 14 January 2008 from *http://www.forbes.com/lists/2007/53/07celebrities_The-Celebrity-100_Rank.html*.

Chapter 9

1. T. Veblen and M. Banta, 2007, *Theory of the Leisure Class,* Oxford's World Classics (New York: Oxford University Press).

2. T. Van Riper, 2007, "The Costs of Online Football: Pure Fantasy," *Forbes,* 26 September, accessed 9 March 2008 from *http://www.forbes.com/leadership/2007/09/26/fantasy-football-office-lead-cx_tvr_0926productivity.html.*

3. A.A. Raney, 2006, "Why We Watch and Enjoy Mediated Sports," in *Handbook of Sports and Media,* ed. A.A. Raney and J. Bryant (Hillsdale, NJ: Erlbaum).

4. "St. Julien Will Be First Black Jockey in 79 Years at Derby," *Sports Illustrated,* 4 May, accessed 16 December 2007 from *http://sportsillustrated.cnn.com/more/horseracing/2000/triplecrown/kentucky/news/2000/05/04/stjulien_derby_ap/.*

5. A. Ritchie, 1996, *Major Taylor: The Extraordinary Career of a Champion Bicycle Racer* (Baltimore: Johns Hopkins University Press).

6. International Boxing Hall of Fame, "George Dixon," accessed 26 December 2007 from *http://www.ibhof.com/dixon.htm*; International Boxing Hall of Fame, "Jack Johnson," accessed 26 December 2007 from *http://www.ibhof.com/jjohnson.htm.*

7. D.L. Fleitz, 2005, *Cap Anson: The Grand Old Man of Baseball* (Jefferson, NC: McFarland); *Cap Chronicled,* Chapter 4: "Cap's Great Shame — Racial Intolerance," accessed 26 December 2007 from *http://www.capanson.com/chapter4.html.*

8. J. Horrigan, "Charles Follis Led Early Black Pioneers in Pro Football," Pro Football Hall of Fame, reprinted by author permission from the *Pro Football Researchers Association Annual,* accessed 26 December 2007 from *http://www.profootballhof.com/history/release.jsp?release_id=1381.*

9. Pro Football Hall of Fame, "African-Americans in Pro Football Pioneers, Milestones and Firsts," accessed 26 December 2007 from *http://www.profootballhof.com/history/general/african-americans.jsp*; M.E. Lomax, 1999, "The African American Experience in Professional Football," *Journal of Social History,* v. 33 (Fall): 163–178.

10. Pro Football Hall of Fame, "Marion Motley," accessed 30 January 2008 from *http://www.profootballhof.com/hof/member.jsp?player_id=156*; Pro Football Hall of Fame, "Bill Willis," accessed 30 January 2008 from *http://www.profootballhof.com/hof/member.jsp?player_id=231.*

11. R. Lapchick, with M. Bustamante and H. Ruiz, 2006, "The 2006–07 Season Racial and Gender Report Card: National Basketball Association," University of Central Florida, College of Business Administration, DeVos Sports Business Management Program, accessed 26 December 2007 from *http://www.bus.ucf.edu/sport/public/downloads/2006_NBA_RGRC_PR.pdf.*

12. J. Quirk and R.D. Fort, 1997, *Pay Dirt: The Business of Professional Team Sports* (Princeton, NJ: Princeton University Press).

13. G. Camponi-Tabery, 2002, "Jump for Joy: Jump Blues, Dance, and Basketball in 1930s African America," in *Sports Matters: Race, Recreation, and Culture,* ed. J. Bloom and M.N. Miller (New York: NYU Press).

14. The subject of consumer (fan) discrimination is among the better-studied in the academic sports economics literature. For examples of the range of this literature, see F. Fizel, ed., 2006, *Handbook of Sports Economics Research* (Armonk, NY: M.E. Sharpe).

15. R. Lapchick and J. Brendan, 2006, "The 2005 Racial and Gender Report Card: College Sports," University of Central Florida De Vos Sports Business and Management Program, 13 December, accessed 30 January 2008 from *http://www.bus.ucf.edu/sport/public/downloads/2005_Racial_Gender_Report_Card_Colleges.pdf.*

16. R.O. Davies, 1994, *America's Obsession: Sports and Society since 1945* (Fort Worth, TX: Harcourt-Brace).

17. ABC News, 2007, "Women's Purse at Wimbledon Now Equals Men's," 24 June, accessed 30 January 2008 from *http://abcnews.go.com/GMA/story?id=3310814.*

18. D.L. Wann, M.J. Melnick, G.W. Russell, and D.G. Pease, 2001, *Sports Fans: The Psychology and Social Impact of Spectators* (New York: Routledge).

19. G. Su-Lin, C.A. Toggle, M.A., Mitrook, S.H. Coussement, and D. Zillman, 1997, "The Thrill of a Close Game: Who Enjoys It and Who Doesn't?" *Journal of Sport and Social Issues,* v. 21: 53–64.

20. Quoted in J.C.H. Jones, D.G. Ferguson, and K.G. Stewart, 1993, "Blood Sports and Cherry Pie: Some Economics of Violence in the National Hockey League," *American Journal of Economics and Sociology,* v. 52, no. 1: 63–78.

21. Ibid.

22. J.C.H. Jones, J.C.H., D.G. Ferguson, and R. Sunderman, 1996, "From the Arena into the Streets: Hockey Violence, Economic Incentives and Public Policy," *American Journal of Economics and Sociology,* v. 55, no. 2: 231–243.

23. B. Gorman and D. Weeks, 2003, "Foul Play: Fan Fatalities in Twentieth-Century Organized Baseball," *NINE: A Journal of Baseball History and Culture,* v. 12, no. 1: 115–132; R.E. Ward, Jr., 2002, "Fan Violence: Social Problem or Moral Panic?" *Aggression and Violent Behavior,* v. 7: 453–475.

24. L. Kutcher, 1983, "The American Sport Event as Carnival: An Emergent Norm Ap-

proach to Crowd Behavior," *The Journal of Popular Culture,* v. 16, no. 4: 34–41.

25. E.L. Thayer, 1888, "Casey at the Bat," *San Francisco Examiner,* 3 June, published under the pen name of "Phin."

26. Ward, "Fan Violence."

27. B.D. Goss, C.B. Jubenville, and J.L. MacBeth, 2003, "Primary Principles of Post-9/11 Stadium Security in the United States: Transatlantic Implications from British Practices," International Association of Assembly Managers, mimeograph, accessed 26 December 2007 from *http://www.iaam.org/CVMS/Post%20911%20Stadium%20Security.doc.*

28. "College Football; Fan Violence Erupts During Victory Celebrations," 2002, *New York Times,* 24 November, accessed 26 December 2007 from *http://query.nytimes.com/gst/fullpage.html?res=9E0DE6DB1E39F936A15752C1A9649C8B63.*

29. Gorman and Weeks, "Foul Play."

30. S. Paolantonio, 2002, "Eagles Preparing to Leave Veterans Stadium," on ESPN.com, 13 December, accessed 26 December 2007 from *http://espn.go.com/nfl/columns/paolantonio_sal/1476046.html.*

31. Wann, Melnick, Russell, and Pease, *Sports Fans.*

Chapter 10

1. The above quote is from a 17 August 1895 letter to a conference concerning proportional representation held in Saratoga Springs, NY, in 1895, and later reprinted in the *National Review.* See L. Courtney, 1895, "To My Fellow Disciples in Saratoga Springs," *National Review* (London), v. 26: 21–26. The origins of the "Lies" quote are not quite clear, although they go back at least to Walter Bagehot, who died in 1884. For an interesting discussion of the quote's history, see University of York, Department of Statistics, 2008, "Lies, Damn Lies, and Statistics," 20 January, accessed 20 February 2008 from *http://www.york.ac.uk/depts/maths/histstat/lies.htm.*

2. A. Schwarz, 2004, *The Numbers Game* (New York: St. Martin's).

3. S. Szymanski and A.S. Zimbalist, 2005, *National Pastime* (Washington, DC: Brookings Institute); Wisden, 2006, "The Wisden Timeline," accessed 23 February 2008 from *http://content-www.cricinfo.com/wisdenalmanack/content/current/story/243911.html.*

4. A.J. Schiff, 2008, "*The Father of Baseball": A Biography of Henry Chadwick* (Jefferson, NC: McFarland).

5. F. Galton, 1902, "The Most Suitable Proportion Between the Value of First and Second Prizes," *Biometrika,* v. 1, no. 4: 385–399.

6. J. Albert, J. Bennett, and J.J. Cochran, eds., 2005, *Anthology of Statistics in Sports* (Cambridge: Cambridge University Press).

7. F. Mosteller, 1952, "The World Series Competition," *Journal of the American Statistical Association,* v. 47, no. 259: 355–380; F. Mosteller, 1997, "Lessons from Sports Statistics," *The American Statistician,* v. 51, no. 4: 305–310.

8. American Statistical Association, "Statistics in Sports," accessed 23 February 2008 from *http://www.amstat.org/sections/sis/.*

9. *Journal of Quantitative Analysis in Sports,* accessed 23 February 2008 from *http://www.bepress.com/jqas/.*

10. S. Lehman, "The Baseball Archive," accessed 23 February 2008 from *http://baseball1.com/.*

11. A. Hald, 2005, *A History of Probability and Statistics and Their Applications before 1750* (Hoboken, NJ: Wiley); The word *statistics* often is attributed a German scientist named Gottfried Achenwall, although there is evidence that the term *statistik* was already in use among German academics by the time Achenwall used it in a 1748 paper. The term dates from at least 1589, when *statistica* was used by Italian historian Girolamo Ghilini. See M.G. Kendall, 1960, "Studies in the History of Probability and Statistics. Where Shall the History of Statistics Begin?" *Biometrika,* v. 47, no. ?: 447–449. Also see V. John, 1883, "The Term 'Statistics,'" *Journal of the Statistical Society of London,* v. 46, no. 4: 656–679.

12. H.W. Eves, 2002, "A Very Brief History of Statistics," *The College Mathematics Journal,* v. 33, no. 4: 306–308.

13. T. Frank, 1924, "Roman Census Statistics from 225 to 28 B.C.," *Classical Philology,* v. 19, no. 4: 320–341.

14. R.L. Plackett, 1958, "Studies in the History of Probability and Statistics: VII. The Principle of the Arithmetic Mean," *Biometrika,* v. 45, no. ?: 130–135.

15. M.G. Kendall, 1960, "Studies in the History of Probability and Statistics: Where Shall the History of Statistics Begin," *Biometrika,* v. 47, no. ?: 447–449.

16. Plackett, "Studies in the History of Probability and Statistics: VII"; Kendall, 1960, "Studies in the History of Probability and Statistics"

17. A. Hald, *A History of Probability and Statistics and Their Applications before 1750.*

18. J. Aubrey, O.L. Dick, and E. Wilson, 1962, *Aubrey's Brief Lives* (Ann Arbor: University of Michigan Press).

19. Hald, *A History of Probability and Statistics and Their Applications before 1750.*

20. From Henry Chadwick's *1869 Beadle's Dime Base-Ball Player*, as quoted in Schiff, "*The Father of Baseball.*"
21. Z.W. Pylyshyn and L. Bannon, 1989, *Perspectives on the Computer Revolution* (Bristol, UK: Intellect Books).
22. Schiff, "*The Father of Baseball.*"
23. Ibid.
24. G.B. Kirsch, 2003, *Baseball in Blue and Gray: The National Pastime during the Civil War* (Princeton, NJ: Princeton University Press).
25. J. Holtzmann, 2005, *Jerome Holtzmann on Baseball: A History of Baseball Scribes* (Champagne, IL: Sports Publishing, LLC).
26. Schiff, "*The Father of Baseball.*"
27. Ibid.
28. Ibid.
29. F.W. Taylor, 1911, *The Principles of Scientific Management* (New York: Harper).
30. R.W. McChesney, 1989, "Media Made Sport: A History of Sports Coverage in the United States," in *Media, Sports and Society*, ed. L.A. Wenner (Newbury Park, CA: Sage).
31. W.J. Goldstein, 1989, *Playing for Keeps: A History of Early Baseball* (Ithaca, NY: Cornell University Press).
32. Schiff, "*The Father of Baseball.*"
33. A. Schwarz, 2004, *The Numbers Game* (New York: St. Martin's).
34. D.L. Westby and A. Sack, 1976, "The Commercialization and Functional Rationalization of College Football: Its Origins," *Journal of Higher Education*, v. 47, no. 6: 625–647.
35. M. Oriard, 1991, *Sporting with the Gods: A Rhetoric of Play and Game in American Culture* (Cambridge: Cambridge University Press).
36. A.A. Stagg and H.L. Williams, 1893, *Scientific and Practical Treatise on American Football* (Hartford, CT: privately printed); S.A. McQuillan and R.A. Smith, 1993, "The Rise and Fall of the Flying Wedge: Football's Most Controversial Play," *Journal of Sport History*, v. 20, no. 1: 57–64.
37. A. Schwarz, 2004, *The Numbers Game* (New York: St. Martin's).
38. F. Leib, 1996, *Baseball as I Have Known It* (Lincoln: University of Nebraska Press); Schwarz, *The Numbers Game.*
39. Schwarz, *The Numbers Game.*
40. Notre Dame University. Spaulding (1891–1940), Barnes (1941–49), and National Collegiate Athletic Association (1950-) annual guides, Rare Books and Special Collections, accessed 1 March 2008 from *http://www.library.nd.edu/rarebooks/collections/sports/football/annuals/spalding_barnes.shtml.*
41. Notre Dame University, Basketball — guide format annuals, Spaulding Guides, Rare Books and Special Collections, accessed 1 March 2008 from *http://www.library.nd.edu/rarebooks/collections/sports/basketball/annuals/spalding.shtml.*
42. P. Williams, 2006, *The Draft* (New York: MacMillan).
43. Notre Dame University, Basketball — guide format annuals.
44. Notre Dame University, Boxing — guide format annuals — Ring Record Book, Rare Books and Special Collections, accessed 1 March 2008 from *http://www.library.nd.edu/rarebooks/collections/sports/boxing/annuals/ring_record.shtml.*
45. It is difficult to find a reference to Siwoff that comments favorably upon his charm. For example, see Dr. Z, 2003, "Logistical Nightmare," *Sports Illustrated*, 10 April, accessed 1 March 2008 from *http://sportsillustrated.cnn.com/inside_game/dr_z/news/2003/04/10/drz_insider/.*
46. Schwarz, *The Numbers Game.*
47. Ibid.
48. STATS, Inc., 2008, "STATS Historical Timeline," accessed 1 March 2008 from *http://biz.stats.com/timeline.asp.*
49. J. Garrett, 2008, "When Stock Meant Stock," *New York Times*, 17 February, accessed 1 March 2008 from *http://www.nytimes.com/2008/02/17/automobiles/collectibles/17speed.html?em&ex=1203310800&en=b5306e31d7adb231&ei=5087%0A.*
50. R. Neyer, 2002, "Red Sox Hire James in Advisory Capacity," accessed 1 March 2008 from *http://espn.go.com/mlb/s/2002/1105/1456563.html.*
51. J. Henry, 2006, "Bill James," 30 April, accessed 1 March 2008 from *http://www.time.com/time/magazine/article/0,9171,1187260,00.html.*
52. M. Lewis, 2003, *Moneyball: The Art of Winning an Unfair Game* (New York: Norton).
53. D. Okrent, 1981, "He Does It by the Numbers (Bill James)," Sports Illustrated, v. 54 (25 May): 40–47.
54. Schwarz, *The Numbers Game.*
55. Ibid.
56. Ibid.
57. D. Everson, 2008, "Tactics: Baseball Taps Wisdom of Fans," *Wall Street Journal*, 7 March, p. W4; St. Louis Cardinals, 2008, "The Official Site of the St. Louis Cardinals: Fan Forum: St. Louis Cardinals One for the Birds," accessed 9 March 2008 from *http://stlouis.cardinals.mlb.com/stl/fan_forum/oneforthebirds_index.jsp.*
58. J. von Chaffrin, 2008, "All to Play for in Fantasy Sports," *Financial Times Deutschland*, accessed 9 March 2008 from *http://www.ftd.de/karriere_management/business_english:Business%20English%20All/294830.html.*
59. From a 4 December 1926 letter to fellow physicist Max Born. F.R. Shapiro, 2006, *The Yale Book of Quotations* (New Haven: Yale University Press).

60. F.N. David, 1955, "Studies in the History of Probability and Statistics I: Dicing and Gaming (a Nnote on the History of Probability)," *Biometrika*, v. 47, no. ?: 1–15.

61. F.N. David, 1998, Games, Gods, and Gambling: A History of Probability and Statistical Ideas (New York: Courier Dover).

62. Ibid.

63. Ibid.

64. A. Hald, 2005, *A History of Probability and Statistics and Their Applications before 1750* (Hoboken, NJ: Wiley).

65. Ibid.

66. Ibid.

67. J. Bernoulli and E. D. Sylla, 2006, *The Art of Conjecturing, Together with a Letter to a Friend on Sets in Court* (Baltimore: Johns Hopkins University Press).

68. W.D. Hill and J.E. Clark, 2001, "Sports, Gambling, and Government: America's First Social Compact?" *American Anthropologist*, v. 3 no. 2: 331–345.

69. R.D. Sauer, 1998, "The Economics of Wagering Markets," *Journal of Economic Literature*, v. 36, no. 4: 2021–2064.

70. H.L. Vogel, 2007, *Entertainment Industry Economics: A Guide for Financial Analysis* (Cambridge: Cambridge University Press).

71. R.D. Hammer, 2001, "Does Internet Gambling Strengthen the U.S. Economy? Don't Bet on It," *Federal Communications Law Journal*, v. 54, no. 1: 103–128, accessed 2 March 2008 from *http://www.law.indiana.edu/fclj/pubs/v54/no1/Hammer.pdf.*

72. S.D. Levitt, 2004, "Why Are Gambling Markets Organized So Differently from Financial Markets?" *Economic Journal*, v. 114, no. 495: 223–246; American Gaming Association, 2008, "Industry Issues Detail: Sports Wagering," accessed 24 February 2008 from *http://www.americangaming.org/Industry/factsheets/issues_detail.cfv?id=16.*

73. Levitt, "Why Are Gambling Markets Organized So Differently from Financial Markets?"; J. Drape, 2002, "Horse Racing; Current Wagering System Leaves Plenty of Room to Maneuver," *New York Times*, 4 November, accessed 24 February 2008 from *http://query.nytimes.com/gst/fullpage.html?res=9D00E1D9153EF937A35752C1A9649C8B63*; A. Weinberg, 2003, "The Case for Legal Sports Gambling," *Forbes*, 27 January, accessed 24 February 2008 from *http://www.forbes.com/business/2003/01/27/cx_aw_0127gambling.html.*

74. J.W. Welte, G.M. Barnes, W.F. Wieczorek, M-C. Tidwell, and J. Parker, 2002, "Gambling Participation in the U.S.— Results from a National Survey," *Journal of Gambling Studies*, v. 18, no. 4: 313–337.

75. Ibid.

76. R.A. Volberg, K.L. Nysse-Carris, and D.R. Gerstein, 2006, "2006 California Problem Gambling Prevalence Survey," California Department of Alcohol and Drug Programs Office of Problem and Pathological Gambling, August, accessed 2 March 2008 from *http://www.adp.ca.gov/OPG/pdf/CA_Problem_Gambling_Prevalence_Survey-Final_Report.pdf.*

77. Gamblers Anonymous, "20 Questions," accessed 2 March 2008 from *http://www.gamblersanonymous.org/20questions.html.*

78. American Psychiatric Association, 2000, *Diagnostic and Statistical Manual of Mental Disorders*, 4th Edition, Text Revision (Arlington, VA: American Psychiatric Association).

79. K.V. DiGregory, 1998, "Statement Concerning Gambling on the Internet before the Subcommittee on Crime," Committee on the Judiciary U.S. House of Representatives, 24 June, accessed 2 March 2008 from *http://www.usdoj.gov/criminal/cybercrime/kvd0698.htm.*

80. L.G. Walters, 2003, "The Law of Online Gambling in the United States — A Safe Bet, or Risky Business?" *Gaming Law Review*, v. 7, no. 6: 445–450; United States Court of Appeals for the Fifth Circuit, 2002, *In Re: Mastercard International Internet Gambling Litigation*, Case No. 01–30389, accessed 2 March 2008 from *http://vlex.com/vid/18408682.*

81. J. Sullum, 2006, "Know When to Fold 'Em," *Reason*, 25 October, accessed 2 March 2008 from *http://www.reason.com/news/show/38400.html.*

82. J. Miller and M. Hyman, 2000, *Confessions of a Baseball Purist: What's Right— and Wrong— with Baseball* (Baltimore: Johns Hopkins University Press); D. Brock, 2006, "Leagues of Their Own," *NINE: A Journal of Baseball History and Culture*, v. 15, no. 1.

83. Schwarz, *The Numbers Game*; J. Albert and J. Bennett, 2003, *Curve Ball: Baseball, Statistics, and the Role of Chance in the Game* (New York: Springer).

84. Schwarz, *The Numbers Game.*

85. S. Walker, 2006, *Fantasyland: A Season on Baseball's Lunatic Fringe* (New York: Viking Penguin); S. Allis, 2006, "Lords of the Games: Fantasy Baseball Indebted to Two Innovators," *Boston Globe*, 12 March, accessed 9 March 2008 from *http://www.boston.com/news/local/articles/2006/03/12/lords_of_the_games/.*

86. Allis, "Lords of the Games"; W. Gamson and N.A. Scotch, "Scapegoating in Baseball," *The American Journal of Sociology*, v. 70, no. 1: 69–72.

87. Schwarz, *The Numbers Game*; Walker, *Fantasyland.*

88. "The History of Fantasy Football," 2007, *Coed Magazine*, 12 November, accessed 9 March

2008 from *http://www.coedmagazine.com/sports/3176.*

89. T. Baker, 2008, "As Super Bowl Approaches, Fantasy Sports Research Provides Insights into Consumer Behavior," University of Mississippi, 20 January, accessed 9 March 2008 from *http://www.olemiss.edu/cgi-bin/news2000/display.pl?id=6736&mode=full.*

90. T.O. Comeau, 2007, "Fantasy Football Participation and Media Usage," University of Missouri-Columbia, Ph.D. dissertation, December, accessed 9 March 2008 from *http://edt.missouri.edu/Fall2007/Dissertation/Comeau T-121407-D8570/research.pdf.*

91. von Chaffrin, "All to Play for in Fantasy Sports."

92. "Sports Traffic No Fantasy for Yahoo," 2007, *ValleyWag Magazine,* accessed 9 March 2008 from *http://valleywag.com/tech/stats/sports-traffic-no-fantasy-for-yahoo-336833.php.*

93. von Chaffrin, "All to Play For in Fantasy Sports."

94. T. Van Riper, 2007, "The Costs of Online Football: Pure Fantasy," *Forbes,* 26 September, accessed 9 March 2008 from *http://www.forbes.com/leadership/2007/09/26/fantasy-football-office-lead-cx_tvr_0926productivity.html.*

95. T. Kee, 2007, "Online Sports Spending to Reach $1 Billion by 2011," *Online Media Daily,* 24 July, accessed 8 March 2008 from *http://publications.mediapost.com/index.cfm?fuseaction=Articles.showArticleHomePage&art_aid=64461.*

96. Comeau, "Fantasy Football Participation and Media Usage."

97. G. Garber, 2006, "Fantasy Craze Creates Awkward Moments for Players," on ESPN.com, 6 December, accessed 8 March 2008 from *http://sports.espn.go.com/nfl/columns/story?columnist=garber_greg&id=2684942.*

98. *International News Service v. Associated Press,* 248 U.S. 215 (1918).

99. Copyright law is given in Title 17 of the U.S. Code.

100. *The National Basketball Association v. Motorola, Inc,* 05 F.3d 841 (2nd Cir. 1997).

101. K. Badenhausen, 2006, "Foul Ball," *Forbes,* 27 February, accessed 9 March 2008 from *http://www.forbes.com/global/2006/0227/025A.html.*

102. A. Schwarz, 2006, "Baseball Is a Game of Numbers, But Whose Numbers Are They?" *New York Times,* 16 May, accessed 9 March 2008 from *http://www.nytimes.com/2006/05/16/sports/baseball/16license.html?_r=1&oref=slogin*; *C.B.C. Distrib. and Mktg., Inc. v. Major League Baseball Advanced Media, L.P.,* 443 F. Supp. 2d 1077 (E.D. Mo. 2006).

103. B. Van Voris, 2007, "Court Won't Reconsider Decision Favoring Fantasy Sports Leagues," Bloomberg News Service, 26 November, accessed 9 March 2008 from *http://www.bloomberg.com/apps/news?pid=newsarchive&sid=aGSQgvgz.LvI*; *C.B.C. Distribution and Marketing Inc. v. Major League Baseball Advanced Media,* 06-3357 and 06-3358, U.S. Court of Appeals for the Eighth Circuit.

Chapter 11

1. St. Augustine and R. Warner. 2001. *The Confessions of St. Augustine,* Book VIII, Chapter 7 (New York: Signet).

2. J.K. Fairbank, 1994. *China: A New History* (Cambridge, MA: Harvard University Press).

3. "Chinese dynasties," on Thinkquest.org, accessed 21 March 2008 from *http://library.thinkquest.org/12255/library/dynasty/dynasty.htm.*

4. Between 1921 and 1964, AL attendance grew from 4.6 million to 11.5 million, while U.S. population grew from 109 million to 184 million. However, AL attendance flagged during the 1950s, while NL attendance increased. See J. Quirk and R.D. Fort, 1997, *Pay Dirt: The Business of Professional Team Sports* (Princeton, NJ: Princeton University Press). Also see U.S. Census Bureau, 2000, *Historical National Population Estimates: July 1, 1900 to July 1, 1999,* Population Estimates Program, Population Division, 11 April; revised 28 June, accessed 22 March 2008 from *http://www.census.gov/population/estimates/nation/popclockest.txt.*

5. Wikipedia entries report total NCAA men's tournament attendance was 141,000 in 1964 and 183,000 in 1975; however these figures may not be reliable — the sources listed in the entries do not themselves include attendance figures. See *http://en.wikipedia.org/wiki/1964_NCAA_Men%27s_Division_I_Basketball_Tournament* and *http://en.wikipedia.org/wiki/1975_NCAA_Men%27s_Division_I_Basketball_Tournament,* both accessed 22 March 2008.

6. Hickok Sports, 2007, "History — NCAA Division I Men's Basketball," 17 December, accessed 22 March 2008 from *http://www.hickoksports.com/history/ncmbask.shtml.*

7. NBA total attendance was just over 1 million during the 1956–57 season and nearly 3.7 million during 1968–69. See Quirk and Fort, *Pay Dirt.*

8. NBA total attendance was 9.9 million during 1979–80 and 17.9 million during 1990–91. See Quirk and Fort.

9. ShrpSports,accessed 21 March 2008 from shrpsports.com; Quirk and Fort, *Pay Dirt.*

10. ShrpSports, accessed 21 March 2008 from shrpsports.com.

11. Total NHL attendance in 1975–76 was 9.1 million, 7.7 million in 1978–79, 10.5 million in 1979–80, 11.0 million in 1982–83, 11.4 million in 1983–84, and 12.6 million in 1989–90. See Quirk and Fort, *Pay Dirt.*

12. Total NHL attendance in 2000–2001 and 2006–7 were 20.3 and 20.9 million, respectively. The 2003–4 lockout apparently had a negligible immediate attendance impact as total league attendance was 20.3 million and 20.9 million in 2002–3 and 2004–5, respectively. See R.D. Fort, 2008, "Sports Business Pages, accessed 29 March 2008 from *http://rodneyfort.com/SportsData/BizFrame.htm.*

13. The Associated Press began to certify the national college football champion in 1936. In 1941, Bill Schroeder, who then was the managing editor of the Helms Athletic Association (later the United Savings and Loan Athletic Association, and then the First Interstate Bank Athletic Association), retroactively selected champions beginning with the 1883 season. See University of Notre Dame, 2008, "Official Athletic Site of the University of Notre Dame," accessed 21 March 2008 from *http://und.cstv.com/sports/m-footbl/archive/nd-m-fb-a-nattit.html.*

14. ShrpSports, accessed 21 March 2008 from shrpsports.com. NFL attendance totaled 4 million in 1961 and 6 million in 1967. See Quirk and Fort, *Pay Dirt.*

15. Pro Football Hall of Fame, "History: Pro Football's Other Undefeated Teams," accessed 26 January 2008 from *http://www.profootballhof.com/history/decades/1940s/undefeated.jsp.* As has so often been the case with rival leagues, the NFL absorbed the Browns as well as two other AAFC teams, the San Francisco 49ers and Baltimore Colts, following the 1949 season. Quirk and Fort, *Pay Dirt.*

16. R.D. Fort, 2006, *The Economics of Sports* (Upper Saddle River, NJ: Pearson Prentice-Hall).

17. A.B. Block, 2007, "How Johnny Depp Became the Highest Paid Actor Ever," *Hollywood Today,* 1 May, accessed 25 January 2008 from *http://www.hollywoodtoday.net/?p=773*; Box officemojo.com, "Pirates of the Caribbean: Dead Man's Chest (2006)," accessed 25 January 2008 from *http://www.boxofficemojo.com/movies/?id=piratesofthecaribbean2.htm.*

18. Golf tournament final standings were derived from a variety of sources.

19. J. Brown, 2007, "Quitters Never Win: The (Adverse) Effects of Competing with Superstars," University of California, Berkeley Department of Economics, November, mimeograph, accessed 26 January 2008 from *http://are.berkeley.edu/~brown/Brown%20-%20Competing%20with%20Superstars.pdf.*

20. T. Bonk, 2008, "Tiger Tale: To Have or Have-not," *Los Angeles Times,* 23 January, accessed 26 January 2008 from *http://www.latimes.com/sports/la-sp-tigertv23jan23,1,2991626.story?coll=la-headlines-sports&ctrack=1&cset=true.*

21. As measured at the official exchange rate. See CIA, 2008, *World Fact Book,* accessed 29 March 2008 from *https://www.cia.gov/library/publications/the-world-factbook/geos/kr.html.*

22. PGA Tour, 2008, "PGA Tour Statistics," accessed 21 March 2008 from *http://www.pgatour.com/r/stats/info/?110.*

23. F.G. Aflalo and H. Peek, 1897, *The Encyclopaedia of Sport* (London: Lawrence and Bullen), accessed 21 March 2008 from books.google.com.

24. International Tennis Hall of Fame, "William Tatem Tilden, 'Bill, Big Bill,'" accessed 21 March 2008 from *http://www.tennisfame.com/famer.aspx?pgID=867&hof_id=140.*

25. International Tennis Hall of Fame, 2006, "Helen Newington Wills Moody Roark, 'Little Miss Poker Face,'" accessed 21 March 2008 from *http://www.tennisfame.com/famer.aspx?pgID=867&hof_id=95.*

26. A. Zimbalist, 1992, "Salaries and Performance: Beyond the Scully model," in *Diamonds Are Forever: The Business of Baseball,* ed. P.M. Sommers (Washington, DC: Brookings Institute).

27. D.J. Berri, M.B. Schmidt, and S.L. Brook, 2004, "Stars at the Gate: The Impact of Star Power on NBA Gate Revenues," *Journal of Sports Economics,* v. 5, no. 1: 33–50; D.J. Berri and M.B. Schmidt, 2006, "On the Road with the NBA's Superstar Externality," *Journal of Sports Economics,* v. 7, no. 4: 347–358.

28. J.A. Hausman and G.K Leonard, 1997, "Superstars in the National Basketball Association: Economic Value and Policy," *Journal of Labor Economics,* v. 15, no. 4: 586–624.

29. ESPNsoccernet, 2007, "Beckham Agrees to Five-year $250M LA Galaxy Deal," 11 January, accessed 25 January 2008 from *http://soccernet.espn.go.com/news/story?id=399471&cc=5901.*

30. This unique structure had to survive an antitrust lawsuit brought by MLS players, and is similar to that used by the WNBA, XFL, and Women's United Soccer Association (WUSA). See R. Sandomir, 2000, "Federal Jury in Antitrust Suit Says M.L.S. Not a Monopoly," *New York Times,* 12 December, p. D2.

31. F. Nietzsche and M. Faber, 1996, *Human, All Too Human: A Book for Free Spirits.* (Lincoln: University of Nebraska Press).

32. The Nobel Foundation, 2002, "Economics 2002," accessed 23 March 2008 from *http://nobelprize.org/nobel_prizes/economics/laureates/2002/*; A. Tversky and D. Kahneman,

1981, "The Framing of Decisions and the Psychology of Choice," *Science,* v. 211 (Jan. 30): 453–458.

33. S. Brosnan, 2006, "Nonhuman Species' Reaction to Inequity and Their Implications for Fairness," *Social Justice Research,* v. 19, no. 2: 153–185.

34. The website for America's Official Rock Paper Scissors League was accessed on 22 March 2008 from *http://www.usarps.com/.*

35. S. Szymanski, 2003, "The Economic Design of Sporting Contests," *Journal of Economic Literature,* v. 41, no. 4: 1137–1187.

36. S. Rottenberg, 1956, "The Baseball Players' Labor Market," *Journal of Political Economy,* v. 64, no. 3: 242–258.

37. W.C. Neale, 1964, "The Peculiar Economics of Professional Sports: A Contribution to the Theory of the Firm in Sporting Competition and in Market Completion," *The Quarterly Journal of Economics,* v. 78, no. 1: 1–14.

38. M. El-Hodiri and J. Quirk, 1971, "The Economic Theory of a Professional Sports League," *Journal of Political Economy,* v. *79,* no. 6 (November-December): 1302–1319.

39. A.R. Sanderson, 2002, "The Many Dimensions of Competitive Balance," *Journal of Sports Economics,* v. 3, no. 2: 204–228.

40. A.S. Zimbalist, 2002, "Competitive Balance in Sports Leagues: An Introduction," *Journal of Sports Economics,* v. 3, no. 2: 111–121.

41. A.S. Zimbalist, 2003, "Competitive Balance Conundrums: Response to Fort and Maxcy's Comment," *Journal of Sports Economics,* v. 4, no. 2: 161–163.

42. R.D. Fort and J. Maxcy, 2003, "Competitive Balance in Sports Leagues: An Introduction." *Journal of Sports Economics,* v. 4, no. 2: 154–160.

43. Zimbalist, "Competitive Balance in Sports Leagues: An Introduction."

44. A.R. Sanderson and J.J. Siegfried, 2003, Thinking about Competitive Balance," *Journal of Sports Eco*nomics, v. 4, no. 4: 255–279.

45. S. Szymanski, 2006, "Uncertainty of Outcome, Competitive Balance, and the Theory of Team Sports," in *Handbook on the Economics of Sport,* ed. W. Andreff and S. Szymanski (Cheltenham, UK: Elgar).

46. C.A. Depken and D.P. Wilson, 2002, "The Uncertainty of Outcome Hypothesis in Division IA College Football," mimeograph, University of Texas — Arlington.

47. G. Knowles, K. Sherony, and M. Haupert, 1992. "The Demand for Major League Baseball: A Test of the Uncertainty of Outcome Hypothesis," *The American Economist,* v. 36, no. 2: 72–80; D. Rascher, 1999, "A Test of the Optimal Positive Production Network Externality in Major League Baseball," in *Sports Economics: Current Research,* ed. J. Fizel, E. Gustafson, and L. Hadley (Westport, CT: Praeger).

48. D. Forrest and R. Simmons, 2002, "Outcome Uncertainty and Attendance Demand in Sport: The Case of English Soccer," *Journal of the Royal Statistical Society, Series D, The Statistician,* v. 51, no. 2: 229–241.

49. K.S. Courneya and A.V. Carron, 1992, "The Home Advantage in Sport Competitions: A Literature Review," *Journal of Sport and Exercise Psychology,* v. 14, no. 1: 13–27.

50. D.R. Smith, 2003, "The Home Advantage Revisited: Winning and Crowd Support in an Era of National Publics," *Journal of Sport and Social Issues,* v. 27, no. 4: 346–371.

51. Ibid.

52. Depken and Wilson, "The Uncertainty of Outcome Hypothesis in Division IA College Football."

53. R.D. Fort and J. Quirk, 1999, "The College Football Industry," in *Sports Economics,* ed. Fizel, Gustafson, and Hadley; J. Quirk, 2004, "College Football Conferences and Competitive Balance," *Managerial and Decision Economics,* v. 25, no. 2: 63–75.

54. A.C. Krautmann, J.H. Lee, and K.G. Quinn, 2008. "Playoff Uncertainty and Playoff Races," mimeograph, 25 March, DePaul University.

55. Y.H. Lee, 2004, "Competitive Balance and Attendance in Japanese, Korean, and U.S. Professional Baseball Leagues," in *International Comparisons in Sports Economics,* ed. R. Fort and J. Fizel (Westport, CT: Praeger).

56. J. Quirk and R.D. Fort, 1997, *Pay Dirt: The Business of Professional Team Sports* (Princeton, NJ: Princeton University Press).

57. S. Szymanski, 2005, "Tilting The Playing Field: Why a Sports League Planner Would Choose Less, Not More Competitive Balance," mimeograph, Tanaka Business School Discussion Papers, TBS/DP05/35 (London), accessed 29 March 2008 from *http://www3.imperial.ac.uk/pls/portallive/docs/1/43004.PDF.*

58. R.C. Levin, G.J. Mitchell, P.A. Volcker, and G.F. Will, 2000, "The Report of the Independent Members of the Commissioner's Blue Ribbon Panel on Baseball Economics," *Major League Baseball,* July, accessed 23 March 2008 from *http://www.mlb.com/mlb/downloads/blue_ribbon.pdf.*

59. Quirk and Fort, *Pay Dirt.*

60. D.J. Berri and M.B. Schmidt, 2006, "On the Road with the National Basketball Association's Superstar Externality," *Journal of Sports Economics,* v. 7, no. 4: 347–358.

61. Quirk and Fort, *Pay Dirt.*

62. Szymanski, "Uncertainty of Outcome, Competitive Balance, and the Theory of Team Sports."

63. For example, see H. Schuman and J. Harding, 1963, "Sympathetic Identification with the Underdog," *The Public Opinion Quarterly*, v. 27, no. 2: 230–241.

64. "The AFL: A Football Legacy," 2001, *Sports Illustrated*, 22 January, accessed 26 March 2008 from *http://sportsillustrated.cnn.com/football/news/2001/01/22/afl_history_2/*.

65. "Super Bowl Stats: TV Ad Rates, Ticket Prices, Player Pay," 2008, *Honolulu Advertiser*, 30 January, accessed 26 March 2008 from *http://the.honoluluadvertiser.com/article/2008/Jan/30/br/br7936501284.html*.

66. CNN-SI, 2008, "Giants-Patriots Most-Watched Super Bowl Ever," 4 February, accessed 26 March 2008 from *http://www.cnn.com/2008/SHOWBIZ/TV/02/04/superbowl.ratings.ap/index.html*.

67. Internet Movie Data Base, "Seabiscuit (2003) Box Office/Business," accessed 26 March 2008 from *http://IMDB.com/title/tt0329575/business*.

68. National Museum of Racing and Hall of Fame. 2004. Accessed 26 March 2008 from *http://www.racingmuseum.org/hall/fame.asp*.

69. European Football Statistics, "EFS Domestic League and Cup," accessed 30 March 2008 from *http://www.european-football-statistics.co.uk/league.htm*.

70. ESPN.com, 2008, "MLB Attendance Report — 2007," accessed 30 March 2008 from *http://sports.espn.go.com/mlb/attendance?sort=home_avg&year=2007&seasonType=2*.

71. R.G. Noll, 2002, "The Economics of Promotion and Relegation in Sports Leagues: The Case of English Football," *Journal of Sports Economics*, v. 3, no. 2: 169–203.

72. European Football Statistics, 2008, "England — Table of Last 25 Seasons," accessed 30 March 2008 from *http://www.european-football-statistics.co.uk/league.htm*.

73. Author calculations based on data from Shrpsports, 2008, accessed 30 March 2008 from *http://shrpsports.com/*.

74. S. Rottenberg, 1956, "The Baseball Players' Labor Market," *Journal of Political Economy*, v. 64, no. 3: 242–258.

75. D. Surdam, 2006, "The Coase Theorem and Movement in Major League Baseball," *Journal of Sports Economics*, v. 7, no. 2: 201–221.

76. S. Szymanski, 2003, "The Economic Design of Sporting Contests," *Journal of Economic Literature*, v. 41, no. 4: 1137–1187.

77. L. Kahane and S. Shmanske, 1997, "Team Roster Turnover and Attendance in Major League Baseball," *Applied Economics*, v. 29, no. 4: 425–431.

78. K.G. Quinn, forthcoming, "Talent Dispersal Drafts," in *The Business of Sports*, Vol. 3, ed. D. Howard and B. Humphreys (Westport, CT: Praeger).

79. R.D. Fort, 2006, *Sports Economics*, 2nd Edition, (Englewood Cliffs, NJ: Prentice-Hall).

80. M. Lewis, 2003, *Moneyball: The Art of Winning an Unfair Game* (New York: Norton); K.G. Quinn, M. Geier, and A. Berkovitz, 2008, "Passing on Success? Productivity Outcomes for Quarterbacks Chosen in the 1999–2004 National Football League Player Entry Drafts," mimeograph, St. Norbert College.

81. Quinn, Geier, Berkovitz, "Passing on Success?"

82. J.R. Crooker and A.J. Fenn, 2007, "Sports Leagues and Parity When League Parity Generates Fan Enthusiasm," *Journal of Sports Economics*, v. 5, no. 2: 139–164; J.G. Maxcy, 2006, "Revenue Sharing in MLB: The Effects on Player Transfers," International Association of Sports Economists Working Paper Series, Paper No. 06–15, September, accessed 2 April 2008 from *http://www.holycross.edu/departments/economics/RePEc/spe/Maxcy_Transfers.pdf*.

83. R. Bradley, "The History of NBA Labor," Association for Professional Basketball Research, accessed 2 April 2008 from *http://www.apbr.org/labor.html*.

84. S. Hall, S. Szmanski, and A.S. Zimbalist, 2002, "Testing Causality between Team Performance and Payroll: The Cases of Major League Baseball and English Soccer," *Journal of Sports Economics*, v. 3, no. 2: 149–168; K.G. Quinn, A. Berkovitz, and M. Geier, 2008, "Superstars and Journeymen: An Analysis of National Football Teams' Allocation of the Salary cap Across Rosters, 2000–2005," online at http://www.holycross.edu/departments/economics/RePEc/spe/Quinn_NFLJourneymen.pdf.

Chapter 12

1. G. Rice, 1923, "Alumnus Football," accessed 5 April 2008 from Profession Football Research Association at *http://nflhistory.net/cgi-bin/dcforum/dcboard.cgi?az=read_count&om=1114&forum=DCForumID64*.

2. J. Rawls, 1999, *A Theory of Justice* (Cambridge, MA: Belknap Press/Harvard University Press).

3. Some writers have opted for the more gender-neutral "sportspersonship." However, the bulk of references in both popular and academic literature maintain the use of "sportsmanship," and this also will be done here.

4. E. Asinof, 1963, *Eight Men Out* (New York: Henry Holt); Blackwell, J.A., 1996, *On Brave Old Army Team: The Cheating Scandal that Rocked the Nation: West Point, 1951* (Novato, CA: Presidio Press); I. Berkow, 1992, "Marge

Schott: baseball's big red headache," *New York Times,* 29 November, S1; Breitbart, 2007, "Shootings, arrests spoil post-NBA All-Star Game party," 19 February, accessed 9 November 2008 from http://www.breitbart.com/article.php?id=070220031716.fq28ybhs&show_article=1; B. Crawford, 2004, *All American: The Rise and Fall of Jim Thorpe* (New York: Wiley); R.O. Davies, 1994, *America's Obsession: Sports and Society Since 1945* (Fort Worth, TX: Harcourt Brace); T. Egan, 1994, "2 men accused of conspiracy to harm Kerrigan: figure skating," *New York Times,* 14 January, A1; ESPN, 2001, "Academic, athletic irregularities force resignation," 15 December, accessed 9 November 2008 from http://espn.go.com/ncf/news/2001/1214/1295624.html; ESPN, 2007, "Tocchet pleads guilty, may avoid jail time," 25 May, accessed 9 November 2008 from http://sports.espn.go.com/nhl/news/story?id=2882460; ESPN, 2008, "Senator wants to know why NFL destroyed Patriots spy tapes," February 2, accessed 9 November 2008 from http://sports.espn.go.com/nfl/news/story?id=3225539; Fainaru-Wada and L. Williams, 2006, *Game of Shadows: Barry Bonds, BALCO, and the Steroids Scandal that Rocked Professional Sports* (New York: Gotham); L. Johnston, 2004, "Ex-Georgia assistant's exam laughable; can you pass?" *USA Today,* 4 March, accessed 9 November 2008 from http://www.usatoday.com/sports/college/mensbasketball/2004-03-03-harrick-exam_x.htm; E. Kalb, 2007, *The 25 Greatest Sports Conspiracy Theories of All-Time: Ranking Sports' Most Notorious Fixes, Cover-Ups, and Scandals* (New York: Skyhorse); J. Longman, 2000, "Olympics; Memo Details Payments Made to Influence Bids," *New York Times,* 27 May, accessed 9 November 2008 from http://query.nytimes.com/gst/fullpage.html?res=9F07E0DC113DF934A15756C0A9669C8B63; M. Maske and L. Carpenter, 2006, "Player arrests put the NFL in a defensive mode," *Washington Post,* 16 December, p. A01, accessed 9 November 2008 from http://www.washingtonpost.com/wp-dyn/content/article/2006/12/15/AR2006121502134.html; C. Nash, 2003, "Webber avoids jail, pleading guilty on a contempt charge," *New York Times,* 15 July, p.D5; L. Shapiro, 2005, "Vikings give new meaning to term 'Love Boat,'" *Washington Post,* 14 October, accessed 9 November 2008 from http://www.washingtonpost.com/wp-dyn/content/article/2005/10/14/AR2005101401674.html; B. Simmons, 2007, "One man out, one league in trouble," ESPN, 23 July, accessed 9 November 2008 from http://sports.espn.go.com/espn/page2/story?page=simmons/070722; "Two Brooklyn gamblers accuses of college basketball bribery," 1945, *New York Times,* 30 January, 1; G. White, 1963, "Football stars banned for bets," *New York Times,* 18 April, 1; D. Whitford, 1989, *A Payroll to Meet: A Story of Greed, Corruption, and Football at SMU* (New York: Macmillan); E. Wong, 2001, "Baseball: Little League tightens its rules," *New York Times,* 12 December, p.S4; E. Zaldua, 2006, "Landis scandal causes dismay in cycling," *Time,* 28 July, accessed 9 November 2008 from http://www.time.com/time/world/article/0,8599,1220390,00.html.

5. J. Kramer and D. Schaap, 1969, *Instant Replay: The Green Bay Diary of Jerry Kramer* (New York: Signet).

6. S. Rosen, 1981, "The Economics of Superstars," American Economic Review, v. 71, no. 5: 845–858.

7. P. von Allmen, 2005, "The Economics of Individual Sports: Golf, Tennis, and NASCAR," In *Handbook of Sports Economics Research,* ed. J. Fizel (Armonk, NY: Sharpe).

8. The winner's curse is derived from the point that the winner of an item via auction will necessarily pay more than he or she can sell the item for — the second-highest bidder's losing offer. However, the term has generally come to be interpreted as meaning that auction winners simply pay too much for a variety of reasons.

9. J.N. Rosen, 2007, *The Erosion of the American Sporting Ethos: Shifting Attitudes toward Competition* (Jefferson, NC: McFarland).

10. K. Zernike, 2002, "With Student Cheating on the Rise, More Colleges Are Turning to Honor Codes," *New York Times,* 2 November, accessed 19 April 2008 from *http://query.nytimes.com/gst/fullpage.html?res=9B03E1DA163EF931A35752C1A9649C8B63.*

11. For example, see A. Daly, 1949, "Sport of the Times," *New York Times,* 26 January, p. 33.

12. "When the Rules of the Game Are Broken: Sports Injuries Related to Illegal Activity," 2008, *Science Daily* 2 March, accessed 12 April 2008 from *http://www.sciencedaily.com/releases/2008/02/080229141827.htm.*

13. Pro-Football-Reference.com, "Bill Walsh Records, Statistics, and Category Ranks," accessed 13 April 2008 from *http://www.pro-football-reference.com/coaches/WalsBi0.htm.*

14. G. Eskenazi, 1989, "Football: Bengals Accused of Pulling a Fast One: No-huddle, Hurry-up Offense," New York Times, 7 January, accessed 13 April 2008 from http://query.nytimes.com/gst/fullpage.html?res=950DE5DE173CF934A35752C0A96F948260&sec=&spon=&pagewanted=all; Pro-Football-Reference.com, 1988, "Cincinnati Bengals Statistics and Players," accessed 16 April 2008 from http://www.pro-football-reference.com/teams/cin/1988.htm.

15. Eskenazi, "Football"; P.E. Scranton, P.P. Scranton, and P.E. Scranton, Jr., 2002, Playing Hurt (Dulles, VA: Brassey's).

16. R. Butcher and A. Schneider, 2003, "Fair Play and Respect for the Game," In *Sports Ethics: An Anthology*, ed. J. Boxill (Malden, MA: Blackwell).

17. M. Smith, 2003, "What Is Sports Violence?" in *The Ethics of Sports,* ed. Boxhill.

18. ESPN.com, 2007, "Dirtiest Professional Team Players." accessed 12 April 2008 from *http://espn.go.com/page2/s/list/readers/dirtiest/players.html.*

19. Heisman.com, "John W. Heisman: An Innovator of the Game," accessed 16 April 2008 from *http://www.heisman.com/history/john-heisman.html.*

20. B. Pennington, 2006, "John Heisman, the Coach behind the Trophy," *New York Times,* 8 December, accessed 16 April 2008 from *http://www.nytimes.com/2006/12/08/sports/ncaafootball/08heisman.html?_r=1&oref=slogin*; F. Litsky, 2006, "In 1916, a Blowout for the Ages," *New York Times*, 7 October, accessed 16 April 2008 from *http://www.nytimes.com/2006/10/07/sports/ncaafootball/07tech.html?partner=rssnyt&emc=rss.*

21. N. Dixon, 2003, "On Sportsmanship and 'Running Up the Score,'" in *Sports Ethics,* ed. Boxill.

22. C.A. Depken and D.P. Wilson, 2002, "The Uncertainty of Outcome Hypothesis in Division IA College Football," mimeograph, University of Texas — Arlington.

23. J. Lindsay, 2002, "BCS Drops Margin of Victory from Ratings Formula — Several Pollsters Expected to Leave BCS," accessed 12 April 2008 from *http://espn.go.com/ncf/news/2002/0621/1397538.html*; R. Sandomir, 2002, "College Football; Margin of Victory Falls in Bowl Rating," *New York Times,* 26 June, accessed 12 April 2008 from *http://query.nytimes.com/gst/fullpage.html?res=9E0DE6DE143EF935A15755C0A9649C8B63.*

24. J.W. Keating, 1964, "Sportsmanship as a Moral Category," *Ethics*, v. 75, no. 1: 25–35.

25. Ibid.

26. "Unsplendid Splinter," 2003, *Sports Illustrated,* 3 June, accessed 12 April 2008 from *http://sportsillustrated.cnn.com/baseball/news/2003/06/03/sosa_ejected_ap/.*

27. ESPN.com, 2003, "Sosa Challenges Suspension with Immediate Appeal," accessed 12 April from *http://espn.go.com/mlb/news/2003/0606/1564235.html.*

28. MLB.com, 1983, "The pine tar game," 24 July, accessed 12 April 2008 from *http://mlb.mlb.com/mlb/baseballs_best/mlb_bb_gamepage.jsp?story_page=bb_83reg_072483_kcrnyy*; R. Weinberg, "Pine Tar Nullifies Home Run, so Brett Goes Ballistic," ESPN 25–67, accessed 12 April 2008 from *http://sports.espn.go.com/espn/espn25/story?page=moments/67*; "George Brett Pine Tar Game Enhanced Box Score," *Baseball Almanac,* accessed 12 April 2008 from *http://www.baseball-almanac.com/boxscore/07241983.shtml.*

29. O. Leaman, 2007, "Cheating and Fair Play in Sport," in *Ethics in Sport,* 2nd Edition, ed. J.M. Morgan (Champaign, IL: Human Kinetics).

30. I. Preston and S. Szymanski, 2003, "Cheating in Contests," *Oxford Review of Economic Policy*, v. 19, no. 4: 612–624.

31. D.G. Kyle, 2004, "Ancient Olympics Guide: Winning at Olympia," *Archeology,* 6 April, accessed 12 April 2008 from *http://www.archaeology.org/online/features/olympics/olympia.html.*

32. J. Swaddling, 2000, *The Ancient Olympic Games* (Austin: University of Texas Press).

33. J.B. Verrengia, 2004, "Ancient Olympics Had Its Own Scandals," Associated Press, 28 July, accessed 12 April 2008 from *http://www.msnbc.msn.com/id/5467740.*

34. B. Lowitt, 1999, "Harding, Kerrigan Are Linked Forever by Skating Incident," St. Petersburg Times, 29 November, accessed 13 April 2008 from http://www.sptimes.com/News/112999/Sports/Harding__Kerrigan_are.shtml.

35. BBC Sport, 2002, "Three-year Ban for Skating Judge," 30 April, accessed 12 April 2008 from *http://news.bbc.co.uk/sport1/hi/other_sports/1959181.stm.*

36. R. Sandomir, 2002, "Figure Skating; Russian Man Is Arrested in Italy in a Plot to Fix Olympics Skating," New York Times, 1 August, accessed 12 April 2008 from http://query.nytimes.com/gst/fullpage.html?res=9C04E5D9163BF932A3575BC0A9649C8B63.

37. NCAA, "Timeline of College and Professional Sports Wagering Cases," accessed 12 April 2008 from *http://www1.ncaa.org/membership/enforcement/gambling/toolkit/chapter_20?ObjectID=42739&ViewMode=0&PreviewState=0.*

38. B.M. Woodland and L.M. Woodland, 1991, "The Effects of Risk Aversion on Wagering: Point Spread versus Odds," *Journal of Political Economy,* v. 99, no. 3: 638–653.

39. A. Feinberg, 1946, "'Fixer' Jailed Here for Bribe Offers to Football Stars," *New York Times,* 16 December, p. 1.

40. "Two Brooklyn Gamblers Accused of College Basketball Bribery," 1945, *New York Times,* 30 January, p.1.

41. R.O. Davies, 1994, *America's Obsession: Sports and Society since 1945* (Fort Worth, TX: Harcourt Brace).

42. "Open Hearings Set to Sift Basketball," 1945, *New York Times,* 14 February, p. 25.

43. Davies, *America's Obsession*; CNN/*Sports Illustrated*, 1998, "Previous Point-shaving Scandals," 27 March, accessed 13 April from *http://sportsillustrated.cnn.com/basketball/college/news/1998/03/27/gambling_sidebar/.*

44. J. Wolfers, 2006, "Point-shaving: Corruption in College Basketball," *American Economic Review*, v. 96, no. 2: 279–283.

45. L. Leonhardt, 2006, "Sad Suspicions about Scores in Basketball," *New York Times*, 8 March, accessed 13 April 2008 from *http://www.nytimes.com/2006/03/08/business/08leonhardt.html?partner=rssnyt&emc=rss*.

46. D. Stickney, 2001, "Gold Club Scandal Serves Athletes' Right," *Daily Nebraskan*, 26 July, accessed 13 April 2008 from *http://media.www.dailynebraskan.com/media/storage/paper857/news/2001/07/26/Sports/Gold-Club.Scandal.Serves.Athletes.Right-1728906.shtml*; B. Simmons, "Idiot's Guide to the Gold Club Trial," accessed 13 April 2008 from *http://proxy.espn.go.com/espn/page2/story?id=1237371*.

47. J. O'Connell, 2007, "Much Required to Become MLB Umpire," on MLB.com, 28 August, accessed 13 April 2008 from *http://mlb.mlb.com/news/article.jsp?ymd=20070827&content_id=2173765&vkey=news_mlb&fext=.jsp&c_id=mlb*.

48. M Stein, 2007, "Donaghy Questions ... and Answers," on ESPN.com, 24 July, accessed 13 April from *http://sports.espn.go.com/nba/columns/story?columnist=stein_marc&id=2947073*.

49. CBC Sports, 2007, "NHL Reinstates Rick Tocchet," 1 November, accessed 13 April 2008 from *http://www.cbc.ca/sports/hockey/story/2007/11/01/tocchet-reinstated.html?ref=rss*.

50. *Humphrey v. Viacom, Inc.*, Case No. 06–2768 (DMC) (D.N.J., June 20, 2007).

51. J. Wolfers, 2007, "Blow the Whistle on Betting Scandals," *New York Times*, 27 July, accessed 13 April 2008 from *http://www.nytimes.com/2007/07/27/opinion/27wolfers.html*; I. Preston and S. Szymanski, 2003, "Cheating in Contests," *Oxford Review of Economic Policy*, v. 19, no. 4: 612–624.

52. T. Dolby, 1982, "She Blinded Me with Science," in Capitol Records, *The Golden Age of Wireless* (CD).

53. "Soccer Robots Compete for the Title," 2008, *Science Daily*, 4 April, accessed 16 April 2008 from *http://www.sciencedaily.com/releases/2008/04/080401110128.htm*.

54. F. Thomas, 1978, "'Iron Byron' Sets Distance Standards," *USGA Green Section Records*, March/April, pp. 5–7, accessed 16 April 2008 from *http://turf.lib.msu.edu/1970s/1978/780305.pdf*.

55. M.S. Bahrke and C.E. Ysalis, 2002, *Performance-Enhancing Substances in Sport and Exercise* (Champaign, IL: Human Kinetics); M.H. Stone, M. Stone, B. Sands, and W.A. Sands, 2007, *Principles and Practice of Resistance Training* (Champaign, IL: Human Kinetics); R. Grucza, 2006, "History of Doping," *Institute of Sport*, May, Warsaw, Poland, mimeograph, accessed 19 April 2008 from *http://www.wada-ama.org/rtecontent/document/Athens_Grucza.pdf*.

56. R.L. Simon, 1984, "Good Competition and Drug-enhanced Performance," *Journal of the Philosophy of Sport*, v. 11, no. 1: 6–13.

57. M.S. Bahrke and C.E. Ysalis, 2002, *Performance-Enhancing Substances in Sport and Exercise* (Champaign, IL: Human Kinetics).

58. Bahrke and Ysalis, *Performance-Enhancing Substances in Sport and Exercise*; J.L. Sylvester, 1973, "Anabolic Steroids at the 1972 Olympics," *Coach and Athletic Director*, reprinted 2006 in *Coach and Athletic Director*, October, pp. 12–13 and 84.

59. F. Hartgens and H. Kuipers, 2004, "Effects of Androgenic-anabolic Steroids in Athletes," *Sports Medicine*, v. 34, no. 8: 513–554.

60. M. Lavin, 2006, "Sports and Drugs: Are the Current Bans Justified?" in *The Ethics of Sports*, ed. Boxhill.

61. R.L. Simon, 2004, *Fair Play: The Ethics of Sport* (Boulder, CO: Westview).

62. M. Duggan and S.D. Levitt, 2002, "Winning Isn't Everything: Corruption in Sumo Wrestling," *American Economic Review*, v. 92, no. 5: 1594–1605.

63. Blood doping involves removing one's own blood prior to an event, and they reinjecting the red blood cells so as to give the athlete an unnatural aerobic advantage over competitors.

64. G. Luschen, 2000, "Doping in Sport as Deviant Behavior and Its Social Control," in *Handbook of Sports Studies*, ed. J.J. Coakley and E. Dunning (London: Sage).

65. S. Meyer, 1980, "Adapting the Immigrant to the Line: Americanization in the Ford Factory, 1914–1921," *Journal of Social History*, v. 14, no. 1: 67–82.

66. Meyer, "Adapting the Immigrant to the Line"; P. Coppola, A. Levesque, and R. Wilmouth, 1998, "Model T, 1908–1827," Bryant College, mimeograph, accessed 20 April 2008 from *http://web.bryant.edu/~ehu/h364proj/fall_98/coppola/index.html*.

67. "Gives $10,000,000 to 26,000 employees," 1914, *New York Times*, p. 1.

68. Meyer, "Adapting the Immigrant to the Line."

69. "Gives $10,000,000 to 26,000 Employees."

70. M. Wise, 1997, "N.B.A. Fines Rodman $50,000 for Remarks on Mormons," *New York Times*, 13 June, accessed 20 April 2008 from *http://query.nytimes.com/gst/fullpage.html?res=9C0CE7D9143FF930A25755C0A961958260*.

71 P.F. Boller and J. George, 1989, They Never Said It: A Book of Misquotes, Fake Quotes, and Misleading Attributions (New York: Oxford U.S.).

72. J. Boxhill, 2003, "The Ethics of Competition," in The Ethics of Sports, ed. Boxhill.

73. J. Merriman and J. Hill, 1992, "Ethics, Laws, and Sport," Journal of Legal Aspects of Sport, v. 2, no. 2: 56–63.

74. J.N. Rosen and D. Wetcher-Hendricks, forthcoming, "Repression at the Ballpark: Sport, Socialization, and the Birth of a New Stadium Etiquette," in *Sport and Social Theory,* ed. E. Smith (Champaign, IL: Human Kinetics).

Chapter 13

1. L. Wigge, 1999, "War of the Worlds — Most of the Best National Hockey League's Players Come from Europe," The Sporting News, 22 March, accessed 23 April 2008 from http://findarticles.com/p/articles/mi_m1208/is_12_223/ai_54245989.

2. N. Longley, 2000, "The Underrepresentation of French Canadians on English Canadian NHL Teams: Evidence from 1943–1998," *Journal of Sports Economics,* v. 1, no. 3: 236–256.

3. Wigge, "War of the Worlds."

4. Players born in Puerto Rico are considered here to be U.S.-born. See P.M. Sommers, 2003, "Baseball's All-Stars: Birthplace and Distribution," *The College Mathematics Journal,* v. 34, no. 1: 24–30.

5. R. Lapchick, 2008, "The 2006–07 Season Racial and Gender Report Card: National Basketball Association," and "The 2008 Racial and Gender Report Card: Major League Baseball," DeVos Sports Business Management Program, University of Central Florida, 15 April, accessed 23 April 2008 from *http://www.tidesport.org/Articles/2008_MLB_RGRC_PR.pdf.*

6 R. Lapchick, "The 2006 Racial and Gender Report Card: Major League Soccer," DeVos Sports Business Management Program University of Central Florida, 22 November, accessed 23 April 2008 from *http://www.tidesport.org/RGRC/2006/2006_RGRC_MLS.pdf.*

7. M.B. Schmidt and D.J. Berri, 2003, "On the Evolution of Competitive Balance: The Impact of an Increasing Global Search," Economic Inquiry, v. 41, no. 4: 692–704.

8. A. Nicholson, 2008, "Gazprom Funds, Forms Russian Rival to National Hockey League," Bloomberg News, 6 February, accessed 23 April 2008 from *http://www.bloomberg.com/apps/news?pid=newsarchive&sid=ajMouFsMLj_c.*

9. R. Westhead, 2007, "Rival Hockey League to Raid the NHL," *The Toronto Star,* 15 December, accessed 23 April 2008 from *http://www.thestar.com/comment/columnists/article/285910.*

10. J. Hawksworth, 2006, "The World in 2050: Implications of Global Growth for Carbon Emissions and Climate Change Policy," Price Waterhouse Coopers, September, accessed 23 April 2008 from *http://www.pwc.com/extweb/pwcpublications.nsf/docid/DFB54C8AAD6742DB852571F5006DD532/$file/world2050carbon.pdf.*

11. CIA, 2008, *The World Factbook,* accessed 23 April 2008 from *https://www.cia.gov/library/publications/the-world-factbook/.*

Bibliography

ABC News. 2007. "Women's Purse at Wimbledon Now Equals Men's." 24 June. Accessed 30 January 2008 from *http://abcnews.go.com/GMA/story?id=3310814.*

Adams, R.L.A., and J.F. Rooney. 1985. "Evolution of American Golf Facilities." *Geographical Review,* v. 75, no. 4: 419–438.

Adams, V. 1954. "News of TV and Radio." *New York Times,* 30 January, p. X15.

Adelman, M.L. 1997. "The Early Years of Baseball, 1845–60." In *The New American Sports History: Recent Approaches and Perspectives,* ed. S.W. Pope. Urbana: University of Illinois Press.

Advanced Media, L.P., 443 F. Supp. 2d 1077 (E.D. Mo. 2006).

"Advertising Age DataCenter: 2007 Marketer Profiles Yearbook," *Advertising Age,* 25 June. Accessed 3 November 2007 from *http://adage.com/images/random/lna2007.pdf.*

"The AFL: A Football Legacy." 2001. *Sports Illustrated,* 22 January. Accessed 26 March 2008 from *http://sportsillustrated.cnn.com/football/news/2001/01/22/afl_history_2/.*

Aflalo, F.G., and H. Peek. 1897. *The Encyclopaedia of Sport.* (ondon: Lawrence and Bullen. Accessed 21 March 2008 from books.google.com.

Ahn, S.C., and Y.H. Lee. 2003. "The Attendance Demand of Major League Baseball." Paper presented at the 2003 Western Economic Association International meeting. Denver, CO, July.

Albert, J. and J. Bennett. 2003. *Curve Ball: Baseball, Statistics, and the Role of Chance in the Game.* New York: Springer.

Albert, J., J. Bennett, and J.J. Cochran, eds. 2005. *Anthology of Statistics in Sports.* Cambridge: Cambridge University Press.

Alexander, C.C. 2002. *Breaking the Slump: Baseball in the Depression Era.* New York: Columbia University Press.

Allis, S. 2006. "Lords of the Games: Fantasy Baseball Indebted to Two Innovators." *Boston Globe,* 12 March. Accessed 9 March 2008 from *http://www.boston.com/news/local/articles/2006/03/12/lords_of_the_games/.*

Allison, M. 2007. "A Need for Speed." *The Telegraph,* February 3 and March 2. Accessed 19 June 2007 from *http://www.telegraph.co.uk/motoring/main.jhtml?view=DETAILS&grid=A1YourView&xml=/motoring/2007/02/03/nosplit/mfspeed03.xml.*

American Gaming Association. 2008. "Industry Issues Detail: Sports Wagering." Accessed 24 February 2008 from *http://www.americangaming.org/Industry/factsheets/issues_detail.cfv?id=16.*

American Psychiatric Association. 2000. *Diagnostic and Statistical Manual of Mental Disorders,* 4th Edition, Text Revision. Arlington, VA: American Psychiatric Association.

American Statistical Association. "Statistics in Sports." Accessed 23 February 2008 from *http://www.amstat.org/sections/sis/.*

American Tobacco Co., 221 U. S. 106 (1911).

Annual TV Households, "Number of TV Households in America." Accessed 25 March 2005 from *http://www.tvhistory.tv/Annual_TV_Households_50–78.JPG.*

Answers.com. "American Football League." Accessed 25 March 2005 from *http://www.answers.com/main/ntquery;jsessionid=13872xegu7jv8?method=4&dsid=2222&dekey=American+Football+League&gwp=8&curtab=2222_1&sbid=lc04b.*

Arledge, R. 2002. *Roone.* New York: HarperCollins.

"Ask Huge Damages of Ball Magnates." 1916. *New York Times,* 30 March, p. 10.

Asinof, E. 1963. *Eight Men Out.* New York: Henry Holt.

Aubrey, J., O.L. Dick, and E. Wilson. 1962. *Aubrey's Brief Lives.* Ann Arbor: University of Michigan Press.

St. Augustine and R. Warner. 2001. *The Confes-*

sions of St. Augustine. Book VIII, Chapter 7. New York: Signet.

Autoracingsport.com. 2006. "Fox Sports and Speed TV to broadcast F1 races in U.S. through 2009." 28 November. Accessed 9 November 2008 from http://autoracingsport.com/uncategorized/fox-sports-and-speed-tv-to-broadcast-fl-races-in-us-through-2009/.

Badenhausen, K. 2006. "Foul Ball." *Forbes,* 27 February. Accessed 9 March 2008 from *http://www.forbes.com/global/2006/0227/025A.html.*

Bader, C., K. Dougherty, P. Froese, B. Johnson, F.C. Mencken, J.Z. Park, and R. Starr. 2006. "American Piety in the 21st Century: New Insights to the Depth and Complexity of Religion in the US." Baylor University, Institute for the Studies of Religion. Accessed 15 January 2008 from *http://www.baylor.edu/content/services/document.php/33304.pdf.*

Bahrke, M.S. and C.E. Ysalis. 2002. *Performance-Enhancing Substances in Sport and Exercise.* Champaign, IL: Human Kinetics.

Baker, T. 2008. "As Super Bowl Approaches, Fantasy Sports Research Provides Insights into Consumer Behavior." University of Mississippi, 20 January. Accessed 9 March 2008 from *http://www.olemiss.edu/cgi-bin/news2000/display.pl?id=6736&mode=full.*

Balio, T. 1996. "Surviving the Great Depression." In *Grand Design: Hollywood as a Modern Business Enterprise 1930–39.* Berkeley: University of California Press, pp. 13–15.

Baran, S.J. "Sports and Television." Museum of Broadcast Communications. Accessed 17 February 2008 from *http://www.museum.tv/archives/etv/S/htmlS/sportsandte/sportsandte.htm.*

Baseball Almanac. "Babe Ruth Baseball Stats." Accessed 4 April at *http://www.baseball-almanac.com/players/player.php?p=ruthba01.*

_____. "Famous firsts in the lively ball era." Accessed 10 February 2008 from *http://www.baseball-almanac.com/firsts/first3.shtml.*

_____. "Famous Night Games." Accessed 15 June 2007 from *http://www.baseball-almanac.com/firsts/first10.shtml.*

_____. "George Brett Pine Tar Game Enhanced Box Score." Accessed 12 April 2008 from *http://www.baseball-almanac.com/boxscore/07241983.shtml.*

_____. "President Franklin Roosevelt Green Light Letter — Baseball Can Be Played during the War." Accessed March 22, 2005 from *http://www.baseball-almanac.com/prz_lfr.shtml.*

_____. "Year in Review: 1934: National League." Accessed 20 June 2007 from *http://www.baseball-almanac.com/yearly/yr1934n.shtml.*

_____. "Year in Review: 1941: American League." Accessed March 22, 2005 from *http://www.baseball-almanac.com/yearly/yr1941a.shtml.*

_____. "Year in Review: 1942: American League." Accessed March 22, 2005 from *http://www.baseball-almanac.com/yearly/yr1942a.shtml.*

"The Base-ball Field." 1883. *New York Times,* 14 October, p. 7.

BaseballLibrary.com. "National League." Accessed October 31, 2005 from *http://www.baseballlibrary.com/baseballlibrary/ballplayers/N/National_League.stm.*

_____. "St. Louis Browns." Accessed 15 June 2007 from *http://www.baseballlibrary.com/baseballlibrary/ballplayers/S/St_Louis_Browns.stm.*

"Baseball Moguls See Dire Changes." 1919. *New York Times,* 14 April, p. 10

"Baseball Season Near." 1903. *New York Times,* 1 March, p. 16.

BBC Sport. 2002. "Three-year Ban for Skating Judge." 30 April. Accessed 12 April 2008 from *http://news.bbc.co.uk/sport1/hi/other_sports/1959181.stm.*

Becker, G., and K. Murphy. 1988. "A Theory of Rational Addiction." *Journal of Political Economy,* v. 96, no. 4, 675–700.

Berkow, I. 1992. "Marge Schott: baseball's big red headache." *New York Times.* 29 November.

Bernoulli, J., and E. D. Sylla 2006. *The Art of Conjecturing, Together with a Letter to a Friend on Sets in Court.* Baltimore: Johns Hopkins University Press.

Berri, D.J., and M.B. Schmidt. 2006. "On the Road with the NBA's Superstar Externality." *Journal of Sports Economics,* v. 7, no. 4: 347–358.

Berri, D.J., M.B. Schmidt, and S.L. Brook. 2004. "Stars at the Gate: The Impact of Star Power on NBA Gate Revenues." *Journal of Sports Economics,* v. 5, no. 1: 33–50.

Blackwell, J.A. 1996. *On Brave Old Army Team: The Cheating Scandal that Rocked the Nation: West Point, 1951.* Novato, CA: Presidio Press.

Blanchard, K. (1985). *The Anthropology of Sport.* South Hadley, MA: Bergin & Garvey.

Block, A.B. 2007. "How Johnny Depp Became the Highest Paid Actor Ever." *Hollywood Today,* 1 May. Accessed 25 January 2008 from *http://www.hollywoodtoday.net/?p=773.*

Block, D. 2006. *Baseball before We Knew It: A Search for Roots of the Game.* Lincoln: University of Nebraska Press.

Bloom, B.M. 2006. "TV Deals OK'd in Quiet Meetings." On MLB.com, 16 November. Accessed 9 February 2008 from *http://mlb.mlb.com/news/article.jsp?ymd=20061116&content_id=1741845&vkey=news_mlb&fext=.jsp&c_id=mlb.*

Boller, P.F., and J. George. 1989. *They Never Said It: A Book of Misquotes, Fake Quotes, and Misleading Attributions.* New York: Oxford U.S.

Bonk, T. 2008. "Tiger Tale: To Have or Have-not." *Los Angeles Times,* 23 January. Accessed 26 January 2008 from *http://www.latimes.com/sports/la-sp-tigertv23jan23,1,2991626.story?coll=la-headlines-sports&ctrack=1&cset=true.*

Bourtros, L. "Phoenician Sports Founded *Olympics* and the *Stadium.*" Accessed 23 July 2005 from *http://phoenicia.org/phoenicianolympics.htm#Stadium.*

Boxhill, J. 2003. "The Ethics of Competition." In *The Ethics of Sports: An Anthology,* ed. J. Boxhill. Malden, MA: Blackwell.

Boxofficemojo.com. Pirates of the Caribbean: Dead Man's Chest (2006). Accessed 25 January 2008 from *http://www.boxofficemojo.com/movies/?id=piratesofthecaribbean2.htm.*

Bradley, R. "The History of NBA Labor." Association for Professional Basketball Research. Accessed 2 April 2008 from *http://www.apbr.org/labor.html.*

Brandweek.com. "NBC, ESPN Snap Up NFL Packages." Accessed 17 May 2005 from *http://www.brandweek.com/brandweek/search/article_display.jsp?schema=&vnu_content_id=1000885303.*

Breitbart. 2007. "Shootings, arrests spoil post-NBA All-Star Game party." 19 February. Accessed 9 November 2008 from http://www.breitbart.com/article.php?id=070220031716.fq28ybhs&show_article=1.

Brewster, M. 2004. "The NFL's MVP: Pete Rozell." *Business Week,* 24 November. Accessed 4 January 2008 from *http://www.businessweek.com/bwdaily/dnflash/nov2004/nf20041124_5773_db078.htm.*

Bridges, H. 1958. "he Robber Baron Concept in American History." *The Business History Review,* v. 32, no. 1: 1–13.

Broadcast History Timeline. "A Timeline Of TV History, 1900–1992." Accessed 25 March 2005 from *http://www.tvhandbook.com/History/History_timeline.htm.*

Brock, D. 2006. "Leagues of Their Own." *NINE: A Journal of Baseball History and Culture,* v. 15, no. 1.

Brooks, A. (2003). "Harvard Stadium, 1903–2003." *Harvard University Gazette.* Accessed 1 April 2007 from *http://www.hno.harvard.edu/gazette/2003/10.23/00-stadium.html.*

Brosnan, S. 2006. "Nonhuman Species' Reaction to Inequity and Their Implications for Fairness." *Social Justice Research,* v. 19, no. 2: 153–185.

Brown, C. 2000. "Golf; Nike Deal for Woods Said to Be the Richest." *New York Times,* 15 September.

Brown, D., and J. Bryant. 2003. "Sports Content on U.S. Television." In *Handbook of Sports and Media,* ed. A.A. Raney and J. Bryant. New York: Erlbaum.

Brown, J. 2007. "Quitters Never Win: The (Adverse) Effects of Competing with Superstars." University of California, Berkeley Department of Economics, November. Mimeograph. Accessed 26 January 2008 from *http://are.berkeley.edu/~brown/Brown%20-%20Competing%20with%20Superstars.pdf.*

Bryant, J., and A.M. Holt. 2006. "A Historical Overview of Sports and Media in the United States." In *Handbook of Sports and Media,* ed. A.A. Raney and J. Bryant. New York: Erlbaum.

Bureau of Economic Analysis, U.S. Department of Commerce. "Regional Economic Accounts, Gross Domestic Product by Metropolitan Area." Accessed 6 January 2008 from *http://www.bea.gov/regional/gdpmetro/.*

Butcher, R., and A. Schneider. 2003. "Fair Play and Respect for the Game." In *Sports Ethics: An Anthology,* ed. J. Boxill. Malden, MA: Blackwell.

Camponi-Tabery, G. 2002. "Jump for Joy: Jump Blues, Dance, and Basketball in 1930s African America." In *Sports Matters: Race, Recreation, and Culture,* ed. J. Bloom and M.N. Miller. New York: NYU Press.

Capasnson.com. *Cap Chronicled.* Chapter 4: "Cap's Great Shame — Racial Intolerance." Accessed 26 December 2007 from *http://www.capanson.com/chapter4.html.*

Cave, M., and R.W. Crandall. 2001. "Sports Rights and the Broadcast Industry." *The Economic Journal,* v. 111, no. 469: F4–F26.

CBC Sports. 2007. "NHL reinstates Rick Tocchet." 1 November. Accessed 13 April 2008 from *http://www.cbc.ca/sports/hockey/story/2007/11/01/tocchet-reinstated.html?ref=rss.*

"The Celebrity 100." 2007. *Forbes,* 14 June. Accessed 14 January 2008 from *http://www.forbes.com/lists/2007/53/07celebrities_The-Celebrity-100_Rank.html.*

Chaffrin, J. von. 2008. "All to Play for in Fantasy Sports." *Financial Times Deutschland.* Accessed 9 March 2008 from *http://www.ftd.de/karriere_management/business_english/:Business%20English%20All/294830.html.*

Cheng, J. 2007. "Report: Video Game Spending to Surpass Music Spending This Year." *Arstechnica,* 23 June. Accessed 3 November 2007 from *http://arstechnica.com/news.ars/post/20070623-report-video-game-spending-to-surpass-music-spending-this-year.html.*

"China through a Lens, Sports in Ancient China and Greece." Accessed 23 July 2005 from *http://www.china.org.cn/english/features/olympics/100651.htm.*

Christesen, P. 2007. *Olympic Victor Lists and Ancient Greek History.* Cambridge: Cambridge University Press.

CIA. 2008. *World Factbook.* Accessed 23 April

2008 from *https://www.cia.gov/library/publications/the-world-factbook/.*

Cialdini, R.B., R.J. Borden, A. Throne, M.R. Walker, S. Freeman, and S.R. Sloane. 1976. "Basking in Reflected Glory: Three (Football) Field Studies." *Journal of Personality and Social Psychology*, v. 34: 366–375.

"Claims Baltimore Club Was Ignored." *New York Times*, 12 June. Sports section, p. 10.

Clapp, C.M., and J.K. Hakes. 2005. "How Long a Honeymoon? The Effect of New Stadiums on Attendance in Major League Baseball." *Journal of Sports Economics*, v. 6, no. 3: 237–263.

Clarke, B. 2006. "Cubs Night Games at Wrigley Field." On Cubdom.com. Accessed 21 June 2007 from *http://www.thecubdom.com/features/wrigleyfieldnightgames.html.*

CMG Worldwide. 1998. "50 Years after His Death, the Legend of the Bambino Lives On." Accessed 22 June 2007 from *http://www.baberuth.com/flash/about/viewheadline.php?id=946.*

CNN.com. 1997. "List of World Land Speed Record Holders." October 15. Accessed 19 June from *http://www.cnn.com/TECH/9710/15/brits.land.speed/list.reut.html.*

_____. 2004. "Birthday Praise for N. Korea's Kim." 16 February. Accessed 2 February 2008 from *http://edition.cnn.com/2004/WORLD/asiapcf/02/16/kim.birthday.reut/.*

CNNMoney.com. 5 Februrary. Accessed 15 January 2008 from *http://money.cnn.com/2007/02/05/news/companies/superbowl_ratings/index.htm.*

CNNSI.com. 1998. "Previous Point-shaving Scandals." 27 March. Accessed 13 April 2008 from *http://sportsillustrated.cnn.com/basketball/college/news/1998/03/27/gambling_sidebar/.*

_____. 2001. "The AFL: A Football Legacy." *http://sportsillustrated.cnn.com/football/news/2001/01/22/afl_history_1/.*

_____. 2008. "Giants-Patriots Most-watched Super Bowl Ever." 4 February. Accessed 26 March 2008 from *http://www.cnn.com/2008/SHOWBIZ/TV/02/04/superbowl.ratings.ap/index.html.*

Coates, D., and B.R. Humphreys. 2005. "Novelty Effects of New Facilities on Attendance at Professional Sporting Events." *Contemporary Economic Policy*, v. 23, no. 3: 436–455.

"Coffin Nails — The Tobacco Controversy in the 19th Century." HarpWeek. Accessed 14 January 2008 from *http://tobacco.harpweek.com/hubpages/CommentaryPage.asp?Commentary=Introduction.*

Cohen, R. 2007. "NBA extends TV deals with ESPN/ABC, TNT, ESPN." 27 June. Accessed 9 November 2008 from http://www.usatoday.com/sports/basketball/2007-06-27-3096131424_x.htm.

"The Collective Bargaining Agreement for Fans. The 1800s." Accessed 31 October 2005 from *http://www.cbaforfans.com/1800s.html.*

College Football Encyclopedia, "Introduction." Accessed 1 April 2007 from *http://www.footballencyclopedia.com/cfeintro.htm.*

"College All-star Football Game." *Encyclopedia of Chicago*. Accessed 15 June 2007 from *http://www.encyclopedia.chicagohistory.org/pages/3215.html.*

"College Football; Fan Violence Erupts during Victory Celebrations." 2002. *New York Times,* 24 November. Accessed 26 December 2007 from *http://query.nytimes.com/gst/fullpage.html?res=9E0DE6DB1E39F936A15752C1A9649C8B63.*

Comeau, T.O. 2007. "Fantasy Football Participation and Media Usage." University of Missouri-Columbia. Ph.D. dissertation, December. Accessed 9 March 2008 from *http://edt.missouri.edu/Fall2007/Dissertation/ComeauT-121407-D8570/research.pdf.*

Consoli, J. 2007. "WNBA Expands TV Rights Deal with ABC/ESPN." On Mediaweek.com, 16 July. Accessed 10 January 2008 from *http://www.wnba.com/media/fever/070716_MediaWeek_wnba.pdf.*

Coppola, P., A. Levesque, and R. Wilmouth. 1998. "Model T, 1908–1827." Bryant College, mimeograph. Accessed 20 April 2008 from *http://web.bryant.edu/~ehu/h364proj/fall_98/coppola/index.html.*

Cornette, K.D. "The Story of the 1870 Red Stockings, Or Why the Red Sox Lost the 1986 World Series." Accessed 15 August 2005 from *http://www.redsoxdiehard.com/story/stockings.html.*

Courneya, K.S., and A.V. Carron. 1992. "The Home Advantage in Sport Competitions: A Literature Review." *Journal of Sport and Exercise Psychology*, v. 14, no. : 13–27.

Courtney, L. 1895. "To My Fellow Disciples in Saratoga Springs." *National Review* (London), v. 26: 21–26.

Crawford, B. 2004. *All American: The Rise and Fall of Jim Thorpe*. New York: Wiley.

Crepeau, R. 2006. "Stuff Another Football in the Turkey." 11 November. Accessed 1 April 2007 from *http://www.poppolitics.com/archives/2006/11/stuff_another_football_in_the.*

Crooker, J.R., and A.J. Fenn. 2007. "Sports Leagues and Parity When League Parity Generates Fan Enthusiasm." *Journal of Sports Economics*, v. 5, no. 2: 139–164.

Daly, A. 1949. "Sport of the Times." *New York Times,* 26 January, p. 33.

DaNavis-Walt, C., Proctor, B.D., and Smith, J. 2007. "Income, Poverty, and Health Insurance Coverage in the United States 2006." U.S. Census Bureau, August. Accessed 3 November 2007 from *http://www.census.gov/prod/2007pubs/p60–233.pdf.*

David, F.N. 1955. "Studies in the History of Probability and Statistics I: Dicing and Gaming (a Note on the History of Probability)." *Biometrika*, v. 47, no. 1/2: 1–15.

Davies, R.O. 1994. *America's Obsession: Sports and Society Since 1945*. Fort Worth, TX: Harcourt Brace.

Day, J.I. 1950. "Horseracing and the pari-mutual." *Annals of the American Academy of Political and Social Science*, v. 269 (May): 55–61.

Deford, F. (1976). *Big Bill Tilden: The Triumphs and the Tradedy*. New York: Simon and Schuster.

DeLong, B. 1998. "Robber Barons." University of California at Berkeley. Mimeograph. Accessed 4 January 2008 from *http://econ161.berkeley.edu/Econ_Articles/carnegie/DeLong_Moscow_paper2.html.*

Depken, C.A., and D.P. Wilson. 2002. "The Uncertainty of OutcomeH in Division IA College Football. Mimeograph. University of Texas — Arlington.

Deseret News. 2007. "WNBA unveils new television contract." Accessed 9 November 2008 from http://findarticles.com/p/articles/mi_qn4188/is_/ai_n19370272.

DiGregory, K.V. 1998. Statement Concerning Gambling on the Internet before the Subcommittee on Crime. Committee on the Judiciary U.S. House of Representatives. 24 June. Accessed 2 March 2008 from *http://www.usdoj.gov/criminal/cybercrime/kvd0698.htm.*

Dixon, N. 2003. On Sportsmanship and "Running up the Score." In *Sports Ethics: An Anthology*, ed. J. Boxill. Malden, MA: Blackwell.

Dolby, T. 1982. "She Blinded Me with Science." *The Golden Age of Wireless*. CD, Capitol Records.

Donavan, J. 2007. "MLB, DirecTV Strike Deal." *Sports Illustrated*, 8 March. Accessed 9 February 2008 from *http://sportsillustrated.cnn.com/2007/writers/john_donovan/03/08/directtv/.*

Dodd, D. *Historical Statistics of the States of the United States*. Westport, CT: Greenwood Press, 1993.

Drape, J. 2002. "Horse Racing; Current Wagering System Leaves Plenty of Room to Maneuver." *New York Times*, 4 November. Accessed 24 February 2008 from *http://query.nytimes.com/gst/fullpage.html?res=9D00E1D9153EF937A35752C1A9649C8B63.*

Duncan, J. 2006. "Political Ploy Gave Birth to Saints 40 Years Ago." *New Orleans Times-Picayune*, 30 October. Accessed 18 December 2007 from *http://www.nola.com/newslogs/tpupdates/index.ssf?/mtlogs/nola_tpupdates/archives/2006_10_30.html.*

Duggan, M., and S.D. Levitt. 2002. "Winning Isn't Everything: Corruption in Sumo Wrestling." *American Economic Review*, v. 92, no. 5: 1594–1605.

"Economic Report of the President." 1947. Appendix B, Table I and Table V. Accessed 19 June 2007 from *http://fraser.stlouisfed.org/publications/ERP/issue/1630/download/7538/ERP_1947_January.pdf.*

Edmunds.com. 2005. "NASCAR Announces New Lucrative Television Contracts, but without NBC." *Edmunds' Inside Line*, 8 December. Accessed 9 February 2008 from *http://www.edmunds.com/insideline/do/News/articleId=108437.*

Egan, T. 1994. "2 men accused of conspiracy to harm Kerrigan: figure skating." *New York Times*. 14 January.

El-Hodiri, M., & Quirk, J. 1971. "The Economic Theory of a Professional Sports League." *Journal of Political Economy*, v. *79*, no. 6 November-December): 1302–1319.

Ellenport, C. 2001. "From Football Field to the Battlefield." On NFL.com. Accessed 15 June 2007 from *http://www.nfl.com/features/2001/military.html.*

Eskenazi, G. 1989. "Football: Bengals Accused of Pulling a Fast One: No-huddle, Hurry-up Offense." *New York Times*, 7 January. Accessed 13 April 2008 from *http://query.nytimes.com/gst/fullpage.html?res=950DE5DE173CF934A35752C0A96F948260&sec=&spon=&pagewanted=all.*

ESPN.com. 2001. "Academic, athletic irregularities force resignation." 15 December. Accessed 9 November 2008 from http://espn.go.com/ncf/news/2001/1214/1295624.html.

_____. 2003. "Top N. American Athletes of the Century." Accessed 3 November 2007 from *http://espn.go.com/sportscentury/athletes.html.*

_____. 2004. "Late Season Games Can Be Moved to Monday Nights." 9 November. Accessed March 25, 2005 from *http://sports.espn.go.com/nfl/news/story?id=1918761.*

_____. 2005. "NASCAR agrees to 8-year deal with ESPN, ABC." 8 December. Accessed 9 November 2008 from http://sports.espn.go.com/rpm/news/story?series=wc&id=2251049.

_____. 2007. "Dirtiest Professional Team Players." Accessed 12 April 2008 from *http://espn.go.com/page2/s/list/readers/dirtiest/players.html.*

_____. "2007 Stadium Naming Rights." Accessed 5 Jan 2008 from *http://espn.go.com/sportsbusiness/s/stadiumnames.html.*

_____. 2007. "Tocchet pleads guilty, may avoid jail time." 25 May. Accessed 9 November 2008 from http://sports.espn.go.com/nhl/news/story?id=2882460.

_____. 2008. "Frequently Asked Questions — ESPNRadio." 7 February. Accessed 10 February 2008 from *http://espnradio.espn.go.com/espnradio/story?storyId=1457975.*

_____. 2008. "MLB Attendance Report—2007." Accessed 30 March 2008 from *http://sports.espn.go.com/mlb/attendance?sort=home_avg&year=2007&seasonType=2.*

_____. 2008. "Senator wants to know why NFL destroyed Patriots spy tapes." February 2. Accessed 9 November 2008 from http://sports.espn.go.com/nfl/news/story?id=3225539.

ESPNsoccernet. 2007. Beckham Agrees To Five-Year $250M LA Galaxy Deal." 11 January. Accessed 25 January 2008 from *http://soccernet.espn.go.com/news/story?id=399471&cc=5901.*

European Football Statistics. "EFS Domestic League and Cup." Accessed 30 March 2008 from *http://www.european-football-statistics.co.uk/league.htm.*

_____. 2008. England—Table of Last 25 Seasons. Accessed 30 March 2008 from *http://www.european-football-statistics.co.uk/league.htm.*

Everson, D. 2008. Tactics: Baseball Taps Wisdom of Fans. *Wall Street Journal,* 7 March, p. W4.

Eves, H.W. 2002. "A Very Brief History of Statistics." *The College Mathematics Journal,* v. 33, no. 4: 306–308.

Fainaru-Wada and L. Williams. 2006. *Game of Shadows: Barry Bonds, BALCO, and the Steroids Scandal that Rocked Professional Sports.* New York: Gotham.

Fairbank, J.K. 1994. *China: A New History.* Cambridge, MA: Harvard University Press.

Fastis, S. 2004. Salaries, Promos and Flying Solo. *Wall Street Journa*l, 9 February, p. R4.

"Federal League Charges a Trust." 1915. *New York Times,* 6 January, p. 14.

Feinberg, A. 1946. "'Fixer'" Jailed Here for Bribe Offers to Football Stars." *New York Times,* 16 December, p. 1.

Feldman, A. "Baseball's Transition to Professionalism." Accessed 31 October 2005 from *http://www.sabr.org/cmsFiles/Files/feldman%20JKA%202002.pdf.*

Findlaw. 2005. "Findlaw's Supreme Court Awareness Survey." Accessed 10 November from *http://public.findlaw.com/ussc/122005survey.html.*

Fizel, J. Ed. 2006. *Handbook of Sports Economics Research.* Armonk, NY: M.E. Sharpe.

Fleitz, D.L. 2005. *Cap Anson: The Grand Old Man of Baseball.* Jefferson, NC: McFarland.

Forrest, D., and R. Simmons. 2002. "Outcome Uncertainty and Attendance Demand in Sport: The Case of English soccer." *Journal of the Royal Statistical Society.* Series D. *The Statistician,* v. 51, no. 2: 229–241.

Fort, R.D. 2003. Personal communication with the author at the Western Economic International meeting. Denver, Colorado, July.

Fort, R.D. 2004. "Subsidies as Incentive Mechanisms in Sports." Managerial and Decision Economics, v. 25, no. 2: 95–102.

_____. 2006. *Sports Economics.* 2nd Edition. Englewood Cliffs, NJ: Prentice-Hall.

_____. "Sports Business Pages. *http://users.pullman.com/rodfort/SportsBusiness/BizFrame.htm.*

Fort, R.D., and J. Maxcy. 2003. "Competitive Balance in Sports Leagues: An Introduction." *Journal of Sports Economics,* v. 4, no. 2: 154–160.

Fort, R.D., and J. Quirk. 1999. "The College Football Industry." In *Sports Economics: Current Research,* ed. J. Fizel, E. Gustafson, and L. Hadley. Westport: CT: Praeger.

Frank, T. 1924. "Roman Census Statistics from 225 to 28 B.C." Classical Philology, v. 19, no. 4: 320–341.

Franklin D. Roosevelt Presidential Library and Museum. Accessed 15 June 2007 from *http://www.fdrlibrary.marist.edu/39.html.*

Freeman, M. 2001. *ESPN: The Uncensored History.* Lanham, MD: Taylor Trade.

Freyer, J., M. Rucker, and J. Thorn. 2005. *Peverelly's National Game.* Mount Pleasant, SC: Arcadia.

Gage, J. 2006. "Racing for Success." *Forbes,* 5 June. Accessed 20 June 2007 from *http://members.forbes.com/forbes/2006/0605/126.html.*

Gage, J. 2007. "The Most Valuable NASCAR Teams." *Forbes,* 15 June.

Gallup Poll. "Religion." Accessed 7 January 2008 from *http://www.gallup.com/poll/1690/Religion.aspx.*

Galton, F. 1902. "The Most Suitable Proportion between The Value of First and Second Prizes." *Biometrika,* v. 1, no. 4 (August): 385–399.

Gamblers Anonymous. "20 questions." Accessed 2 March 2008 from *http://www.gamblersanonymous.org/20questions.html.*

Gamson, W., and N.A. Scotch. 1964. "Scapegoating in Baseball." *The American Journal of* Sociology, v. 70, no. 1: 69–72.

Garber, G. 2006. "Fantasy Craze Creates Awkward Moments for Players." On ESPN.com, 6 December. Accessed 8 March 2008 from *http://sports.espn.go.com/nfl/columns/story?columnist=garber_greg&id=2684942.*

Garcia, J. 2008. "What to Watch: Obama Need Second Term to Fix BCS." Accessed 9 November 2008 from http://www.mysananton io.com/sports/What_to_Watch_Obama_Need_Second_Term_to_Fix_BCS.html.

Garrett, J. 2008. "When Stock Meant Stock." *New York Times,* 17 February. Accessed 1 March 2008 from *http://www.nytimes.com/2008/02/17/automobiles/collectibles/17speed.html?em&ex=1203310800&en=b5306e31d7adb231&ei=5087%0A.*

General Mills. "Wheaties History." Accessed 16

June 2007 from *http://www.wheaties.com/history/index.aspx.*

"Gives $10,000,000 to 26,000 Employees." 1914. *New York Times,* p. 1.

Go.HR.com. Accessed 10 August 2005 from *http://go.hrw.com/ndNSAPI.nd/gohrw_rls1/pKeywordResults?ST9%20Cities%201900.*

Goldstein, W.J. 1989. *Playing for Keeps: A History of Early Baseball.* Ithaca, NY: Cornell University Press.

Golf Links to the Past. "Biography—Bobby Jones." Accessed 5 April 2007 from *http://www.golfspast.com/page/E/CTGY/HBJB.*

Gorant, J. 2007. "New flavors." On Golf.com. 7 September. Accessed 8 January 2008 from *http://www.golf.com/golf/tours_news/article/0,28136,1660194,00.html.*

Gorman, B. 2007. "Does NFL Sunday Night Scheduling Help Ratings?" Accessed 15 January 2008 from *http://tvbythenumbers.com/2007/11/11/does-nfl-sunday-night-scheduling-help-ratings/1723.*

Gorman, B., and D. Weeks. 2003. "Foul Play: Fan Fatalities in Twentieth-Century Organized Baseball." *NINE: A Journal of Baseball History and Culture,* v. 12, no. 1: 115–132.

Gorn, E. (1997). "Sports through the Nineteenth Century." In *The New American Sports History: Recent Approaches and Perspectives,* ed. S.W. Pope. Urbana: University of Illinois Press.

Goss, B.D., C.B. Jubenville, and J.L. MacBeth. 2003. "Primary Principles of Post-9/11 Stadium Security in the United States: Transatlantic Implications from British Practices." International Association of Assembly Managers. Mimeograph. Accessed 26 December 2007 from *http://www.iaam.org/CVMS/Post%20911%20Stadium%20Security.doc.*

Gough, P.J. 2004. "NFL Inks $11.5 Billion in Pacts with CBS, Fox, DirecTV." *Hollywood Reporter,* 9 November. Accessed 9 February 2008 from *http://www.hollywoodreporter.com/hr/search/article_display.jsp?vnu_content_id=1000708995.*

Greater Mansfield Chamber of Commerce, Inc. "History of Mansfield." Accessed 21 June 2007 from *http://www.mansfield.org/history.htm.*

Gronow, P. 1983. "The Record Industry: Growth of a Mass Medium." *Popular Music,* v. 3: 53–75.

Grucza, R. 2006. "History of Doping." Institute of Sport. Warsaw, Poland. May. Mimeograph. Accessed 19 April 2008 from *http://www.wada-ama.org/rtecontent/document/Athens_Grucza.pdf.*

Guttman, A. 1996. *The Erotic in Sports.* New York: Columbia University Press.

Hadley, L.H. 2004. "Review: Zygmont and Leady, "When Is the Honeymoon Over?" Western Oregon University. Mimeograph. Accessed 6 January 2008 from *http://www.roadsidephotos.com/baseball/hadley04.htm.*

Hagstrom, R.G. 2001. *The NASCAR Way: The Business That Drives the Sport.* Somerset, NJ: John Wiley & Sons.

Hald, A. 2005. *A History of Probability and Statistics and Their Applications before 1750.* Hoboken, NJ: Wiley.

Hall, S., S. Szmanski, and A.S. Zimbalist. 2002. "Testing Causality between Team Performance and Payroll: The Cases of Major League Baseball and English Soccer." *Journal of Sports Economics,* v. 3, no. 2: 149–168.

Hammer, R.D. 2001. "Does Internet Gambling Strengthen the U.S. Economy? Don't Bet On It." *Federal Communications Law Journal,* v. 54, no. 1, pp. 103–128. Accessed 2 March 2008 from *http://www.law.indiana.edu/fclj/pubs/v54/no1/Hammer.pdf.*

Hardin, M. 2005. "Survey Finds Boosterism, Freebies Remain Problem for Newspaper Sports Departments." *Newspaper Research Journal,* v. 26, no. 1 (Winter).

Harris, M. 2004. "Source: ABC, ESPN to extend TV contract with IRL." *USA Today.* 26 May. Accessed 9 November 2008 from http://www.usatoday.com/sports/motor/irl/indy500/2004-05-26-notebook_x.htm.

Hartgens, F., and H. Kuipers. 2004. "Effects of Androgenic-Anabolic Steroids in Athletes." *Sports Medicine,* v. 34, no. 8: 513–554.

Harvard Business School. Exhibits—19th Century Trade Cards—Historical Collections—Baker Library. Accessed 14 January 2008 from *http://www.library.hbs.edu/hc/19th_century_tcard/.*

Harvey, A. 2004. *The Beginnings of a Sporting Culture in Britain, 1793–1850.* London: Ashgate.

Hausman, J.A., and G.K Leonard. 1997. "Superstars in the National Basketball Association: Economic Value and Policy." *Journal of Labor Economics,* v. 15, no. 4: 586–624.

Hawksworth, J. 2006. "The World in 2050: Implications of Global Growth for Carbon Emissions and Climate Change Policy." Price Waterhouse Coopers. September. Accessed 23 April 2008 from *http://www.pwc.com/extweb/pwcpublications.nsf/docid/DFB54C8AAD6742DB852571F5006DD532/$file/world2050carbon.pdf.*

Heisman.com. "John W. Heisman: An Innovator of the Game." Accessed 16 April 2008 from *http://www.heisman.com/history/john-heisman.html.*

Hemphill, L. 2008. "No Card This Month." On Thestate.com. 12 January. Accessed 15 January 2007 from *http://www.thestate.com/sports/story/282573.html.*

Hendricks, T. 2003. "Sport in the Later Middle Ages." In *Sport*, ed. E. Dunning and D. Malcolm. London and New York: Routledge.

Henry, J. 2006. "Bill James." 30 April. Accessed 1 March 2008 from *http://www.time.com/time/magazine/article/0,9171,1187260,00.html.*

Herbert, B. 1996. "In America; Nike's Pyramid Scheme." *New York Times*, 10 June.

HickokSports.com. "Baseball History — The First Major League (1876–1889)." Accessed 4 January 2008 from *http://www.hickoksports.com/history/baseba04.shtml.*

_____. "Baseball History — The Professionals Take Over." Accessed 15 August 2005 from *http://www.hickoksports.com/history/baseba03.shtml.*

_____. "History — Auto Racing — Early History." Accessed 20 June 2007 from *http://www.hickoksports.com/history/autorace01.shtml.*

_____. "History — Bareknuckle Boxing in America." Accessed 4 April 2007 from *http://www.hickoksports.com/history/boxing02.shtml.*

_____. "History — College Bowl Games." Accessed 4 April 2007 from *http://www.hickoksports.com/history/collbowl.shtml.*

_____. 2007. "History — NCAA Division I Men's Basketball." 17 December. Accessed 22 March 2008 from *http://www.hickoksports.com/history/ncmbask.shtml.*

_____. "The Pro Bowl." Accessed 15 June 2007 from *http://www.hickoksports.com/history/probowl.shtml.*

Hiestand, M. 2007. "NASCAR Ratings Drop Again; Remain Strongest in the South." *USA Today*, November 13. Accessed 27 January 2008 from *http://www.usatoday.com/sports/columnist/hiestand-tv/2007-11-13-nascar-ratings_N.htm.*

Higgs, R. 1990. "Wartime Prosperity during World War II?" Presented at Economics in Times of Crisis, Cliometric sessions at the 1990 Allied Social Science Associations meetings, Washington, DC. Accessed 19 June 2007 from *http://eh.net/Clio/Conferences/ASSA/Dec_90/Higgs%20Abstract.*

Hill, W.D., and J.E. Clark. 2001. "Sports, Gambling, And Government: America's First Social Compact?" *American Anthropologist*, v. 3 no. 2: 331–345.

"The History of Fantasy Football." 2007. *Coed Magazine*, 12 November. Accessed 9 March 2008 from *http://www.coedmagazine.com/sports/3176.*

"History of the MLB All-Star Game — 1933." *The Sporting News*. Accessed 15 June 2007 from *http://archive.sportingnews.com/features/allstar/1933.html.*

Holtzman, J. 2005. *Jerome Holtzman on Baseball: A History of Baseball Scribes*. Champagne, IL: Sports Publishing, LLC.

Homerunweb. "Excerpts from the *Book of Baseball Literacy*." David Martinez, *The Book of Baseball Literacy*, 2nd Edition. Authorhouse. Accessed 25 March 2005 from *http://www.homerunweb.com/ch3text.html.*

Hooker, R., "History of the Minoans." Accessed 23 July 2005 from *http://www.wsu.edu:8080/~dee/minoa/history.htm.*

Horrigan, J. "Charles Follis Led Early Black Pioneers in Pro Football." Pro Football Hall of Fame. Reprinted by author permission from the *Pro Football Researchers Association Annual*. Accessed 26 December 2007 from *http://www.profootballhof.com/history/release.jsp?release_id=1381.*

Houthakker, H.S., and L.D. Taylor. 1966 and 1970. *Consumer Demand in the United States, 1929–1970*. Cambridge: Harvard University Press.

Huston, L. 1955. Theatre and boxing ruled subject to antitrust laws. *New York Times*, 1 February, p. 1.

Inberger, J. 1948. "The Money Spent for Play: An Index of Opinion." *The Public Opinion Quarterly*, v. 2, no. 2: 249.

Indianapolis Motor Speedway. "History of the Indianapolis Motor Speedway." Accessed 20 June 2007 from *http://www.indianapolismotorspeedway.com/history/.*

Innaccone, L. 1998. "Introduction to the Economics of Religion." *Journal of Economic Literature*, v. 36, no. 3: 1465–1496.

International Boxing Hall of Fame. "George Dixon." Accessed 26 December 2007 from *http://www.ibhof.com/dixon.htm.*

_____. "Jack Dempsey." Accessed 4 April 2007 from *http://www.ibhof.com/dempsey.htm.*

_____. "Jack Johnson." Accessed 26 December 2007 from *http://www.ibhof.com/jjohnson.htm.*

International Tennis Hall of Fame. "William Tatem Tilden: 'Bill, Big Bill.'" Accessed 21 March 2008 from *http://www.tennisfame.com/famer.aspx?pgID=867&hof_id=140.*

_____. 2006. "Helen Newington Wills Moody Roark: 'Little Miss Poker Face.'" Accessed 21 March 2008 from *http://www.tennisfame.com/famer.aspx?pgID=867&hof_id=95.*

Internet Movie Data Base. "Babe Ruth." Accessed 20 June 2007 from *http://www.imdb.com/name/nm0751899/bio.*

_____. "Biography for Babe Ruth." Accessed 20 June 2007 from *http://www.imdb.com/name/nm0751899/.*

_____. "Biography for Johnny Weismuller." Accessed 20 June 2007 from *http://www.imdb.com/name/nm0919321/bio.*

_____. "Jack Dempsey (I)." Accessed 20 June 2007 from *http://imdb.com/name/nm0218727/.*

_____. "Seabiscuit (2003) Box Office/business." Accessed 26 March 2008 from *http://imdb.com/title/tt0329575/business.*

_____. "Trivia for: Boxing (1892)." Accessed 22 June 2007 from *http://www.imdb.com/title/tt0241266/trivia.*

Irwindale Speedway. "NASCAR Brand Review." Accessed 20 June 2007 from *http://www.irwindalespeedway.com/ISdemo05.pdf.*

Jacobsen, J.P. 2007. *The Economics of Gender.* 3rd Edition. Malden, MA: Blackwell.

Jay, K. 2006. *More Than Just a Game.* New York: Columbia University Press.

John, V. 1883. The Term "Statistics." *Journal of the Statistical Society of London*, v. 46, no. 4: 656–679.

Johnston, L. 2004. "Ex-Georgia assistant's exam laughable; can you pass?" *USA Today.* 4 March. Accessed 9 November 2008 from http://www.usatoday.com/sports/college/mensbasketball/2004-03-03-harrick-exam_x.htm.

Johnston, L.D., and S.H. Williamson. 2005. "The Annual Real and Nominal GDP for the United States, 1790—Present." Economic History Services. Accessed 21 June 2007 from *http://www.eh.net/hmit/gdp/.*

Jones, J.C.H., D.G. Ferguson, and K.G. Stewart. 1993. "Blood Sports and Cherry Pie: Some Economics of Violence in the National Hockey League." *American Journal of Economics and Sociology*, v. 52, no. 1: 63–78.

Jones, J.C.H., D.G. Ferguson, and R. Sunderman. 1996. "From the Arena into the Streets: Hockey Violence, Economic Incentives and Public Policy." *American Journal of Economics and Sociology,* v. 55, no. 2: 231–243.

Journal of Quantitative Analysis in Sports. Accessed 23 February 2008 from *http://www.bepress.com/jqas/.*

"Judge Landis May End Baseball War." 1915. *New York Times*, 27 April, p. 10.

Kahane, L., and S. Shmanske. 1997. "Team Roster Turnover and Attendance in Major League Baseball." *Applied Economics,* v. 29, no. 4: 425–431.

Kahn, L. 2007. Sports League Expansion and Consumer Welfare." *Journal of Sports Economics*, v. 8, no.2: 115–138.

Kalb, E. 2007. *The 25 Greatest Sports Conspiracy Theories of All-Time: Ranking Sports' Most Notorious Fixes, Cover-Ups, and Scandals.* New York: Skyhorse.

Keating, J.W. 1964. Sportsmanship as a Moral Category." *Ethics*, v.7 5, no. 1: 25–35.

Keating, R.J. 1999. "Sports Pork: The Costly Relationship between Major League Sports and Government." The Cato Institute Policy Analysis No. 339. April 5. Accessed 5 January 2008 from *http://www.cato.org/pubs/pas/pa339.pdf.*

Kee, T. 2007. "Online Sports Spending to Reach $1 Billion by 2011." *Online Media Daily*, 24 July. Accessed 8 March 2008 from *http://publications.mediapost.com/index.cfm?fuseaction=Articles.showArticleHomePage&art_aid=64461.*

Kelley, B. "About Golf." Accessed 16 August 2006 from *http://golf.about.com/b/a/234789.htm.*

Kendall, M.G. 1960. "Studies in the History of Probability aAnd Statistics. Where Shall the History of Statistics Begin?" *Biometrika*, v. 47, no. 3/4: 447–449.

Kennickell, A.B. 2006. "Currents and Undercurrents: Changes in the Distribution of Wealth, 1989–2004." Federal Reserve Board. Accessed 4 January 2004 from *http://www.federalreserve.gov/pubs/oss/oss2/papers/concentration.2004.5.pdf.*

Kiley, D. 2007. "NBC: Blindsided by Notre Dame." *Business Week*, 20 December 2007. Accessed 9 February 2008 from *http://www.businessweek.com/magazine/content/07_53/b4065037218411.htm.*

Kirsch, G.B. 2003. *Baseball in Blue and Gray: The National Pastime during the Civil War.* (Princeton, NJ: Princeton University Press.

Knowles, G., K. Sherony, and M. Haupert. 1992. "The Demand for Major League Baseball: A Test of the Uncertainty oOf Outcome Hypothesis." *The American Economist*, v. 36, no. 2: 72–80.

Kramer, J., and D. Schaap. 1969. *Instant Replay: The Green Bay Diary of Jerry Kramer.* New York: Signet.

Krautmann, A., and L. Hadley. 2006. Demand Issues: The Product Market for Professional Sports." In *Handbook of Sports Economics*, ed. J. Fizel. Armonk, NY: M.E. Sharpe.

Krautmann, A.C., J.H. Lee, and K.G. Quinn. 2008. "Playoff Uncertainty and Playoff Races." DePaul University. Mimeograph. 25 March.

Kurian, G.T. Ed. 2004. *Datapedia of the United States: American History in Numbers.* 3rd Edition. Lanham, MD: Bernan Press.

Kutcher, L. 1983. "The American Sport Event as Carnival: An Emergent Norm Approach to Crowd Behavior." *The Journal of Popular Culture*, v. 16, no. 4: 34–41.

Kyle, D.G. 2004. "Ancient Olympics Guide: Winning at Olympia." *Archeology,* 6 April. Accessed 12 April 2008 from *http://www.archaeology.org/online/features/olympics/olympia.html.*

LaMonica, P.R. 2007."CBS Scores with Super Bowl Ratings." On CnnMoney.com, 5 February.

Lapchick, R. 2006. "The 2006–07 Season Racial and Gender Report Card: National Basketball Association." University of Central Florida, College of Business Administration, DeVos Sports Business Management Program. Accessed 26 December 2007 from *http://www.bus.ucf.edu/sport/public/downloads/2006_NBA_RGRC_PR.pdf.*

Lapchick, R., and J. Brendan. 2006. "The 2005 Racial and Gender Report Card: College Sports." University of Central Florida De Vos Sports Business and Management Program. 13 December. Accessed 30 January 2008 from *http://www.bus.ucf.edu/sport/public/downloads/2005_Racial_Gender_Report_Card_Colleges.pdf.*

Lavin, M. 2006. "Sports and Drugs: Are the Current Bans Justified?" In *The Ethics of Sports: An Anthology,* ed. J. Boxhill. Malden, MA: Blackwell.

Leaman, O. 2007. "Cheating and Fair Play in Sport." In *Ethics in Sport,* 2nd Edition, ed. J.M. Morgan. Champaign, IL: Human Kinetics.

Lee, Y. H. 2004. "Competitive Balance and Attendance in Japanese, Korean, and U.S. Professional Baseball Leagues." In *International Comparisons in Sports Economics,* ed. R. Fort and J. Fizel. Westport, CT: Praeger.

Leeds, M., and P. von Allmen. 2005. *The Economics of Sports.* Boston: Pearson Addison Wesley.

Lehman, S. "The Baseball Archive." Accessed 23 February 2008 from *http://baseball1.com/.*

Leib, F. 1996. *Baseball as I Have Known It.* Lincoln, NE: University of Nebraska Press.

Leonhardt, L. 2006. "Sad Suspicions about Scores in Basketball." *New York Times,* 8 March. Accessed 13 April 2008 from *http://www.nytimes.com/2006/03/08/business/08leonhardt.html?partner=rssnyt&emc=rss.*

Lesko, J. 2005. "League History." AAGPBL Players Association, Inc. Accessed 22 June 2007 from *http://www.aagpbl.org/league/history.cfm.*

Levin, R.C., G.J. Mitchell, P.A. Volcker, and G.F. Will. 2000. The Report of the Independent Members of the Commissioner's Blue Ribbon Panel on Baseball Economics. Major League Baseball. July. Accessed 23 March 2008 from *http://www.mlb.com/mlb/downloads/blue_ribbon.pdf.*

Levitt, S.D. 2004. "Why Are Gambling Markets Organized So Differently from Financial Markets?" *Economic Journ*al, v. 114, no. 495: 223–246.

Lewis, M. 2003. *Moneyball: The Art of Winning an Unfair Game.* New York: Norton.

Library of Congress. "American Treasures of the Library of Congress." Accessed 15 August 2005 from *http://www.loc.gov/exhibits/treasures/tri077.html.*

Lindsay, J. 2002. "BCS Drops Margin of Victory from Ratings Formula — Several Pollsters Expected to Leave BCS." Accessed 12 April 2008 from *http://espn.go.com/ncf/news/2002/0621/1397538.html.*

Litsky, F. 2006. "In 1916, a Blowout for the Ages." *New York Times,* 7 October. Accessed 16 April 2008 from *http://www.nytimes.com/2006/10/07/sports/ncaafootball/07tech.html?partner=rssnyt&emc=rss.*

Lomax, M.E. 1999. "The African American Experience in Professional Football." *Journal of Social History,* v. 33 (Fall): 163–178.

"Long Baseball War Is Settled." 1915. *New York Times,* 23 December, p. 10.

Longley, N. 2000. "The Underrepresentation of French Canadians on English Canadian NHL Teams: Evidence from 1943–1998." *Journal of Sports Economics,* v. 1, no. 3: 236–256.

Longman, J. 2000. "Olympics: Memo Details Payments Made to Influence Bids." *New York Times.* 27 May. Accessed 9 November 2008 from http://query.nytimes.com/gst/fullpage.html?res=9F07E0DC113DF934A15756C0A9669C8B63.

Lowitt, B. 1999. "Harding, Kerrigan Are Linked Forever by Skating Incident." *St. Petersburg Times,* 29 November. Accessed 13 April 2008 from *http://www.sptimes.com/News/112999/Sports/Harding__Kerrigan_are.shtml.*

Luschen, G. 2000. "Doping in Sport as Deviant Behavior and Its Social Control." In *Handbook of Sports Studies,* ed. J.J. Coakley and E. Dunning. London: Sage.

Magazine Publishers of America. "2006 Average Total Paid and Verified Circulation for Top 100 ABC Magazines." Accessed 10 February 2008 from *http://www.magazine.org/circulation/circulation_trends_and_magazine_handbook/22175.cfm.*

"Major League Soccer." DeVos Sports Business Management Program, University of Central Florida (22 November). Accessed 23 April 2008 from *http://www.tidesport.org/RGRC/2006/2006_RGRC_MLS.pdf.*

Mandell, R.D. 2003. "Europe, 500–1750." In *Sport,* ed. E. Dunning and D. Malcom. London and New York: Routledge.

Martin, E.S. 1899. "This Busy World." *Harper's Weekly,* 19 August, p. 809.

Maske, M. and L. Carpenter. 2006. "Player arrests put the NFL in a defensive mode." *Washington Post.* 16 December. Accessed 9 November 2008 from http://www.washingtonpost.com/wp-dyn/content/article/2006/12/15/AR2006121502134.html.

Massey, K. "Freeze of 1948." Museum of Broadcast Communications. Accessed 17 February 2008 from *http://www.museum.tv/archives/etv/F/htmlF/freezeofl/freezeofl.htm.*

Maxcy, J.G. 2006. "Revenue Sharing in MLB:

The Effects on Player Transfers." *International Association of Sports Economists Working Paper Series*, Paper No. 06–15. September. Accessed 2 April 2008 from *http://www.holycross.edu/departments/economics/RePEc/spe/Maxcy_Transfers.pdf.*

McCarty, B. "Football's Greatest Decade." *College Football Historical Society Journal*, v. 1, no. 1: 2–6. Accessed 15 June 2007 from *http://www.aafla.org/SportsLibrary/CFHSN/CFHSNv01/CFHSNv01n1b.pdf.*

McChesney, R.W. 1989. "Media Made Sport: a History of Sports Coverage in the United States." In *Media, Sports and Society*. ed. L.A. Wenner. Newbury Park, CA: Sage.

McDonald, M.A., and D. Rascher. 2000. "Does Bat Day Make Cents? The Effect of Promotions on Demand for Major League Baseball." *Journal of Sport Management*, v. 14, no. 1: 8–27.

McQuillan, S.A., and R.A. Smith. 1993. "The Rise and Fall of the Flying Wedge: Football's Most Controversial Play." *Journal of Sport History*, v. 20, no. 1: 57–64.

Meacham, S. (2006). "Old Division Football, the Indigenous Mob Soccer of Dartmouth College." *Dartmo*. Accessed 1 April 2006 from *http://www.dartmo.com/football/Football_Meacham.pdf.*

"Media Timeline —1921–1925." Accessed 4 April 2007 from *http://www.ketupa.net/timeline3.htm.*

Merriman, J., and J. Hill. 1992. "Ethics, Laws, and Sport." *Journal of Legal Aspects of Sport*, v. 2, no. 2: 56–63.

Meyer, S. 1980. "Adapting the Immigrant to the Line: Americanization in the Ford Factory, 1914–1921." *Journal of Social History*, v. 14, no. 1: 67–82.

Miller, J., and M. Hyman. 2000. *Confessions of a Baseball Purist: What's Right— and Wrong— with Baseball.* Baltimore: Johns Hopkins University Press.

Mills, J. 1987. "Radio's All-Sports Gamble." *The New York Times*, 4 August. Accessed 10 February from *http://query.nytimes.com/gst/fullpage.html?res=9B0DEFD91639F937A3575BC0A961948260.*

Minorleaguebaseball.com. "History: Timeline." On MinorLeagueBaseball.com. Accessed 15 June 2007 from *http://web.minorleaguebaseball.com/milb/history/timeline.jsp.*

MLB.com. 1983. "The Pine Tar Game." 24 July. Accessed 12 April 2008 from *http://mlb.mlb.com/mlb/baseballs_best/mlb_bb_gamepage.jsp?story_page=bb_83reg_072483_kcrnyy.*

_____. 2007. "MLB, DIRECTV expand multi-year agreement." 8 March. Accessed 9 November 2008 from http://mlb.mlb.com/news/press_releases/press_release.jsp?ymd=20070308&content_id=1833910&vkey=pr_mlb&fext=.jsp&c_id=mlb.

Mosteroller, F. 1952. "The World Series Competition." *Journal of the American Statistical Association*, v. 47, no. 259: 355–380.

MSNBC. 2007. "NBA Finals TV Ratings Were Record Low." Accessed 26 January 2008 from *http://www.msnbc.msn.com/id/19253444/.*

Mullin, B.J., S. Hardy, and W.A. Sutton. 2007. *Sports Marketing*. Champaign, IL: Human Kinetics.

NASCAR. "Evolution of the Stock Car: Part I." Accessed 19 June 2007 from *http://www.nascar.com/2002/kyn/history/evolution/02/06/stockcar/index.html.*

Nash, C. 2003. "Webber avoids jail, pleading guilty on a contempt charge." *New York Times*. 15 July.

National Baseball Hall of Fame and Museum. "Baseballs Like Concrete." Accessed 15 June 2007 from *http://www.baseballhalloffame.org/exhibits/online_exhibits/baseball_enlists/concrete.htm.*

_____. "A New Ball Game." Accessed 15 June 2007 from *http://www.baseballhalloffame.org/exhibits/online_exhibits/baseball_enlists/new.htm.*

_____. "Origins of the Baseball Hall of Fame and Museum." Accessed 15 August 2005 from *http://www.baseballhalloffame.org/about/history.htm.*

_____. "War Dominates Baseball." Accessed 15 June 2007 from *http://www.baseballhalloffame.org/exhibits/online_exhibits/baseball_enlists/dominates.htm.*

"National Basketball Association." DeVos Sports Business Management Program University of Central Florida (9 May). Accessed 23 April 2008 from *http://www.tidesport.org/Articles/2006_NBA_RGRC_PR.pdf.*

National Basketball Association. The 2008 Racial and Gender Report Card: Major League Baseball. DeVos Sports Business Management Program University of Central Florida (15 April). Accessed 23 April 2008 from *http://www.tidesport.org/Articles/2008_MLB_RGRC_PR.pdf.*

National Endowment for the Arts. 2004. "2002 Survey of Public Participation in the Arts," Table 28. Research Division Report #45.

National Football League. "NFL History." Accessed 5 April 2007 from *http://www.nfl.com/history/chronology/1869–1910.*

National Museum of Racing and Hall of Fame. 2004. Accessed 26 March 2008 from *http://www.racingmuseum.org/hall/fame.asp.*

Nauright, J. "The Emergence of Golf as a Sporting Spectacle 1904–1935." Accessed 5 April 2006 from *http://www.aafla.org/SportsLibrary/NASSH_Proceedings/NP2002/NP2002s.pdf.*

_____. 1996. "Writing and Reading American

Football: Culture, Identities, and Sports Studies." Accessed 1 April 2007 from *http://www.aafla.org/SportsLibrary/SportingTraditions/1996/st1301/st1301k.pdf.*

NCAA. "NCAA Broadcast Information." On NCAA.com. Accessed 25 March 2005 from *http://www.ncaasports.com/broadcast/mlacrosse.*

_____. "Timeline of College and Professional Sports Wagering Cases." Accessed 12 April 2008 from *http://www1.ncaa.org/membership/enforcement/gambling/toolkit/chapter_20?ObjectID=42739&ViewMode=0&PreviewState=0.*

_____. 2007. "National Collegiate Athletic Association Revised Budget for Fiscal Year Ended August 31, 2007." Accessed 3 November 2007 from *http://www1.ncaa.org/finance/2006-07_budget.pdf.*

NCAAfootball.com. 2008. "TV Ratings and Bowl Games Highlight America's Passion for College Football in 2007." Accessed 26 January 2008 from *http://www.ncaafootball.com/index.php?s=&url_channel_id=34&url_article_id=11994&change_well_id=2.*

Neale, W.C. 1964. "The Peculiar Economics of Professional Sports: A Contribution to the Theory of the Firm in Sporting Competition and in Market Competition." *The Quarterly Journal of Economics,* v. 78, no. 1: 1–14.

Neal-Lunsford, J. 1992. "Sport in the Land of Television: The Use of Sport in Network Prime-time Schedules, 1946–1950." *Journal of Sport History,* v. 19, no. 1: 56–76.

Neilson Media Research. 2008. "Neilson's Recap of 2008 Super Bowl Advertising." 7 February. Accessed 27 February 2008 from *http://www.nielsenmedia.com/nc/portal/site/Public/menuitem.55dc65b4a7d5adff3f65936147a062a0/?vgnextoid=697760772bfe7110VgnVCM100000ac0a260aRCRD.*

"New York Radio History." Accessed 9 June 2006 from *http://www.tangentsunset.com/newyorkradiohistory.htm.*

Neyer, R. 2002. "Red Sox Hire James in Advisory Capacity." Accessed 1 March 2008 from *http://espn.go.com/mlb/s/2002/1105/1456563.html.*

"NHL All-Star Teams." Hickok Sports. Accessed 15 June 2007 from *http://www.hickoksports.com/history/nhlallstarteams.shtml.*

Nicholson, A. 2008. "Gazprom Funds, Forms Russian Rival to National Hockey League." Bloomberg News, 6 February. Accessed 23 April 2008 from *http://www.bloomberg.com/apps/news?pid=newsarchive&sid=ajMouFsMLj_c.*

Nietzsche, F., and M. Faber. 1996. *Human, All Too Human: A Book for Free Spirits.* Lincoln: University of Nebraska Press.

Noll, R. 1982. "Major League Sports." In *The Structure of American Industry,* ed. W. Adams. New York: Macmillan.

Noll, R.G. 2002. "The Economics of Promotion and Relegation in Sports Leagues: The Case of English Football." *Journal of Sports Economics,* v. 3, no. 2: 169–203.

_____. 2003. "The Economics Of Baseball Contraction." *Journal of Sports Economics,* v. 4, no. 4: 367–388.

Northwestern University Readership Institute. 2001. "Newspaper Industry Content Analysis Report: Data Tables and Definitions." Accessed 7 January 2008 from *http://www.readership.org/content/content_analysis/data/industry_content_report.pdf.*

The Nobel Foundation. 2002. "Economics 2002." Accessed 23 March 2008 from *http://nobelprize.org/nobel_prizes/economics/laureates/2002/.*

Notre Dame University. "Basketball — guide Format Annuals." *Spaulding Guides.* Rare Books and Special Collections. Accessed 1 March 2008 from *http://www.library.nd.edu/rarebooks/collections/sports/basketball/annuals/spalding.shtml.*

Notre Dame University. "Boxing — guide Format Annuals — Ring Record Book." Rare Books and Special Collections. Accessed 1 March 2008 from *http://www.library.nd.edu/rarebooks/collections/sports/boxing/annuals/ring_record.shtml.*

Notre Dame University. *Spaulding Annual Guide* (1891–1940), *Barnes Annual Guide* (1941–49), and *National Collegiate Athletic Association Annual Guide* (1950-). Rare Books and Special Collections. Accessed 1 March 2008 from *http://www.library.nd.edu/rarebooks/collections/sports /football/annuals/spalding_barnes.shtml.*

Noyes, G. "American Broadcasting Company." Museum of Broadcast Communications. Accessed 17 February 2008 from *http://www.museum.tv/archives/etv/A/htmlA/americanbroa /americanbroa.htm.*

NPD Group. 2007. "2006 U.S. Video Game and PC Game Retail Sales Reach $13.5 Billion, Exceeding Previous Record Set in 2002 by Over $1.7 billion." Press Release, 19 January. Accessed 3 November 2007 from *http://www.npd.com/press/releases/press_070119.html.*

"#2 Tiger Woods." 2007. *Forbes.* Accessed 22 June 2007 from *http://www.forbes.com/lists/2007/53/07celebrities_Tiger-Woods_WR6D.html.*

O'Connell, J. 2007. "Much Required to Become MLB Umpire." On MLB.com. 28 August. Accessed 13 April 2008 from *http://mlb.mlb.com/news/article.jsp?ymd=20070827&content_id=2173765&vkey=news_mlb&fext=.jsp&c_id=mlb.*

Officer, Lawrence H., and Samuel H. Williamson. 2007. "Purchasing Power of

Money in the United States from 1774 to 2006." On MeasuringWorth.Com.
O'Keefe, B. 2005. "America's Fastest Growing Sport." *Fortune,* 5 September.
Okrent, D. 1981. "He Does It by the Numbers (Bill James)." *Sports Illustrated,* v. 54 (25 May): 40–47.
Onereed.com. 2002. "Ancient Calendars and the Race against Time." Accessed 23 July 2005 from *http://www.onereed.com/articles/vvflolympics.html.*
"Open Hearings Set to Sift Basketball." 1945. *New York Times,* 14 February, p. 25.
Oriard, M. 1991. *Sporting with the Gods: A Rhetoric of Play and Game in American Culture.* Cambridge: Cambridge University Press.
_____. 1993. *Reading Football: How the Popular Press Created an American Spectacle.* Chapel Hill: University of North Carolina Press.
Ours, R.M. "Introduction: A Brief History of College Football." *College Football Encyclopedia.* Accessed 28 December 2007 from *http://www.footballencyclopedia.com/cfeintro.htm.*
Owens, J.W. 2006. "The Coverage of Sports on Radio." In *Handbook of Sports and Media,* ed. A.A. Raney and J. Bryant. New York: Erlbaum.
Pacey, P.L. 1985. "The Courts and College Football: New Playing Rules off the Field?" *American Journal of Economics and Sociology,* v. 44, no. 2: 145–154.
Paolantonio, S. 2002. "Eagles Preparing to Leave Veterans Stadium." On ESPN.com. 13 December. Accessed 26 December 2007 from *http://espn.go.com/nfl/columns/paolantonio_sal/1476046.html.*
Pappas, D. 1997. "1997: 75 Years of National Baseball Broadcasts." *Outside the Lines.* National SABR Business of Baseball Community Newsletter. Accessed 20 June 2007 from *http://roadsidephotos.sabr.org/baseball/nationalbroadcast .htm.*
Paton, J. 2008. "Mammoth Sales." *Rocky Mountain News,* 21 March. Accessed 23 April 2008 from *http://www.rockymountainnews.com/news/2008/mar/21/mammoth-sales/.*
PCL 100. "Centennial News: The Formation of the Pacific Coast League." Accessed March 25, 2005 from *http://www1.infinitydesign.net/virtual/pclbaseball.com/www/pcl100/news/?id=2277.*
Penelope P. 2003. "NASCAR Pulls into Prime Time." *Forbes,* 7 October. Accessed 9 February 2008 from *http://www.forbes.com/2003/10/07/cx_pp_1007nascar.html.*
Pendergast, S., and T. Pendergast. Eds. 2002. *Bowling, Beatniks, and Bell-Bottoms: Pop Culture of 20th Century America.* Farmington Hills, MI: UXL.
Pennington, B. 2006. "John Heisman, the Coach behind the Trophy." *New York Times,* 8 December. Accessed 16 April 2008 from *http://www.nytimes.com/2006/12/08/sports/ncaafootball/08heisman.html?_r=1&oref=slogin.*
Pew Research Center. 2005. "Box Scores and Bylines: A Snapshot of the Newspaper Sports Page." 22 August.
_____. 2006. "Americans to the Rest of the World: Soccer Not Really Our Thing." 14 June.
PGA Tour. 2008. "PGA Tour Statistics." Accessed 21 March 2008 from *http://www.pgatour.com/r/stats/info/?110.*
"The PGA Tour: Where's the Green?" 2002. *Business Week,* 20 May. Accessed 9 February 2008 *http://www.businessweek.com/magazine/content/02_20/b3783108.htm.*
Pietruza, D. 1997. *Lights On! The Wild Century-Long Saga of Night Baseball.* Lantham, MD: Scarecrow.
Plackett, R.L. 1958. "Studies in the History of Probability and Statistics: VII. The Principle of the Arithmetic Mean." *Biometrika,* v. 45, no. 1/2: 130–135.
Plunkett, J.W. 2007. *Plunkett's Sports Industry Almanac 2008.* Houston: Plunkett Research.
Polling Report.com. Accessed 10 November 2007 from *http://www.pollingreport.com/sports.htm.*
Porter, P.G. 1969. "Origins of the American Tobacco Company." *The Business History Review,* v. 43, no. 1: 59–76.
"Powdered Wigs. 2007. *Economist,* 13 December.
Preston, I., and S. Szymanski. 2003. "Cheating in Contests." *Oxford Review of Economic Policy,* v. 19, no. 4: 612–624.
PRnewswire.com. 1999. "CBS Sports and National Collegiate Athletic Association Reach Long-Term Agreement for NCAA Division I Men's Basketball Championship." 18 November. Accessed 9 November 2008 from http://www.prnewswire.com/cgi-bin/stories.pl?ACCT=104&STORY=/www/story/11-18-1999/0001079506&EDATE=.
Pro Football Hall of Fame. "African-Americans in Pro Football: Pioneers, Milestones and Firsts." Accessed 26 December 2007 from *http://www.profootballhof.com/history/general/african-americans.jsp.*
Professional Football Researchers Association. "All-American Football Conference." Accessed 24 March 2005 from *http://www.footballresearch.com/articles/frpage.cfm?topic=aafc.*
Pro Football Hall of Fame. "Bill Willis." Accessed 30 January 2008 from *http://www.profootballhof.com/hof/member.jsp?player_id=231.*
_____. "Football and America: World War II." Accessed 15 June 2007 from *http://www.prof*

ootballhof.com/history/general/war/worldwar2/page1.jsp.

_____. "History: Pro Football's Other Undefeated Teams." Accessed 26 January 2008 from *http://www.profootballhof.com/history/decades/1940s/undefeated.jsp.*

_____. "History — Providence Steam Roller." Accessed 22 June 2007 from *http://www.profootballhof.com/history/decades/1920s/providence.jsp.*

_____. "Marion Motley." Accessed 30 January 2008 from *http://www.profootballhof.com/hof/member.jsp?player_id=156.*

_____. "Nov. 12 — Birth of Pro Football." Accessed 1 April 2007 from *http://www.profootballhof.com/history/general/birth.jsp.*

Pro-Football-Reference.com. "1988 Cincinnati Bengals Statistics and Players." Accessed 16 April 2008 from *http://www.pro-football-reference.com/teams/cin/1988.htm.*

_____. "Bill Walsh Records, Statistics, and Category Ranks." Accessed 13 April 2008 from *http://www.pro-football-reference.com/coaches/WalsBi0.htm.*

"Pulliam Is President." 1902. *New York Times*, 13 December, p. 11.

Pylyshyn, Z.W., and L. Bannon 1989. *Perspectives on the Computer Revolution*. Bristol, UK: Intellect Books.

Quinn, K.G. Forthcoming. "Talent Dispersal Drafts." In *The Business of Sports,* Volume 3, ed. D. Howard and B. Humphreys. Westport, CT: Praeger.

Quinn, K.G., and D. Surdam. 2007. "The Case of the Missing Fans: St. Norbert College and University of Northern Iowa." St. Norbert College. Mimeograph.

Quinn, K.G., A. Berkovitz, and M. Geier. 2008. "Superstars and Journeymen: An Analysis of National Football Teams' Allocation of the Salary Cap across Rosters, 2000–2005." Online at http://ideas.repec.org/p/spe/wpaper/0722.html.

Quinn, K.G., P.B. Bursik, C.P. Borick, and L.M. Raethz. 2003. "Do New Digs Mean More Wins? The Relationship between a New Venue and a Professional Sports Team's Competitive Success." *Journal of Sports Economics,* v. 4, no. 3: 167–182.

Quinn, K.G., M. Geier, and A. Berkovitz. 2008. "Passing on Success? Productivity Outcomes for Quarterbacks Chosen in the 1999–2004 National Football League Player Entry Drafts." St. Norbert College. Mimeograph.

Quirk, J. 2004. "College Football Conferences and Competitive Balance." *Managerial and Decision Economics,* v. 25, no. 2: 63–75.

Quirk, J., and R.D. Fort. 1997. *Pay Dirt: The Business of Professional Team Sports.* Princeton, NJ: Princeton University Press.

Rader, B. (1983). *American Sports: From the Age of Folk Games to the Age of Spectators.* Englewood Cliffs, NJ: Prentice-Hall.

Radio Advertising Bureau. 2007. *Radio Marketing and Fact Book 2007–2008.* 11 October. Accessed 10 February 2008 from *http://www.rab.com/public/MediaFacts/2007RMGFB-150-10-11.pdf.*

Raney, A.A. 2006. "Why We Watch and Enjoy Mediated Sports." In *Handbook of Sports and Media,* ed. A.A. Raney and J. Bryant. Hillsdale, NJ: Erlbaum.

Rascher, D. 1999. "A Test of the Optimal Positive Production Network Externality in Major League Baseball." In *Sports Economics: Current Research,* ed. J. Fizel, E. Gustafson, and L. Hadley. Westport: CT: Praeger.

Rawls, J. 1999. *A Theory of Justice.* Cambridge, MA: Belknap Press/Harvard University Press.

RecordingHistory.org. "The History of Recording Technology." Accessed 4 April 2007 from *http://www.recording-history.org/HTML/phono_technology1.php.*

Referenceforbusiness.com. "Company Histories: Wirtz Corporation." Accessed 27 December 2007 from *http://www.referenceforbusiness.com/history/Vi-Z/Wirtz-Corporation.html.*

Rice, G. 1923. "Alumnus Football." Accessed 5 April 2008 from Professional Football Research Association at *http://nflhistory.net/cgi-bin/dcforum/dcboard.cgi?az=read_count&om=1114&forum=DCForumID64.*

Ritchie, A. 1996. *Major Taylor: The Extraordinary Career of a Champion Bicycle Racer.* Baltimore: Johns Hopkins University Press.

Robbins, L. 2007. "A Football Final Four." *New York Post,* 17 July. Accessed 9 February from *http://www.nypost.com/seven/07172007/sports/a_football_final_four_sports_lenn_robbins.htm.*

Roberts, R. (2003). *Jack Dempsey, the Manassa Mauler.* Urbana: University of Illinois Press.

Robinson, D.W. 1961. "The Economics of Fashion Demand." *The Quarterly Journal of Economics,* v. 75, no. 3: 376–398.

Romano, A. 2004. "Regional Appeal." *Broadcasting and Cable,* 15 March. Accessed 17 February 2008 from *http://www.broadcastingcable.com/article/CA403509.html.*

Room, R. 1987. "Alcohol Monopolies in the U.S.: Challenges and Opportunities." *Journal of Public Health Policy,* v. 8, no. 4: 509–530.

"Rose Bowl Stadium." Accessed 4 April 2007 from *http://www.rosebowlstadium.com/RoseBowl_history_154_facts.htm.*

Rosen, J.N. 2007. *The Erosion of the American Sporting Ethos: Shifting Attitudes toward Competition.* Jefferson, NC: McFarland.

Rosen, J.N., and D. Wetcher-Hendricks. Forthcoming. "Repression at the Ballpark: Sport,

Socialization, and the Birth of a New Stadium Etiquette." In *Sport and Social Theory,* ed. E. Smith. Champaign, IL: Human Kinetics.

Rosen, S. 1981. "The Economics of Superstars." *American Economic Review,* v. 71, no. 5: 845–858.

Rottenberg, S. 1956. "The Baseball Players' Labor Market." *Journal of Political Economy,* v. 64, no. 3: 242–258.

Rovell, D. 2003. "Seven Licensees Will Pay the Bulk of the Fees." On ESPN.com. 4 August, updated 6 August. Accessed 26 April 2008 from *http://espn.go.com/sportsbusiness/news/2003/0804/1590167.html.*

St. John, A. 1999. Home away from Home: A Yankee Fan's Guide to Fenway Park. The Villiage Voice. Accessed 15 June 2007 from *http://www.villagevoice.com/news/9927,stjohn,6888,3.html.*

"St. Julien Will Be First Black Jockey in 79 Years at Derby." 2007. *Sports Illustrated,* 4 May. Accessed 16 December 2007 from *http://sportsillustrated.cnn.com/more/horseracing/2000/triplecrown/kentucky/news/2000/05/04/stjulien_derby_ap/.*

St. Louis Cardinals. 2008. "The Official Site of the St. Louis Cardinals: Fan Forum: St. Louis Cardinals One for the Birds." Accessed 9 March 2008 from *http://stlouis.cardinals.mlb.com/stl/fan_forum/oneforthebirds_index.jsp.*

Sanderson, A.R. 2002. "The Many Dimensions of Competitive Balance." *Journal of Sports Economics,* v. 3, no. 2: 204–228.

_____. 2004. "The Puzzling Economics of Sports." May 3. Accesed 27 April 2008 from *http://www.econlib.org/library/Columns/y2004/Sandersonsports.html.*

Sanderson, A.R., and J.J. Siegfried. 2003. "Thinking about Competitive Balance." *Journal of Sports Economics,* v. 4, no. 4: 255–279.

Sandomir, R. 1998. "TV Sports; It's a Summer Doubleheader for Babe Ruth Fans." *New York Times,* 14 July.

_____. 2000. "Federal Jury in Antitrust Suit Says M.L.S. Not a Monopoly." *New York Times,* 12 December, p. D2.

_____. 2002. "College Football; Margin of Victory Falls in Bowl Rating." *New York Times,* 26 June. Accessed 12 April 2008 from *http://query.nytimes.com/gst/fullpage.html?res=9E0DE6DE143EF935A15755C0A9649C8B63.*

_____. 2002. "Figure Skating; Russian Man Is Arrested in Italy in a Plot to Fix Olympics Skating." *New York Times,* 1 August. Accessed 12 April 2008 from *http://query.nytimes.com/gst/fullpage.html?res=9C04E5D9163BF932A3575BC0A9649C8B63.*

_____. 2003. "OLYMPICS: NBC's Olympic Run Is Extended to 2012 With $2 Billion Bid." *New York Times.* 7 June. Accessed 9 November 2008 from http://query.nytimes.com/gst/fullpage.html?res=9E00E6D91739F934A35755C0A9659C8B63&sec=&spon=&&scp=3&sq=olympics%20tv%20rights%20deal&st=cse.

_____. 2007. "N.B.A. Renews Pacts, Adding Links to Digital Use." *New York Times,* 28 June. Accessed 10 January 2008 from *http://www.nytimes.com/2007/06/28/sports/basketball/28sandomir.html?fta=y.*

_____. 2008. "Versus extends contract with N.H.L." *New York Times.* 23 January. Accessed 9 November 2008 from http://www.nytimes.com/2008/01/23/sports/hockey/23versus.html?ref=sports.

Sauer, R.D. 1998. "The Economics of Wagering Markets." *Journal of Economic Literature,* v. 36, no. 4: 2021–2064.

Scanlon, T.F. 2006. Sports and Mdia in the Ancient Mediterranean." In *Handbook of Sports and Media,* ed. A.A. Raney and J. Bryant. New York: Erlbaum.

Schiff, A.J. 2008. *"The Father of Baseball": A Biography of Henry Chadwick.* Jefferson, NC: McFarland.

Schmidt, M.B., and D.J. Berri. 2003. "On the Evolution of Competitive Balance: The Impact of an Increasing Global Search." *Economic Inquiry,* v. 41, no. 4: 692–704.

Schudson, M. 1978. *Discovering the News: A Social History of American Newspapers.* New York: Basic.

Schuman, H., and J. Harding. 1963. "Sympathetic Identification With the Underdog." *The Public Opinion Quarterly,* v. 27, no. 2: 230–241.

Schwartz, L. "Man o' War Came Close to Perfection." On ESPN.com. Accessed 4 April 2007 from *http://espn.go.com/sportscentury/features/00016132.html.*

Schwarz, A. 2004. *The Numbers Game.* New York: St. Martin's Press.

_____. 2006. "Baseball Is a Game of Numbers, but Whose Numbers Are They?" *New York Times,* 16 May. Accessed 9 March 2008 from *http://www.nytimes.com/2006/05/16/sports/baseball/16license.html?_r=1&oref=slogin.*

Scranton, P.E., P.P. Scranton, and P.E. Scranton, Jr. 2002. *Playing Hurt.* Dulles, VA: Brassey's.

Sears, E.S. 2001. *Running through the Ages.* Jefferson, NC: McFarland.

Sears, H.D. 1992. "The Moral Threat of Intercollegiate Sports." *Journal of Sport History,* v. 19, no. 3 (Winter).

Seidman, J. 2007. "Sports Ratings: Challenged at the National Level." 5 September. Accessed 15 January 2008 from *http://tvbythenumbers.com/2007/09/05/ted-asks-why/502.*

Seigfried, J., and Zimbalist, A. 2000. "The Economics of Sports Facilities and Their Communities." *Journal of Economic Perspectives,* v. 14, no. 3: 95–114.

Sessa, D. 2006. "Baseball expands TV coverage with Fox, Turner deals." Bloomberg News. 11 July. Accessed 9 November 2008 from http://www.bloomberg.com/apps/news?pid=20601089&sid=a4weBYzzyNtc&refer=home.

Shapiro, F.R. 2006. *The Yale Book of Quotations.* New Haven: Yale University Press.

Shapiro, L. 2005. "Vikings give new meaning to term 'Love Boat.'" *Washington Post.* 14 October. Accessed 9 November 2008 from http://www.washingtonpost.com/wp-dyn/content/article/2005/10/14/AR2005101401674.html.

Shea, S. 2007. "Cubs Broadcast History." Society for American Baseball Research, Business of Baseball Committee. 26 July. Accessed 10 February 2008 from *http://bob.sabrwebs.com/index2.php?option=com_content&do_pdf=1&id=119.*

Simmons, B. "Idiot's Guide to the Gold Club Trial." Accessed 13 April 2008 from *http://proxy.espn.go.com/espn/page2/story?id=1237371.*

Simmons, B. 2007. "One man out, one league in trouble." ESPN. 23 July. Accessed 9 November 2008 from http://sports.espn.go.com/espn/page2/story?page=simmons/070722.

Simon, R.L. 1984. "Good Competition and Drug-enhanced Performance." *Journal of the Philosophy of Sport,* v. 11, no. 1: 6–13.

_____. 2004. *Fair Play: The Ethics of Sport.* Boulder, CO: Westview.

"Sirius Satellite Will Broadcast NASCAR." 2005. *USA Today,* 22 February. Accessed 9 February 2008 from *http://www.usatoday.com/sports/motor/nascar/2005-02-22-sirius-nascar_x.htm.*

Smith, D. R. 2003. "The Home Advantage Revisited: Winning and Crowd Support in an Era of National Publics." *Journal of Sport and Social Issues,* v. 27, no. 4: 346–371.

Smith, M. 2003. "What Is Sports Violence?" In *The Ethics of Sports: An Anthology,* ed. J. Boxhill. Malden, MA: Blackwell.

Smith, R.A. 1988. "A Failure of Elitism: The Harvard-Yale Dual League Plan of the 1890s." *The New England Quarterly,* v. 61, no. 2.

_____. 2001. *Play-by-Play: Radio, Television, and Big-Time College Sport.* Baltimore: Johns Hopkins University Press.

_____. 2001. *Sports and Freedom: The Rise of Big Time College Athletics.* Oxford: Oxford University Press.

Smith, T.W. 1998. "A Review of Church Attendance Measures." *American Sociological Review,* v. 63, no. 1: 131–136.

Smithsonian Institution. "Human Ancestors Hall—*Homo Sapiens.*" Accessed 1 April 2007 from *http://www.mnh.si.edu/anthro/humanorigins/ha/sap.htm.*

SNL Archives. Accessed 21 June 2007 from *http://snl.jt.org/.*

Snyder, E.D., and E. Spreitzer. 1974. "Sociology of Sport: An Overview." *The Sociological Quarterly,* v. 15, no. 4: 467–487.

"Soccer Robots Compete for the Title." 2008. *Science Daily,* 4 April. Accessed 16 April 2008 from *http://www.sciencedaily.com/releases/2008/04/080401110128 .htm.*

Sommers, P.M. 2003. "Baseball's All-Stars: Birthplace and Distribution." *The College Mathematics Journal,* v. 34, no. 1: 24–30.

Soonhwan, L., and H. Chun. 2002. Economic values of professional sports franchises in the United States. Online at thesportjournal.org.

"Sosa Challenges Suspension with Immediate Appeal." Accessed 12 April from *http://espn.go.com/mlb/news/2003/0606/1564235.html.*

Spadafora, V. 2006. "Football under the Lights." *The World Almanac 2007.* Accessed 21 June from *http://www.worldalmanac.com/blog/2006/11/football_under_the_lights.html.*

Sport Journal, v. 5, no. 3. Accessed 28 December 2007 from *http://www.thesportjournal.org/2002Journal/Vol5-No3/economic-values.asp.*

Sports Business Journal. 2006. *2006 Sports Business Resource Guide and Fact Book.* Charlotte, NC: Street & Smith's.

Sports Illustrated. 1968. 22 July.

"Sports Traffic no Fantasy for Yahoo." 2007. *ValleyWag Magazine.* Accessed 9 March 2008 from *http://valleywag.com/tech/stats/sports-traffic-no-fantasy-for-yahoo-336833.php.*

Stagg, A.A., and H.L. Williams. 1893. *Scientific and Practical Treatise on American Football.* Hartford, CT: privately printed.

STATS, Inc. 2008. "STATS Historical Timeline." Accessed 1 March 2008 from *http://biz.stats.com/timeline.asp.*

Stein, M. 2007. "Donaghy Questions . . . and Answers." On ESPN.com. 24 July. Accessed 13 April 2008 from *http://sports.espn.go.com/nba/columns/story?columnist=stein_marc&id=2947073.*

Stickney, D. 2001. "Gold Club Scandal Serves Athletes Right." *Daily Nebraskan,* 26 July. Accessed 13 April 2008 from *http://media.www.dailynebraskan.com/media/storage/paper857/news/2001/07/26/Sports/Gold-Club.Scandal.Serves.Athletes.Right-1728906.shtml.*

Stone, M.H., M. Stone, B. Sands, and W.A. Sands. 2007. *Principles and Practice of Resistance Training.* Champaign, IL: Human Kinetics.

Strasser, J.B. 1993. *Swoosh! The Unauthorized Story of Nike and the Men Who Played There.* New York: HarperCollins.

Substance Abuse and Mental Health Administration. 2007. *Results from the 2006 National Survey on Drug Use and Health: National*

Findings. Office of Applied Studies, NSDUH H-32, DHHS Publication No. SMA 07-4293.

Su-Lin, G., C.A. Toggle, M.A., Mitrook, S.H. Coussement, and D. Zillman. 1997. "The Thrill of a Close Game: Who Enjoys It and Who Doesn't?" *Journal of Sport and Social Issues*, v. 21: 53–64.

Sullum, J. 2006. "Know When to Fold 'Em." *Reason*, 25 October. Accessed 2 March 2008 from *http://www.reason.com/news/show/38400.html.*

"Sunday Baseball Barred." 1904. *New York Times*, 3 March, p. 7.

"Super Bowl Stats: TV Ad Rates, Ticket Prices, Player Pay." 2008. *Honolulu Advertiser*, 30 January. Accessed 26 March 2008 from *http://the.honoluluadvertiser.com/article/2008/Jan/30/br/br7936501284.html.*

Surdam, D. 2006. "The Coase Theorem and Movement in Major League Baseball." *Journal of Sports Economics*, v. 7, no. 2: 201–221.

_____. 2007. "Mr. Keynes, Meet Mr. Ruppert: The New York Yankees during the Great Depression." Presented at the annual meeting of the Social Science History Association, Chicago, IL. November.

Suzanne, B. 1998. "Characters of Plato's Time and Dialogues: Pindar." Accessed 2 February from *http://plato-dialogues.org/tools/char/pindar.htm.*

Swaddling, J. 2000. *The Ancient Olympic Games*. Austin: University of Texas Press.

Sylvester, J.L. 1973. "Anabolic Steroids at the 1972 Olympics." *Coach and Athletic Director.* Reprinted 2006 in *Coach and Athletic Director*, October, pp. 12–13 and 84.

Szymanski, S. 2003. "The Economic Design of Sporting Contests." *Journal of Economic Literature*, v. 41, no. 4: 1137–1187.

_____. 2005. "Tilting the Playing Field: Why a Sports League Planner Would Choose Less, Not More Competitive Balance." Mimeograph. Tanaka Business School Discussion Papers: TBS/DP05/35. London: Tanaka Business School. Accessed 29 March 2008 from *http://www3.imperial.ac.uk/pls/portallive/docs/1/43004.PDF.*

_____. 2006. "Uncertainty of Outcome, Competitive Balance, and the Theory of Team Sports." In Handbook on the Economics of Sport, ed. W. Andreff and S. Szymanski. Cheltenham, UK: Elgar.

Szymanski, S., and A.S. Zimbalist. 2005. *National Pastime*. Washington, DC: Brookings Insitute.

The Tarzan Movie Guide. 1995 and 2001. "The Weismuller Films (1932–1948)." Accessed 20 June 2007 from *http://www.tarzanmovieguide.com/index.htm.*

Taylor, F.W. 1911. *The Principles of Scientific Management*. New York: Harper.

tcdtrade.com. 2001. "Licensing Industry Prospers, but Sports, Entertainment Categories Soften." Accessed 7 January 2008 from *http://www.tdctrade.com/imn/01062802/trade01.htm.*

"Team Marketing Report." Accessed 3 November 2007 from *www.teammarketing.com.*

"The Tennis Grand Slam." Accessed 22 June 2007 from *http://www.all-about-tennis.com/tennisgrandslam.html.*

That's Racin.' 2008. "Media Center: NASCAR on 2008 Fox Schedule." 25 January. Accessed 27 January 2008 from *http://www.thatsracin.com/119/story/10203.html.*

Thayer, E.L. 1888. "Casey at the Bat." *San Francisco Examiner*, 3 June. Published under the pen name of "Phin."

Thebaseballpage.com. "Tracing the Origins of Baseball." Accessed 15 August 2005 from *http://www.thebaseballpage.com/features/2001/origins/origins.htm.*

Thinkquest.org. "Chinese dynasties." Accessed 21 March 2008 from *http://library.thinkquest.org/12255/library/dynasty/dynasty.htm.*

Thomas, F. 1978. "'Iron Byron' Sets Distance Standards." *USGA Green Section Records*, March/April, pp. 5–7. Accessed 16 April 2008 from *http://turf.lib.msu.edu/1970s/1978/780305.pdf.*

Touregypt.net. "Egypt: Ancient Sports." Accessed 23 July 2005 from *http://www.touregypt.net/historicalessays/ancsportsindex.htm.*

"Transatlantic Implications from British Practices." International Association of Assembly Managers. Mimeograph. Accessed 26 December 2007 from *http://www.iaam.org/CVMS/Post%20911%20Stadium%20Security .doc.*

Tuff Stuff, 2007, December. (Collectibles guide magazine.)

Tversky, A., and D. Kahneman. 1981. "The Framing of Decisions and the Psychology of Choice." *Science*, v. 211 (30 Jan.): 453–458.

"Two Brooklyn Gamblers Accused of College Basketball Bribery." 1945. *New York Times*, 30 January, p. 1.

"The Uncertainty of Peace." National Baseball Hall of Fame and Museum. Accessed 15 June 2007 from *http://www.baseballhalloffame.org/exhibits/online_exhibits/baseball_enlists/peace.htm.*

United States Golf Association. "USGA history 1931–1950." Accessed 20 June 2007 from *http://www.usga.org/aboutus/usga_history/1931_1950.html.*

University of Notre Dame. 2008. "Official Athletic Site of the University of Notre Dame." Accessed 21 March 2008 from *http://und.cstv.com/sports/m-footbl/archive/nd-m-fb-a-nattit.html.*

University of York Department of Statistics. 2008. "Lies, Damn Lies, and Statistics." 20 January. Accessed 20 February 2008 from *http://www.york.ac.uk/depts/maths/histstat/lies.htm.*

"Unsplendid Splinter." 2003. *Sports Illustrated,* 3 June). Accessed 12 April 2008 from *http://sportsillustrated.cnn.com/baseball/news/2003/06/03/sosa_ejected_ap/.*

U.S. Census Bureau. Various years. *Statistical Abstract of the United States.*

_____. 2000. *Historical National Population Estimates: July 1, 1900 to July 1, 1999.* Population Estimates Program, Population Division. 11 April; revised 28 June. Accessed 22 March 2008 from *http://www.census.gov/population/estimates/nation/popclockest.txt.*

U.S. Department of Education, Office of Post-Secondary Education. "Equity in Athletics Data Analysis Cutting Tool Website." Accessed 3 November 2007 from *http://ope.ed.gov/athletics/.*

U.S. Department of Labor, Bureau of Labor Statistics; U.S. Department of Commerce, Bureau of Economic Analysis.

UPI. 2008. "NBC Sports extends NHL TV contract." Accessed 9 November 2008 from http://www.upi.com/Sports_News/2008/04/24/NBC_Sports_extends_NHL_TV_contract/UPI-13211209063880/.

VanGierzen, R., and A.E. Schrenk. 2001. "Compensation from before World War I through the Great Depression." *Compensation and Working Conditions,* Fall. Accessed 18 June 2007 from *http://www.bls.gov/opub/cwc/cm20030124ar03p1.htm.*

van Ours, J.C. 1995. "The Price Elasticity of Hard Drugs: The Case of opium in the Dutch East Indies, 1923–1938." *The Journal of Political Economy,* v. 103, no. 2: 261–279.

Van Riper, T. 2007. "The Costs of On-Line Football: Pure Fantasy." *Forbes,* 26 September. Accessed 9 March 2008 from *http://www.forbes.com/leadership/2007/09/26/fantasy-football-office-lead-cx_tvr_0926productivity.html.*

Van Voris, B. 2007. "Court Won't Reconsider Decision Favoring Fantasy Sports Leagues." Bloomberg News Service, 26 November. Accessed 9 March 2008 from *http://www.bloomberg.com/apps/news?pid=newsarchive&sid =aGSQgvgz.LvI.*

Vaughn, J.L. 2002. "Baseball's Importance during the Great Depression." Master's thesis, Central Connecticut State University. Accessed 18 June 2007 from *http://fred.ccsu.edu:8000/archive/00000016/01/etd-2002–16.pdf.*

Veblen, T., and M. Banta. 2007. *Theory of the Leisure Class.* Oxford's World Classics. New York: Oxford.

Verrengia, J.B. 2004. "Ancient Olympics Had Its Own Scandals." Associated Press, 28 July. Accessed 12 April 2008 from *http://www.msnbc.msn.com/id/5467740.*

Vogel, H.L. 2007. *Entertainment Industry Economics: A Guide for Financial Analysis.* Cambridge: Cambridge University Press.

Volberg, R.A., K.L. Nysse-Carris, and D.R. Gerstein. 2006. "2006 California Problem Gambling Prevalence Survey." California Department of Alcohol and Drug Programs Office of Problem and Pathological Gambling. August. Accessed 2 March 2008 from *http://www.adp.ca.gov/OPG/pdf/CA_Problem_Gambling_Prevalence_Survey-Final_Report.pdf.*

von Allmen, P. 2005. "The Economics of Individual Sports: Golf, Tennis, and NASCAR." In *Handbook of Sports Economics Research,* ed. J. Fizel. Armonk, NY: Sharpe.

Vrooman, J. 1997. "Franchise Free Agency in Professional Sports Leagues." *Southern Economic Journal,* v. 64, no. 1: 191–219.

Waddington, I., and M. Roderick. "American Exceptionalism: Soccer and American Football." *The Sports Historian* (University of Leicester Center for Research into Sport and Society), no. 16. Accessed 1 April 2006 from *http://www.aafla.org/SportsLibrary/SportsHistorian/1996/sh16f.pdf.*

Walker, S. 2006. *Fantasyland: A Season on Baseball's Lunatic Fringe.* New York: Viking Penguin.

"When the Rules of the Game Are Broken: Sports Injuries Related to Illegal Activity." 2008. *Science Daily,* 2 March. Accessed 12 April 2008 from *http://www.sciencedaily.com/releases/2008/02/080229141827.htm.*

White, G. 1963. "Football stars banned for bets." *New York Times.* 18 April.

Whitford, D. 1989. *A Payroll to Meet: A Story of Greed, Corruption, and Football at SMU.* New York: Macmillan.

Wolfers, J. 2006. "Point-shaving: Corruption in College Basketball." *American Economic Review,* v. 96, no. 2: 279–283.

_____. 2007. "Blow the Whistle on Betting Scandals." *New York Times,* 27 July. Accessed 13 April 2008 from *http://www.nytimes.com/2007/07/27/opinion/27wolfers.html.*

Wong, E. 2001. "Baseball: Little League tightens its rules." *New York Times.* 12 December.

Wong, S. 2005. *Smithsonian Baseball: Inside the World's Finest Collections.* New York: Harper Collins.

Woodland, B.M., and L.M. Woodland. 1991. "The Effects of Risk Aversion on Wagering: Point Spread versus Odds." *Journal of Political Economy,* v. 99, no. 3: 638–653.

Yastine, J. 2007. "Superbowl-sized Sports Memorabilia Sales." *Nightly Business Report,* 2 February. Accessed 7 January 2008 from *http://www.pbs.org/nbr/site/onair/transcripts/070202c/.*

Z, Dr. 2003. "Logistical Nightmare." *Sports Illustrated,* 10 April. Accessed 1 March 2008 from *http://sportsillustrated.cnn.com/inside_game/dr_z/news/2003/04/10/drz_insider/.*

Zaldua, E. 2006. "Landis scandal causes dismay in cycling." *Time.* 28 July. Accessed 9 November 2008 from http://www.time.com/time/world/article/0,8599,1220390,00.html.

Zernike, K. 2002. "With Student Cheating on the Rise, More Colleges Are Turning to Honor Codes." *New York Times,* 2 November. Accessed 19 April 2008 from *http://query.nytimes.com/gst/fullpage.html?res=9B03E1DA163EF931A35752C1A9649C8B63.*

Zimbalist, A. 1992. "Salaries and Performance: Beyond the Scully Model." In *Diamonds Are Forever: The Business of Baseball,* ed. P.M. Sommers. Washington, DC: Brookings Institute.

_____, Ed. 2001. *The Economics of Sport.* Northampton, MA: Elgar.

Zimbalist, A.S. 2002. "Competitive Balance in Sports Leagues: An Introduction." *Journal of Sports Economics,* v. 3, no. 2: 111–121.

_____. 2003. "Competitive Balance Conundrums: Response to Fort and Maxcy's Comment." *Journal of Sports Economics,* v. 4, no. 2: 161–163.

Zoss, J., and J. Bowman. 2004. *Diamonds in the Rough: The Untold Story of Baseball.* Lincoln: University of Nebraska University Press.

Zuglad, J. 2004. "Business of the NHL—League's TV Deal May Suffer." *Minneapolis Star-Tribune,* 21 January. Accessed 25 March 2005 from *http://www.startribune.com/stories/1330/4330146.html.*

Zygmont, Z.X., and J.C. Leadley. 2005. "When Is the Honeymoon Over? Major League Baseball Attendance 1970–2000." *Journal of Sport Management,* v. 19, no. 3: 278–299.

Index